YURI
ANDROPOV

YURI ANDROPOV

A SECRET PASSAGE
INTO THE KREMLIN

Vladimir Solovyov
and Elena Klepikova

Translated by Guy Daniels, in collaboration with the authors

Macmillan Publishing Company

NEW YORK

Collier Macmillan Publishers

LONDON

Copyright © 1983 by Vladimir Solovyov and Elena Klepikova

Macmillan Publishing Company
866 Third Avenue, New York, N.Y. 10022
Collier Macmillan Canada, Inc.

Library of Congress Cataloging in Publication Data

Solovyov, Vladimir.
    Yuri Andropov, a secret passage into the Kremlin.

    1. Andropov, $\widehat{IU}$. V. ($\widehat{IU}$riĭ Vladimirovich),
1914—   . 2. Heads of state—Soviet Union—
Biography. I. Klepikova, Elena. II. Title.
DK275.A53S64 1983   947.085'4'0924 [B] 83-12034
ISBN 0-02-612290-1

10 9 8 7 6 5 4 3 2

Designed by Jack Meserole

Printed in the United States of America

To our dear friend Willy,
who has been a source of consolation for us
in hard times, and who takes a particular
pleasure in sharing times of joy with us—
a Russian-born émigré calico cat.

The best and easiest way to find out what is good in a man, and what is bad, is to look closely into what he strove for under another ruler. —The Emperor Galba in naming his successor, as quoted by Tacitus

God knows, my son,
By what by-paths and indirect crook'd ways
I met this crown. —SHAKESPEARE, *Henry IV*, Part 2

Contents

Foreword

Churchill's well-known phrase about Russia—that it is "a riddle wrapped in a mystery inside an enigma"—may well be applied to the USSR's present ruler, even if he wants to appear more mysterious than in fact he is. The latter possibility is not to be ruled out, either vis-à-vis Andropov or in regard to the country he now heads up. On that subject, there is a popular joke the gist of which is that Russia's chief secret is that it has no secrets. And in the past century, the poet Fyodor Tyutchev wrote a fine quatrain—about nature but also applicable to Russia:

> Nature's a sphinx, and her ordeal by riddle
> All the more surely devastates a man
> In that, perhaps, she really has no riddle,
> And never has had since the world began.

In one way or another, since he first became head of the Soviet empire, Andropov has been seen as a sphinx—one about whom world public opinion has been sharply divided. In America's best-known newspaper, a famous American journalist welcomed him as a "closet liberal," while an American general said he was "nastier than a snake." The rumors swirling about the Kremlin's new occupant, each one less plausible than the last, have given rise to two opposed hagiographies; and it has been hard to tell which is closer to reality—which is the true portrait, and which is apocryphal.

While all this was going on, our hero, whenever he appeared at a ceremony of great moment (beginning with the burial of his predecessor beside the Kremlin Wall in Red Square), was accompanied by a short man carrying a black suitcase. This lent Andropov an even more mysterious air, since everyone would like to know what was in that suitcase. The control device for launching ICBMs? A secret telephone switchboard? Drugs of choice for treating angina pectoris, diabetes, and nephritis—with all of which Andropov is afflicted? For some reason, no one has suggested that the black suitcase was empty. Yet that, too, is a possibility.

The first thing Andropov did when he came to power was to ban a new production, at Moscow's avant-garde Taganka Theater, of *Boris Godunov*, based on Pushkin's historical verse play. Although the drama is set in the late sixteenth and early seventeenth centuries, its theme has been topical throughout Russian history: the struggle for power, its usurpation, its arrogation. In *Boris Godunov* political history unfolds quite separately from that of the people: significantly, the last line in Pushkin's drama (a stage direction) is "The crowd remains silent." And its plot is based on a rumor that Boris Godunov, so that he could become tsar, had ordered the murder of Ivan the Terrible's epileptic son, the tsarevich Dmitri. What parallel in that plot seemed so threatening to Andropov that he made haste to deprive the audience of Pushkin's play?

Our guess is that today he would ban any drama dealing with a power struggle, whether it was written by Shakespeare, Pushkin, Jean Anouilh, Victor Hugo, Schiller, or Count Aleksei Tolstoy—anyone at all. Because they are still too fresh—the traces of that spasmodic struggle for power he had to wage while Brezhnev was yet alive. Will a new Shakespeare or Pushkin turn up to describe how Andropov came to power? After all, the story is no less dramatic than the chronicle plays of those poets.

Our own approach to the personality of our hero is, rather, a historical and journalistic one, combined with a political analysis of his "works and days." Here and there, however, we were unable to avoid those novelistic devices imposed by the story line of our book, since the way a biography is written is dictated by the behavior of its subject. If we had been writing a book about Roosevelt, Churchill, or de Gaulle, everything would have been different; and the tried-and-true mode of biography would not have run the risk of taking on, from time to time, aspects of the detective story. Again, along with our hero's penchant for intrigue, the fact that he was head of the secret police for a full fifteen years (from May 1967 to May 1982) could not but have affected his character and habits. Finally, the deeds in our chronicle take place in the Soviet Union, where the supreme power is attained neither through free elections nor through succession to the throne, as in monarchies. That is why, in Russia, the upward path is steeper, more tortuous, and more dangerous than anywhere else: from any of the heights, a fall is possible; and once he has fallen, a man can never climb back up.

Of course, as Pascal said, "In any game of chance, there is no doubt as to the risk, but winning is doubtful." And he was quite right. But he also said: "Wherever there is infinity, and not an infinity of chances of losing against the chance of winning, one must not vacillate: one must wager all." And that was just what each of Andropov's predecessors had done, regarding the supreme power in the Kremlin as "infinity," and wagering all, sometimes including their own lives. Nor was Andropov an exception: he was following a fixed Soviet tradition. Struggling for power in the Kremlin is like walking a tightrope at a vertiginous height.

That tradition is not only Soviet but Russian, despite the official succession to the throne in prerevolutionary Russia. Consider the greater part of the eighteenth century, after the death of Peter the Great in 1725, when Russia was ruled by women. Behind those empresses who succeeded one another, we find military juntas who preferred to have a woman on the throne because she was easier to deal with. From time to time the army would put forth from its ranks the most attractive males, who would see to it that the empress remained obedient. On the surface this "regiment of women" was a permanent military dictatorship with recurrent military coups, murders of legitimate heirs, tsarinas in barracks wearing men's military uniforms, and infighting among army factions. And all this in total disregard of the basic principle of the autocracy: the hereditary succession to power. Instead of that succession there was a long series of military coups, the last of which was the "December Revolution" of 1825. It was unsuccessful, but its social nature was the same as that of earlier coups. In that respect, the Decembrists were not revolutionaries but conservatives: they came out of the military tradition of the eighteenth century, and their political consciousness was limited by it. The eighteenth century, along with the first quarter of the nineteenth, was a period of coups and usurpations. Legitimate tsars were murdered, and after Peter the Great all rulers but Paul were usurpers, including Catherine the Great. She broke two tsarist lines, killing Ivan VI and her husband, Peter III; and she blocked access to the throne for her own son, Paul (a kind of Russian Hamlet), under whom she was entitled to be only a regent, and then not for long. This kind of thing went on until the reign of her grandson, Alexander I, who came to power via the murder of his own father, that same unfortunate Paul. Incidentally, Alexander I's successor, Nicholas I, after overcoming the Decembrists, became emperor through bypassing his older brother, Konstantin; and the whole matter is still a murky one. If memory serves us right, Madame de Staël said somewhere that government in Russia was a tyranny interrupted now and then by a strangling.

We have sketched here, in a few brief strokes, the historical background without which our hero's adventures might seem bizarre and improbable. Nay, more: information about him is fragmentary and not always reliable; so that as his biographers we have had to steer between the Scylla of "disinformation" and the Charybdis of a total lack of information. Nor is there any hope that sometime in the future, accurate information about the secrets of the Kremlin court will surface. After all, it never did in the case of Stalin, or Catherine the Great, or Ivan the Terrible; and their biographers have had to rely not so much on documents as on their own intuition. As biographers of Andropov, it has been hard for us to keep a checkrein on our imagination and stick to analysis. And although we have made much use of information received from Russia (some of it via secret channels), it has by no means been easy to select those items that are reliable.

As for the book's story line, it was not (we repeat) provided by us but by our main character. All we did, as authors, was to try and bring secret things out into the open. Hence we have very good reason to call Yuri Vladimirovich Andropov our coauthor. Not to say as much here would be most ungrateful.

YURI
ANDROPOV

The Hungarian

Début

I

After the demand made by the government (Imre Nagy),
we nevertheless found it feasible to pull our troops out of
Budapest, but to position them at the airport. So we had no
troops in Budapest. But we had a presence there: our
ambassador was in Budapest.
— NIKITA KHRUSHCHEV, *Memoirs*

In the lives of major political figures, there is always
a moment that marks the beginning of their real political biography, as
if from that point on, fate itself were clocking their time. Looking
back, Yuri Andropov must feel grateful for the incident which, in
1953, caused him to be removed from the close-ranked cohort of
Moscow *apparatchiki* and transferred to the Soviet embassy on Bayza
Street in Budapest, although at the time the new assignment could
scarcely have pleased him.

Only two years before, he had been brought into the Central Committee from the Karelo-Finnish Republic, where he had spent a good
ten years in various posts under the sponsorship of Otto Kuusinen, an
old Finnish Social Democrat and member of the Comintern. In
Moscow some enticing prospects opened up for the ambitious thirty-
seven-year-old—although, if we take Stalin's destruction of the Party
into account, those prospects were not without their dangers. But
after Stalin's death, as a result of the shuffling of key personnel,
Andropov found himself outside the boundaries of that little play-
ground where the big political games are played—games whose outcome determines the fate, if not of all mankind, then of at least half of
it. For an ambitious man, a transfer from the Central Committee's
apparatus to diplomatic work—and in a neighboring socialist country
at that—usually meant the end of his Party career. According to simple statistics, the most that Andropov could count on was to become
one of the many deputy ministers of foreign affairs toward the end of
his diplomatic career. Ordinarily, however, all he could manage—if it
suited Moscow—would be to get promoted from a socialist country to

a capitalist one. This happened, for example, in the case of Stepan Chervonenko, the Soviet ambassador to Czechoslovakia, who for his zeal during the suppression of the Prague Spring in 1968 was named ambassador to France (despite the protests of the French). The only exception was Andrei Gromyko, minister of foreign affairs for more than a quarter century, who during the war years was Soviet ambassador to Washington. But Washington is not Budapest: there was no road back from Budapest into the Kremlin. Moreover, although Andropov himself was sent to Hungary as a result of Khrushchev's chessboard manipulations of the key personnel he inherited from Stalin, being shifted from Party work to diplomacy was also a kind of exile for Moscow bureaucrats who were being penalized or were in disgrace. It was the first stage of disfavor, and had been widely employed by Stalin in the early period of his rule (later on he preferred less liberal methods of punishment), as well as by Khrushchev, Brezhnev, and Andropov himself when he finally reached the summit of power. Thus Andropov's "excommunication" from Moscow bore the stamp of disgrace, even if it was not disgrace of a personal nature.

For that matter, there is a rumor that Andropov, being a provincial without experience in Moscow intrigues, was at the time a victim of the post-Stalin power struggle between Premier Malenkov and Party Secretary Khrushchev. This version has it that Malenkov, trying to strengthen his own position, decided to remove the Party boss of Lithuania, Antanas Snechkus, whom he found objectionable, and instructed Andropov to prepare a report on him. But instead of the compromising report that Malenkov expected, Andropov submitted an objective one, thereby saving Snechkus and sacrificing his own career—more likely from lack of experience than out of principle. Either that, or one must credit Andropov with a special prophetic gift that enabled him to foresee or guess Khrushchev's victory over Malenkov, and the former's grateful sponsorship of Andropov in later years. Most probably, this rumor is of recent origin—one of those which, with hindsight, elucidates certain obscure phases in the new Soviet chieftain's life story, based on what he wants today. In other words, it is the kind of rumor that he is now spreading about himself. (As we shall see later, this is a specialty in which Andropov has surpassed all his predecessors.)

There is yet another rumor that Andropov cannot be suspected of spreading, since it is not in his present interests. According to this story, the young careerist from Petrozavodsk (the capital of the Karelo-Finnish Republic) struck the passionate anti-Stalinist Khrushchev as an adherent to the old Stalinist methods of leadership. The ideal of a police state proclaimed by Andropov immediately after his accession to supreme power in the USSR tends to confirm this rumor rather than the former one. It would seem, in fact, that in the fifties Andropov was opposed to the policy of "liberalization" that Khrushchev had adopted.

It was a period when, for the first time after a quarter century of unquestioning obedience to Stalin's orders, the Party bureaucrats had to make up their minds whose side they were on, since the entire remainder of their careers depended on it. At the top, in the Kremlin, a fight to the death was going on between the anti-Stalinists and the neo-Stalinists—one that stirred up the lower Party ranks and compelled them to choose their own positions. What was called for now was not blind obedience but swift ideological orientation. The majority in the ruling Politburo were Stalinists. And although one of them, Beria, was physically eliminated a few months after Stalin's death, the others—Molotov, Kaganovich, Malenkov, and Voroshilov—would have overthrown Khrushchev four years later, had it not been for the military intervention of Marshal Zhukov. It was these years of fluctuation after Stalin's death that were the formative ones, ideologically, for Andropov. The position he had taken resulted in his "exile" to Hungary. Yet Hungary was precisely the place where it was necessary to revive Stalinist methods of governing the empire: first to pacify the Hungarians, then to do the same to the other peoples of Eastern Europe. And it was just then that Khrushchev finally recognized Andropov's talents, utilizing them and promoting their possessor, since at that time he had begun to back off, crablike, from the policy of de-Stalinization he himself had proclaimed. In order to balance things, the liberal Khrushchev had to have a gendarme at his side—especially in troubled East European matters. Andropov became just such a gendarme after the brilliant performance of his mission in Hungary.

When he first came there, however, nothing foreshadowed the abrupt upturns his career would take in the future; and at first he looked on his life in Budapest as nothing more nor less than exile. Sandor Kopacsi, then chief of the Budapest police, recalls that for formal receptions at the Soviet embassy, Andropov would summon the police force's gypsy orchestra and would sing along with the gypsies in a thin tenor. But even more than the heart-rending gypsy love songs, he liked the Hungarian ballad about the crane that left its mate and flew off to distant lands. This was hardly nostalgia for Russia, since in his tastes Andropov was more of a cosmopolite than a jingois- tic patriot. (Indeed, after his return to Moscow in 1957 he missed Hungary; and at first he often went there on private visits.) Nor was he lonely for his family: as an ambassador, he had his family with him there in Budapest. His nostalgia was strictly political. He missed the political fighting from which he had been forcibly separated. Because politics was not only his job, it was his passion. On this point there is unanimity among all who knew him, both his admirers and his critics. In view of his subsequent triumphant return to the "high society" of Moscow politics, his life in Budapest can be compared to the biblical story of Joseph in the pit. It was, in fact, a fall for him; but that fall marked the beginning of his rise.

More precisely, his rise began three years later, when a revolution swept over Hungary. Its suppression became his personal victory.

Although more than a quarter century has passed since the Hun- garian revolution, disputes are still going on about the role played in its suppression by the then Soviet ambassador to Budapest—disputes stimulated by his apotheosis, which was unexpected by the Hun- garians (and, for that matter, by many Russians).

Just what was Andropov in the autumn of 1956? Was he an initia- tor or merely an obedient executor of orders? He could not have been an initiator. The decision to put down the Hungarian revolution by military force was made in Moscow by the then Soviet leadership, headed by Khrushchev, which did not include Andropov. On the other hand, however, he was not a mere executor of orders—the blind instrument of Soviet imperialism. Otherwise, there could be no expla- nation for his subsequent swift climb up the Party ladder immediately after the events in Hungary—a climb that ended at the very top of the ladder.

Let us again recall the career of his colleague Stepan Chervonenko, Soviet ambassador to Czechoslovakia during the Prague Spring, who, a few months after Andropov became general secretary of the Commu- nist Party, left his post of Soviet ambassador to France. Chervonenko had by no means been a passive observer of the Soviet occupation of Czechoslovakia in 1968. He had taken part in it to the fullest extent of his capacities, serving as a pointsman who coordinated the actions of the military command with cloakroom intrigues, and searching out collaborationists and puppets among Czechs and Slovaks. Beyond a doubt, Andropov did the same kind of thing in Hungary. The only questions is: What else did he do? What did he do to earn the trust and admiration of both Khrushchev and Brezhnev? First, of Khrushchev, who made him chief of the Central Committee's Department for Liaison with Ruling Communist Parties (actually, overseer of the Kremlin's unruly East European vassals), and subsequently Central Committee secretary. Then, of Brezhnev, who named him to head up the most important department in the Soviet structure, the secret police, and brought him into the Politburo. Why, in reward for Hungary, was the former Soviet ambassador to Budapest not given a further career in diplomacy but a career as a gendarme? What precisely, in Andropov's Hungarian experience, prompted Brezhnev to appoint him chief of the KGB? What kind of person did Andropov have to be in Hungary so as, twenty-five years after the revolution there, to become the fifth Soviet *vozhd* (great chief)? His subsequent career (unprecedented for an ambassador) turns the searchlight back on his secret mission in Budapest. For a biographer, this is a reliable guide to understanding the role that he played not only in putting down the Hungarian revolution but in that explosion itself—in bringing it about.

Actually, the Hungarian uprising was the first East European challenge to the Soviet empire, if one doesn't count the workers' riots in East Germany in the summer of 1953, which were mostly a matter of wages and prices. At regular intervals of twelve years, such uprisings were repeated in 1968 in Prague and in 1980 in Gdansk and Warsaw. If the Polish schism was the most massive and prolonged (the issues still haven't been finally settled, despite General Jaruzelski's military coup), and if the Czechoslovak challenge was dangerous in that it germinated within the ranks of the ruling Party and came from Communists, the distinguishing feature of the Hungarian revolution was its radicalism, its intransigence, and its armed, brutal character. That is why such a tragic revolution provokes more sympathy than admiration. Unlike the Prague Spring and the Polish trade-union anarchy, in Hungary there was a genuine armed uprising against the Russians and their local collaborationists. The streets flowed with blood, sometimes innocent blood—as, for example, during the enraged mob's lynching of Party activists and secret-police recruits on the Square of the Republic. And the Hungarian premier, Imre Nagy, under pressure from the people, managed—in the few days granted him by fate, history, and the Kremlin—to hand the Soviet ambassador, Andropov, a declaration of Hungary's neutrality and its withdrawal from the Warsaw Pact, and to make a radio announcement about the war between the Hungarians and the Russians. Those few decisive days in early November 1956 demanded of Andropov that he bring all of his capacities into play under great stress: an iron will, instant presence of mind, absolute cynicism, self-control, a willingness to take risks, and ruthlessness. If he hadn't possessed those traits he would have gained nothing, personally, from the Hungarian loss to the Russians, even if the revolution had nonetheless been crushed by Soviet tanks.

It least befits a biographer, however, to ignore the role of the individual and lean toward historical determinism, claiming that what happened was inevitable just because it happened. If Andropov's services in putting down the Hungarian revolution were so great as to earn him the admiration of both Khrushchev and Brezhnev, plus a swift rise in the Party hierarchy, one is entitled to ask: Would the Hungarian revolt have been crushed without Andropov?

But we have to begin with a different question that is more complex and subtle: Would that revolt have broken out at all, had it not been for the secret activity and ambiguous role of Yuri Andropov, the Soviet ambassador to Hungary? As the reader will soon see, we have very good grounds for posing that question.

Not long before his appointment to Hungary (first as counsellor, then a few months later as ambassador), Andropov was sent on a mission to East Germany, where before his very eyes (and perhaps with his participation) the Soviet occupying troops brutally crushed the workers' revolt of June 17, 1953. Some 267 men and women were killed in street fighting, hundreds were wounded, 18 were sentenced to death by military tribunals and executed, and more than 1,100 were sent to prison. This marked the collapse of the ideological illusions of the leftist German intellectuals, who after World War II had returned from emigration to "the best of the Germanies" and found themselves in a Communist ersatz Prussia. In the aftermath of this uprising, the famous German playwright Bertholt Brecht wrote this bitter epitaph:

> After June 17th,
> People brought to the Secretary of the Writers Union
> Leaflets found in Stalinallee

Saying that the people
Had lost the trust of the government,
And that only by creative labor
Could they win it back.
It would surely have been simpler for the rulers
To relieve that people of their obligations
And seek out another one for themselves.

It was only natural that the leaders of the Soviet empire should draw from that uprising a totally different kind of lesson from that drawn by the leftist German antifascists; namely, that what was needed was a harsher policy toward the unruly East European herd. In view of this, it is all the more astounding that a few days after the suppression of the German revolt, the Hungarian leaders—headed up by Party boss and Premier Matyas Rakosi—were summoned to Moscow, where they were given a dressing-down by their superiors for their harsh methods of governing, lack of flexibility, forcible collectivization, economic mistakes, and even for violating laws and arresting innocent people. Thus it was in Hungary that the process of de-Stalinization in the Soviet empire began. Hungary was almost three years ahead, not only of the other East European vassals of Moscow, but of Russia itself. (The anti-Stalinist Twentieth Party Congress in Moscow did not take place until February 1956.)

How explain the fact that the Kremlin chose Hungary as a pioneer in the anti-Stalinist movement? Because the regime there was more harsh than in the other satellite countries? Because the Hungarian leadership was clinging closer to Stalinism? Because the scope of repressions was broader? But by all these criteria, Hungary was somewhere in the middle among the other East European countries, scarcely differing from them. What it all boiled down to was that, unlike the other East European Stalinists, Matyas Rakosi—who had spent sixteen years in Admiral Horthy's prisons, and for whose release the Kremlin had traded some military trophies (regimental colors captured by the Russian army when the Hungarian revolution of 1848–49 was put down)—was of Jewish origin.

When the Kremlin leaders met with the Hungarian delegation, they had before them copies of a detailed report on the situation in Hungary that had been drawn up by Andropov's predecessor, Yevgeniy Kiselev, then Soviet ambassador to Budapest. That report showed, in black and white, that the chief cause of the troubles in

Hungary was the fact that all of the four men governing that country, headed by Rakosi, were Jews.

"Listen, Rakosi," said Beria, chief of the secret police. "We know that Hungary has been ruled by Turkish sultans, Austrian emperors, Tatar khans, and Polish kings. But so far as we know, Hungary has never been ruled by a Jewish tsar. And yet you are becoming just such a tsar. But bear in mind that we can't allow that."

On that occasion Khrushchev supported Beria, his most dangerous rival, who a few days later, on Khrushchev's orders, was shot in the basement of the Lubyanka (the Moscow political prison), where he had been absolute master until just shortly before.

The Soviet leaders agreed to let Matyas Rakosi remain Party boss, but insisted that as premier he be replaced by a non-Jew. So it was that they appointed as head of the Hungarian government the future leader of the Hungarian revolution, Imre Nagy, who suited them primarily because he was of non-Jewish origin. (Later—in fact, quite soon—the Soviet Union would have to pay dearly for this anti-Semitism.)

This was a strictly bureaucratic approach to the question. One may even say that the Kremlin acted out of idealistic principles (if anti-Semitic ones can be so called), ignoring expediency and its own interests. Because the Jew, Rakosi, was much more devoted to the Russians than the Hungarian, Nagy; and his Jewishness had never stopped him from following the Kremlin line blindly and without demur, even if that line was anti-Semitic. When Stalin, a few months before his death, dreamed up and produced a grandiose anti-Semitic show based on the "Doctors' Plot" in which Kremlin doctors were accused of trying to kill top leaders on orders from Zionist organizations and Western espionage centers, Rakosi lost no time in arresting Dr. Benedek, director of the Jewish Hospital in Budapest, along with other Jewish doctors in that city, so that he could put on a similar show in Hungary, following the Soviet script. Thus because of their anti-Semitic stance, Khrushchev, Beria, Malenkov, and the rest of the Kremlin cohort weakened the power of their loyal ally, giving a considerable part of it to a more-than-dubious ally, Imre Nagy.

The first to realize this was Yuri Andropov. When he took up his post in Hungary he looked at the situation sensibly, without anti-Semitic prejudices and strictly in accordance with the interests of the Soviet empire, whose representative in Hungary he was. Unlike his predecessor, Kiselev, and in defiance of instructions from Moscow, which was continuing to support Nagy against Rakosi, Andropov resolutely took the side of the latter. And then, a year after being named premier, Nagy laid before the Central Committee and Parliament a program that provided for closing the concentration camps, political amnesty, economic decentralization, and allowing peasants to leave the kolkhozes. Now the Kremlin had much greater cause for alarm than in June 1953. Hungary was not only several months ahead of Moscow in the process of de-Stalinization; it had carried that process farther than the Soviet Union ever would. The Hungarian reality and its slanted reflection in Andropov's reports produced their effect. On January 7, 1955, the Hungarian leaders were again summoned to Moscow, and again reprimanded harshly. But this time the defendant was Nagy, whom the Kremlin prosecutors—Khrushchev, Malenkov, Mikoyan, Molotov, Kaganovich, and Bulganin—charged with all the mortal sins in the Soviet political code: revisionism, belittling the role of the Communist Party, bourgeois nationalism, breaking up the kolkhozes, and even reducing the nation's military potential. As in the summer of 1953, each Soviet leader had before him on the table a neatly prepared dossier from which he drew his charges, arguments, and proofs. And one must give Andropov due credit: the dossier on Nagy had been prepared in a highly professional way, with very great thoroughness, so that no doubts were left as to the crimes of the Hungarian premier. He was blamed for everything, ranging from a patriotic quotation from the Hungarian poet Sandor Petefi, that Nagy had been incautious enough to have published in the Party newspaper, *Szabed Nep*, to an anti-Soviet demonstration that had spontaneously broken out during a game of water polo between Hungarians and Russians.

Shortly after his return from Moscow, Nagy had a heart attack; and in April he was retired from the Politburo and removed from his post as premier. In an unusual *démarche*, the chief Soviet idealogue, Mikhail Suslov, came from Moscow to Hungary and, sitting at Nagy's bedside, tried to persuade him to recant publicly. Nagy refused, and was expelled from the Party. But to Matyas Rakosi, the victory he had won with Andropov's help seemed to fall short of a complete triumph. He drew up a list of four-hundred persons to be proscribed, and demanded their immediate arrest in the name of public tranquility and order. The first name on the list was that of Imre Nagy.

We do not know what position Andropov took in this matter. Did he support his protégé's demand for the arrest of his rival? As for the Kremlin, it restrained the triumphant ardor of its puppet and did not sanction the arrest of Nagy.

Rakosi had been trying to save his own skin and please Moscow; but he had made a mistake: the winds blowing from Moscow, although changeable, were often warm. Nagy discerned them more keenly. A few weeks before the historic Twentieth Party Congress opened in Moscow, he completed the final draft of his political theses and sent ten copies to the Central Committee of the same Party from which he had been expelled six months before. Also, he sent one copy to the Soviet embassy on Bayza Street. Andropov promptly made more copies of the document, which from his viewpoint discredited Nagy. He sent one of them to Moscow stamped "Top Secret" (he knew that, so stamped, the document would be given due attention), and another to Rakosi personally. (Later those theses would figure in Nagy's trial as the most incriminating evidence against him.)

Andropov did the same thing with the excerpts from Nagy's memoirs that the latter sent to the Soviet embassy for forwarding to the Kremlin leaders: he immediately sent one copy off to Rakosi by messenger.

But in Moscow, right then, no one had any time to give to denunciations. In late February 1956, at a closed session of the Twentieth Party Congress, Khrushchev delivered his secret speech on the crimes of Stalin. Thus began the period of the Russian "Thaw," which affected Eastern Europe as well—especially Poland and Hungary. It was a time when the amplitude of the political oscillations in the Soviet empire was at its greatest. The impossible came to seem possible, although the possible still continued to be impossible. Imre Nagy, who with his political theses had anticipated Khrushchev's anti-Stalinist speech by several weeks, was still a Party pariah in Hungary. Andropov continued to send detailed reports from Budapest to Moscow. He was betting on Rakosi, and went on characterizing Nagy as a troublemaker and revisionist.

To guess what the Kremlin's next step would be, to forecast its reaction, to predict the next sharp turn in its policy, was impossible. Those who made no mistakes at the time did so only by chance. Khrushchev himself, cramped in his movements by his colleague-rivals, could not with any accuracy have said one day what he would do the next. Or, more precisely, what he could do the next day if he managed to overcome the resistance of the Stalinists in the Politburo. Or again, what *they* might do if they managed to overcome *his* resistance—and perhaps himself into the bargain. And Andropov was no exception. Given such wide ideological and political oscillations, the safest thing was to take a wait-and-see position, not openly displaying one's own point of view. He had already got burned in Moscow, when he had openly taken a stand and had paid for it with his Hungarian exile. But he was a gambler and knew you couldn't win without taking risks. Also, he had already placed his bet—not really so much on Rakosi as against Nagy—and it was too late to withdraw it. Meantime, he had succeeded in persuading Moscow to follow his advice in Hungarian affairs, despite the liberal winds blowing from the Soviet capital. At this juncture Khrushchev even recognized the veteran anti-Stalinist Tito and agreed to a rapprochement with Yugoslavia; but at the same time he continued to support the Stalinist Rakosi in Hungary. When, in the summer of 1956, Tito came to Moscow, he tried hard to persuade Khrushchev to disown Rakosi. Later, two weeks after Soviet tanks had crushed the Hungarian revolution, Tito recalled his talks in the Kremlin with the Soviet leaders:

We declared that the Rakosi regime—and Rakosi himself—lacked the qualifications to head up the Hungarian state or achieve national unity, and that the continued existence of that regime might lead to very serious consequences. But unfortunately, the Soviet comrades did not believe us. They noted that Rakosi was an old revolutionary and an honest man. The Soviet comrades said he was an intelligent man and would succeed, and that they didn't know anyone else in that country on whom they could count.

"The Soviet comrades" gave more credence to "their man in Budapest" than to the honored guest from Yugoslavia. If the opposite had happened, and Khrushchev had heeded Tito rather than Andropov, the Hungarian revolution might have been avoided. Rakosi would have been replaced several months earlier by Nagy, who by means of gradual liberal reforms would have steered Hungary along the tortuous course between the Kremlin decrees and the demands being made by the Hungarian people.

After all, during that same period a revolution was avoided in Poland, where in mid-October 1956, after the workers' riots in Poznan, the revolutionary situation was close to the one that developed in Hungary in late October. But the October Plenum, invoking emergency powers, co-opted Wladyslaw Gomulka (only recently released from prison, rehabilitated, and restored to Party membership) into the Central Committee, and elected him a member of the Politburo and first secretary. As soon as word about the changes in Poland reached Moscow, the Soviet troops stationed in Poland and along the Soviet-Polish border started moving toward Warsaw. And early on the morning of October 19, without warning, a Soviet plane landed at a military airfield near the Polish capital. From it emerged the Kremlin leaders: Khrushchev, Molotov, Mikoyan, Kaganovich, and Marshal Konev. They got into limousines which took them at high speed through still-sleeping Warsaw to the Belvedere, the magnificent presidential palace dating from the eighteenth century, where they had a face-to-face confrontation with the Polish leaders.

"Traitors!" shouted Khrushchev, in so much of a rush that he didn't even greet anyone. "We spilled blood to liberate your country, and now you want to give it to the Americans! But you won't get away with it! That will never be! We won't allow it!"

At that moment Khrushchev noticed among the Poles a stranger who like himself was as bald as a billiard ball. "And just who are you?"

"I'm Gomulka, the man you kept in prison for three years. And now you're trying to prevent my return to political life."

Such was their first meeting.

Meantime, the Soviet troops were moving closer to the Polish capital. And when the Soviet arguments against the Poles had been exhausted, Khrushchev broadly hinted that in that case the matter could be settled only by the Red army. But Gomulka had taken that possibility, too, into account; and he told Khrushchev that the workers in the Warsaw plants were already armed. Their roles had been reversed: it was now the new Polish leader who was negotiating from a situation of strength.

His last ultimatum to Khrushchev was: "Withdraw your forces immediately. Otherwise, we will break off our talks with you and lead the Polish people in combat against the occupying troops."

Khrushchev had no choice but to order the troops to halt their advance on Warsaw.

What had happened in Poland spurred the Hungarians on. If the Poles had succeeded in returning Gomulka to power despite the resistance of the Russians, why couldn't the same thing be done with Imre Nagy? Events in Hungary followed roughly the same scenario as had those in Poland, and were directly tied in with them, but it was a cause-and-effect relationship. Because of that, they lagged several days behind the Poles. "This was the revolution of the lost forty-eight hours," one of those who had taken part in it said later. Also, there was the personal counteraction of the Soviet ambassador, Andropov. Actually, the lag amounted to about a week. For example, Nagy was restored to the post of premier five days after Gomulka's return to power in Poland. After the suppression of the Hungarian revolution, there were those who went so far as to claim that the Hungarians had saved the Poles by taking the full force of the blow dealt by the Soviet empire, which was incapable of putting down two centers of resistance at the same time. It seems more likely, however, that Russia was taking out its resentment on the Hungarians—restoring in Budapest the imperial vanity that had just been wounded in Warsaw.

And yet the most important lag was not behind Poland but behind reality: Soviet concessions were not keeping up with Hungarian demands. And in that lag lay the cause of the tragedy that was fated to be played out in the streets of Budapest.

At long last, the Kremlin leaders heeded Tito's advice and sacrificed Matyas Rakosi. At long last, they ordered that Imre Nagy be restored to membership in the Party. At long last, the Soviet ambassador, against his own will and wishes, on direct instructions from Moscow, sent Nagy an invitation to come and see him at the embassy. At long last, all this was done; and if it had been done sooner, it might have helped Hungary to avoid the tragedy. But by now all these acts were like the lamentations of the chorus in a Greek drama—a chorus that cannot interfere with, or prevent, the unfolding of the tragic action.

And so they finally met: the two antipodes, the two enemies, the two who would be the main characters in the Hungarian revolution, the two upon whom its outcome would depend. One was a man appointed by the empire as its viceroy in Hungary; the other, a man called upon by his people to lead the uprising against the empire. Even physically (if we leave out the fact that they both wore glasses), they offered a rare example of opposites: the short, stocky Hungarian with the drooping mustaches; and the tall, rather plump, smooth-shaven Russian with something elephantine in his general appearance.

Andropov had very good reasons for personally hating Nagy. If the latter proved to be as successful as Gomulka, it would mean the end of

Andropov's political career. If he had not received direct orders from Moscow, Andropov would never, on his own initiative, have summoned the Hungarian leader who, only a year and a half before, had been cashiered on the basis of his (Andropov's) personal denunciation. But in his three years as a diplomat, Andropov had learned diplomatic etiquette, and perhaps even surpassed other envoys in that respect. Almost all those who met him noticed that his face wore a permanent smile that made it even more inscrutable. For the people who knew him in Hungary, Andropov remained a mystery, although he certainly did not keep out of view, and was not a stay-at-home or unsociable.

Quite the contrary. He even managed while living in Hungary to become fond of that shard of the Austro-Hungarian empire which, via the manipulations of the great powers at Yalta and Potsdam, had come into new hands. Unlike his colleagues in other Soviet embassies in Eastern Europe, who preferred to remain in the capitals, learning about the countries to which they were accredited chiefly from the local newspapers, he made many trips around the country, visiting villages, farms, and plants, and talking with peasants, blue-collar workers, and engineers. He even took lessons in the Hungarian language, which, along with Finnish and Estonian, belongs to the Finno-Ugric subfamily—the most difficult for a foreigner to learn. His children—his son Igor and his daughter Irina—attended a school in Budapest and made friends with Hungarians. In the summer, the entire Andropov family went off to the picturesque shores of Lake Balaton. And even after he had been recalled to Moscow, he sometimes vacationed (and underwent treatment for his diabetes) at Hungarian resorts, although he preferred Varna in Bulgaria or Karlovy Vary in Czechoslovakia.

In general, he was fond of Eastern Europe, through which he often had occasion to travel in later years on official business. He was fond of it, however, not as something foreign but as a part of the Soviet empire—his favorite part of it. In his tastes he was what is called, somewhat quaintly, a "Westernizer." He was always fashionably dressed. For receptions at the embassy, he issued instructions that the guests be served in the continental style, including French wines. A courteous host, he went from table to table, joking with the men, complimenting the ladies—to whom, when the dancing began, he would offer himself as a partner in a rather ceremonious, old-world manner. The ladies were all aflutter about him—because of his gentle, ingratiating way of talking; because of his compliments; but above all, because of something unexpected: instead of being a Russian bumpkin, he was a Soviet "dandy."

And the men liked him, too. Unlike his predecessor, he never raised his voice. In disputes he tried to persuade his opponent, not to outshout him. He was tolerant and attentive: he listened more than he talked. This was the new breed of Soviet official—a breed the Hungarians had not met up with before. Those people who talked with him, including some Hungarians of radical bent, were usually left with the impression that he was on their side, although most of the time he was taciturn. But his silence was ascribed to his official status as ambassador, which prevented him from openly supporting Hungarian advocates of reform.

In Hungary he learned how to conceal his thoughts and smile—two traits that played a fateful role in the Hungarian revolution. That is why he seemed "one of theirs" not only to the reformers in Budapest but to the Stalinists in Moscow. While feeding the hopes of the Hungarians, he heightened the sense of alarm among the Russians. So that along with the objective factors, he personally helped to create in Hungary a revolutionary situation from which he derived a maximum of benefit for his own career. Even in the last days of the uprising, when its outcome was virtually decided, he seduced the Hungarians with false hopes, blunting their viligance or provoking them into risky actions—something that Moscow needed as a pretext for military intervention. At the same time that many Hungarian revolutionaries and reformers were accepting him as "one of theirs," he was enjoying increasing trust on the part of the Kremlin. There is good reason why Khrushchev, in his memoirs, names him as the man who single-handedly replaced the Soviet army when the Soviet leaders, either for tactical reasons or because they were vacillating, withdrew the army from Budapest a few days before the final assault on the Hungarian capital.

Did Imre Nagy accept Andropov as "his man"? Most likely he knew that the Soviet ambassador had tried, personally, to undermine him. But during that interval when they met almost regularly, several times on some days, and when, more and more, hope alternated with despair in the heart of that tragic premier of Hungary, he preferred to believe Andropov, even if he surmised that the latter would deceive him. He preferred to be deceived, rather than look the hopeless truth in the eye. No one knows what they talked about tête-à-tête for several hours running during that portentous meeting that put an end to Nagy's disgrace and, at the same time, marked the beginning of the Hungarian revolution.

On October 24, at 8:13 A.M., Radio Budapest reported Nagy's appointment as premier. One half hour later the new leader of Hungary declared martial law in the country, trying to bring the anarchy of the revolution into the channel of legality and order. But it was too late. Events that had been held in check for too long, as if making up for lost time, developed spontaneously and uncontrollably.

The day before, a wave of demonstrations had swept through Budapest. The slogan most often shouted by the enraged mob was: "Imre Nagy to the government, Rakosi into the Danube!" Near the city park the demonstrators threw steel cables around the neck of a bronze Stalin and dragged the hated statue from its pedestal, leaving on it only a gigantic pair of Russian boots—the triumphant symbol of a revolution that was later lost. Hooting, the mob dragged the tyrant's statue through the streets to the National Theater. The Hungarian revolution began with a carnival, but all too quickly turned into a bloodbath. The intervention of the Soviet tanks changed its course, politically. The civil war became a war of liberation against the occupying troops; and the slogan most heard now was *"Ruszki, haza!"* (Russians, go home!) The Hungarian army started going over to the side of the insurgents.

At 2:00 P.M. on October 24, Soviet tanks appeared on Academy Street in front of the Central Committee headquarters. Two of them disgorged a pair of distinguished guests from the Kremlin, Mikhail Suslov and Anastas Mikoyan. The former was a Stalinist, and the latter an advocate of de-Stalinization, so that in their contradictory pairing they reflected the contradictions among the Soviet leaders. They spent several days in the Hungarian capital, looking into the situation and taking part in sessions of the Politburo and the government. Since they were pragmatists, they tended increasingly to favor Nagy and his policy of conciliation and reforms. On October 30 Suslov and Mikoyan returned from Moscow, where they had gone to report to the Politburo on the situation in Hungary; and they brought back with them to Budapest a declaration from the Soviet government on equality and nonintervention in relations among the socialist countries.

The next day Nagy announced on the radio that the pullout of Soviet troops from Hungary was beginning. It was a total defeat for Andropov. But the defeat was short-lived, lasting only a few hours.

As early as the evening of November 1, it began to be reported that a Soviet force had crossed the Hungarian border and was advancing deep into the country: tanks, trucks carrying troops and ammunition, armored cars, artillery—a force much bigger than the one that had been pulled out the day before. Early the next morning, Nagy summoned Andropov and demanded an explanation. What was going on? Why was the Soviet government violating its own declaration?

Here is what had happened.

While Suslov and Mikoyan were going around Budapest in tanks—visiting the Central Committee headquarters or Parliament in the morning, then going back at night to the airport where the Soviet troops were positioned—Moscow was on the receiving end of a constant flow of dispatches from Andropov, each more alarming than the one that had come in before. Those dispatches told of anarchy and chaos, atrocities committed by the mob, the hunting-down of former secret police agents, mass lynchings in the streets, the defilement of monuments to Soviet soldiers, the release of criminals from prisons, the return of Hungarian fascists (followers of Horthy) to the country, and a bloodbath on the Square of the Republic that cost the lives of old Party members and very young draftees who had only recently been called up for military service. (Among the victims, it must be said, was the very honest Imre Mezo, Party secretary of Budapest and a supporter of Nagy, who was a veteran of the Spanish Civil War and had been acclaimed for the part he had taken in the French Resistance.)

In the absence of Mikoyan and Suslov, who had gone back to Budapest bearing the Moscow declaration on equality and nonintervention, the Politburo, on the basis of information from Andropov, unanimously voted to use military force in putting down the Hungarian revolution—which in Moscow was of course called a "counterrevolution."

Needless to say, it would be inaccurate to ascribe the Soviet invasion of Hungary solely to Andropov's covert efforts. There is no doubt but that various factors were involved. Probably, if instead of Mikoyan and Suslov, Khrushchev himself had flown to Budapest (as he had flown to Warsaw a few days earlier), and had personally promised Nagy not to intervene, his word would have carried more weight than

the promise of Suslov and Mikoyan, and would have been harder to
renege on. At the time, however, Khrushchev was under pressure
from all directions. From the military, who saw Hungary as the Soviet
empire's western bridgehead, with bases for ground troops and the air
force, and were afraid of losing it. From the satraps of the other East
European countries, who were thrown into a real panic by the events
in Poland and Hungary, so that the anti-Hungarian articles in the
Bucharest *Scinteia* and the East Berlin *Neues Deutschland* had a much
sharper tone than those in *Pravda*. And finally, from the Kremlin
Stalinists, headed by Molotov and Kaganovich, who were demanding
a return to the earlier methods of governing the empire. Hungary was
their trump card in the battle against Khrushchev. "This," they no
doubt said, "is what his liberal policy has brought us to." And the
secret information sent from the building on Bayza Street in Budapest
to the one on Red Square in Moscow supplied the needed arguments
to the Soviet military, the Kremlin true believers, and, indirectly, to
the East European leaders with their fear of the chain reaction which
would inevitably be set off by the events in Hungary if they were not
stopped in time.

Naturally, Andropov was very familiar with the alignments of
forces in the Kremlin; and with his compromising reports he was
making a bid for the attention of the anti-Khrushchev faction headed
by Molotov and Kaganovich, and not that of Khrushchev, who only
three years before had sent him into exile in Hungary. For Khrushchev himself, the Hungarian question was a *Lebensfrage*—a matter
on which his political survival depended. In agreeing with the arguments of Andropov and the neo-Stalinist faction behind him, he
postponed the decisive power struggle until a year later, when he had
grown strong enough to overcome his enemies and drive them out of
the Politburo.

As to just how much vacillation there was in the Kremlin at that
time, we have the testimony of Khrushchev himself, in the memoirs
that he later dictated on a tape recorder. At one point he summoned
Marshal Konev, commander-in-chief of the Warsaw Pact Forces, and
asked him how much time the army would need to restore order in
Hungary. Konev's answer was "Three days." But Khrushchev dismissed him without issuing a definitive order. On another occasion he
invited a group of Chinese Communists headed by Liu Shaoqui to
Moscow, and argued all night with them at Stalin's former dacha,

called the *Lipka*. The Chinese kept making telephone calls to Peking to consult Mao Zedong—who, like an owl, didn't sleep at night but worked instead. Finally, toward morning, they persuaded Khrushchev not to use force against the Hungarians. But the Politburo, when he reported to it on his conference with the Chinese, undid that bit of persuasion. On the stormy night of November 2, accompanied by Malenkov, Khrushchev took a plane to Yugoslavia to see Tito, who was then vacationing on the island of Brioni in the Adriatic. Their plane avoided crashing only by a miracle. Then they had a bumpy ride in a car, followed by a still rougher one in a motor launch, so that when they finally reached the island they were more dead than alive.

Once again, an all-night discussion was held—this time with the Yugoslav dictator. They needed to gain his support, although by this time the decision had already been made—something Khrushchev was unwilling to acknowledge to Tito.

All of these fluctuations in the Kremlin were at the same time fluctuations in the political life of Yuri Andropov. For him, it had been a period demanding a tremendous amount of groundwork, which he did in his office at the embassy on Bayza Street. By November 1, when the Birnam Wood of the Red army had started to move and crossed the Hungarian border, the fate of Hungary was sealed; and all that remained for Andropov to do was to add the finishing touches to the work of art he had created.

In response to Nagy's first question, Andropov calmly replied that he had no accurate information on the situation that had developed. He promised, however, that he would immediately ask his government for an explanation.

At 11:00 A.M. he returned to the Parliament building, where the Hungarian premier was, and told him that the movements of the Soviet forces were of a routine kind, and that given the time of year, they were a usual phenomenon in no way associated with the events in Hungary.

"And even if there is a connection," he added with a smile, "it is not to the prejudice of Hungary. To the contrary, we are doing it in order to avoid incidents in the pullout of Soviet military units from Hungary. That is our obligation: to assure the orderly withdrawal of the forces."

"But why have tanks and armored cars encircled our airports?" Nagy asked.

For this, too, Andropov had a ready answer.

"To ensure the safe evacuation, by air, of the sick and wounded. You will surely agree, Mr. Prime Minister, that things are not very peaceful in your country right now."

For Nagy, to be addressed as "Mr." (*gospodin*) was like a stab. All of the Soviet officials, including Ambassador Andropov, had always called him "Comrade." But this was not the time to worry about personal nuances. Nagy preferred to believe Andropov: there was nothing else he could do. He asked the ambassador to get additional information from Moscow, and at the same time to convey to the Kremlin his protest in connection with the movement of Soviet troops through the territory of Hungary.

At 2:00 P.M. Nagy again telephoned the Soviet embassy and called Andropov to the phone. This time he gave the ambassador an ultimatum: if the Soviet Union did not immediately begin to withdraw its forces from Hungary, the Hungarian government would announce its withdrawal from the Warsaw Pact. He asked that his ultimatum be promptly conveyed to Moscow.

At 5:00 P.M., not yet having had a return call from Andropov, Nagy convened a session of the Council of Ministers, which unanimously passed a resolution declaring Hungary to be a neutral country. But Nagy himself realized how pregnant with consequences that resolution was; and he kept putting off its official announcement from one hour to the next. He was still waiting for Andropov—still hoping.

The Soviet ambassador finally arrived, and read the Kremlin's answer aloud. Nagy instantly translated it into Hungarian, and dictated it to an aide.

Moscow's reply was that the Soviet declaration of October 30 on equality and nonintervention was still in force. Also, it proposed that two joint commissions be set up: one to deal with the political problems resulting from Hungary's decision to withdraw from the Warsaw Pact, and the other to handle the technical details involved in the pullout of Soviet forces from the territory of Hungary.

Andropov had to gain time at any price. First, to prevent military resistance by the Hungarians against the Soviet army, and thereby reduce the number of Russian casualties. Second, to finish the job of seeking out Hungarian quislings for setting up a new government to counterbalance the Nagy regime. Andropov took upon himself the responsibility for settling the Hungarian crisis. His version of things had been accepted by Moscow. And now he alone had taken the place, in Budapest, of the Soviet army, the organs of state security, and the entire Politburo. The fate of the whole Soviet empire, and of each Soviet soldier, now depended upon him—personally. And any means for achieving such a lofty end were regarded by him as acceptable. Lying was the most harmless of the means he had to use during those fateful days in Budapest.

Nagy and the members of his cabinet listened to Moscow's answer, which consisted of five paragraphs, and then once again demanded of Andropov the immediate pullout of Soviet troops. The most stinging comment was that made by Janos Kadar: "What will happen to me is of absolutely no importance. But, being a Hungarian, I'm ready to fight if I must. If your tanks again enter Budapest, I'll go out on the street and fight them with my bare hands."

That same day, Kadar spoke on the radio—more frankly and passionately than Nagy: "In the course of this uprising, our people have overthrown the Rakosi regime. Those taking part in the uprising have gained freedom for the people and independence for the country. . . . We are proud that we have honorably fulfilled our duty in this armed uprising."

It was already late, and the cabinet dispersed. Kadar got into a car along with Ferenc Munnich. While riding in the car, they began to quarrel sharply about something. They were already nearing Kadar's home, when he told the driver to turn around and go to Bayza Street. They spent the night at the Soviet embassy, and in the morning a Soviet tank took them to the military air base of Tokol on Csepel Island. From there a special plane took them to the Soviet (formerly Hungarian) city of Uzhgorod, near the border.

On the morning of November 2, when Nagy learned not only of the disappearance of Kadar and Munnich but of more crossings of the Hungarian border by Soviet troops, he again summoned Andropov to his office. For the first time, that Soviet fashion plate was not up to his usual natty appearance. He looked tired, worn-out. He was unshaven, and his necktie was sloppily tied. It seemed as if he hadn't even gone to bed the night before. But at that moment, Nagy couldn't give his attention to such details, so he didn't make any connection between the nocturnal vanishing of two of his cabinet members and the unusual appearance of the Soviet ambassador. Nagy spoke nervously and yet with gravity. He realized that the Soviet empire stood behind Andropov's back, and he hurled one charge after another at him.

By contrast, Andropov listened absentmindedly and answered purely for the sake of form, listlessly and often irrelevantly, not even bothering to come up with more or less credible arguments. The only real effort he made was in trying to play down the Soviet military threat. "When you talk about a massive invasion, you're obviously exaggerating. It's just that some units are being replaced by others. But they, too, will soon be pulled out. The whole question isn't worth a wooden kopeck."

Nagy's patriotic fervor struck Andropov as out of place, especially now. Some of the premier's questions he simply left unanswered. He looked straight into the eyes of that doomed man and wearily—not so much politely as mechanically—smiled. He was already thinking of something else. His Hungarian game was over.

On the night of November 3, Nagy slept in the Parliament building. At 4:00 A.M. he was awakened and told that Soviet troops were assaulting Budapest. At 5:20 he went on the radio to address his fellow citizens:

> This is Imre Nagy, chairman of the Council of Ministers of the Hungarian People's Republic.
> Today, at dawn, Soviet troops attacked the capital with the evident intention of overthrowing the legitimate democratic government of Hungary.
> Our troops are fighting.
> The government is remaining at its post.
> I am reporting these events to the people of our country and to the world.

A half hour later, Nagy learned that a pro-Soviet government, headed by Janos Kadar, had been formed. Did the Hungarian premier then recall that the Soviet ambassador, Andropov, looked worn-out, as if he hadn't slept, the morning after Kadar had sought refuge in the mysterious building behind the wrought-iron gate on Bayza Street?

Nor had Kadar slept that night. He was the only Hungarian to whom the professionally secretive Andropov had revealed the whole story. That Nagy's game was up, and he was done for. That the Soviet troops had already been ordered to crush the uprising. And that Janos Kadar had no choice: if he refused to collaborate with the Russians, he would suffer the same fate as Nagy.

"It was Andropov who talked to Kadar first, and it was Andropov who persuaded Kadar to go over to the Soviet viewpoint," recalls Miklos Vasarhelyi, Nagy's press aide.

On that cold autumn night, equally cold calculation, cynicism, and perfidy gained the upper hand over the romanticism, naïveté, and political infantilism of the Hungarian revolution.

Imre Nagy found asylum in the Yugoslav embassy. Some twenty-two days later, having received a guarantee of personal safety from the authorities, he emerged. But he never reached home: he was seized by agents of the Soviet secret police. Eighteen months later he was convicted of treason; and on the night of June 15, 1958, he was executed.

Some of Nagy's surviving aides have told of their encounters with the Soviet proconsul during the last days—and even the last hours—before the fall of Budapest. Major-General Bela Kiraly, formerly chairman of the Council of National Defense and commander-in-chief of the Hungarian National Guard, had this to say. On November 2 Andropov made a telephone call complaining that disorderly hooligans were threatening the security of the embassy and its personnel, and declaring that if the Hungarian government was not able to maintain order, he would have to call upon Soviet troops for help. Consequently, General Kiraly, accompanied by motorized infantry and armored cars, was sent to the Soviet embassy. When they reached the building on Bayza Street, they didn't find a single person near the embassy. A dead silence reigned in the area around it, and there was no sign of life. They knocked for a long time on the heavy oak door until it was finally opened. On the threshold appeared a stately man in a dinner jacket. It was Andropov. Behind him, lined up as if for some kind of ceremony, stood the entire embassy staff. Andropov immediately withdrew his complaint, saying that it was the result of a misunderstanding, and even joked, telling them that the only Hungarians who had threatened the Soviet embassy that day were two old ladies looking for some place to get warm because of the cold, windy weather.

Andropov invited General Kiraly to come up with him to his office. "Believe me, General, the Soviet people are Hungary's best friends," said the Soviet ambassador. And he proposed the immediate beginning of talks about withdrawing Soviet troops from Hungary. Throughout this conversation, it seemed to General Kiraly that Andropov was hypnotizing him.

Andropov escorted him back downstairs, then gave him a firm handshake. And Kiraly left with no doubt in his mind that the Soviet ambassador was on the side of the Hungarian revolution. "He was masterful in conveying the impression of being sincere and natural."

The talks proposed by Andropov were begun the next day at the Soviet military base of Tokol on Csepel Island. They continued until midnight, when KGB agents broke into the room and arrested the Hungarian delegation. Its head, General Pal Maleter, a hero of the Hungarian revolution, was executed.

A quarter century later, Bela Kiraly remembers Andropov's false smile and his cold, gray-blue eyes and their hypnotic power. Today he feels that they were the eyes of an inquisitor. "You knew immediately that he could smile at you or kill you with the same ease."

But he adds: "And yet, Andropov showed considerable courage in [earlier] going to the prime minister's office even as Soviet forces were invading the country. He definitely put himself in danger. He could have been lynched.

"Here was this man Andropov who clearly understood what was going on," Kiraly said bitterly, "yet he pretended until the last moment to me and to the prime minister and to others that everything was business as usual. Even pirates, before they attack another ship, hoist a black flag. He was absolutely calculating.

"Andropov is a symbol of the reign of terror that followed the Soviet invasion. He made Hungary silent—like a graveyard. He deported thousands to Russia and had hundreds of defenseless young men hanged."

Colonel Sandor Kopacsi, then chief of the Budapest police, whom Andropov had met at receptions at the Soviet embassy, and with whose wife he had danced, remembers: "Andropov gave the impression of being pro-reform. He smiled often, had honeyed words for reformers, and it was hard for us to tell whether he was only acting on instructions or was following his own personal inclination. He was well mannered and personable. Instead of ordering this or that, as his predecessor had done, Andropov always 'suggested' and 'recommended' things. But I felt something cold in him. His eyes seemed to change color. And there was a chilly flame in those eyes hidden behind the spectacles."

The last meeting between Sandor Kopacsi and Yuri Andropov took place on the last day of the Hungarian revolution. As Kopacsi and his wife were hurrying toward the Yugoslav embassy, where they hoped to find political asylum, they were arrested on the street by KGB agents and taken to the Soviet embassy. Andropov greeted them cheerfully and affably, and explained that Janos Kadar, who was now forming a new government, wanted to see Kopacsi. Colonel Kopacsi believed his old acquaintance. But instead of taking him to Kadar, the Soviet armored car took him to prison. He wasn't released until seven years later, in 1963, by a general amnesty. He has never forgotten how Andropov, standing on an upper landing of the staircase, smiled and waved good-bye to him.

Georg Heltai, deputy minister of foreign affairs in Nagy's cabinet, noting Andropov's intelligence and coolness, is of the opinion that the Soviet ambassador was "the ultimate power who decided who and how many people should be executed."

And he adds: "I'm sure that he had an absolutely free hand to deal with the revolutionaries, so the reign of terror in Hungary was the reign of terror of Yuri Andropov. It's bound to his name forever."

Almost all of the Hungarians who had occasion to meet the Kremlin *gauleiter* during the revolution are reminded by that of the historical episode, in 1544, when the Turkish sultan Suleiman invited a Hungarian nobleman, Balint Torok, to dinner. The guest did not trust his host overly much, and several times he got up from the table, intending to go home. Each time he did the host, smiling, insisted that he stay for a while. "But you haven't yet tried our black soup," he would say—meaning coffee. When the "black soup" was finally served, some janissaries seized the Hungarian and put him in fetters. Since then, in the Hungarian language, "black soup" has meant the vilest kind of perfidy and treachery.

A Lucky Ticket: The KGB

2

"And don't all animal-trainers go about it like that?"
"By no means all. They have two methods, or schools:
the wild, or *wilde Dressur*, using fire and iron, and the tame,
or *zahme Dressur*, which not only rules out shooting but even
cracking the whip in the air for the sake of appearances. And
yet the most brilliant results are achieved: the wild beasts are
as meek as lambs, and the audience is tranquil and
complacent."   — NIKOLAI LESKOV,
                                 "Administrative Grace (*Zahme
                                 Dressur* . . . in a Gendarme
                                 Arrangement)," 1893

There is one particular fact about Andropov's political career that predetermined its steady progression and triumphal
character: in changing posts, he did not change his former functions
but merely expanded them. Over a period of thirty years, beginning
with his Hungarian assignment, his political itinerary was essentially a
matter of broadening his official duties, until finally he reached the
post that marked the bourn of that movement. For him, henceforth,
the expansion of his career was possible only by means of the territorial expansion of the Soviet empire.

It suffices to compare Andropov's career with that of any of his
Party colleagues, to get an idea of how expansionist and aggressive was
his climb up the political ladder: his movement upward was at the
same time a movement in breadth. For example, even Brezhnev's
ascent to the Kremlin Olympus involved much more discontinuity
and zigzags. When he got a new job, he inevitably lost the preceding
one. Thus right after the war he was named Party boss of the
Zaporozhe Oblast; two years later he was transferred to a similar post
in the neighboring Dnepropetrovsk Oblast, where he was born; three
years later he became Party leader of the Moldavian Republic (although he was not a Moldavian); and four years after that he was
appointed to the same kind of position in another republic, Kazakhstan (although he was not a Kazakh). Ultimately, Brezhnev became

[26]

a Soviet vozhd, but this was rather due to the anti-Khruschchev intrigues of his colleagues, headed by Suslov, than to his own efforts. Things were quite otherwise with Andropov. There was an inexorable logic about the way in which he arrived at the supreme power; and he was indebted to no one but himself for achieving that power.

Actually, his path to the Kremlin was one of an accumulation of official duties, until their quantity spilled over into quality. This was not a matter of chance but rather the inevitable—one might almost say arithmetical—result of all his previous cumulative activities.

From 1953 on, indeed, he did not suffer any of those losses that are usually attendant upon almost any official career in the USSR. He was appointed counsellor in Budapest, and in less than a year he became Ambassador Extraordinary and Plenipotentiary. In other words, his duties and responsibilities in Hungary were broadened and consolidated. After the brilliant fulfillment of his secret mission there, he was named, in the summer of 1957, head of the Central Committee's Department for Liaison with Ruling Communist and Workers' Parties. That meant he was put in charge of overseeing Moscow's vassals—the East European countries, Mongolia, China, North Korea, and North Vietnam. (Yugoslavia was also included here, although this was a matter of wishful thinking.) Andropov made frequent trips to those countries, at first accompanying Khrushchev and later, after Khrushchev's downfall, accompanying his successors, Brezhnev and Kosygin; or he would visit them alone. No one after Lenin had spent as much time abroad before becoming the Soviet vozhd as had Andropov; and yet not once did he step across the border of the socialist camp. Ironically, that border was for Andropov even more impassable than for the other Soviet citizens, who (a tiny minority of them, naturally) cross it as tourists, diplomats, journalists, spies, emigrants, or defectors. Perhaps it was also in part for personal reasons that he had an interest in strengthening that border. During the night of August 12, 1961, the last escape hatch from Eastern Europe into Western Europe was sealed off: a living chain of fifty thousand soldiers cut off the Soviet sector of Berlin from the rest of the world. In the place of that cordon there soon arose the Berlin Wall, twenty-five kilometers long, with barbed wire entanglements, anti-tank barriers, mine fields, and watchtowers. It was built by soldiers; but its chief architects were Walter Ulbricht, then the leader of East Germany, and Yuri Andropov, then imperial overseer of the socialist countries.

And so, even after Andropov's departure from Hungary, it remained under his wardship, along with eleven other countries. Many years later, when he was already close to the Olympian leap in his unusual career, and when rumors (each one contradicting the next) were completely obscuring his real activities, among the other things that were being ascribed to Andropov was the coauthorship, along with Janos Kadar, of Hungarian "goulash socialism" or "socialism with a bourgeois face"—a paraphrase of the "socialism with a human face" that existed in Prague during several months of 1968, until it was crushed by the treads of Soviet tanks. That is hardly likely. In view of the job he had done in Hungary, Andropov was given the role of a sheepdog responsible for driving stray sheep back into the flock, while such complex questions as granting reforms were decided by the shepherd himself, who at the time was Khrushchev. For that matter, whoever may have sanctioned the construction in Hungary of "the happiest barracks in the socialist camp," it was due not to liberalism but to pragmatism—since, as one Roman emperor opined, a good shepherd shears his sheep but he doesn't strip their hides off them.

The Department of the CC (Central Committee) for Liaison with Ruling Communist Parties was new, as if it had been specially set up for Andropov because of the successful job he had done in Hungary and with a premonition of future difficulties in relations with the socialist countries. Under the leadership of Andropov, and in view of the growing divergence of opinion between the Soviet Union on the one hand and Yugoslavia, China, Albania (and, soon, Rumania) on the other, that department assumed prime importance. This was indirectly reflected in the very fact that Andropov was elected a member of the CC at a regular Party congress in 1961 and a secretary of the CC at the next congress, while still retaining his post as head of the department. During that period he published several sharply worded articles against the East European schismatics: against the Yugoslavs in the May 1960 issue of the magazine *Kommunist*, and against the Albanians in *Pravda* for December 2, 1961.

Again, unlike his colleagues, he gained more while losing nothing. It is simply that at the time, especially in view of the schism between the Soviet Union and China, the importance of the CC department headed by Andropov had grown so much that it was necessary to have someone in the secretariat itself to oversee those matters. And among those whom the Soviet leaders had been keeping their eye on, there was no one more suitable for that post than Andropov. By being elected a secretary of the CC in 1962 while at the same time retaining his post as head of a department of the CC, Andropov became, as it were, his own superior—a unique combination in the Soviet Party structure.

In passing, we should note yet another anomaly in Andropov's career: he was elected a full member of the CC without having passed through a probationary period as an alternate member. Nor was this the first time he had done such "leapfrogging." Thus in 1938 he became first secretary of the Yaroslavl Oblast Committee of the Komsomol when he was still not a Party member, although according to the Party rules then in force, no one who did not have a minimum of four years' membership in the Party could be named to that post. Yet Andropov did not become a Party member until 1939. A year later, however, he was named first secretary of the Komsomol of the Karelo-Finnish Republic—again in violation of the Party rules, since five years' membership in the Party was a prerequisite to that appointment. The fact that in those days he was able to leap up several rungs of the ladder at once is no doubt due to the scope of Stalin's purges: there were too many positions left open. Stalin needed new, young, reliable cadres; and at the outset of his career, Andropov figuratively walked over the corpses of his predecessors. This was especially true of the Komsomol, where he made his début. The old all-union Komsomol leadership, headed up by Kosarev, perished to a man in the period of the Great Terror (Kosarev was personally arrested by Beria); and many republic and provincial Komsomol organizations were destroyed. What in fact happened was that the former Komsomol, with its Leninist traditions, was completely replaced by a new Stalinist Komsomol, one of whose activists and leaders was Yuri Andropov.

It is more difficult to understand why, in 1961, Andropov became a full member of the CC, bypassing the freshman stage as an alternate member. Perhaps that was yet another reward for the services he had rendered in Hungary. Or else he had managed to earn it in his new post as head of a CC department; because in and of itself, the idea of the Berlin Wall, phenomenal in its crude strength, was worthy of a reward. One thing, however, is clear: by now Andropov was indispensable to Khrushchev—as a Stalinist, police-style corrective to his relatively liberal and, in any case, anti-Stalinist regime. Andropov was one of the counterpoises to that regime—something needed to offset the liberal undertakings of Khrushchev, who undoubtedly displayed a political Ménière's syndrome. And yet Khrushchev's fall came about because he, afraid of losing his balance, surrounded himself with too many Stalinist counterpoises; he fell in the opposite direction from that in which he was afraid he would fall. And it was precisely that downfall in the "Little October" of 1964 (so-called to distinguish it from the "Big October" of 1917) that became yet one more decisive moment in the political life of Yuri Andropov.

Khrushchev, with his sharp opposition to Stalinism, was an outspoken rebel sitting in the armchair of the prime minister and Party boss; and his rebellion was aimed against Russian imperial history. His liberal reforms threatened the very existence of the empire. In other words, Khrushchev's anti-Stalinist policy was out of place in Russia, and was resolutely rejected by that country. One may even say that the cause of his downfall was his voluntarism toward the Russian tradition; and that his Party colleagues, who in the autumn of 1964 carried out a palace revolution, were (perhaps without even being aware of it) accomplishing the will of history.

Behind them was the ice block of the Russian past; and that is why the dissent that arose at such a high level was put down. Khrushchev—and not Solzhenitsyn or Sakharov—was the first Soviet dissident. And the strange thing is not that he finally fell, but that he fell in 1964 and not in 1957, when the majority of his comrades-in-arms rose up against him, and he was saved only by Marshal Zhukov's resolute, forceful move.

If even the anti-Stalinist Khrushchev, who did not particularly like Andropov, could nonetheless not get along without him and his services, the Party team which replaced Khrushchev, and which got the country back on course, bringing it again into the main channel of Russian imperial history, valued Andropov for the services he had rendered. On May 19, 1967, less than three years after the October palace coup, at age fifty-two, Yuri Andropov was named chairman of the KGB. And a month later *Pravda* announced that the new head of the KGB had been elected a candidate-member of the Politburo—a clear sign of the heightened importance (as compared with the Khrushchev era) that the new Kremlin leaders attributed to the KGB and to Andropov personally. Because since Lavrenty Beria was shot in 1953, not so much as one head of the secret police had been elected to the Politburo, even on the candidate level, without the right to vote.

The man whom Andropov replaced as chief of the KGB was Vladimir Semichastny, famous for what he had said (during his previous tenure as boss of the Komsomol) about Boris Pasternak, after the latter had published his novel *Doctor Zhivago* abroad; namely, that even a hog doesn't shit in his own pigsty, whereas Pasternak had shat. But of course it was not for that "contribution" to literary criticism that Semichastny was fired. He had already made enough mistakes which, from the viewpoint of Brezhnev and Company, were more serious. Many observers think that his biggest mistake was his failure to prevent the defection of Stalin's daughter, Svetlana Alliluyeva. But this could not have been the cause of his dismissal; at the very most, it provided an occasion for it. The important thing here is that Semichastny was the protégé of Alexander Shelepin, who had preceded him both in the Komsomol and at the KGB, and was stubbornly keeping him in tow as he moved upward, naming him to posts that he himself had had to vacate, since he (Shelepin) was filling ever higher and more responsible ones.

Alexander Shelepin was called "Iron Shurik" (Shurik being a diminutive of Alexander). He tried to extend the methods of the KGB (which he had once headed) to the whole country, explaining this by the necessity for a strong regime and discipline—a program close to that announced by Andropov when he came to power. Shelepin called his movement the "Workers' Opposition." He campaigned for a return from the bureaucratic dictatorship to the dictatorship of the proletariat and pure socialism; and he was ready personally to lead a crusade against the intellectuals-turned-bourgeois and the cosmopolitan Jews. But his appearance on the political stage was premature, and his challenge to Brezhnev's power was inapposite. Shelepin's swift rise was followed by an equally swift fall: first secretary of the Komsomol, chairman of the KGB, secretary of the CC (with simultaneous membership in the Politburo), and then, suddenly, Trade-Union chairman. The last-named post was merely nominal; but he couldn't hang on even to that one, and fell into political oblivion.

Shelepin's ambition was overweening, his will to power was in fact an iron will, and in addition he had almost complete control over the KGB organs and the key posts in the Party apparatus. His impatience was his undoing; and his removal was Brezhnev's greatest political victory. Naturally, the struggle with Shelepin was at the same time a struggle with his protégés, the most dangerous of whom was KGB chief Semichastny. Almost simultaneously with Semichastny's dismissal came that of Komsomol boss Sergei Pavlov, another Shelepin protégé, who had tried to transform the Party's filial youth organization into a kind of *Hitlerjugend*. But with no Hitler at the head of the nation, this meant getting dangerously far out in front of his real power. In response to official criticism, he usually said that the Komsomol was the Party's watchdog and was duty-bound to run ahead of its master. He was dismissed just at the moment when he was trying to introduce a special uniform for Komsomol members, and to form detachments of storm troopers from among his Brownshirts.

To come back to Semichastny, the process of his neutralization had begun long before his official removal from office, with Andropov playing a leading role in that process. As a secretary of the CC, in addition to his regular duties, the latter had the job of keeping an eye on the KGB organs, with the result that on the Party level he became a kind of backup man for Semichastny, in several cases fully replacing him, and in all cases monitoring him. It is most probable that this happened sometime in the middle of 1966, a year before Andropov's official appointment as head of the secret police, succeeding Semichastny. It was just then that Andropov, who by virtue of his job as CC secretary for liaison with the socialist countries had to take part in various conferences with leaders of "fraternal" Communist parties, suddenly disappeared from view—for more than four months. His last public appearance before that was on April 13, 1966, when Brezhnev met with a Cuban delegation. His subsequent vanishing from public view was obviously not due to his being in disfavor, even temporary, because in June he was elected as a deputy of the Supreme Soviet (something that did not require a public appearance); and in July his signature was one of those appended to the official obituary of Rudakov, who had been CC secretary for heavy industry. Nor would this seem to have been a case of prolonged illness. Andropov's next appearance before the public did not occur until August 27, at a meeting with the West German Communist Max Reiman—with whom, actually, he was not obliged to meet, since his duties included overseeing ruling Communists but not such hopeless oppositionists as Max Reiman.

There are bits of circumstantial evidence tending to show that Andropov spent those four months learning his new trade and squeezing out Semichastny. One of them comes from Vladimir Sakharov, a former Soviet diplomat and KGB agent, who defected in 1971. He is not a very reliable source of information, and we will later have an opportunity to explain why. And yet, since he was a friend of Andropov's son Igor and was on occasion the guest of Igor and his father, Sakharov sometimes provides quite good information. In particular, he is of the opinion that although Andropov's appointment as head of the KGB was officially announced in 1967, it actually dates from 1964 or 1965, " . . . because I remember a party celebrating his new appointment at about that time."

The only doubtful thing in that statement is the date. Andropov could not have been named KGB chief in either 1964 or 1965, because it was precisely during those two years that he was most intensively occupied with trips to the socialist countries. Among the places he visited: Hungary (twice); Brioni Island, for a meeting with Tito; Belovezhskaya Forest, on the border between Poland and the USSR, for a meeting with Gomulka; East Berlin, for the celebration of the one hundredth anniversary of the First International; Warsaw, for a session of the Consultative Council of the Warsaw Treaty Organization; North Vietnam; Peking; North Korea, for a discussion of the Vietnamese question; Warsaw (again), as a member of the Party-government delegation; and finally, Bucharest, for the Ninth Congress of the Rumanian Workers' Party. And then in the autumn of 1966, right after his four months of absence from public view, the frequency of Andropov's junkets abroad dropped sharply. This means that throughout 1964 and 1965 he remained CC secretary for the socialist countries, but that in the spring of 1966 he was transferred to a new job—with the KGB. Sakharov's inaccuracy is easy to explain. The interview in which he told about the party at Andropov's home to celebrate his appointment as head of the secret police was conducted in 1982, more than a decade and a half after that party. For that matter, he does not insist that he is accurate, and by way of guesswork names two years, 1964 and 1965. This leaves open the possibility of at least one other date; and the most likely one, it seems to us, is 1966.

Another bit of circumstantial evidence tending to show that Andropov was named chief of the KGB prior to the official announcement of that appointment is to be found in an article that the Rumanian "conductor," Nikolai Ceausescu, published in the Bucharest Party newspaper *Scinteia* on May 7, 1967. In that article, the Rumanian dictator complains about the subversive activity of some Communist countries against others. He does not explicitly name the Soviet Union, but there is no doubt that it is the USSR he is talking about. Just at this time came the discord between Moscow and Bucharest that was more and more disquieting the Kremlin. Together with two other schismatic countries, Yugoslavia and Albania, Rumania forms a kind of gap in the Soviet empire's march or borderland defensive zone extending from the Black Sea to the Adriatic. Not only that, but Rumania, which was becoming more and more independent both politically and militarily, was breaking the USSR's territorial tie with its loyal vassal, Bulgaria. It is very likely that after taking on his new job, Andropov first of all tried to use his new powers and means to take revenge for his failure when he was in his previous post, and drive the stray sheep back into the Warsaw flock—this time not through suasion. And again he failed. Just how sensitive he was to that defeat, and just how rancorous Andropov is, can be judged from the fact that sixteen years later, two and a half months after he became general secretary of the Party, he again tried to discipline the unruly Rumania, and failed yet once again. On January 31, 1983, the Rumanian security service, Sekuritane, discovered a Moscow-inspired plot by several generals of the Rumanian army to assassinate Ceausescu. By February 3 the pro-Moscow plotters had already been executed.

But the exact dating of Andropov's appointment as chairman of the KGB is not so important as the precise reasons for which he was named to that post. And it is not even so much reasons involving personality that are at issue here, since they are more or less obvious: Andropov had made a good showing in Party and diplomatic work as a proponent of a hard line and uncompromising decisions; and it was just such a person that was needed in that post. But what about the professional reasons? After all, Andropov had no background either as a military man or a KGB man. Therefore, his appointment was bewildering to the majority of Western journalists and experts, who could find only one, strictly personal explanation for it: that Andropov was an intimate co-worker of Brezhnev's. Actually, however, the professional reasons for Andropov's transfer from the CC's department for liaison with the socialist countries to the secret police can be explained by the close kinship between the functions performed by these two organs of the Soviet regime.

After all, the very existence of such a colossal apparatus of coercion as the Committee of State Security (KGB) is due, first of all, to the necessity of keeping the satellite peoples (more precisely, the people of the marches) within the boundaries of the empire. In other words, there is a double borderland zone: the union republics within the USSR and the socialist countries on its frontiers. As for Russia proper, the present regime is a creation of the Russians and meets their social, political, moral, and psychological needs. If this were not so, we would have to resort to a mystical explanation of the origins of that imperial totalitarianism which, under various names that have not changed its essence (autocracy, dictatorship of the proletariat), has with variable success existed on the territory of Russia for a good many centuries. That which for a Czech, a Pole, an Estonian, a Hungarian, or an Afghan is the worst form of imperial totalitarianism is for the Russians (as for an imperial people) a form of *elemental democracy* in keeping with their notions of what is lawful, their historical traditions, and their daily needs. The empire puts this people (in many respects backward) on a level with advanced peoples. It forces others to take the Russians into account, and gives the latter a feeling of equality or even superiority. So that for them, giving up the empire would mean relinquishing their own historical significance as a great people.

To put it another way, the empire is the result of a historical choice. As between it and freedom, the Russians chose the empire, because within the limits of a country that is territorially one, the coexistence of unfreedom for the subjugated peoples and freedom for the subjugator-people is quite impossible. Likewise impossible is a voluntary union of the satellite peoples among themselves or, *a fortiori*, one headed up by the imperial people. If there were no apparatus of coercion, such a union would fall apart instantly, since the bonds among the peoples making it up (to use Herzen's phrase) are "based on their mutual repulsion." One may even risk saying that if the 250 million inhabitants of the vassal nations of the *Pax Sovietica* live in involuntary servitude, the remaining 138 million who constitute its Russian population live in voluntary servitude. For freedom is the price that the Russian people paid—and are still paying—for their choice, although that tragic choice has not brought happiness either to those who made it or (especially) to those who were victimized by someone else's choice, having become the slaves of a slave. The Russian empire is a boomerang that comes back to wound the one who threw it. As Karl Marx acutely remarked, "A people that enslaves another people, forges its own chains." The chains that the Russian people forged are the most durable and most perfect in the world. Regardless of how they are called—the *oprichnina* in the times of Ivan the Terrible or the Committee of State Security in our day—they must be ranked among the great creations of the Russian people, along with Mendeleyev's Periodic Table, *War and Peace, The Brothers Karamazov,* the Russian ballet, and the sputniks.

The demographic paradox of the world's last empire consists in the fact that it was founded as a *Russian* empire but has turned out to be a *multinational* empire in which the Russians have been pushed into the background when it comes to population figures, although politically they remain in the foreground—with the help of the organs of coercion. Therefore, it has not only been the borderland uprisings against the empire that have had a vividly nationalist/ethnic character (the repeated Polish, Ukrainian, Hungarian, and Czechoslovak rebellions, plus the current one in Afghanistan). The uprisings in the hinterland have also had a nationalist/ethnic coloration. For example, the jacqueries of Stenka Razin under Tsar Aleksei Mikhailovich in the seventeenth century, and of Emelyan Pugachev under Catherine the Great in the next century were primarily revolts of national minorities (the Mari, the Chuvash, the Mordvinians, the Tatars, the Cossacks) against the Russian denomination. Some Russian writers have even opined that if Catherine the Great had not acquired Poland late in the eighteenth century, and Poland's Jews along with it, the revolution of 1917 might have been avoided. The very similar conclusion that Solzhenitsyn draws from this—one as to the imported nature of that revolution—is based on the fact that among its makers there were fewer Russians than Jews, Poles, Georgians, Latvians, and other *minoritaires* all lumped together. But what kind of import was it if the Jews, Poles, Georgians, and Latvians were citizens of the same empire as the Russians, although they got less out of it than the Russians; that is, they did not enjoy equality with them, either in rights or in rightlessness. It was that state of affairs which impelled them to act against an empire which, politically, was not *theirs*—carrying along with them the malcontents among the Russians. Thus the crude notion that the Russians defend the empire while the national minorities destroy it is not so far from reality. But that, of course, does not rule out the active participation of Russians in its destruction (Lenin is the most striking example), and of non-Russians in defending it and restoring it. (It was under Stalin's hegemonic dictatorship that the Russian revolution countermarched, destroying its own model en route.) On the whole, however, the Russians have an imperial immunity to revolutionary contagion; and any revolt by a subjugated people is perceived by most of them as above all anti-Russian—which, by the way, is absolutely true.

So that to maintain order among the Russian inhabitants of the empire, the regular police suffice (with negligible exceptions, like the tiny group of Moscow dissidents with whom Andropov efficiently coped in the late seventies). But to put down the Hungarians in 1956 and the Czechoslovaks in 1968, it was necessary to throw in the whole mighty apparatus of the KGB organs, along with the army. And this means that while working as Party secretary for the socialist countries—chiefly those that form the Soviet empire's zone of defense—Andropov was already fulfilling a part (indeed, the most important part) of the functions he inherited when he became chairman of the Committee of State Security. His appointment to that post involved a natural and logical continuation of his previous work; and the Kremlin leaders, in naming him head of the KGB, took into account not only his personal traits but the duties he had already performed. His new appointment, like his earlier ones, did not mean a switch to completely new work but the expansion of his earlier functions and powers. Previously, he had carried out his pacifying, gendarme-type functions vis-à-vis the peoples of Eastern Europe. Now, in his new post, he had to carry them out vis-à-vis all the other peoples of the Union of Soviet Socialist Republics, including Russians—but especially vis-à-vis non-Russians. And the same inexorable logic mentioned *supra* is easy to discover in the appointment, fifteen years later, of the KGB chief as leader of the Soviet Union. For in fact he had already become the leader in the late seventies, when he transformed his agency (which had fallen into disfavor under Khrushchev) into the same all-powerful instrument it had been under Stalin, although without the scope of the Stalinist terror. The Number One gendarme's self-appointment as the Russian vozhd definitively exposed the Soviet Union as a police state. Thus Andropov's transfer to the secret police in 1967 (more accurately, a year earlier) was his lucky ticket. But he didn't get it by chance: he had earned it.

There is something definitely symbolic about the meeting that the new KGB chief chaired in the Kremlin on June 21, 1967—a day which marked the end of a two-day plenum of the CC at which Andropov was elected a candidate-member of the Politburo. This was a meeting with twenty representatives of the Crimean Tatars, a people who had been totally and forcibly resettled in Central Asia by Stalin, allegedly for collaboration with the Germans during World War II. Almost half of them, chiefly women and children, perished en route to their place of exile.

Many of the Tatar delegates took notes on that meeting. Among them was Aishe Seitmuratova, with whom one of the authors of this book conducted a detailed interview.

They were led into the conference room of the Presidium of the USSR Supreme Soviet and given seats at a long table covered with green baize. They didn't have to wait long. Soon the door was opened, and three men came in. The tallest of them—slightly stooped, with thick-lensed glasses and wearing an expensive-looking suit of dark gray—opened the meeting.

"Let's get acquainted. On my right is Comrade Shchelokov, minister of internal affairs. On my left is Comrade Rudenko, general procurator. My name is Andropov. I am chairman of the Committee of State Security."

The delegates of the Crimean Tatars were amazed when they found out that their demand for political rehabilitation and return to the Crimea was to be dealt with by the three chiefs of the punitive organizations of the Soviet Union. It was as if a compliant by mice were to be dealt with by cats. This was an open demonstration of force; and when Andropov suggested that a delegate state his complaints, one of them rose to his feet and said: "In what capacity are you personally serving on this commission? As a candidate-member of the Politburo or as chairman of the KGB?"

Andropov smiled faintly. "Does that make any difference?" Then he explained: "All three of us are members of the Central Committee. And each of us has a specific official position besides."

He was plainly being coy, playing down the importance of the dread organization that he bossed, and putting it on the same level with other punitive organs.

"But it does make a difference," the Tatar delegate insisted. "If you're here as a candidate-member of the Politburo, we'll tell you what's on our minds. But if you're here as chairman of the KGB, we'll leave this room without getting into any talks."

Andropov, who had always preferred the possession of secret strength to any external, ambitious manifestation of it, instantly took back what he had said. "I," he agreed, "was of course named head of the commission as a candidate-member of the Politburo." And again he smiled his elusive smile.

In this way the Tatars learned that Andropov was not simply one of the members of the commission assigned to deal with their complaints but its chairman. This was clearly confirmed by the pourparler that followed: he alone conducted it, his colleagues only putting in a word now and then.

Andropov's correct tone, his tractability, and his smiles disposed the Tatars toward openness. It was roughly the same effect that his manners had produced, eleven years before, on the Hungarians he talked to. This was the first time the Crimean Tatars had been granted an audience on such a high level; and it was the first time anyone had talked with them as equals, not threatening them but listening closely to what they had to say. Therefore, even the most intractable of the delegates, who had just expressed doubts about Andropov's authority and his membership in the CC commission, now relaxed and said: "Well, then, we can begin. But we have no leader, and no one person has been designated to speak for us. We were all granted the same degree of authority in representing our people, so you'll have to listen to all of us."

"Of course!" Andropov readily agreed. Then he added, smiling again: "But on one condition: that each of you speak one at a time, and not all of you in chorus."

That broke the ice. For the next four hours, the commission patiently heard out each of the Crimean Tatar petitioners in turn. The members of the commission listened more than they talked.

Toward the end of the talks, Andropov said: "We realize, Comrades, that your people want to return to its homeland and preserve its national integrity, language, and culture. And you are entitled under Soviet law to try for a full and definitive settlement of your national question. Last night the Politburo held a session on that subject, and I can inform you that in the matter of the political rehabilitation of the

Crimean Tatars, the opinion of the Politburo members was unanimous. But in the matter of your return to the Crimea, opinion was divided."

Aishe Seitmuratova got quickly to her feet. "Yuri Vladimirovich, may I ask a question?"

"What might your name be?" Andropov asked. And when Aishe introduced herself, he knit his brow slightly. "Your name seems to ring a bell for me."

"On the same day that you were named chairman of the KGB, I was released from your boarding house."

That was in fact what had happened. On May 19, 1967, after nine months of preventive detention in Lefortovo Prison, Aishe had been convicted of stirring up nationalist feelings and sentenced to three years probation. She was released from custody right there in the courtroom.

"Yes, yes, I remember," Andropov said good-naturedly. "And what is your question?"

"Which members of the Politburo were in favor of our return to the Crimea, and which ones were against it?"

"Even if you take me like that," said Andropov, putting his hand to his throat, "I won't tell you." And he added: "We'll arrange all conditions for your life in Uzbekistan."

"But there's nothing in Uzbekistan for us!" exclaimed one of the delegates. "We want to go home to the Crimea."

At this point, Shchelokov broke in: "Comrades, don't refuse what's being offered you. The seedlings have to be planted. It will be easy to transplant them later on."

Andropov promptly tried to soften his colleague's overly blunt remark. It was plain to see that he was a man whose style and tastes were totally different. "So here you are with your national question, which as a matter of fact is already ripe—"

"Overripe, Yuri Vladimirovich!" interrupted one of the completely undaunted petitioners.

"All right, overripe. I'm not going to argue. You know best. But I should point out that in recent years I've become a specialist on national questions. I've been assigned to handle just such questions, as my comrades will tell you." At this point, he nodded toward Rudenko and Shchelokov. "Eleven years ago I was the ambassador to Hungary. Do you remember what happened in Hungary?"

"But we're not Hungarians. We're Crimean Tatars who are Soviet citizens."

"True enough. But your problem is not the only one. Do you know, for example, that in the East we're sitting on a powder keg?"

At that time, relations with China were steadily worsening. On the border, there was growing tension, which less then twenty months later produced a bloody conflict on a tiny island in the Ussuri River, which the Chinese called Chenpao and the Russians called Damansky. As CC secretary for liaison with the socialist countries, Andropov had taken part in several talks with the Chinese, all of which ended in failure.

There was no point in talking about the Chinese to the Crimean Tatars, who couldn't have cared less. So Andropov changed the subject. "Well, then, if I understand you correctly, you want the Crimea and nothing more. Is that right?"

Aishe recalls that all of them, without any discussion, promptly answered in chorus: "That's right! The Crimea, and nothing more!"

Andropov promised that a decree on the political rehabilitation of the Crimean Tatars would soon be published. Then the delegates asked whether, upon their return to Uzbekistan, they would be allowed to hold a mass meeting and report the results of their trip to their people. Andropov, amicably smiling for the last time, replied: "What's the problem? If you want, I'll be happy to call Rashidov myself so you can get the best auditorium in Tashkent—the Navoi Theater—for your meeting."

Andropov undoubtedly did make a call to Tashkent; either to Rashidov, the Party boss of Uzbekistan, or to one of his deputies, or (most likely of all) to the chief of the Uzbek KGB, Andropov's immediate subordinate. But the welcome given the Crimean Tatar delegation in Uzbekistan was altogether different from what they expected after Andropov's encouraging smiles. Not only did they not get the Navoi Theater as a forum where they could report back to those who had sent them to Moscow, they were not even allowed to hold an open-air meeting. They were dispersed, beaten, hauled off to the police station, and prosecuted. And although by the decree of the Presidium of the USSR Supreme Soviet dated September 5, 1967, the groundless charge of treason that had been made against the Crimean Tatars was finally withdrawn, that decree at the same time effectively destroyed the nationhood of the Crimean Tatars, using the language "citizens of

Tatar ethnic origin who formerly inhabited the Crimea." That decree was the result of the Crimean Tatars' long struggle for their national rights, and simultaneously the beginning of the definitive suppression of that struggle. Now, when Tatars came to Moscow with petitions, they were picked up, beaten, and sent back to Uzbekistan. And in Uzbekistan itself, Crimean Tatar meetings and demonstrations were dispersed by the police and soldiers. But those who had the worst of it were the thousands of people who had dared to return to their home-land, the Crimea. They were thrown out of the homes they had bought; they were beaten; they were robbed; they were again de-ported to Uzbekistan; and their homes were razed by bulldozers, without their even being compensated for the value of those homes. In the Crimea a very real anti-Tatar psychosis set in, exacerbated by the xenophobia of the local Ukrainians and Russians. Anti-Tatar pogroms became a daily occurrence. More than three hundred persons were arrested and convicted on trumped-up charges. And the entire anti-Tatar campaign was directed by local branch offices of the KGB. A few years later the USSR Council of Ministers passed a draconian decree tightening very severely the internal passport regulations on the territory of the Crimea. The local inhabitants were prohibited, under threat of resettlement, to allow into their homes any representa-tives of the people that had been in possession of the Crimea for many centuries. Such is the epilogue to the meeting between the delegation of Crimean Tatars and the CC commission headed by Yuri Andropov.

In 1971 Aishe Seitmuratova was again arrested. This time she was sentenced to three years of incarceration: not a suspended sentence, but a real one. The investigator on her case was KGB Major Alexander Sevostyanov. When she mentioned the year 1937, the peak of the Stalinist terror, which was carried out by the organs of state security, he riposted in a malicious tone: "We're sick of being reproached for '37! Then we put in too much salt, and now we're not putting in enough."

Apparently, the notion of putting in too much salt (overdoing things) and not putting in enough (leaving things underdone) was not the personal discovery of Major Sevostyanov. Rather it was a phrase commonly used at the headquarters of the KGB after Yuri Vladimirovich Andropov had taken charge there. Moreover, it is likely that it struck him and his people as objective and just, since it con-tained an admission of past shortcomings in their organization because of which, in effect, it had to pull back somewhat and weaken its position. In other words, "oversalting" under Stalin led to "under-salting" in the Khrushchev era. Both were extremes; and it was necessary to get back for the secret police its former significance and prestige in the state, while yet not allowing excesses in the direction of senseless terror, which usually proved harmful, on the rebound, to secret police agents. "And do you know how many of our comrades perished during Stalin's purges?" was the standard argument of KGB agents in response to mentions of that organization's former destructive activity when it existed under different names and abbreviations. The list runs as follows: ChK (Extraordinary Commission), GPU (State Political Administration), NKVD (People's Commissariat of Internal Affairs), NKGB (People's Commissariat of State Security), MGB (Ministry of State Security), and finally, KGB. Such a frequent changing of names was dictated, *inter alia*, by that organization's constant disavowals of its own activity and its attempts, if one may so express it, to start life anew each time.

It was an organization of which the Soviet leaders had a vital need and, at the same time, a deadly fear, so that they had a kind of KGB syndrome. Under Stalin it had absolute authority. When Andropov's sponsor, Otto Kuusinen, the fictive prime minister of a Finland that the USSR never conquered in the "Winter War" of 1939–40, came to Stalin to intervene for his arrested son, the great vozhd, taking his extinguished pipe out of his mouth, said: "That's a terrible thing, but what can I do with them? They've already put half of my relatives behind bars, and I'm powerless to save them."

During Andropov's tenure at the KGB, a joke was making the rounds in Moscow. It seems that in the course of a Politburo session, Premier Kosygin whispered to General Secretary Brezhnev: "Be on your guard with Andropov. They say he's a stoolie." That joke was not only witty but prophetic. As we shall see later, Kosygin's apprehensions turned out to be fully justified, although Brezhnev did not heed his warning. Or perhaps he did heed it, but when it was already too late. . . .

Andropov's appointment as head of the KGB meant that the need for that organization had prevailed over the Kremlin leaders' fears that it might, given the scope of its functions—total surveillance on all Soviet citizens (including the dwellers in the Kremlin), guarding the frontiers, espionage abroad, and even monitoring the armed forces—

ultimately became a state within a state, as had happened before. True, the attempts by Beria and Shelepin to set the secret police up against the Party apparatus had been nipped in the bud. Apparently, Brezhnev and his colleagues were hoping that this time, too, in case of necessity, they could take emergency measures against the head of the KGB. But as later developments showed, they failed to allow for many attendant circumstances—above all, the fact that Andropov had learned his lesson from the unhappy experience of his predecessors. His appointment to the KGB was, indeed, his lucky ticket in the Kremlin lottery; and at the same time it was an unlucky one for those who were hoping, by means of that appointment, to put an end to the political fluctuations of the first post-Khrushchev years. In the well-known words of Karl Marx, one may say that Brezhnev and his colleagues bred their own grave digger.

Unlike all those who had preceded him as head of the secret police, who were totally lacking in risibility, Andropov had a sense of humor, although it was rather sinister for those toward whom it was directed. One of the first victims of that humor was Mikola Sharygin-Bodulyak, of Ukrainian origin, a subject of Her Majesty the queen of England, and the representative of an English commercial firm. He was arrested in Moscow as a suspected spy. But at his first interrogation, the KGB investigator cynically told him: "The charge is hogwash. Just sign an agreement to work for the motherland, and back you go to the hotel—with our compliments."

For about six months Mikola was the object of suasion, alternating with threats to prosecute him on a charge of high treason, although his own country was England, where he had been taken as a young child. One day the investigator warned him that Yuri Vladimirovich Andropov, chairman of the Committee of State Security, was going to talk to him. The prisoner was led from one floor to another, and through one corridor after another.

Upon entering the huge office, he was asked: "Well, haven't you changed your mind yet? Do you still refuse to work for the motherland?"

"My motherland is Great Britain," Mikola replied quietly.

"If that's the way things are, put him on trial!" Andropov said to a short man standing beside him. "Take him away."

"But he really is a British subject," Andropov's assistant meekly objected to him.

As Mikola was being led out of Andropov's office, he heard the latter's answer—spoken loud enough so that the prisoner, Mikola, could hear it: "I trust the queen of England will not declare war on us because of Sharygin."

Andropov was right: the queen of England did not declare war on the Soviet Union. As for Mikola Sharygin-Bodulyak, he served ten years in prison and strict-regimen labor camps for espionage. After being released, he spent another several months fighting desperately to get back to England. (He was offered a Soviet passport so that he would stay in his "motherland.")

If we didn't know Andropov better, we could only guess why he felt it necessary to smile at the Crimean Tatars before leading a crusade against them—or to joke about a man he was sending off for a long prison sentence. But let us not forget Hungary. Andropov is a gendarme in a dinner jacket, wearing white gloves, with a jesuitic smile on his face.

Our job, however, is to write his political biography, not to draw a psychological portrait. For the latter, the reader should go to Dostoyevsky, with his jesuitic realism and underground characters: there he will find the key he needs to understand the "mysterious Russian soul" of the new Kremlin vozhd.

That said, let us go back to the late 1960s, when the head of the imperial secret police was faced with a much more severe "on the job" test than organizing the genocide of the Crimean Tatars. That test arose from the fact that the Khrushchevian "Thaw," which after the palace coup of 1964 had been followed by frosts throughout the Soviet Union, nonetheless persisted in the borderlands of the empire—in the countries of Eastern Europe. And in one of them it even became the Prague Spring, so called although it began in the depth of winter in 1968 and lasted until midnight of August 20, when troops from five Warsaw Pact countries (not including Rumania) invaded Czechoslovakia from all sides, so that by morning the country was occupied.

Andropov's role in Czechoslovakia was much like the one he played in Hungary in 1956, despite the radical difference between the Prague Spring and the Hungarian revolution. In Czechoslovakia there was no fighting in the streets; Stalinists were not hunted down and lynched at intersections or in public squares; monuments to Soviet soldiers were not defiled; and there were not even any scurrilous anti-Soviet slogans. It was the most proper, gentlemanly revolution in the

Soviet empire—partly because the Czechs and Slovaks had been lessoned by previous uprisings against Russian overlordship, and also because of their even-tempered, European national character (unlike that of the Poles and Hungarians). And it was to this special kind of revolution that the Hungarian stereotype, derived from Andropov's experience as ambassador in 1956, was applied. But since the stereotype and reality did not coincide, the Committee of State Security had to fit them together in a hurry; and to make them fit, it was of course the Czechoslovak reality that had to be most radically distorted.

As early as July 29, at a meeting between the Party-government delegations of Czechoslovakia and the Soviet Union in the East Slovak border village of Cierna-nad-Tisou, a member of the Soviet Politburo, the Ukrainian Party boss Petr Shelest, had handed to the leader of the Prague Spring, Alexander Dubcek, "the politician with the sad eyes," a leaflet—allegedly printed in Czechoslovakia and smuggled into the Soviet Union—calling for the Transcarpathian Ukraine to secede from the USSR. It was such an obvious forgery that Shelest had to apologize the next day.

Then came a report that the East German intelligence service had intercepted a letter from Simon Wiesenthal in Vienna, director of the Jewish Center for Research on Nazi Crimes, in which he admitted that the Prague Spring was the work of Zionists. Needless to say, Simon Wiesenthal never wrote such a letter, nor could he have.

This was followed by the discovery, not far from the town of Sokolovo in northern Bohemia, of a stockpile of weapons, allegedly sneaked in by the Americans for the Czechoslovak counterrevolution. The Dubcek government took a very serious view of this find, surmising who was behind the whole thing and what its purpose was. The weapons did in fact turn out to be American. But the lubricants on them were from East Germany; and the knapsacks lying nearby were clearly labelled in Russian "Number Such-and-Such."

Nietzsche once remarked that the Germans do not have the fingers for nuances. Andropov had had neither the fingers nor the time for nuances: it wasn't a moment for nuances of any kind, so he hadn't bothered with them. The episode in the Czech town of Sokolovo was something to be remembered in the future. Fifteen years later, the main argument of those claiming that the KGB had no hand in the attempt on the Pope's life in St. Peter's Square would be that the workmanship was too crude to have been that of the KGB. In our view, to use East German lubricants on planted American weapons and leave, next to them, Soviet knapsacks with Russian lettering on them is much cruder workmanship than to hire a right-wing Turkish terrorist through the Bulgarians. The KGB does not have the fingers for nuances.

The differences between Czechoslovakia and Hungary were also "nuances" for Andropov. Hence the haste and heedlessness with which the Prague Spring was made to fit the Hungarian image. Whom was the KGB trying to convince? The Czechs and Slovaks, who knew better than anyone else what was going on in their own country? The Soviet citizenry, who after the occupation of Czechoslovakia were convinced that the Red army had got there just two hours ahead of the Bundeswehr? Or the Politburo, which in the case of Czechoslovakia had even more reason to vacillate than during the events in Hungary, so that the final decision to use force was passed only by a simple majority of seven to five? Apparently, it was indeed the Politburo which was the main target of the inflammatory propaganda campaign launched on an unprecedented scale by Andropov and his henchmen. Because to convince the Czechoslovak public of that country's need for the "friendly help" of the Warsaw Pact nations was impossible. As for public opinion in the USSR, it didn't exist as such. For example, many Soviet soldiers who in 1956 participated in the blitzing of Hungary mistook the Danube for the Suez Canal, because the propaganda campaigns against the Hungarian revolution and the joint Anglo-Franco-Israeli military action coincided, and the soldiers confused the two events. (One wonders what, in late August 1968, the Soviet soldiers took the Vltava River to be?)

Present in Prague at that time, along with the Soviet ambassador Stepan Chervonenko, was Andropov's personal representative, Ivan Udaltsov, a high-ranking KGB officer. Chervonenko did the "clean" work, intriguing among Czechoslovak leaders during the Yuletide hunting in the preserve of the ancient castle of Konopiste near Prague, or forging anonymous letters against the reformists. All of the dirty work was assigned by Andropov to Udaltsov. He wanted Udaltsov to do the same thing he himself had done in Hungary, the only difference being that then Andropov was acting largely on his own, whereas Udaltsov was working under the direct supervision of the KGB chairman. There are reports that on several occasions Andropov visited Prague incognito, and that during the critical days he was constantly in the city, personally directing all operations. That would accord with his position. It is reliably known, for example, that during the Hungarian revolution the then KGB chief, General Ivan Serov, was in Budapest and personally took part in the arrest of the Hungarian military delegation headed by General Pal Maleter during the talks with the Soviet military delegation on Csepel Island.

But Andropov was a man of a different stamp: he did not personally take part in the arrest of Alexander Dubcek and his comrades. Former KGB Major Stanislav Levchenko, who defected in 1979, said in an interview published in *Der Spiegel*:

> Andropov is a very secretive man. He is not eager to have anything at all known about him, preferring to remain inscrutable. Even in his own work— although he directs all operations personally, and everything that happens in the KGB is done only with his knowledge and under his direction—he often prefers to remain in the shadows, letting his assistants handle the technical side of things.

The anonymity of Andropov's work probably helps to explain the fact that the Czechoslovak leaders did not see the basic threat as coming from the KGB chief himself but from his representative, Ivan Udaltsov, and even from Stepan Chervonenko. At Cierna-nad-Tisou, Iosef Smrkovsky, chairman of the Czechoslovak National Assembly, told Brezhnev: "Comrade Brezhnev, those two representatives of the Soviet Union are rendering a bear's services★ to our friendship. You are being wrongly informed.

"Come and visit us, Comrade Brezhnev. Come to Prague, Ostrava, Brno, Pilsen, or Bratislava. Choose the place you want to visit. We'll go with you. You'll see how our people support the Communist Party, socialism, and concord with the Soviet Union. Travel around, and you'll see for yourself that the information you have is nothing but gossip, slander, and trivial details picked up from all over—things that in no way determine the way we live."

As in Hungary, everything depended on the kind of information the vacillating Politburo got on the events in Czechoslovakia. But since there was much more vacillation this time, it demanded consid-

---

★This untranslatable locution derives from an old fable (best known, perhaps, in the versions by Krylov and La Fontaine) about a recluse who, being lonely, strikes up a friendship with a bear. One day the bear, seeing a fly alight on the forehead of his sleeping friend, hits the fly with a heavy rock, crushing his friend's skull. (Translator's note.)

erably more work on the part of Andropov to convince the vacillators. One may venture the guess, for example, that if Khrushchev had been in Brezhnev's place, he would not have sent troops into Czechoslovakia, just as he did not send them into Poland, although the scope of the events there was distinctly more dangerous to the empire than those of the Prague Spring. Brezhnev was easier to convince; yet even so, it required substituting for the real Czechoslovakia a kind of similitude of Hungary. We think in terms of associations. We look to the past for analogies with the present, and we act on the basis of our previous experience. When the analogy "Czechoslovakia-Hungary" that Andropov presented was activated in the brains of the majority of the Politburo members, the Soviet troops occupied Czechoslovakia without firing a single shot.

The fact that not a single shot was fired must also be credited to the agency headed by Andropov and its representatives in the army.

First, the invasion took the Czechoslovaks completely by surprise. To quote once again from Iosef Smrkovsky's memoirs, which he managed to get on tape shortly before his death: "I can say that before 11:30 on the night of August 20th, I never heard, either directly or through an intermediary, that they had decided to enter our territory and occupy our country."

And Alexander Dubcek, first secretary of the Communist Party of Czechoslovakia, was undoubtedly sincere when he said: "Comrades, how can you think for a moment that a fraternal socialist country would attack us?"

That old cynic Janos Kadar was amazed by the naïveté of his Czechoslovak colleagues. "Don't you realize the kind of people you're dealing with?" he asked Dubcek. But he never could shake Dubcek's internationalist faith in the Russians.

Second, the Czechoslovak army received secret orders from the Supreme Command of the Armed Forces of the Warsaw Treaty Organization to "effect the concentration of your forces along the border with West Germany and thereby assure the defense of Czechoslovakia and of the entire socialist camp in view of the immediate threat of an attack by the Bundeswehr and the NATO forces stationed in West Germany."

Between July 15 and August 15, virtually all of the Czechoslovak army—eleven out of twelve divisions, armed with the most modern products of technology—was shifted to the western border. As soon as this maneuver was completed, six hundred thousand "friendly" troops, supported by seven thousand tanks, swept into the country from all the other borders.

Third, even before Soviet troops occupied the country, the Czechoslovak minister of defense, Martin Dzur, was arrested by the KGB so that he could not order the Czechoslovak army to resist. (He was the first of the Czechoslovak leaders to be arrested.)

Fourth, although the Soviet partocrats could not at first find quislings among their Czechoslovak colleagues, Andropov had, throughout the crisis, his own local collaborationists operating out of the building on St. Bartholomew Street that served as headquarters for the police and the KGB. One of Ivan Udaltsov's primary duties was to keep in constant touch with Viliam Salgovic, chief of the Czechoslovak security organs. In any case, all arrests of members of the Czechoslovak government were made by KGB agents, with the direct participation of Czechoslovak secret-police agents who served as guides.

From that point on, however, everything followed a somewhat different scenario from the one proposed by that rationalist and scholastic, Andropov, who was trying fully to re-create the Hungarian model on Czechoslovak soil. It proved impossible to promptly set up a worker-peasant revolutionary government and oppose it to the Dubcek government: there was no Janos Kadar among Dubcek's colleagues. It also proved impossible to put Dubcek and his comrades on the defendants' bench and try them as traitors to the cause of socialism; i.e., to repeat the tragic spectacle that had been put on with Imre Nagy and his comrades. And there is no doubt but that Andropov had planned to stage just such a show trial. One of the Czech volunteers from the Ministry of Internal Affairs who accompanied the KGB's punitive squad told the arrested men—Dubcek, Smrkovsky, Kriegel, and other Czechoslovak leaders—that within two hours they would be hauled up before a revolutionary tribunal. And he even told them who would be president of the tribunal: the neo-Stalinist Alois Indra.

But very soon there was a change in the way the KGB's high-ranking prisoners were being treated; and from it they sensed that under the pressure of various circumstances, the Kremlin leaders had had to give up the idea of settling their personal fates in such a radical manner. When they were taken to Moscow, their status changed from that of political prisoners to one of "participants in talks." The only one of them who refused to take part in this spectacle was Dr. Frantisek Kriegel, chairman of the National Front. Zdenek Mlynar, who did take part in the Moscow "talks," later had this to say about Kriegel: "As future developments showed, his behavior was much more in keeping with the actual situation than ours was. We were in fact being blackmailed by gangsters. But we solaced ourselves with the illusion that we were still politicians with whom politicians from another country were holding talks."

Having failed in his plan to take immediate reprisals against all the leaders of the Prague Spring, Andropov decided to get his own back against one of them: Frantisek Kriegel. While the other distinguished prisoners were being given the Playboy Club treatment, with cognac, vodka, caviar, sturgeon, and even (courtesy of the KGB) seductive young ladies in see-through negligees who came to their rooms at bedtime, Kriegel, separated from the rest of the delegation, was being held in the KGB prison. Even after the signing of a communiqué—one that was humiliating for Czechoslovakia—they didn't want to let him go back to Prague with the others. They tried to make a scapegoat of him—all the more so since he, unlike the other members of the delegation, was Jewish. And when the Czechoslovaks nonetheless defended their comrade against the Kremlin gangsters, the latter found a collective scapegoat of the same ethnic origin. KGB journalists put out a *White Book* (modelled after a similar one about the Hungarian revolution) declaring that Jews were directly responsible for the very emergence of the Prague Spring. In *Molodaya gvardiya* (Young Guard), one of the popular Moscow magazines with close ties to the security organs, it was even stated that "the Prague Zionists galvanized the literary corpse of Kafka to combat Communism."

It should be recalled that in Poland, in the same year as the Prague Spring, by way of response to student riots, the minister of internal affairs, Mieczyslaw Moczar, organized an anti-Semitic campaign unprecedented in postwar Eastern Europe. The result was the expulsion from Poland of almost every one of the small number of Jews who had managed, by a miracle, to survive there after Hitler had annihilated three million of them.

Thus in two vassal states at once, Andropov verified in practice the coordination of the work being done by a secret police force common to the whole Soviet empire. For nothing in that empire—not the economy, and not even the armed forces—has achieved such a degree of integration as the organs of the state security, which within its limits is international in the fullest sense of the word. As the famous Polish aphorist Stanislav Jerzy Lec used to say: "All shackles in the world are joined together." And this applies even more so to the shackles of the Warsaw Pact countries. (Clearer proof of the connections between the secret police forces of those countries would be offered to the world on May 13, 1981, in St. Peter's Square in Rome.) Toward the end of 1968, it was being rumored that Brezhnev had summoned Andropov immediately after the Soviet occupation of Czechoslovakia and asked him if he had a blacklist of people who should be promptly arrested in case of a war. Andropov answered in the affirmative.

"Then you may take it that war has broken out," said Brezhnev.

"Is that to be understood as an order to arrest several thousand suspect individuals?" Andropov is supposed to have asked.

"Yes, you can go ahead!"

Then Andropov supposedly objected that for such a massive arrest he had to have something more than Brezhnev's oral instructions: he needed a decision by the Politburo.

Thus the chairman of the Committee of State Security allegedly saved many writers, scientists, actors, and artists from reprisals for their political unreliability.

That rumor is not only a fiction but a transmogrification. The two people involved in that fictive conversation behave very differently from what might be expected on the basis of what we know about them. Of the two, Andropov was the hawk. And he was a hawk whose appetite had not yet been surfeited, since his Hungarian prescription for the empire's Czechoslovak illness had been accepted only in part. As for Brezhnev, he must have felt quite satisfied. For that matter, he was not an insatiable dictator, as can be seen from his subsequent reign. His political thinking was perfunctory: he was content with the appearance of order where there was actual, or impending, disorder. Also, the Soviet system of information flow, whereby it passes through many stages and reaches the Kremlin leaders in idealized form, so as not to disquiet them and jeopardize the bearers of bad tidings, screened Brezhnev and his closest comrades-in-arms off from reality.

By contrast, Andropov, as head of the secret police, was thoroughly familiar with the empire's situation; and that situation made him fearful of what might happen to it. He knew that it had to be strengthened from within, since just as a fish's head is the first part of it to rot, so the parent state is the first part of an empire to break down. The dissent in Eastern Europe had begun with Khrushchev's "Thaw." Therefore it was essential to destroy all vestiges of the preceding era of political vacillation and concessions. Not only personally but professionally he was a proponent of stern and resolute measures. It was not for nothing that he had served as head of the secret police, which had always proposed more radical solutions than could be adopted by the Party leadership (except for the Stalin era, when "Party" and "police" coincided). But his personal experience, too, led him to the same conclusions. He remembered Hungary. If (he felt) they had listened to him and not supported Nagy, there would have been no revolution: Andropov and Rakosi would not have allowed it. And there wouldn't have been any revolutions at all, had it not been for the Twentieth Party Congress, with its exposure of Stalin. Dissent in the Soviet empire represented a metastasis of Khrushchevian liberalism that was not excised resolutely and in time.

So that the talk between Brezhnev and Andropov about which rumors were circulating through Moscow in August 1968 probably did actually take place, since where there's smoke, there's fire. But the casting of the actors was very different. The proposal for arresting people on the basis of a blacklist must have come from the one who drew up that list. It could not have been otherwise. In a totalitarian state, the chief gendarme is always more royalist than the king. Andropov had very good reason to be dissatisfied with the way things were going in the domain he was in charge of. And as a man responsible for order in the empire, he was quite right.

His convictions were reinforced when his apprehensions were justified.

On the day when Czechoslovakia was occupied, Nikolai Ceausescu, who had refused to follow the orders of the Supreme Command of the Warsaw Treaty Organization and take part in the punitive expedition against the erring country, standing on a balcony above the Square of the Republic in Bucharest, delivered a fiery anti-Soviet speech before a crowd of thousands of his subjects: "They are saying that a threat of counterrevolution has arisen in Czechoslovakia. And tomorrow somebody will probably turn up and say that counterrevolutionary tendencies have surfaced among us here, at this meeting. But we will reply to everyone: the Rumanian people will never let anyone encroach upon the territory of our fatherland! Just look!"

At this point he gestured toward the comrades standing behind him. "You see here before you our entire Central Committee, the State Council, the government. . . . Believe me, we will never become traitors to our fatherland, traitors to the interests of our people."

A few days later, on Sunday, August 25, a demonstration in defense of Czechoslovakia was held right in Red Square. All eight of the demonstrators were immediately seized by KGB agents. Later they were tried, convicted, and sentenced to various terms. That demonstration in fact marked the beginning of the dissident movement in the Soviet Union; and it took Andropov an entire decade to squash it. But it is an ill wind that blows no good. In combatting sedition within Russia, the KGB sharpened and perfected its tools, making them more sophisticated. Andropov did not abandon *wilde Dressur*. But because of the discredit brought upon the KGB after Stalin's death and the restrictions imposed on its activities, he combined *wilde Dressur* with *zahme Dressur*. He was, at one and the same time, a master of both methods of animal training, as practiced by gendarmes.

Much more complex and dangerous was the situation in the East, where there was an explosion of that powder keg about which Andropov had tried, unsuccessfully, to talk with the Crimean Tatars—so deeply was he concerned by it. The border guards, who came under the jurisdiction of the KGB chairman, got into bloody conflicts with the Chinese on the Ussuri River. Apparently this was a test of strength undertaken by Andropov. But this one, too, was forestalled by the Kremlin pragmatists: in September 1969, Premier Aleksei Kosygin unexpectedly flew to Peking, where he met with his Chinese counterpart, Zhou Enlai, and they agreed on a ceasefire.

Just at that time, a joke about the scariest dream Brezhnev had ever had was circulating in Moscow. It seems he dreamed that a Czech was squatting in Red Square, eating Jewish matzo balls with Chinese chopsticks. That dream was not Brezhnev's personal nightmare but a collective dream of the Soviet empire, which perceives its fear of retribution—and passes it off—as a defensive fear of aggression. Russia's frantic fear of the peoples it has subjugated is the hangman's fear of his victims, the master's fear of his slaves, the persecutor's persecution mania. In the same way, and even sooner than Brezhnev, with his perfunctory way of thinking, Andropov could have had the same kind of dream—especially since right then, immediately after the invasion of Czechoslovakia, it is likely that in his imagination he was trying on, for the first time, the imperial crown. There can hardly be any other explanation for the fact that he hastened to dissociate himself from the Czechoslovak action and its consequences, spreading through Moscow the rumor about a talk with Brezhnev—a rumor in which he ascribed to his Party chief his own proposal, and to himself Brezhnev's pragmatic (or rather, perhaps, *pro forma*) rejection of further repressions.

Later Andropov would repeatedly use this tried-and-true device of putting the blame on someone else—right up to the invasion of Afghanistan in the Christmas season of 1979. He had been one of the initiators of that invasion during Brezhnev's serious illness, but he did not hesitate to ascribe it entirely to his Party chief.

The Soviet top cop, if he wanted some day to become the Kremlin great chief, needed to keep in reserve a reputation as a liberal.

3

Russian Nationalism: The KGB's Ideological Stake

Russia's national leaders, foreseeing the threat of a war with China, will in any case have to rely on patriotism and only patriotism. Don't forget that when Stalin veered in that direction during the war, no one was even surprised, and no one pined away after Marxism. Everyone accepted it as something that was quite natural—something that was ours, Russian! When faced with a great danger, it is wise to regroup one's forces—beforehand, and not later.

— ALEXANDER SOLZHENITSYN, "Letter to the Leaders of the Soviet Union," September 5, 1973

The Minotaur in the Cretan Labyrinth devoured criminals. And once every year, as a special treat, he got a tribute from Athens: seven boys and seven girls. Human sacrifices were indispensable to the Phoenician Moloch, the Chinese Dragon, and almost every other mythological monster. But for that modern monster, the KGB, human sacrifices are not enough: its inner engine also requires ideological fuel. Without it—in the Khrushchev era, say, or early in Brezhnev's reign—that motor often comes close to dying. When Andropov became head of the KGB, he realized that—with all the perceptiveness of his imperial mode of thinking.

The fuel that had been used earlier—the Communist ideology—considerably boosted the productivity of the secret police in the late 1930s, during the Great Terror. But it was all used up by the time of the war, when Stalin tried (and Solzhenitsyn is absolutely right), by way of an emergency measure, to replace it with another kind of ideological fuel: great-power nationalism. He did not, however, manage to complete the job—he died. And his successor, Khrushchev, sharply cut down deliveries of ideological fuel—not only to the KGB but to the whole country. Memories of former feats, a history of impunity, and a tradition of absolutism made it impossible for the KGB to be content with its new status in the post-Stalin era. That weakened organization had to find an ally to restore its former might. It was well provided, however, with personnel and technological tooling; all it lacked was ideological inspiration. But the Pegasus that the KGB was to saddle had already been waiting impatiently in the stables, champing at the bit.

It must be said at the outset that Andropov was not original in his choice of an ally: in the political history of Russia, impulses toward a police state have always been accompanied by hysterical upsurges of great-power nationalism. That kind of thing happened not only under Stalin but under the reign of such reactionary emperors as Nicholas I, Alexander III, and Nicholas II. For example, "The Protocols of the Elders of Zion," that international masterpiece of anti-Semitism, was the handiwork of the Russian secret police, who in 1905 organized armed bands of pogromists (the "Black Hundreds")—forerunners of Hitler's storm troopers. Thus the national chauvinists were not only the natural and inevitable but the *traditional* allies of the secret police. And together they constituted, on the one hand, a strong counterpoise to the liberal mind-set in the parent state and the national-separatist one in the borderland republics and, on the other hand, opposition to the official regime, which was too complacent toward those tendencies so destructive of the empire.

As a matter of fact, it was in its aspect as counterpoise and opposition that Russian national chauvinism resurfaced in the 1960s, when it was promptly picked up on, and secretly supported by, the KGB, then headed by Shelepin and (after him) Semichastny. Chauvinist sentiments, especially among the military and the writers, were unchannelled; and it was up to Andropov, when he took over the KGB, to channel them and give them legal status.

As we know, an idea comes into being in response to its absence. The "Russian Idea" arose during a prolonged ideological hiatus, when not only the KGB but the state bureaucratic system itself felt an acute need for new stimuli to replace those of Communism, which had grown weak and if they continued to be operative at all, did so only through inertia. Moreover, in Russia by the early 1970s there was not one but two gaps—two Torricellian vacuums into which, like mercury in a barometer, new ideas and slogans rushed: an ideological vacuum

and a political one. The first was due to the withering away of the
Communist ideology, and the second (coming slightly later) to the
physical frailty of the Kremlin gerontocrats. Under such favorable
conditions, it would indeed have been amazing if an opposition movement had not arisen, with pretensions to spiritual leadership and political power. Given the USSR's lack of freedom, both as a political
reality and as a historical tradition, that opposition necessarily had to
come from the right, as a corrective applied to the Soviet regime by
the secret police. It was a response not only to the country's lack of an
ideology but to signs of an embryonic liberalism. And it was no less
natural that an ideology claiming that it would strengthen the regime
in a multinational empire should take on great-power traits. Moreover,
the revival of Russian national chauvinism was somewhat belated as
compared to the growth of Jewish, Ukrainian, Lithuanian, Georgian,
and other "little nationalisms," because it was a response to them and
(so it seemed to its idealogues) a defensive reaction.

This must be rightly understood. The Russians have demonstrated, time and again—both during the "great patriotic wars"
against Napoleon and Hitler, and during the more peaceful times of
the Polish uprisings in the past century or the Hungarian and Czechoslovak revolts in our time—their militant readiness to defend the empire against enemies from the outside (the French, the Germans) or
those from within (the Poles, the Hungarians, the Czechoslovaks). For
that empire is their only political offspring, their supreme political
achievement of the past few centuries; and it is as dear to them as is,
say, democracy to the Americans. For the sake of building that empire, they were willing to overtax themselves to a colossal extent, and
make unprecedented human sacrifices; and they will not give it up
without a struggle. The empire's chronic fear of collapse is perceived
at various levels of the imperial consciousness as a fear of vanishing
from the earth as a nation; since in their recent historical memory, the
Russians have known no other form of existence than the imperial.

Therefore, a growth of centrifugal forces provokes the strengthening of centripetal, coercive bonds; that is, greater integration on the
level of ideology, the bureaucracy, the military, and the secret police.
In other words, Russian national chauvinism is the empire's con-
structive response to the destructive tendencies within it that are actively supported from without—above all, by its principal rival in the
world, the United States of America. This, at any rate, is the way

things look from Moscow: from the windows of the Kremlin, or from those of the neoclassical building on Dzerzhinsky Square housing the headquarters of the Committee of State Security and the office of its erstwhile chairman, Yuri Vladimirovich Andropov.

From without, of course, things look different: Russian chauvinism is an ideology of fear. But it is a perfectly natural fear of collapse which in the final analysis becomes a national stimulus to the empire, both on the government level and on that of the people as a whole (meaning, naturally, the imperial people).

Incidentally, the nationalist movements in the Soviet republics and the satellite countries (like the Russian liberals in Moscow and Leningrad) would have had a much greater chance of success—or at least of survival—if they had been opposed only by the Party orthodox and bureaucrats. After all, it was against them that they began their resistance after Stalin's death; and they did not at first notice that with their struggle they had awakened the dozing monster of Russian national chauvinism. It was as if Russian history itself, out of an instinct of self-preservation, had sprouted that frightful tusk. The same thing happened with the KGB. When the ideological ferment in Russia began, that organization was discredited, weakened, and divided into two parts (like Berlin): the secret police and the regular police. But in combatting dissent, the Committee of State Security sharpened its weapons, restored its reputation, and strengthened its position in the country.

Another thing that played an important role in the rise of great-power nationalism was the fact that demographically, the Russians are being pushed into the background in the country where they hold the supreme power. (In Stalin's words, the "elder brother" in the family of Soviet peoples is the Russian people.) In terms of numbers, they are now inferior to the totality of the peoples (including those of Eastern Europe) who are subordinate to them and, at the same time, opposed to them. And this demographic regression of the Russians is irreversible if we take into account the falling birthrate among the Slavs and the increasing rate among the Soviet Moslems, along with the empire's new territorial acquisitions; e.g., Afghanistan, with its population of fifteen million. To this we can add the demographic—or, more accurately, military-demographic—fear of China, to which fear Afghanistan fell a victim in late 1979. Hence the primary coloration of this Russian nationalism: it is great-power chauvinism, imperialistic and colonialistic, with inevitable traits of xenophobia and anti-Semitism. It is even breaking the traditional ties with Slavophilism, the most widespread form of Russian nationalism in the nineteenth century, since today other Slavs—the Poles, Czechs, Slovaks, Ukrainians—are just as much enemies (potentially, military enemies) as the non-Slavs: the Hungarians, Afghans, Estonians, Georgians, or Rumanians. One can therefore readily understand the influence of Russophile propaganda in the armed forces and its sponsorship not only by Andropov but by such famous military leaders as Marshal Chuikov and General Epishev, both passionate adepts of national chauvinism.

Marshal Chuikov, hero of the Battle of Stalingrad, stood beside the cradle of the Russian nationalist movement in the sixties. He was its godfather. At first, however, he had no direct kinship with it. He was a man from the sidelines—but precisely those sidelines that gave the movement confidence and scope. Officially, that high-ranking sponsor held the post of honorary president of the All-Russian Association of *Rodina* (Motherland) Societies, which from the late sixties began to proliferate all through Russia with catastrophic swiftness, like mushrooms after a rain. Officially (again) they were founded in order to promote the preservation of ancient monuments of Russian culture and history, and were organized on a voluntary basis, their membership consisting of enthusiasts and fanatics. But these societies were headed up by carefully selected nationalist ideologues who were highly paid and officially came under the jurisdiction of the Ministry of Culture, while secretly (and actually) they came under that of the KGB. But then, it could not have been otherwise. In a country permeated by the secret police, there was no possibility for the founding of an independent organization; and these societies very soon entirely abandoned their "official" obligations to preserve monuments and became totally involved in setting up, in the one-party Soviet system, a quasi-official, quasi-oppositionist group which soon openly gave itself the name of the Russian Party (as a counterpoise to the Communist Party). It was Andropov's illegitimate, experimental offspring. He kept it at his beck and call and, at the same time, at a respectful distance. On a lower level, however, his own organization was not shy about acknowledging its kinship with the "Russites." Boris Pavlovich Chudinov, an agent of the Leningrad KGB, once said to one of the authors of this book (Vladimir Solovyov): "We have two subsidiaries:

the Palestine Liberation Organization and the Russian Party."

The Rodina societies served as the basic cells of the Russian Party, just as the Roman catacombs did for the early Christians.

For that matter, the Russian Party used real catacombs: they held weekly meetings in the ruins of the ancient Andronnikov Monastery in Moscow. There they got into heated theoretical debates, discussed plans, and elected central organs of the Russian Party and even shadow cabinets in case they should suddenly come to power. Beginning in the early seventies, similar (but more local) meetings, often nocturnal, were held at the offices of organizations where representatives of the Russian Party were influential. There are reports of such meetings at the editorial offices of the magazines *Avrora* (Dawn), *Detskaya literatura* (Children's Literature), and *Sovetskaya muzyka* (Soviet Music). At other editorial offices—those of *Nash sovremennik* (Our Contemporary), *Moskva* (Moscow), and *Molodaya gvardiya* (Young Guard)—where they were in the majority, there was no need for conspiracy. There was such a coincidence between what was official and what was underground, that meetings of the editorial board became meetings of the local cell of the Russian Party. (At the magazine *Moskva*, it was suggested to the sole Jewish staffer that she resign, with the blunt explanation that when she was present, the other members of the editorial staff could not have frank discussions.)

From the very outset the Russian nationalist ideology enjoyed even more privileged conditions in the armed forces, where it was passionately supported by the Stalinists. Stalin's rehabilitation in military circles, a decade after his exposure by Khrushchev, began with his rehabilitation as a military leader. When his name was mentioned at a meeting of high-ranking officers in Moscow, they all leaped to their feet as if by command and applauded for a long time—a defiantly long time: as long as they had when he was alive—in that way alleviating their acute political nostalgia for the dead and discredited tyrant. Feelings like this were so strong that pro-Stalin verses even appeared in the official press. The author of one bit of versifying, a "military poet" (pilot) by the name of Felix Chuyev, proposed that a Stalin Pantheon be erected in Moscow—apparently in addition to (or perhaps to replace) Lenin's Tomb, where Stalin had been buried for several years before he was expelled from it in disgrace by a decision of the Twenty-second Party Congress. Chuyev's verses read:

Let whoever enters this place know
how he depends on Russia in all things.
Among us is the Generalissimo
with his great marshals, statelier than kings.

When, one dark October night, Stalin's body was removed from
Lenin's Tomb under reinforced guard and placed in a "simple" Party
grave beside the Kremlin Wall, the then-rebellious poet Yevgeniy
Yevtushenko, in a poem published in *Pravda*, called for a tripling of
the guard at the grave, "so Stalin won't rise up/and with Stalin, the
past." Alas, the poet's fears were fully justified: the guard detail was
plainly inadequate.

The military cult of Stalin was only part of the Stalinist patriotic
cult. His admirers were soon recalling the postwar campaign against
"cosmopolites and Zionists" that he carried on under the badge of
great-power nationalism. A few months before his death he even
dreamed up a nationwide pogrom, arresting some Kremlin doctors—
the "murderers in white coats"—who had allegedly tried to do away
with him and all his comrades-in-arms. So that when Stalin died, his
death was called "the Jews' luck," although of course it was a lucky
thing for all the peoples of the USSR, including the Georgians, his
own people, and the Russians, in whose name he had acted. Nonetheless, the new cult of Stalin in the late sixties and early seventies attracted more and more followers, from Party bureaucrats to pensioners, from policemen to chronic drunks. The alcoholics hoped that
with a return to the way things had been in Stalin's time they would
stop drinking and get back to a normal life and discipline in their
work, either under ideological hypnosis or from fear of punishment.
(Those punishments had been abolished by the liberal Khrushchev.
They were to be partially restored by Andropov when he came to
power.) Pensioners remembered the battle for Berlin, forgetting about
the Red army's massive retreat during the first months of the war, and
the twenty million Soviet lives lost during the four years that it lasted.
Young cab drivers, born after Stalin's death and knowing of him only
by hearsay, hung his photograph on their windshields, and contrasted
the imposing tyrant with the decrepit Brezhnev, whose health was
getting worse every year. ("It's shameful to look at TV. Are we a great
power, or aren't we?") And on trains making long runs, a passenger
could buy, for one ruble, a homemade calender of the type depicting a
saint's life, with a picture of Stalin on each page.

Then, after Khrushchev's downfall, Stalin's image began to appear more and more often, even officially: in books, on television, in films, and even in an official calendar. Nor could it have been otherwise: Stalin's rehabilitation began at the bottom. At the top, meantime, some leaders cautiously held it in check, whereas others (and Andropov was among them) just as cautiously supported it. The dream of Stalin's rehabilitation was not one centered on his personal rehabilitation; it was centered on restoring his way of governing. It was, that is, a dream about a powerful regime, about discipline; an imperial people's dream about a secure empire. Stalin seemed to be a panacea for all those imperial ills that people noticed every day, all around them and in themselves. If he had miraculously come back to life and, like Napoleon at Fréjus, debarked on the shore of the Black Sea, the Baltic Sea, or even the Bering Strait, he would have been assured a triumphal progress across all of Russia, and been borne aloft by the crowd into the Kremlin. And his stay there would not have been any mere One Hundred Days.

We might have compared Stalin to the main characters in those horror films so dear to the Americans, like the Mummy or Frankenstein's monster. Instead, however, we shall remain loyal to the Russian tradition and borrow an image from one of Tchaikovsky's ballets. In the late sixties, Stalin was like the Sleeping Beauty, and princes of various political bloodlines were hurrying from all directions to reawaken him to political life and enlist his implied support. Among the pretenders to the hand of the Sleeping Beauty, the military were the favorites. Andropov and his "Young Turks" joined forces with them for more than just ideological reasons. He had made his Komsomol career thanks to Stalin's prewar purges, and his Party career because he used Stalinist methods in putting down Hungary and Czechoslovakia in post-Stalinist times. But considerations of a strictly careerist kind had also played their role; and now the neo-Stalinist brand of national chauvinism struck him as the best political bet. And so once again, as in Hungary and Czechoslovakia, he was in harness with the army, but this time as chairman of the Committee of State Security. This moment marks the beginning of the close collaboration between Andropov and the chief military ideologue, General Aleksei Epishev, director of the Political Administration of the Armed Forces; in other words, their political commissar. Just how successful and fruitful that alliance was can be judged from the fact that almost a decade later,

Andropov and Epishev, without waiting for the Politburo's sanction, would become the prime movers of the blitzkrieg in Afghanistan—Andropov as its ideological sparkplug, and Epishev as its military architect.

It should be noted that Epishev, in the same measure as Andropov, stubbornly remained a Stalinist even in anti-Stalinist times. When the Khrushchevian "Thaw" was at its warmest, both the armed forces and the secret police were resolutely opposed to the democratic reforms. And the Kremlin leaders had to put up with it in view of both the external and internal dangers threatening the empire, because the reforms might weaken those two organizations that were defending it.

On his home ground in the armed forces, General Epishev introduced his own system of censorship, which was quite independent of the regular state system. He banned things that were permitted (for the time being) in the civilian world; and he allowed things that were (for the time being) banned there. The former was what happened to the Moscow magazines *Novy Mir* (The New World) and *Yunost* (Youth), the two main forums of Russian liberalism. General Epishev laid a very strict ban on them in the armed forces, up to and including disciplinary punishment for any soldier or officer found in possession of them. The opposite happened with the film *What Is Secret, and What Is Plain to See*, based on a screenplay by Dmitri Zhukov, a former Soviet spy in the Middle East and then one of the Russian Party's chief propagandists. Zhukov was the first writer to use extensive passages from Nazi authors in his articles, although out of caution, he did not employ quotation marks or cite his sources. And it was precisely a Nazi propaganda film that this violently anti-Semitic movie was modelled after, although it made use of contemporary Russian examples. The opening shot shows the healthy, flowering tree of Russian life that Jews have entangled in a sticky spiderweb, so that it will very soon die unless something is done immediately. (We are using the metaphorical, allegorical language of the film itself.) Among the individuals shown as bearers of evil are the Social Revolutionary Fanya Kaplan, who shot at Lenin; Leon Trotsky; Golda Meir; and even Franz Kafka in the role already familiar to us—as the posthumous instigator of the Prague Spring. (That image was directly borrowed, for use in the film, from Andropov's old stockpile of propaganda.) The movie was so inflammatory that Party officials had well-founded apprehensions as to how a mass audience might react upon seeing it: because the natural and direct conclusion to be drawn from it was that a pogrom should be launched immediately. The authorities banned any public showing of *What Is Secret, and What Is Plain to See*, in spite of Andropov's vigorous, stubborn support of it. The ban was due not only to fears of an uncontrollable audience reaction to that leaflet-film but to pure chance as well. Among those who saw it at a private screening was a cameraman who, during the war, had been assigned as a photojournalist to the Fourth Ukrainian Front (army group), where Brezhnev was commissar. The cameraman, shaken by what he had seen at the screening, appealed to his former military superior; and by Brezhnev's imperial edict the movie was banned. Right on top of this came another imperial edict, this time from General Epishev, directing that the film be shown everywhere in the armed forces. So that among the military, Andropov was at least partially avenged for his defeat in the world of civilians.

For him, however, there was something even more important than his ties with the armed forces: his alliance with the press. Whereas before, according to Lenin's oft-quoted dictum, to seize power one had to get control of the postal service, the telegraph offices, and the bridges, now it sufficed to infiltrate the organs of propaganda: the magazines, newspapers, and publishing houses. It was natural that the founders of the Russian Party should have been chiefly journalists and writers. (To quote Lenin again: when filling out a questionnaire, he put down as his profession "a man of letters.") They were, that is, professionally talkative people, unlike Andropov, who was profession-ally closemouthed and preferred to remain in the shadows. But it was just such tight-lipped and reclusive types as Andropov who needed people skilled at phrasing new political slogans in a country where political activity was banned. Andropov had inherited the nationalist cadres from his predecessors, Shelepin and Semichastny, the "Komso-mol" heads of the secret police: and he was mindful of what had befallen those two. Hence although he continued to support and use the "Russites," he kept them at a distance, preferring not to risk his career.

The second half of the sixties was the period when the Russian Party's underground activities were most intensive. The cutoff point for them came in the early seventies, when with the help of the KGB that Party emerged from the underground. During the rest of the seventies it was given increasing leeway, both in the censored Soviet press and more broadly—in the KGB-controlled social and political spheres. Also, the stronger the suppression of liberal activities, the greater the freedom for national-chauvinistic ones. This inverse ratio was produced by the political seesaw, with the dwindling liberals at one end and the evermore robust national chauvinists at the other. It was because of that seesawing that the political atmosphere of the first post-Khrushchevian years was so vague, fluctuating, and unstable. But all this bouncing up and down came to an end one August night in 1968. Soviet tanks went into Czechoslovakia. And Andropov, not having got the Politburo's sanction for immediate reprisals against dissidents on the basis of the blacklist he had drawn up long before, placed a secret ideological and political bet on the Russian Party. It was right then, in the summer of 1968, that the three groups—the neo-Stalinists in the armed forces, the civilian national chauvinists, and the secret police—having discovered their inner kinship, realized the necessity for a practical alliance.

This agreement was helped along by yet another international event that had taken place a year before at a much greater distance from the Soviet Union than Czechoslovakia. That event was the Six Day War of 1967, when the USSR took a position that was openly anti-Israeli, anti-Zionist, and essentially, in terms of its long-range results, anti-Semitic. (At this point, the Russian Party's propagandistic help came in very handy indeed.) For that matter, the relationship here was more likely an inverse one: anti-Semitism was the main reason why the Soviet Union took a hard anti-Israeli line, and even broke off diplomatic relations with Israel.

Anti-Semitism was the point at which the two ideologies—the official and the Russophile—came closest together, even coinciding completely. The Russian Party was the wheelhorse of the team; and on the basis of its carefully prepared plan, an anti-Semitic propaganda campaign was carried out whose scope was nationwide. Things which earlier had been printed only in illegal, samizdat periodicals like *Veche* (Popular Assembly) were now being published with impunity in the leading Moscow and Leningrad magazines, and by the big publishing houses. In the late sixties stencil duplicators were used for the underground publication (with the knowledge and sanction of the KGB) of *Mein Kampf*, the masterpiece of Nazi literature, and that classic anti-Semitic forgery "The Protocols of the Elders of Zion." But by the seventies the Russophiles no longer had anyone to hide from. The mask of secrecy was dropped as unnecessary, and the conditions of their ideological existence kept improving, not from day to day but from hour to hour. There was no longer any need to use stencil duplicators, in the depth of the night, to print *Mein Kampf*, when one could openly cite another Nazi manifesto, Alfred Rosenberg's *The Myth of the Twentieth Century*, in the literary monthly *Moskva*, or quote from the Nazi theorist Werner Sombart in the weekly *Ogonyok* (Little Light), which had a circulation of a million. The newspaper for young people, *Komsomolskaya pravda*, published an article in which the author pedantically calculated how many Jews, half-Jews, and Jewish converts to Christianity there were in the U.S. government. In a book called *Foreign Voices on the Air*, issued in a printing of one hundred thousand copies by the Russian Party's own publishing house, *Moloduya gvardiya*, the Soviet reader is told that Jews have seized control of the radio, television, and press in the United States. In *The Legend of Israel and Reality*, a book that all armed forces libraries are required to have on their shelves, author Leon Korn (his real name is Lev Korneyev) declares that all one hundred thousand Iranian Jews are secret agents of Israel, while at the same time they spy for the United States and China. In Valentin Pikul's historical novel *At the Last Boundary*, which became a best-seller in the USSR as soon as it was serialized in a magazine, all the blame for the calamities that have befallen Russia is put on the tsar's favorite, Grisha Rasputin ("the Holy Devil"), who was allegedly the front for a worldwide Zionist plot. Ivan Artamonov's book *The Weapons of the Doomed* offers the following sensational discoveries, among others: that the Zionists welcomed Hitler's advent to power and used the services of the Gestapo, the SS, and the Abwehr; that Admiral Wilhelm Canaris, the Wehrmacht's chief of counterintelligence, scattered Jewish spies throughout the Allied countries; that Zionist agents were sent on special missions to the death camps of Maidanek and Auschwitz, and were accomplices in the mass murders; that Adolf Eichmann knew Hebrew and Yiddish, and was closely linked to the Zionists; that Babi Yar, where about seventy thousand Ukrainian Jews were exterminated, would always remain a symbol not only of Nazi cannibalism but of the indelible shame of their accomplices and successors, the Zionists; that Menachem Begin's political idols are Hitler and Mus-

solini; and so on—365 pages in that same vein. Revelations of this
kind were pictorially summarized in a painting by Mikhail Savitsky
which was put on exhibit and then promptly reproduced in a newspaper. In it, a German officer and his helper, wearing a striped prison
uniform with a Star of David on his chest, are smiling conspiratorially
at each other across a heap of naked children's corpses. At the picture's compositional center, drawing the viewer's attention, is the un-
circumcised penis of one of the victims. The conclusion to be drawn
from this symbolic painting is inescapable: that in the death camps,
the Jews were not the victims but the murderers.

Examples of this kind could be multiplied indefinitely. But if we
did so, we would stray from our story line and lose sight of our main
character—although there is no doubt as to a direct relationship between him and the witches' Sabbath of propaganda; it would not have
been possible without instructions from him. So we shall mention
nothing more beyond two books by Vladimir Begun, *The Creeping
Revolution* and *Intervention Without Weapons*, both required reading
for the indoctrination of new draftees. They present, for the first time
since the revolution, a vindication of anti-Semitic pogroms, which
". . . may take place as a spontaneous reaction of the oppressed
masses of the laboring population in response to their barbarous ex-
ploitation by the Jewish bourgeoisie." Then comes the corresponding
conclusion: "Today we are not sorry that our fathers, grandfathers,
and great-grandfathers, driven to desperation, treated their oppressors
with no respect whatsoever. . . ."

The whole question is (to paraphrase Shelley): If vindication of
pogroms comes, can their revival be far behind?

Andropov made at least two attempts to support the anti-Semitic
orchestration (secretly incited by him) with resolute anti-Semitic actions. In the summer of 1970 at Smolny Airport in Leningrad, just as
passengers were about to board an airplane, a squad of KGB agents
arrested twelve persons (the majority of them Jews), who were later
charged with attempting to hijack the plane. And in the spring of
1977, in Moscow, KGB agents—defiantly, right on the street and
before the eyes of foreign correspondents—arrested the Jewish
"refusenik" Anatoly Shcharansky, who was charged with the traditional "Jewish" crime: treason.

It should be recalled that both of the two previous attempts to hold anti-Jewish show trials in Russia were brought to nought: the "Doctors' Plot" in 1953 by the death of Stalin, and the Beilis case in 1913 by the verdict of the jury, which acquitted the defendant of the vicious, false charge of ritually murdering a Russian boy.

Andropov would have quite a bit more success than his predecessors, but by no means total success. His chief failure was in the attempt to carry out direct KGB actions (with sound effects provided by the Russian Party) and, using the Jews as scapegoats, to put an end once and for all to the "fifth column" within the country. (Doubtless this action would not have been limited to Jews: it's just that they always receive the first blow.)

The two chief "hijackers," Eduard Kuznetsov and Mark Dymshitz, were sentenced by a Leningrad court to the death penalty. But under pressure from world public opinion—which, just one day before, had got Generalissimo Franco to repeal the death sentences of some Basque terrorists—the sentences of the potential hijackers were commuted to fifteen years' imprisonment. In 1979 they were freed in exchange for two Soviet spies caught in the United States. (Of all those involved in "the airplane case," only the two non-Jews—the Russian, Yuri Fedorov, and the Ukrainian, Aleksei Murzhenko—were left to serve out their terms, presumably on the principle of "divide and conquer.")

Likewise, in the second case Andropov failed to get Shcharansky sentenced to death, the supreme penalty for treason under Soviet law. He was given a term of thirteen years, which he is now serving out in Chistopol Prison on the Kama River, five hundred miles from Moscow.

The important thing, however, is not the fact that these harsh sentences were still less harsh than those Andropov had wanted. Rather, it is the fact that those trials did not become, as he had planned, show trials; that they did not serve as a signal for going into action; that they turned out to be isolated actions by the KGB which did not metastasize into similar trials throughout the country; and that they were not accompanied by either pogroms, the expulsion of the Jews, or anything of the kind. That Andropov had dreamed up a more grandiose and sinister spectacle is beyond doubt. Such an inference can be drawn from articles in the government newspaper *Izvestia* that were couched in detective-story language, with detailed descriptions of the special equipment (invisible ink, etc.) allegedly used by the "spy" Shcharansky; of secret places for meeting with foreigners; of a special code; etc.

At about the same time, Leonid Lyubman, another Jew, was arrested in Leningrad on the same charge of treason but for an even more innocent meeting with a foreigner—a girl. This love affair was made to look like espionage, and Lyubman was sentenced to fifteen years. Preparations were also being made for similar trials of Jews in Kiev, Odessa, Novosibirsk, and Minsk.

A like picture of preparations for a grandiose anti-Semitic spectacle can easily be reconstructed from the trial of the "airplane people," as the potential hijackers were called in the Soviet Union. In both this case and Shcharansky's, vigorous use of the press, radio, and (especially) television were planned in order to stir up the passions of the common people. But Andropov was not allowed to do any of this. Indeed, between the two trials, a quarter of a million Jews were permitted to emigrate from the USSR. This was due to (1) the Kremlin pragmatists' desire to somehow alleviate the Jewish problem in connection with the rapid growth of anti-Semitism incited by the KGB and (2) the beginnings of détente between the West and East at that time. Jewish emigration was a most painful defeat for Andropov, who as chairman of the KGB realized very well that it is impossible to maintain the same pressure in communicating vessels if one of them has begun to leak. So that for him, the entire decade of the seventies was a period of combatting emigration. And finally, in the very early eighties, when he had become the all-powerful regent under the sick and feeble Brezhnev, he managed to stop up that dangerous leak in the totalitarian state—bearing, as he did, direct responsibility for order in it. His campaign against emigration was carried on at the same time as those against dissent and détente; and he was victorious on all three fronts—which is why he came to power. But in the seventies he was defeated in both the matter of the "Jewish trials" and of Jewish emigration. The Kremlin leaders held his gendarme's zeal in check—just as they had before, when he proposed to them the "Hungarian model" for pacifying Czechoslovakia, or the blacklist of suspect citizens to be arrested immediately.

The only thing Andropov could do against Jewish emigration in those days was to further foster anti-Semitism. The number of anti-Semitic articles and publications increased; draconian measures were taken to keep Jews from enrolling at prestigious universities, and it became harder for Jews to find employment. To the Politburo, Andropov justified these measures with the old Russian saying: "No matter how much you feed a wolf, he keeps looking back toward the forest." That is, he keeps trying to get back to his historical homeland, or to go to the United States, which fact was stirring up anti-Semitism (already natural) among the Russian population, since the Russians did not have the way out via emigration that the Jews (with certain limitations) had got. Some of them were leaving not for religious or ethnic reasons but for economic ones; and the economic status of the Russian population in the USSR was lower than that of the Jews. In view of Russia's worsening situation in regard to the economy, demography, and even day-to-day living, it had turned out that the Jews, like rats, were leaving the sinking ship.

On this score, one of the chief poets of the Russian Party addressed himself in verse to his ideological and ethnic enemies:

> You have a place where you can live,
> We have a place where we can die!

Naturally, unlike the Russophile poet, neither the ideologues of the Russian Party nor their highly placed sponsor from the KGB could permit themselves such eschatological sentiments. Despite the resistance of the Party authorities, their political dreams were coming ever closer to reality. Of course there were losses along the way—sometimes big ones. For example, Dmitri Polyansky, a strong supporter of the Russites, was removed from the Politburo and sent off to exile as ambassador to Japan. But even without him the Russites had plenty of sympathizers in the Central Committee and its apparatus. Naturally it sometimes happened that one of their fraternity would stumble and even fall into official disfavor because of an overly zealous chauvinistic article, not on account of its being openly anti-Semitic and anti-liberal (you didn't get fired for that) but because it was, at the same time, covertly anti-Communist. So it was that one of the most unbridled stalwarts of the Russian Party chanced to lose his job. A few months later, however, he resurfaced in another editorial position as good as the one he had lost. (Andropov never failed to come to the rescue when one of his overly fervent foster children got into trouble.)

The important thing, though, is that what Lenin once called "the accursed era of Aesopian language" came to a happy end, for the

Russian chauvinists, in the seventies. It also ended then for the liberals, but with a simultaneous loss of the gift of speech. The Soviet regime could allow only an opposition that it regarded as a possible heir. Such, at any rate, was Andropov's evaluation of the Russian Party's political chances. He himself was not an ideologue (unless the police ideal of a state be considered an ideology); and his view of Russian nationalism was, instead, mercenary and cynical. For him it was a means, not an end. As a secretive and calculating man, Andropov must have been rather unsettled by the wild schemes, lack of restraint, and unprofessionalism of those he had under his wing. But for him, in the struggle for power all means were good. The Russian "Young Turks" had already rendered him good service as a counterpoise to the liberals and the Jews. Now he was hoping to use them in order to weaken the Kremlin partocrats, whose dependence on threadbare Communist slogans had not strengthened their position but rather enfeebled it.

Andropov realized just how risky was his alliance with the Russian Party. But he was counting on his own political professionalism and his rare ability to maneuver and intrigue. He was in fact an insidious ally, and he was hoping he could push the genie of Russian chauvinism back into the bottle from which he had let it out, if that genie began to threaten his own power or even his own reputation. Moreover, he knew from history that there had been chauvinists in Russia before, but that they had never come to power. The distribution of ideological forces, however, had been different—especially just before the revolution. At that time political competition had been relatively free, and the national chauvinists had strong rivals. In the competition, they didn't hold up against anyone: neither the Constitutional Democrats, the Social Revolutionaries, nor the Bolsheviks. But now the Russian nationalists were alone in a clear field: they had no rivals, thanks to the lack of freedom in the USSR and to Andropov's stern suppression of all other opposition movements. As for the official Communist ideology, it no longer stirred any sincere response in anyone. (There is no country in the world where Communist slogans are treated with more indifference than in the Soviet Union.) Ideological quarrels were overshadowed by ethnic concerns; and in the place of abstract ideological enemies, there appeared concrete ethnic ones.

First, the Jews—ethnically, and at the same time more broadly, symbolically—representing the opposition. There was a time in old

Rus when any "furriner" was called a "German"—and even before that, a "Tatarin." In the same way, "Jew" has now become the label for an enemy of the empire: a dissenter, a liberal, and even a Jew. When, on August 25, 1968, a number of Soviet citizens gathered in Red Square to protest the occupation of Czechoslovakia, KGB agents rushed at them, shouting, "They're all Jews! Beat up the anti-sovietchiks!" And yet most of the demonstrators were not Jews.

Second, China, the fear of which was yet one more cause of the success enjoyed by "Russian ideas" and their conversion into official ones. At that time, a war with China was perceived as inevitable at various levels of Soviet society and of the Russian consciousness. It was the bugaboo of both Soviet and Russophile propaganda. This "preventive fear" can only be compared to the feeling of catastrophe during World War II.

Third and last, since the Soviet Union comprises almost as many nations as the UN, it was not only the Jews and the Chinese who were the enemies but any of the other peoples on the empire's territory or along its far-flung borders. Thus we again come to that frightful dream that Brezhnev once dreamed, but that Andropov had even more reason to dream, being more concerned with the fate of the empire than any of his colleagues in the Soviet leadership were. In that joke there are two characters with permanent roles, the Jew and the Chinese, and one who is supersedable: the symbolic Czech squatting in Red Square with his Chinese chopsticks and Jewish matzo balls. He can be replaced by a Pole, a Lithuanian, a Georgian, a Hungarian, or any other of the Soviet vassals, leaving to his understudy his fearful weapons: the matzo balls and the chopsticks.

All these imperialist complexes predetermined the success of "Russian ideas" in Soviet society.

It already seemed that the Russian Party would not have to wage any struggle for power: that it would fall into the Party's hands of its own weight, like an overripe apple. But instead of a drastic upheaval, what took place was a special kind of revolution: one that progressed steadily but in low gear, as it were. It can be compared not to one of Ovid's fabled metamorphoses but to that whereby a caterpillar becomes a butterfly; and this was the chrysalis stage. The Russian Party did not suddenly seize power. Rather, it gradually moved into the seat of power, although no special changes among the top leadership seemed to be taking place. The Russian Party not only moved into the seat of power, it became an everyday reality of Soviet life, permeating all its levels and institutions. By now there were no other, opposed tendencies in the country whose complexion differed very much from that of the Russophile movement. The main source of Russophile cadres was the Central Committee of the Komsomol, with its ramified bureaucratic apparatus and strong network of newspapers, magazines, and publishing houses. Once they had turned forty, the Komsomol "chiefs" and activists continued their careers in the Party CC and oblast committees, the ministries, the armed forces, and the KGB. There is good reason why, in the Soviet Union, Komsomol members are called "the successors." The most striking example of that is Andropov himself, who began his rise by mounting every step of the Komsomol ladder. It is hence not surprising that, thanks to Komsomol "graduates," the number of the Russian Party's supporters grew rapidly in the secret police, among the top officers of the armed forces, and in the Party apparatuses of Moscow, Leningrad, and the oblast centers.

In his day Lenin happily paraphrased the well-known French saying *"Grattez la peau d'un Russe et vous trouverez un Tartare,"* tailoring it to fit certain of his comrades-in-arms, like Stalin: "Scratch a Russian Communist, and you'll find a great-power chauvinist." Stalin didn't even have to be scratched: Communism slid off him like water off a duck's back. No Russian vozhd was such a fierce Russian chauvinist as the Georgian Iosif Dzhugashvili. We shall not try here to guess at the chief cause of that—whether it was due to a complex of ethnic inferiority sublimated into the great-power nationalism of another people, or to a realization of his responsibility toward the Russian imperial tradition. Was Stalin an anomaly in Russian history? Or was he summoned forth by it to counteract, in a monstrous way, the destructive revolutionary forces that were hostile to it? The fact that in the late seventies the atmosphere of national chauvinism, so like the atmosphere in Stalinist times, began to thicken, suggests that for all the vividness of Stalin's personality, he was rather an instrument of Russian history than an original creator.

By that time the situation had become more dangerous and fraught with risk than Andropov could have foreseen, and it might very well have escaped his control at any moment. He was equally threatened, now, by two possibilities: a victory of the Russian Party, which would have left him on the sidelines of a political power struggle, since he was not a fervent adept of the thriving ideology; and its defeat, which would have put an end to his political career because of his support, both covert and overt, of the "Young Russians." (During that interval, the shades of Andropov's deposed predecessors must have appeared to him at night.) In that extremely tense situation, instead of reining in his protégés, or disowning them entirely, Andropov adopted a more crafty stratagem. He began to use them as political kamikazes; that is, he assigned them to carry out the most hazardous operations against the Kremlin leaders—operations that would compromise both them and their targets.

Toward the very end of the 1970s, KGB agents and members of the Russian Party spread through Moscow a rumor (which may have been true) that Brezhnev's wife was Jewish. Given the anti-Semitic context of the time, it is hard to imagine anything more damaging to the Soviet vozhd, except perhaps to pin the Jewish label on the leader himself. (But in Brezhnev's case, this was impossible, because of both his biography and his facial features.)

In early 1979 a letter signed "Vasily Ryazanov" was printed on a stencil duplicator and sent out to a huge number of influential people belonging to the intellectual, military, and Party elite. The fictive "Vasily Ryazanov" wrote: "Not only in the U.S. Senate but in our own Central Committee, there is a powerful Zionist lobby. They won't allow anyone to attack them, under the pretext that it would lead to anti-Semitism, plus a negative reaction in terms of public opinion, and would hurt the policy of détente."

Two weeks later a large number of pamphlets (likewise printed on a stencil duplicator) were left in the entrance hallways of Moscow and Leningrad apartment buildings, at doorways, and even in places right in the streets—pamphlets in which it was declared that Zionists had seized control of the Politburo, and that the principal Zionist was none other than Brezhnev himself. The author further declared that the only real Russians on the Politburo were Premier Aleksei Kosygin, the Party ideologue Mikhail Suslov, and Leningrad Party boss Grigori Romanov.

One should bear in mind that in the Soviet Union the unofficial printing and distribution of any materials (to say nothing of political matter) is forbidden and punishable under the law. You have to get special permission even to have invitations printed. Also, access to such printing equipment as stencil duplicators is restricted and tightly controlled.

Andropov himself, who at the time was already a member of the Politburo, was of course not mentioned in those anonymous leaflets: the head of the secret police was not so naïve as to betray their origin. Yet the very fact that he was not named among the "positive" members of the Politburo could have revealed his coauthorship of the pamphlet. To understand that, however, required a rather complex intellectual makeup, like that of a chess player, or perhaps an inveterate reader of suspense novels. And certainly, of all the members of the Politburo, Andropov himself was the only one capable of such a reading of the anti-Brezhnev pamphlet. He counted on the lack of sophistication of the other Politburo members, whom he had by now had time to study thoroughly, and therefore covered his tracks in the crudest way, which in their case was appropriate.

In addition to compromising both Brezhnev and his chauvinistic opponents, the leaflet had another purpose: to implant hostility in the Politburo, play its various factions off against one another and mutually weaken them.

Although the pamphlet alleging that the Politburo had been taken over by Zionists headed by Brezhnev was signed "The Russian Liberal Movement," this was as much of a pseudonym as "Vasily Ryazanov," the name signed to the earlier document. The anti-Brezhnev leaflet was most likely not a Russian Party document but a counterfeit of one. The political opinions expressed in both pamphlets smacked of nationalism; but the style was too rational and lacked the emotional excesses typical of the Russian chauvinists. They were composed not by a lunatic or a fanatic but by a painstaking, calculating person. If they were not the handiwork of Andropov himself, he undoubtedly edited them, because the stamp of his distinct individuality is to be found in both documents, even stylistically.

As for the style of his protégés, it was metaphorical even in direct political appeals. On the six hundredth anniversary of the Battle of Kulikovo between the Russians and the Tatars (in which nine out of every ten Russian soldiers were killed), the magazine *Nash sovremennik*, the chief literary organ of the Russian Party, published a poem by Alexander Bobrov called "War Song." The poet openly expresses doubts as to the ability of the Kremlin gerontocrats to lead the people in case of war, and calls for their replacement by younger and more resolute men whom he dubs "the young princes," alluding to their ties with the Russian historical (and, especially, military) tradition.

> I cast an anxious gaze toward the East,
> And an equally anxious one toward the West.
> I fear that tomorrow we shall set out
> Along a road lighted by campfires.
> Who is ready to lead us in this campaign?
> Are the young princes yet in the saddle?

And yet the question was purely rhetorical. Such a "war song" could not have appeared in the official Soviet press if the "young princes" were not already in the saddle, ready to issue forth onto the stage where Brezhnev still stood, creating the optical illusion of being in power. But the same man who, with the aid of his all-powerful organization, had put them in the saddle was now, while continuing to use them, discrediting them in every way he could, perceiving them no longer as reliable allies but as dangerous rivals in the struggle for power.

It is in this context that we should take a look at what happened on April 20, 1982, in Pushkin Square, when Andropov overcame all of his rivals, members not only of the Russian Party but of the Communist Party, headed by its nominal chief, Leonid Ilich Brezhnev. We are deliberately breaking the time sequence and getting far ahead of the story in order to show the reader how political marriages of convenience can end up.

As compared with Red Square, so grand and imposing, Pushkin Square, located only several blocks away, is one of the coziest and most intimate spots in downtown Moscow. Here, at the foot of the monument to the great Russian poet, lovers make dates, and pensioners feed the pigeons, read the latest edition of the evening paper, *Izvestia* (whose editorial offices are located on the square), discuss the news, and tell jokes. And yet this idyllic impression is deceiving. From time to time, Pushkin Square throws down the gauntlet to Red Square. In and of itself, the challenge is usually negligible. But because of the absence of political freedom in Russia, and the presence of foreign correspondents, the challenge is exaggerated by the hollow echo it produces.

In the liberal Khrushchev era, young poets gathered here (as they did in nearby Mayakovsky Square) to read their poems to passersby—poems that had been rejected by the official press because of their unofficial political content. And beginning ten years later every December 5th, dissidents headed by Andrei Sakharov would come here and bare their heads—a symbolic gesture in memory of the Stalinist constitution, which was "given to the people" on December 5th, 1936, but never lived up to. The authorities usually sent either snowplows or street sprayers (depending on the weather) to drown out the speakers and disperse the audience. Increasingly harsh measures were taken against both groups, until finally the most active participants in these meetings under the open sky found themselves far, far away from that little square. Some had managed to emigrate, others had been put behind bars or (internally) exiled.

By the late seventies it seemed that Moscow's Hyde Park had lost its political significance. Then, one spring day in 1982, a most unusual demonstration was held there. Like many others in the past, this one was being held on an anniversary, but not that of Pushkin or the Stalinist constitution. What was being celebrated was the one hundredth anniversary of Hitler's birth. Hitler could least of all have expected such tender concern from the Russians. It was almost as unnatural as if Hitler's birthday were to be celebrated by Jews. Nonetheless, several dozen long-haired young people in brown shirts, with swastikas on their service caps, gathered in Pushkin Square and celebrated the anniversary of the birth of the Nazi dictator. Moreover, unlike what had happened on the occasion of earlier demonstrations, this time (strangely enough) the police did not try to stop it, although all unofficial rallies are forbidden in the USSR. And one would think this would apply with particular force to Nazi rallies. (Moscow is not Chicago!) To top it all off, it was known beforehand that this demonstration was to be held, and parents and teachers had warned young people not to take part in it.

But the most amazing thing was just who took part in this Nazi rally: most of the participants were the children of high Party officials, including members of the Central Committee.

At this point, the question naturally arises: Why didn't Stalin suffice as a political ideal for the Russian fascists? (Incidentally, the one hundredth anniversary of his own birth, two and a half years earlier, was celebrated only in his native country of Georgia—not in the center of Moscow.) After all, it was Stalin who with an incredible effort managed to restore the empire, which had fallen into ruin as a result of the 1917 revolution, when almost all of the peoples in the "prison of nations" (as Lenin called prerevolutionary Russia)—Poles, Finns, Ukrainians, and the Baltic, Caucasian, and central Asian peoples—were fleeing from it. There was good reason why Stalin was called "the father of peoples." He brought these prodigal sons back under the paternal roof; and they were soon joined by the peoples of Eastern Europe, including the prodigal sons of another empire that had fallen apart: Austro-Hungary. For all this, Stalin is remembered and loved in Russia. The trouble is, however, that although he yielded nothing to Hitler in his imperial-nationalistic enthusiasm for villainy, he was basically a practical man and did not leave behind him a *Mein Kampf*—a political program. His propaganda was hypocritical: xenophobia put on the mask of internationalism; imperial conquests were carried out under the slogans of freedom, equality, and fraternity; and the slaughter of entire strata of the Soviet population was explained as an aggravation of the class struggle.

True, in the Russia of the thirties a man did show up who welcomed the degeneration of the revolution into the Stalinist regime and gave it an accurate label: "National Bolshevism." But the man in question—a former Constitutional Democrat, Nikolai Vasilyevich Ustryalov—paid for this with his life, because Stalin preferred clever camouflage to the naked truth. Unfortunately, none of Ustryalov's likely followers knew anything about his political program, or about the man himself. Today's Russian fascists—a relatively small fraction of the Russian Party, consisting mostly of the sons of top Party officials—needed something more than a new, living Stalin or a new, living Hitler. They needed a program for action, a theoretical rationale; in short, *Mein Kampf*. In principle, of course, Stalinism and Hitlerism were siblings: there was no basic difference between them. It's no wonder the two dictators so easily found a common tongue in 1939, when they concluded a nonaggression pact and proceeded to divide up Europe. Hitler was the only man in the world that the paranoid Stalin trusted up until the very end—when Wehrmacht troops had already crossed the Soviet border, and Stukas were bombing Soviet cities.

Hitler's Russian admirers, however, are easier to understand than their high-ranking sponsor, without whom the Nazi demonstration in

Moscow could never have taken place. Or, if it had been held without his sponsorship, the demonstrators would have been harshly punished. Undoubtedly, Andropov not only knew about the rally beforehand but secretly incited it.

Why?

Two days later Andropov himself took part in the celebration of another anniversary—this time openly. Moscow was celebrating, in the grand style, the 112th anniversary of the birth of yet another famous politician of the twentieth century, Lenin. The main speech was delivered by Andropov. Although it was his third birthday speech about Lenin, this one—in the context of a fierce power struggle—was perceived as a sign that Andropov had clearly outstripped his rivals. That impression was reinforced when Andropov, as he came back down from the speaker's platform to where the other members of the Politburo were sitting (headed by Brezhnev—already mentally incompetent, or nearly so), was effusively congratulated on his speech by Minister of Defense Dmitri Ustinov. The TV cameras recorded that moment in detail and significantly, as if to demonstrate the unity between the secret police and the armed forces in the power struggle.

A month later it was officially announced that Andropov, after fifteen years of service in the KGB, was returning to the Party Central Committee (but this time to fulfill the functions of Brezhnev, who could no longer cope with them himself). And just as, earlier, he had begun to function as head of the secret police some time before his appointment was officially announced (although *de jure* his predecessor still held the post), he became the *de facto* leader of the USSR while Brezhnev was still alive. This happened about mid-April 1982, when he had finally overcome all his rivals after some complex maneuvers—a matter of which we shall give a separate account. His chief device in this struggle was to smear his opponents, most often through their children. He had done that with Andrei Kirilenko, Grigori Romanov, and Brezhnev himself. The Nazi demonstration in Pushkin Square was devised with the same purpose in mind: to use the young demonstrators in order to discredit their highly placed parents—who included, if not Andropov's rivals, at any rate enemies of his—and in that way completely to neutralize their efforts to block his advent to power. That demonstration, however, was thought up when the power struggle was at its height; but it was held when the latter was already coming to an end. The rally was a move he had kept back for an emergency; and when there was no longer any need for it, he had sent out (through KGB agents) information about the demonstration soon to be held, so that parents and teachers would restrain adolescents from taking part in it. But it was too late: for those young people, permission from the secret police rated higher than advice and no-no's from parents and teachers. It was like a puppet show that the marionettes act out on their own, without the puppeteer, even though it has been cancelled.

The "puppeteer" was lenient toward them and their independent action: none of the demonstrators was punished. But that Nazi rally put an end to the collaboration between Andropov and the Russian national chauvinists—in any case at that stage of the power struggle, which in the spring of 1982 culminated in Andropov's victory. Having served its purpose as an offensive weapon against the dissent of the national minorities and the liberals—and partly to weaken and compromise Andropov's orthodox partocrat rivals in the Kremlin—national chauvinism was mothballed. To vary the metaphor, the watchdog of great-power chauvinism was put back on his chain until a new need for him arose—if indeed it did arise.

Three years before that, Andropov had received unexpected support—along with a prompting—from the Number One Russian nationalist, whom he had expelled from the USSR in 1974. Speaking on the BBC, writer-in-exile Alexander Solzhenitsyn explained to his Russian audience that in his "Letter to the Leaders of the Soviet Union," he was not, ". . . actually, addressing myself to those leaders. I was trying to lay out another path that might be followed by other leaders in lieu of them—who might suddenly take their place."

This was like a direct call for a coup by the military and the secret police, vindicated by the Chinese threat, domestic ferment, political instability, economic troubles, and other symptoms of imperial decline in the Brezhnev era.

"In our country," the writer-politician went on, "I am counting on that degree of enlightenment which has already spread among our people, and which could not but have reached, also, the military and administrative spheres. After all, the people are not just the millionfold masses down below but their individual representatives holding key posts. There are sons of Russia up there, too. And Russia expects that they will do their filial duty."

As future developments showed, that appeal was heeded—pre-

cisely by him to whom it was addressed, although in early 1979 Solzhenitsyn could scarcely have guessed which particular individual would
be the one to act on it. It is plain, however, that the idea of a coup
occurred to Andropov quite a bit earlier than it did to Solzhenitsyn.

But before deciding on such a coup, he had to rehearse it thoroughly—and more than once. The places that Andropov chose for
those rehearsals were far from Moscow: two Caucasian republics,
Georgia and Azerbaijan.

Andropov's Caucasian "Rehearsals":

4

The Police Blitzkrieg in Azerbaijan and in Stalin's Homeland

You can do everything with bayonets, Sire, but sit on them. — Talleyrand to Napoleon

Politically, in the parent state of the Soviet empire the decade of the seventies was peaceful, monotonous, and dull— Brezhnev's favorite view, at which he gazed with satisfaction from the big windows of his Kremlin office. Like many rulers who are faint-hearted and none too clever, he figured that the monotony and drab-ness of the Soviet political scene were signs that everything there was fine. No internal cataclysm, no abyssal displacements disturbed the mirrorlike surface of the Soviet empire. Or so, at any rate, it seemed to Brezhnev. His political thinking was marked by a limp optimism neatly noted in a well-known joke about the three personal methods of Soviet leadership. It seems that Stalin, Khrushchev, and Brezhnev were riding on a train in the same compartment. Suddenly the train ground to a halt out in the middle of nowhere; and it stayed there for a long time. The first one to lose his patience was Stalin. He left the compartment, but soon came back: "Everything's taken care of. I gave orders to have the engineer shot." But still the train didn't move. The next to leave was Khrushchev. When he got back to the compartment, he announced confidently: "Everything's taken care of. The engineer has been posthumously rehabilitated." Yet even now, the train didn't budge. Finally, Brezhnev pulled down the window curtain, leaned back in his seat with great satisfaction, and said: "Everything's taken care of. We're moving."

This cabdriver's joke shrewdly sums up the eighteen years of Brezhnev's tenure, although it was made up in the middle of that era.

Brezhnev was a man given to wishful thinking and fudging in the face of reality, not only in his convictions but in governmental acts— affixing a seal, passing a resolution, signing a decree of the Central Committee. His comforting self-deception came even more easily to him because he was quite helpless without an army of advisors who supplied him with complete information before he made any decision, met any foreign delegation, or set off on a trip—whether abroad or through the union republics. (He was equally ignorant in both cases.) Of course those advisors, aware of his opportunist attitude toward facts, fed them to him only after they had been "doctored" and homogenized, thereby helping him to indulge his self-deception.

One of those advisors was Yuri Andropov, head of the KGB, whose job it was to deal with the enemy's subversive activities both within the Soviet Union and abroad. It was he who quickly calmed down the frightened general secretary after a nerve-wracking incident that happened in early 1969. On Red Square itself a policeman by the name of Ilyin, instead of protecting his country's leader, as was his duty, shot at him with a pistol. (He didn't hit Brezhnev, although he wounded his chauffeur.) With that efficiency he always showed in critical moments, Andropov promptly offered proof that Ilyin was quite insane and had already been sent off to a madhouse. Also, that there were no plots or subversive activity in Moscow; and that there could be none, so long as that "vigilant watchman," the KGB, was keeping a keen eye on the whole empire from Dzerzhinsky Square— from "the Center."

Incidentally, one of the first steps Andropov took after becoming general secretary was to deal with that same Central Committee International Information Office that had supplied Brezhnev with practical and overt intelligence about the West, as against the secret (and often fantastic) intelligence supplied to Andropov by his "fighters on the invisible front" scattered throughout the world. Those two rival sources had provided opposite kinds of information about the West. The CC International Office had presented the West as a partner in matters of trade, culture, and sports with whom one could have political talks. The network of KGB agents had presented it as a covert enemy constantly waging a secret war against the USSR—one which, however, was neutralized by the KGB's secret war against the West. That explains why, when he came to power, Andropov promptly dissolved (or, according to some rumors, radically pruned back) the CC International Office, regarding its activities as "disinformational," since his knowledge of the West differed radically from that offered by Brezhnev's minions, with their anachronistic bent toward détente.

From Andropov's viewpoint, that period (the late sixties and early seventies) was devoid of hope for his plans, both immediate and long-range, to make it into the ranks of the Kremlin partocrats. At the KGB his career prospects were dead-ended: it was an illumination watchtower not plugged in to the main control console. The very thing that now gave him strength—his position as head of the secret police—was an obstacle to power on a higher level. After the devastating years of the terror wrought by his predecessors in that post—Yagoda, Yezhov, and Beria—it had become a political tradition not to admit a chief of the secret police into a governmental body, and to keep him at a certain remove from the Politburo. In the not-so-far-distant past, that punitive machine had with each new chief gained such strength, and had so completely penetrated everywhere, that everyone was vulnerable, up to and including the country's leader. Thus in the thirties the NKVD (the KGB's predecessor) had gobbled up the entire Leninist leadership of the country, except for Stalin but including Trotsky. A Chekist* saying has it that "the arm of the law is longer than the traitor's leg"; and indeed that long arm did reach Trotsky—across the ocean and the Mexican border. And each time the Kremlin vozhds— Stalin, Malenkov, and Khrushchev—had physically destroyed the head of the state security apparatus and his closest collaborators. This was not a power struggle: only the instinct of self-preservation was at work here. So it was that historical experience did not favor Andropov.

Andropov was searching for solid ground to stand on. He astonished the Party leaders with his demonic capacity for work, staying on the job day and night while they revelled in their power. (He himself never revelled in power—not even when he had obtained it in full

---

*Strictly speaking, a member of the Cheka (All-Russian Extraordinary Commission for Combatting Counterrevolution and Sabotage), the original Soviet secret-police force. But "Chekist" is commonly used to designate any member of the Soviet secret police, past or present. (Translator's note.)

measure.) He made them aware that he was irreplaceable; he sought for chinks and gaps; he tried several random probing moves—and he invariably ran up against the partocrats' system of couplings, where everything held together because of a collective instinct of political survival. Not being in a position for individual defense, they used their collective predatory grasp to defend themselves against any sudden attack from the outside—any infringement on their share of power. Whatever Andropov undertook to further his career, he had to adhere strictly to the "general Party line" so as not to provoke Brezhnev's suspicions, or merely his dissatisfaction. Under Brezhnev no reforms of even the most cautious kind were possible: not economic reforms, and certainly not political ones. Having succeeded the expansionist reformer Khrushchev, and remembering the fate that had befallen the man himself and all his undertakings, Brezhnev had an ungodly fear of all reformers—even such moderate ones as Kosygin, with his program for limited economic decentralization, that he had to abandon under pressure from the bureaucratic opposition. Since he instinctively took a cautious attitude toward any innovation, it was not just reformers that Brezhnev could not abide. The same went for personal initiatives, asserted sincerely and openly: these he quietly checkmated. In politics, he would not tolerate any rough gestures, strong phrases, or the prominence of any political groups—even those with the most patriotic of aims. The men who violated this protocol disappeared, one by one, from the political horizon: former Politburo members Shelepin and Polyansky, Pavlov ("the rosy-cheeked Komsomol boss"), and Leningrad Party boss Tolstikov, who had shown too much initiative.

The image of the empire as a swamp, where there were neither undertows nor storms, was to Brezhnev's liking, and had a soothing effect on him. Being a total ignoramus in statesmanship, he did not even suspect that the stagnation of a swamp—which represents a period of active putrefaction in a state's organism, not its healthful growth—engenders some very odd microorganisms, and quite specific flora and fauna. It was precisely from such political stagnation (which Brezhnev called stability) that such an unusual and unexpected enemy as Andropov could crop up. When he named the civilian Andropov, instead of a professional officer, head of the KGB, Brezhnev must have thought he was being very prudent. It didn't occur to him that after such a long period of service, even a man less able than Andropov would inevitably become a professional, since professionals are not born but made. After appointing Andropov to that post, Brezhnev deliberately installed him in the building where he himself lived, in the apartment above his own. As a crude and unsubtle Party intriguer of the old school, Brezhnev preferred to keep potentially dangerous people near at hand. Then, too, the side of Andropov that he saw was always the same one: the Andropov who was industrious, obliging, and supremely loyal.

His mind at rest regarding his personal security and that of his throne, Brezhnev (according to many witnesses) was fond of gazing out of his office windows, with their snow-white, billowing curtains, at the Kremlin's crenellated walls; Red Square, with its ancient, oblong paving stones; the brightly hued onion domes of St. Basil's Cathedral; and the modern, concrete, hulking buildings across the Moscow River—all of his "quagmire state,"* militarized from top to bottom— and felt, as he gazed on this scene, a proud satisfaction and aesthetic pleasure. He looked, and he invited foreign guests to look.

But another panoramic view of old Moscow, no less picturesque and redolent of history, was completely wasted; because the man whose office offered such a good view of this memorable corner of the empire was supremely indifferent to the sights to be seen through his windows. That indifference was due not only to his progressive blindness (which, by the seventies, had made his gait awkward and cautious) but to his tremendous inner concentration on his plans and their elaboration down to the last touch—even if they were plans for the distant future. Like many armchair strategists and people given to abstract thought, Andropov had acquired the habit, when a plan occurred to him, of pacing back and forth in his office with his hands clasped behind his back—going through variants, settling details, and distributing them rhythmically along the main lines of the plan. He would walk up to the window, but he wouldn't see anything, because he possessed only far-reaching mental vision. He took no notice of that outside world of which Brezhnev, for example, was so fond. Later, this would account for the failure of some of his long-range plans. Although they were ideally roughed out, he was not always able to

---

*The phrase comes from Krylov's "The Frogs Who Asked for a Tsar," a reworking of the well-known Aesopian fable. The first Tsar Jupiter provides them with is ideally calm and dignified: a tree stump. (The Russian word for it also means "blockhead.") (Translator's note.)

allow for the inevitable errors in applying a fixed scheme to a change-able reality.

In groping for a way to penetrate into the closed ranks of the Kremlin partocrats, Andropov was driven to the point of desperation: there were no chinks. The men at the top were united not only by the mutual guarantee of power but by nepotism, long-standing friendship, and shared memories. (The cohort from Dnepropetrovsk, headed up by Brezhnev, is a case in point.) Finally, there was something else even stronger than any oath of loyalty: bonds of kinship. The wife of Georgian Party boss Vasily Mzhavanadze was the sister of Ukrainian Party boss Petr Shelest's wife; and both of these women were friends of Brezhnev's wife. She, in turn, was the sister of Semyon Tsvigun's wife—which is why Brezhnev deliberately palmed Tsvigun off on Andropov as his deputy (actually, as a spy).

Even though he held the high post of KGB chief, Andropov was bound hand and foot. His every move was monitored; his authority was intentionally limited; and he was surrounded by overseers, rang-ing from his downstairs neighbor, Brezhnev, to the latter's in-law and "landsman," Tsvigun. In all that, he saw the bitter paradox of his own fate. He was the head of the secret police, a specialist in intrigues, plots, and underground operations, and on the receiving end of infor-mers' reports from everywhere in the world. Yet he himself was the object of constant tailing and surveillance. He could make no move on his own without being "snitched on" by his first deputy, who would either report that move to Brezhnev personally, or do so indirectly: through his own wife to Brezhnev's wife, who would then report it to "himself." Ultimately, all this turned out sadly for Tsvigun. Because for a chief of secret police to have a fink as his deputy was just too burdensome—especially at a critical moment in a power struggle. So in early 1982 Andropov was obliged to do away with Tsvigun.

Earlier, at the very end of the sixties, after soberly weighing his possibilities, Andropov realized that since he was at least twenty rungs from the top of the Kremlin ladder, he had absolutely no chance of outstripping his mighty rivals. Nor did the situation change in 1973, when he became a full member of the Politburo and was about ten rungs from the top of the ladder: the Kremlin chiefs were still invul-nerable to him. Even with all his experience as a master of intrigue and undermining others, if he had joined in the power struggle he would

certainly have failed and lost everything he had so long and assidu-
ously labored to acquire.

It was then, after pondering all possible plans of action and finding
himself in a cul-de-sac, that he made the remarkable discovery which
brought him out of the pitch darkness of theories and hypotheses into
the bright light of the truth. He discovered the point at which all of
the top partocrats were vulnerable, and invented an all-purpose
weapon to use against them. Thus began his famous (although initially
covert) campaign against corruption in the southern Soviet republics,
which served him as proving grounds where he could test his campaign against political corruption on a union-wide scale. In the late
seventies he brought the show to Moscow, where one after another he
neutralized or eliminated his political rivals in the Kremlin, under the
same cover of a campaign against corruption and abuse of power. It
was the perfect pretext, and it yielded 100 percent productivity. In a
country with shortages of everything—from edibles and clothing to
apartments and cars—any person in an executive position is fair game
for charges of corruption. And even if he is honest as the day is long,
one can always find at least one relative of his who has taken advantage
of his high position to obtain privileges and goodies, thereby compromising him.

For the moment, however, there could be no question for Andropov of doing battle against the Kremlin Mafia—even though, for
example, the *dolce vita* and almost royal privileges enjoyed by Brezhnev's daughter Galina were not only evident but on display. He did not
yet have enough authority to use his all-purpose weapon, the armor,
against a political opponent in Moscow, not to mention the Kremlin.
He had to begin from afar—in the literal, geographic sense of the
word.

Azerbaijan and Georgia are two Transcaucasian republics remote
from Moscow, one on the shore of the Caspian Sea, the other on the
shore of the Black Sea. One is noted for its oil rigs, the other for
having the USSR's biggest deposit of manganese and for producing 95
percent of the country's tea. One has a Moslem population, the other's
religion has long been Russian Orthodox. One has, in the course of its
history, undergone international engrafting and a certain degree of
Russification; the other has preserved the purity of its unique language and its ethnic heritage. It was these two republics, so different

from each other in many ways, that Andropov chose as stages where he could rehearse his battle against the partocrats under the guise of a campaign against corruption. These republics suited his purposes not only because of their remoteness from the parent state and their proximity to his birthplace, but for another reason no less important in justifying punitive measures. In both republics, corruption, bribery, graft, and protectionism had become the stuff of folklore, and had deep ethnic and historical roots. Both the Georgian black-market millionaires and the foreign-currency speculators of Baku, the capital of Azerbaijan, had become legendary figures throughout the Soviet Union. For that matter, "the fish swam right into the net": Azerbaijan became an issue as soon as Andropov had become personally acquainted with Geidar Aliyev, then head of the Azerbaijani KGB.

THE POLICE BLITZKRIEG IN AZERBAIJAN

When the two men became closely acquainted, Aliyev made a very strong impression on Andropov—which is why he was chosen to carry out the first experimental police coup in the USSR.

In 1967, when Aliyev was in charge of the state security apparatus in Azerbaijan (that same year Andropov became his chief, being officially named head of the all-union KGB), he was one of the youngest officials in the country to hold such a high post, and with the rank of general besides. His background is remarkable in that during the entirety of his adult life, from age eighteen on, the Azerbaijani Geidar Ali Rza ogly Aliyev had served in the secret police, having graduated from a SMERSh* school and been tempered by wartime intelligence work. Aliyev, along with Georgian Minister of Internal Affairs Eduard Shevardnadze, represented the highest human breed developed in the KGB's underground "nurseries." It was a breed of internationalists who were true believers in the empire, though their names sounded weird even to Russians. Both men had attended Russian schools; and both were devoid of any close attachment to their own soil, or any ethnic roots. Each one looked upon his own republic as an integral part of the Soviet empire. Both (but especially Aliyev) were intolerant toward the ethnic traits, traditions, character, and style of their own peoples. For them, those things were nothing more than prejudices,

---

*SMERSh, an acronym for *Smert shpionam* ("Death to the Spies"), was a World War II counterintelligence organization. (Translator's note.)

vestiges of the past, vexing obstacles (which had to be removed) in the way of setting up a universal and supranational Soviet empire. This is the typical KGB outlook. (It may well be shared by Andropov himself, because his ideological flirtation with the Moscow chauvinists was merely a means, not an end.) This new breed of secret-police officer, as personified by Aliyev and Shevardnadze, is distinguished by a very high degree of executive competence, organizational talents, and an outstanding capacity for work—which plainly shows how much energy the "organs" of state security can squeeze out of its functionaries. Both men were extremely ambitious (which also increased their energy potential); and their ambition was of a higher order than that of their Moscow colleagues. In order to be appointed to posts in Moscow, they had to perform exemplarily in their own republics before crossing their borders in a northwesterly direction. For them, their native republics were something like launching pads. Their ambition, like their mode of thought, had a scope that was imperial and international, in no way restricted by national boundaries.

KGB General Aliyev, unlike his Georgian colleague, who had more humane traits, was an almost ideal mechanical instrument: he had no apprehensions about a misfire, and no convictions other than the official minimum of the imperial ideology. He was as charged with energy as a still-quivering arrow just before being loosed from the bow. In 1969, having waited for just the right moment, Yuri Andropov finally loosed that arrow, naming Azerbaijan's chief of secret police Party boss of the republic.

This was a complete bypassing of, and in flagrant contradiction with, Khrushchev and Brezhnev's policy for key appointments, whereby mostly Party officials were named to high posts in the KGB, but never vice versa. Not to mention the fact that four Party secretaries who had better claims to the post of first secretary than did the outsider Aliyev, were passed over. But in this case, Andropov had personally laid the groundwork both for the removal of Aliyev's predecessor—a weak-willed and obsequious functionary named Veli Akhundov who had gone along with Brezhnev's theory of "reconciling contradictions"—and for his replacement by the professional KGB officer Aliyev. He did this by proving to Brezhnev, with facts ready at hand (with Brezhnev he always used the method of direct persuasion) that in Azerbaijan corruption, embezzlement, and violations of Leninist Party protocol had gone so far (and, most important, had penetrated so deeply) that only severe police measures could "air out the nation." (Here we have used a phrase from Lichtenberg to clarify Andropov's thought.) At this point he laid before Brezhnev a dossier that Azerbaijani KGB chief Aliyev had put together on his Party boss, Veli Akhundov, and showed him the most striking examples of how much corruption there was in Azerbaijan.

Item: one Mamedbekov, a justice of the Supreme Court, had been found guilty of taking bribes in the amount of a million rubles.

Item: the president of the republic, Iskenderov, had himself accepted huge sums of money for pardoning persons sentenced to death.

Item: Allakhverdiyev, secretary of the Baku municipal committee of the Party, had bought up gold from the foreign-currency speculator Rokotov, who was subsequently shot.

Item: Dadashev, chairman of a trade-union council, had bought up foreign currency through front men.

Item: the manager of a fruit-juice plant had put out his product without any fruit, and had pocketed more than a million rubles— exactly the sum that should have been spent on buying fruit over a period of two years.

Item: students had had to pay bribes not only to matriculate at a college but to graduate from it; in fact they had to pay for each examination they took.

Item: in the republic's hospitals, graft had got to the point where one patient died from peritonitis because he hadn't been fast enough in coming up with the money to pay a surgeon for an emergency operation.

And so on: Andropov's presentation to Brezhnev was considerably longer than our summary of it.

By way of exerting more psychological pressure, Andropov added a few belittling touches to the personal file of Veli Akhundov, who before entering upon his Party career had been a doctor. But his doctoral dissertation had been ghosted for him by a professor from an institute of microbiology—a service for which he got two apartments: one for himself and one for his son.

Then Andropov played on the imperial xenophobia of the Kremlin vozhd, maintaining that the only way to govern national minorities was by using police measures. As a result, Andropov got what he wanted: Akhundov was dismissed and replaced by KGB General Geidar Aliyev. That order set the precedent that Andropov needed:

appointing a chief of secret police Party boss. Now it was time to rehearse methods of police government.

Just one month after he was appointed first secretary, Aliyev delivered a speech to Azerbaijan's Party leadership in which he sounded rather pessimistic as compared to his predecessor, and even as compared to his Party colleagues from other republics and oblasts. His pessimism had to do with the economic and ideological condition of the republic. It seemed that "things are bad in almost every sector of the economy"; that the ministries were not coping with the work incumbent upon them; and that a great many local officials were taking bribes and providing cover for criminals. Aliyev then announced the new policy of the police government: "We must tear the mask off the subversives, the slanderers, the plotters, and the careerists who are doing serious damage to our cause. We must do battle, resolutely and inflexibly, against all incidents of graft in our republic, and root out the conditions that lead to them."

This marked the beginning of the purges in Azerbaijan—of a reign of terror throughout the republic. At first the purges were carried out in local "nests," selected more or less at random. But gradually they were shifted to bigger targets, and there was a continuous series of dismissals, already at the ministerial level. Thus the minister of industrial construction was sent into forced retirement; and two months later the minister of public health was fired on the rather serious grounds of "falsifying reports, unsatisfactory organization of public health, and a low level of medical services." In a demonstration of his own incorruptibility, Aliyev dismissed the minister of internal affairs, his close co-worker in the days when he himself was chief of the parallel department, the KGB. And along with him, he fired the minister's two deputies, completely replacing the leadership of the ministry.

Finally, after seven months of constant purges at all levels of the republic's leadership, Aliyev took on the Party's central organ, the Politburo of Azerbaijan. The old, sacred emblem of the KGB had been "the sword and shield of the Party." But now, for KGB General Aliyev—as later for the Georgian Shevardnadze and still later for the USSR's chief of secret police, Yuri Andropov—the KGB had ceased to be the Party's shield. Instead, it became a sword turned against those it was supposed to defend—the top partocrats.

Aliyev immediately removed several members of the Politburo, including the chairman of the council of ministers and Party secretary for Baku. At that time, according to Aliyev's own admission, there was "covert resistance" to his tough police measures at the highest Party level. In order to wipe out sedition at one stroke, he dismissed the president of the republic and promptly expanded the scope of Party purges down to the regional and municipal level, where he would first of all fire Party secretaries and then, quite often, all of their deputies and closest aides.

In a year and a half Aliyev had completely changed the republic's Party and government leadership, filling the vacated posts with his own people, who were usually no older than fifty and mostly from the Azerbaijani KGB. It was a new generation of leaders and, more important, a new type. These men were cynical, ambitious, and totally loyal to Aliyev—and through him, to Andropov.

Aliyev invented a new approach to governing. His large-scale campaign against corruption, accompanied by instant dismissals of high Party officials and often by arrests, was presented for public review throughout Azerbaijan. He saw to it that the press played its own role in the endless series of purges. The Party-government newspaper, *Bakinskiy rabochiy* (The Baku Worker), regularly reported cases of graft, the theft of state property, the existence of entire "underground" private factories and plants, and nepotism among Party leaders. It also reported the punishments meted out, up to and including the death penalty, which Aliyev made a fixture of day-to-day life in the republic.

In this way the "Red bourgeoisie" of Azerbaijan was exposed and put on trial before the public. In this way the harsh police measures used in exposing and punishing lawbreakers were justified—for both the past and the future. In this way the interval was shortened between a person and the state, between prison and home, between life and death. No one was any longer protected, whether by money or a high position, against exposure and punishment. Aliyev had introduced a completely new style in talking to the public and with his Party colleagues: a tone of stern directness, righteousness, and complete openness in sketching the real situation in the republic, emphasizing the minuses and not the pluses, as earlier secretaries of the republic had done when speaking to the public. For example, he was the first to publicize the scandalous fact that not once since World War II had Azerbaijan fulfilled the five-year plan. (Although the republic

had apparently coped with the latest five-year plan—that of 1965–70—
it had done so because, at the last moment, the output norms were
lowered so much that their fulfillment could hardly be counted a great
achievement.) This was an unusually direct and frank kind of talk
between the republic's leader and the public. He wanted to show the
real state of affairs, to stir up feelings of guilt and responsibility among
the people, and to justify the harsh measures he had been compelled to
take in order to root out the evil. In summing up the results of the
republic's performance during the five-year-plan period, Aliyev ac-
knowledged that only one industrial enterprise out of six was working
at full capacity.

When, in late 1982, Andropov began to talk to the entire Soviet
people in this same sober, demanding tone, it produced a very strong,
stunning effect—the effect of waking up from a long sleep and coming
back to reality. Brezhnev's ideas had died out even more rapidly than
his corpse decayed, so antediluvian and irrelevant did his style of
governing seem as compared to the modern and refreshing (not to say
freezing) style of the former KGB chief. The same effect of novelty
and modernism had been felt a decade before by the inhabitants of the
Caucasus, when KGB generals took over as first secretaries in Azerbaijan and Georgia. Very soon, however, the police regime here exhausted its effective and quick-acting but nonetheless limited creative
means. It became just as perfunctory and bureaucratic as—even more
so than—the previous republic regimes of Brezhnev's satraps.

Since Andropov is now setting out on the path toward a police
state, it will be useful to see where that path took Aliyev in Azerbaijan which, for his chief, Andropov, was a kind of proving ground.

Aliyev had carried out his police coup in such a short time and
with such brutal methods, he had made such a clean sweep of the
republic's leadership, and the camouflaging of his war against political
opponents as a "campaign against corruption" was so transparent,
that it worried even Andropov—who of course had been closely ob-
serving the police experiment of his overly zealous and hyperactive
protégé. He was worried, however, not about Aliyev but about himself
because Brezhnev, concerned for the empire's outward stability, had
been roused to suspicion by the fragmentary reports reaching him,
telling of Aliyev's harsh reprisals against the entire Party apparatus of
Azerbaijan. It became important to convince Brezhnev that Aliyev's
police-type regime was successful. And Andropov, knowing all of

Brezhnev's foibles, suggested to Aliyev a move that was crude but impressive.

Aliyev, who only a short time before had fired the minister of internal affairs for his "optimistic statistics," was now himself obliged to resort to "doctoring" reports and working various combinations with the figures. In a word, he had recourse to "optimistic statistics" rather than the pessimistic variety favored by his KGB-man mentality. This was done so that toward the end of his first year as Party secretary he could report to Moscow on the republic's amazing achievements under his rule. The results were too good to be credible. Industrial production had risen 10 percent as compared to the 1969 level—twice the annual growth rate under the previous leadership. Labor productivity had doubled. And the plan for agricultural production—which according to Aliyev had been in a pathetic state in 1969—had finally been fulfilled.

Aliyev didn't even worry about the credibility of that rosy picture—those high indexes attained in the course of only one year. The important thing for him was that they should impress Brezhnev as the best proof of how effective his harsh measures and republic-wide purges had been in an Azerbaijan riddled with corruption. And Brezhnev *was* impressed: the new secretary had proven his zeal as the master of Azerbaijan. And yet Brezhnev never got over the distrust and dislike he felt for Aliyev personally, and toward his KGB policies. He was put on guard by Aliyev's very zeal and his ideal efficiency, in which there was something impersonal, automatic. And by that inexhaustible energy (like the energy of a smoothly functioning machine) with which, over a period of thirteen years, he "purged" the republic of corruption. (Actually, he never did clean it up completely, since the old corruption was replaced by a new variety.) Brezhnev had the feeling that Aliyev stood for a new class very different from the generation of Party bureaucrats he was used to. He vaguely sensed that the youthful-looking, broad-shouldered Party leader of Azerbaijan, who was absolutely unflappable, represented the rising generation—those "iron young men" who had already begun to surface in Moscow, and from whom he instinctively shied away. Which is why he so stubbornly opposed Andropov's insistence that the energetic Aliyev, as a valuable "republic cadre," be brought into the central leadership: the Politburo. He had nothing he could offer as an objection to Aliyev, directly; but he vaguely discerned in him a threat, an alien style, something hard-boiled in his way of thinking. And he did everything he could to put off Aliyev's promotion until, in 1976, seven years after Aliyev had taken over as Party boss in Azerbaijan, Brezhnev was forced—under the pressure of those same optimistic statistics—to make him a candidate-member of the Politburo. (Aliyev never did become a full member of the Politburo during Brezhnev's lifetime, despite help from Andropov and his own efforts.)

Merely during the first three years of his rule in Azerbaijan, Aliyev fired hundreds of high officials. One might think that he would have pulled himself up short at that point and begun, with the republic's fully renewed leadership, to reorganize the economy, whose condition he continued to deplore on his own turf—in contrast to his reports to Moscow. But he stuck closely within the confines of police methods of governing. It is true that a police regime, using nothing but coercive means of tightening discipline and increasing worker responsibility, yields higher labor productivity and economic indexes than does an indifferent, bureaucratic regime. But here two important factors come into play. First, once those indexes have reached a certain level, they have no further capacity for growth. Second, in order to keep them at that level, recourse must be had to new and even harsher methods. It turns out that a police-type regime can effectively get rid of symptoms of a disease but cannot get at its real cause. The radical shifts in the government of Azerbaijan that Aliyev called for during his first days as Party boss resulted in the radical removal of symptoms, while leaving their causes untouched. That marked the limit of his possibilities, since the professional KGB officer Aliyev had no knowledge or experience of other methods of leadership and government. But quite apart from Aliyev, it also marked the limit of the very concept of a police state—or, more precisely, the utopia of a police state—in which he and his Moscow master piously believed as the only reality. José Ortega y Gasset, after quoting Talleyrand's famous remark to Napoleon about the impossibility of sitting on bayonets, adds:

Governing is not sword-rattling, not the threat of force, but its quiet employment. In short, to govern means to *sit*: on a throne, in a minister's armchair, on the Holy See. Contrary to naïve notions, governing demands not force so much as the ability to sit firmly. A state, in the final analysis, is held together by firm public opinion. It is a question of stable equilibrium.

Today we can address these words to Andropov himself, just as in the early seventies they could have been addressed to his protégé from Azerbaijan.

Aliyev, however, as a disciplined time-server and a man never troubled by doubts, was not discouraged by the discovery that there were limits to his police-type regime. He drew only one lesson from that experience: in order to keep labor productivity, and economic production in general, at the level reached thanks to police measures, more purges were required. With some bitterness, he admitted that the new people he had put in office (including former KGB men) had, in their turn, been infected with corruption and bribery. Having exhausted all the productive possibilities of a police-type regime, he again, in a kind of mechanical repetition, resorted to personnel shake-ups.

He began by removing those few ministers who had survived the first wave of dismissals. Then, like someone under a spell, he fired the same regional and municipal Party secretaries whom, not so long before, he himself had appointed. No longer concerned with any serious grounds for charges, he brought in a new protégé to replace an erstwhile close confrere of his whom he had named first secretary of the Baku Municipal Committee in 1970. Now it was the turn of the republic's two police ministries, and Aliyev was already stealing up on them. But a purge proved unnecessary. Unexpectedly, events outstripped the zealous satrap, and everything was settled very efficiently. On June 29, 1978, a prison warden, unhappy about the results of an inspection, stormed into the office of the minister of internal affairs and, right there on the spot, shot him and his two aides: his deputy and a high KGB official. What with the constant purges, trials, and shootings, this extraordinary event did not attract any special attention on the part of the Azerbaijanis, who by that time had developed a kind of immunity to everything that happened in the loftier reaches of the regime.

There were so many purges, so many firings, and so many trials throughout the republic, that the Azerbaijanis began to think their Party leader was possessed by the idea of a "permanent purge." From Aliyev's viewpoint, however, that was his only recourse: to retain, by means of new police purges, what had been gained by earlier ones. In principle, these practices should have led to a police-type dictatorship;

but this was prevented by Azerbaijan's subordination to Moscow within the system of the Soviet empire.

Essentially, for about eight years, Aliyev ruled the republic by momentum, with the motor idling, carrying out a series of repeated purges under the guise of a campaign against corruption. And those purges had their own mechanical rhythm: first a slacking off, then a paroxysm—as happened toward the end of Aliyev's rule in Azerbaijan, when he suddenly wiped out the entire leadership of the prosecutor's office. (And it was done physically: all the accused officials were shot.)

With his endless housecleaning, his monotonous devices of leadership, the severity of his penalties, and his brutal style, Aliyev had squeezed his republic like a lemon: it could no longer yield a higher productivity. In order to keep that republic at an exemplary level (nothing less would do), he had worked out a virtually automatic system for its government by the secret police. It had no more need for him, personally; and he could easily have turned it over to one of his deputies. Moscow was his goal. And in this, his chief and sponsor, Andropov, was doing everything he could to help him: but he was unable to overcome the rocklike resistance of Brezhnev. The oldster in the Kremlin could not abide the fact that during the empire's most tranquil period, at a time of outward (economic and political) stability—behind which Andropov discerned, with anxiety, signs of decay—there were constant changes of Party leadership in one of the Soviet republics. Because such changes meant disorder.

Nonetheless, Andropov was hoping that at the Twenty-sixth Party Congress in 1981 he could bring Aliyev into the Politburo. Knowing Brezhnev's senile weakness for fulsome flattery, he advised Aliyev to constantly interrupt his speech at the congress with praises of "dear Leonid Ilich," using flowery compliments sweet to the old man's ear. At that congress Aliyev tried so hard to please Brezhnev that he set a record for slavish flattery: in the course of his fifteen-minute speech, he contrived to mention Brezhnev's name thirteen times. None of the other thirty-nine speakers could compare with him in either the frequency, or the effusiveness, of his praise for the decrepit Soviet vozhd.

But instead of helping, the flattery put Brezhnev on his guard—so much was it at odds with General Aliyev's stiff, martinet-like bearing. He didn't become a member of the Politburo until ten days after Brezhnev's death. Two days later he was named first deputy prime minister. Azerbaijan might be able to get along without him, since he had left it in the reliable hands of his well-schooled compeers; but Andropov couldn't get along without him in Moscow because Aliyev possessed traits not to be found in any of the men close to the new Soviet leader, and not even to be found in him.

Here we must backtrack a bit. About two years after Geidar Aliyev had begun to rule Azerbaijan, Andropov had available a neat scenario, already acted out, for a police coup conducted under the guise of a campaign against corruption. But the scenario used in Azerbaijan had been too ideal, *too* neat, really. It lacked the lifelike details—and the alternative versions for test purposes—that the USSR's chief of secret police required. So that he had need of yet another police coup in the Caucasus: in neighboring Georgia.

IN STALIN'S HOMELAND:
DIAMONDS, BOMBS, AND CITRUS FRUITS

Sometime early in 1972 Eduard Shevardnadze, chief of the regular police in Georgia and directly accountable to "the Center," laid on Andropov's desk a thick dossier on Vasily Mzhavanadze, the first secretary of Georgia. Andropov had planned the operation to remove Mzhavanadze more thoroughly and carefully, with more camouflage and "redundancy" (to use NASA language), then the similar, relatively smoother, operation in Azerbaijan. And it was carried out accordingly.

For nineteen years Mzhavanadze had "ruled" Georgia as an indolent Eastern princeling might have ruled his fief: perfunctorily, with outward propriety. From time to time at Party congresses, when under heavy pressure from Moscow, he would break out into indignant philippics against the graft, nepotism, nationalism, and clannish favoritism that had flourished under his indulgent regime on a scale that was truly fantastic. The basic rules by which he governed were Brezhnevian, with some colorful Georgian touches added by way of adjustment: to avoid all decisions and prompt measures, and to compromise in difficult situations. Also, in many ways he resembled Brezhnev, whose friend he was. Like him, Mzhavanadze had been a political commissar in the army during the war, and he had been Party boss in Georgia throughout the Brezhnev era. Their wives even had the same names—something that must have tickled the vein of irony in Andropov when he tried (at great risk) to sow strife between the two Victorias during a probing attempt to undermine the general secretary. And Mzhavanadze, fully armed with Communist demagogy, was so skillful at diverting Brezhnev's attention from Georgia's failures to fulfill the five-year plan (for that matter, Brezhnev "was glad to deceive himself") that right up to the beginning of Shevardnadze's purges, Georgia was regarded, along with Armenia, as a model Soviet republic.

Mzhavanadze's wife, who unlike him was strong-willed with expensive tastes, took such great advantage of his high position—everything from accepting lavish gifts to taking direct part in black-market operations involving millions—that the period of Mzhavanadze's rule was called "the Victorian Era." Her very close friend Otari Lazishvili, famous throughout Georgia as a Soviet capitalist and big businessman, owned several underground factories where clothing was manufactured from raw material stolen from the state. The workers were delivered to these underground factories by taxi. Among the items manufactured there were raincoats, stylish sweaters, scarves, and varicolored nylon net bags that were not available from state factories. They were, however, sold illegally at state shops, or on the black market, where they were instantly snapped up. (For the sake of appearances, Lazishvili ran a small laboratory where new synthetic fabrics were tested.)

The black-market millionaire gradually acquired so much influence in the republic that his advice was heeded in appointing and dismissing officials, including members of the Council of Ministers and even leaders of the Communist Party of Georgia. By spreading huge bribes around, he mined all the approaches to himself that might have been taken by enforcers of the law in Georgia. Even General Shevardnadze, chief of the regular police for the entire republic, was powerless before the almighty Lazishvili, who had bought off members of both the legislative and executive branches in Georgia. When Shevardnadze issued several tentative warnings to him, the enraged Lazishvili declared that if Shevardnadze went on trying to undermine him, he would have him demoted from general to private.

The dealings of Lazishvili and his many accomplices provided Andropov with grounds for carrying out yet another police coup in the

Caucasus. But in order to eliminate the Party boss of Georgia, the underground machinations of a Georgian millionaire were not of themselves enough to go on.

Chance, however, came to the aid of Shevardnadze—and of Andropov as well. At a dinner party given by Mzhavanadze for his Party elite and some foreign guests, Shevardnadze noticed on the finger of the first secretary's wife an antique, priceless, eight-carat diamond ring that had been stolen in a European country and was being sought by Interpol. He soon found out that the ring had been given to Mzhavanadze's wife by the black-market capitalist Lazishvili. Now Andropov could show Brezhnev that there were sufficient grounds for removing the Party leader of Georgia; and he could do so without arousing any suspicions as to his having a personal interest in that dismissal. In this case the police coup was ideally camouflaged as a campaign against corruption at the top level.

In order to make everything even more convincing, Andropov and Shevardnadze had recourse, at the last minute, to a device that was literally explosive. The Georgian Party newspaper, *Zarya Vostoka* (Dawn of the East), reported the discovery of several underground firearms factories not far from Sukhumi, the famous Black Sea resort. The article provided ominous details as to how the machine tools for manufacturing rifles and revolvers, including miniaturized pistols resembling fountains pens, were stolen from government plants. And the reporter declared that entire armed bands were roaming about near the outskirts of big cities, "threatening the lives of citizens and their security." The article had been published on orders from Shevardnadze, and used information supplied by him.

Andropov showed it to Brezhnev. And of course there could have been nothing more horrible for the general secretary than to learn of armed subversive activities in one of the Soviet republics. Mzhavanadze's fate was sealed. In August 1972 Police General Eduard Shevardnadze, Andropov's direct protégé and close co-worker, became first secretary of Georgia.

We come now to the most fascinating phase of this Georgian affair—one that demonstrates Andropov's ambitious impatience and his penchant for intrigue.

Shevardnadze, having become (with Andropov's help and blessing) the leader of Georgia, at this stage almost completely imitated his Azerbaijani predecessor. He immediately started to wage war against

corruption in high places as well as low: against extortion, bad leadership, and graft: the familiar assortment of charges under a police
regime. At forty-four he was the youngest of the republic Party bosses.
He had no ethnic prejudices, although in Georgia (unlike Azerbaijan)
nationalist feelings run high. He believed in the strength and effectiveness of coercive devices and police methods. He was honest and austere in his tastes. Unlike his predecessor, Mzhavanadze, he did not
take part in any of those famous Georgian Saturnalias that last for
several days—something else that set him apart from most of his
compatriots, with their Epicurean proclivities.

We shall not try to guess at Shevardnadze's motives—whether he
was animated by puritanism or political ambition, or both. In every
ethnic group there are individuals devoid of clannish prejudices who
look upon their own people from an alien viewpoint: "phobes" and
not "philes." Shevardnadze was a critic of his own people, capable of
looking at their vices from the outside, soberly and disapprovingly. In
Georgia he was universally disliked precisely because he was anti-
Georgian. And there was yet another reason for that dislike: in Stalin's
homeland he was rather a Leninist than a Stalinist. Thus at the
Twenty-fifth Party Congress in Moscow, the only anti-Stalinist speech
was the one made by Shevardnadze.

His predecessor had owned a splendid town house and seven
dachas. He, by sharp contrast, lived in a wretched Soviet apartment
on the fourth floor of a building without an elevator. And he refused to
move from it into quarters more in keeping with his position until (as
he declared rather bombastically) "every Georgian family has its own
apartment." (Incidentally, both of the present writers were often in
Georgia and had an opportunity to observe, personally, all phases of
this Georgian political experiment.)

He was very energetic; but his was not the rather frightening and
mechanical energy of an Aliyev: he showed more personal initiative
and inventiveness. His extensive police experience was helpful to him
in discovering "nests" of lawbreakers. He slept little; he would make
unexpected appearances in the most remote parts of Georgia; and by
the end of his first year in power he was dead tired.

In the course of a year and a half he, like Aliyev, had carried out a
complete purge among the partocrats. He got rid of about three-
quarters of the top officials, including twenty ministers and Central
Committee members, forty-four out of sixty-seven regional secre-

taries, three secretaries of municipal committees, and ten mayors and their deputies. It was a real political coup with the total removal of the republic's leadership. Shevardnadze filled the vacancies with people from the KGB and the regular police, technocrats, and young Party members—people he regarded as at least "honest."

Then, finally, he took reprisals against the Georgian *capo di tutti capi*, Otari Lazishvili. He approached him slowly, gradually tightening the ring, arresting one member after another of his underground gang. Sensing danger, Lazishvili secretly flew to Moscow to seek protection against the boss of Georgia from his old acquaintance, USSR General Prosecutor Roman Rudenko. (This is the same Rudenko mentioned in an earlier chapter as a member of the government troika, headed by Andropov, which held talks with a delegation of Crimean Tatars.) Rudenko undoubtedly had more power in Moscow than the Party secretary of any union republic. So that, once again, Andropov had to intervene personally. For him it was a rather delicate matter, since actually he was entering the lists against a union-wide underground network: one in which the general prosecutor was involved, more or less indirectly. Besides, Rudenko was older than Andropov, was known throughout the country, and had served as the chief Soviet prosecutor at the Nuremberg trials.

By taking a direct part in Georgian affairs and supporting his man Shevardnadze, Andropov was in many ways risking more than the former. But then his stake in the political game was higher. What Andropov did on this occasion was to arrest the Georgian mafioso right in the waiting room of his friend, the USSR general prosecutor.

One might think that this marked the end of the Lazishvili case: he was sentenced to fifteen years,* and Shevardnadze could finally get back to his pressing duties in the republic. But he had to take up the Lazishvili case yet once more, this time on Andropov's personal orders.

Scarcely had Shevardnadze become Party boss of Georgia, scarcely had he worked up a plan for rooting out corruption everywhere in the republic, when Andropov ordered him to investigate the murky affair

---

*The public prosecutor demanded the death penalty, as was usual in Georgia under Shevardnadze, even for much less serious economic crimes against the State. But the prudent Lazishvili had managed in advance to buy off the judiciary; and the Supreme Court of Georgia, which at the same time handed down sentences to about 100 of Lazishvili's accomplices, gave him a relatively light sentence.

of the diamond. At issue was that same stolen eight-carat diamond ring that Lazishvili had once given to Mzhavanadze's greedy wife. It is hardly likely that Shevardnadze, who at the time was busy with critical problems of the economy and personnel shake-ups, and was introducing the police style of government, was the one who initiated this investigation, which from his vantage point was even awkward. His predecessor had gone into honorable retirement, taking along his wife and the Order of the October Revolution. In Georgia, as in many Levantine or Eastern countries, where the code of honor is strong, it is against custom to finish off and humiliate, for the second time, an opponent who has already been defeated. *A fortiori*, one must not make him pay "twice for one and the same thing." Finally, even if one posits a personal vengefulness on the part of Shevardnadze, such an investigation was not in keeping with his character; and he had more weighty evidence as to how Mzhavanadze had abused his position—if only that of the seven villas in the countryside.

But Andropov insisted on investigating the "diamond affair," and on prosecuting not Mzhavanadze but his wife. Shevardnadze was somewhat taken aback by Andropov's stubborn insistence on poking into what was a local, strictly Georgian, matter. But he of course followed orders and called in Mzhavanadze's wife for an interrogation during which she was asked questions about the diamond. Things went so far that the frightened Victoria Mzhavanadze, immediately after her interrogation, flew to the Ukraine to the home of her sister, the wife of Ukrainian Party boss Petr Shelest. The system of nepotism set up by Brezhnev in Moscow, which had walled out Andropov, had also begun to function on the republic level. But by that time Petr Shelest, like Mzhavanadze, had been removed from his post as Party boss by Brezhnev, and expelled from the Politburo. And in his role as a has-been, he was more vulnerable to Andropov's machinations.

In these events one can hear echoes of a Shakespearian drama: two sisters, the wives of overthrown rulers of republics, pursued by an implacable fate in the person of the man heading up the union-wide secret police. Andropov demanded that Shevardnadze continue the criminal investigation he had begun. The stolen diamond, which had once sparkled on the finger of Victoria Mzhavanadze at grand receptions in Tbilisi, had in some strange way stirred up our hero's imagination. Shevardnadze had to request approval from the Kremlin itself for the extradition of the criminal, Mzhavanadze's wife, who at the moment was living in the Ukraine. And despite the damning proofs that he submitted, he got a categorical refusal: from Brezhnev himself.

This was Andropov's first probing attempt to undermine Brezhnev. The reason for his stubborn insistence on investigating the case of the stolen diamond was that he knew—from Shevardnadze—that Victoria Mzhavanadze, who got the antique diamond ring as a gift from the underground millionaire Lazishvili, had in turn presented it to Brezhnev's wife. It is hard to imagine a better place for concealing stolen goods than the Kremlin chief's apartment, although it was only a few stair steps away from the apartment occupied by the top-ranking Soviet gendarme, who was busy looking for that diamond ring. Being in possession of such piquant information, Andropov could not resist the temptation to quietly blackmail, frighten, or even pressure his downstairs neighbor with the help of that stern and jealous guardian of the law, that altruistic fighter against corruption in all levels, that Georgian knight from the KGB, Eduard Shevardnadze.

When Brezhnev blocked further investigation of the "diamond affair," did he have a premonition that ten years later, a few months before his death, he would have to undergo the same sad fate as Vasily Mzhavanadze? There would even be a complete parallel with the infamous "affair of the diamond." But this time—a slight change in Andropov's plans in view of the advanced age of Brezhnev's wife—the one involved would be his daughter. She, too, while her father was still alive, and while he was invested with the supreme power, would be dragged in for interrogation on account of a cache of diamonds (likewise stolen) that was in her possession. And Brezhnev would be powerless to come to the aid of his own daughter.

By the way, this literal coincidence between the two diamond stories casts doubt on whether there really were any stolen diamonds in the second case, involving Brezhnev's daughter. The whole thing is just too neat to be real. One version follows another, and there are just too many diamonds. It's as if the action were taking place, not in the setting of a realistic Moscow, but in *The Three Musketeers*.

Here we must point out one more significant trait of Andropov's mode of thought. Since over a period of many years he had no opportunity to act directly and work out his strategy on the spot, he got used to a wait-and-see position, with repeated rehearsals of a future action and a very thorough elaboration of long-range plans. He acquired the habit of thinking only in terms of distant goals. It differed, for example, from the ad hoc thinking of Brezhnev, who was always content with quick results and local improvements. But in Andropov's long-range thinking, there is a hidden defect due to his long service in the world of bureaucratic formulas and the routine of accountability. After scrupulously working out his plan of action down to the tiniest detail, and trying out its "rough draft" in reality, Andropov is capable—several years or even a whole decade later—of applying that plan to a reality that has changed, without bothering to allow for the unavoidable errors. We have already seen examples of that bureaucratic rigidity in his thinking: when he applied the Hungarian model to the Czechoslovak revolution, which was a very different kind of reality; and his attempt, soon thereafter, to apply it to Poland when the worker riots broke out there. We shall also see in more detail how he took the old smear scheme developed for use against Mzhavanadze and, with a rare degree of pedantry, applied it to the Brezhnev family, although in that case it would prove impossible to tie up all the loose ends. In particular, the matter of the diamonds would, in the context of Moscow and the Kremlin, sound a stridently false note.

Here another important trait of Andropov's long-range thinking comes into play. Once he has made a plan for a future action and then stored it away in one of the safes of his capacious memory, he feels obligated to make use of it at some time or other. Even if the situation has changed so much that there is no longer any practical need for the plan, he will get it out and, after somehow adjusting it to reality, put it into action. It is a kind of formal obligation he feels toward a plan—the need to tick off an item in his ledger book. Also at work in such cases is yet another trait of Andropov's, this one emotional, his abiding vengefulness.

With his secret, stubborn harassment of Mzhavanadze and his wife, Andropov did a bad turn to Shevardnadze, through whom that harassment was effected. Because from that point on, Brezhnev took a strong dislike toward the new secretary of Georgia; and later on it cost Andropov a good deal of effort to incline Brezhnev more favorably toward his (Andropov's) Georgian protégé. For unlike the campaign against corruption in Azerbaijan, the one in Georgia was a dramatic, sharp struggle. It led to a crisis, attempts on Shevardnadze's life, and even the dynamiting of a monument to the "liberation" of Georgia from the Mensheviks by the Russian Bolsheviks in 1921.

Unlike Aliyev, with the rigidity he displayed in his industriousness, and his tough policy of exposure and punishment in Azerbaijan, Shevardnadze was more inventive in his vigorous attempts to restore "socialist legality" and clean out what he called "the capitalist pigsty of our republic." He launched his crusade against Georgian corruption immediately after taking over his post. At his first meeting with Georgia's Party and government leaders, he asked them to raise their left hands in a vote. "Now hold them up for a little while," he said. Then, slowly making his way around the conference table, he looked at one wrist after another: Seiko, Rolex, Omega. . . . On each wrist gleamed an expensive, foreign-made watch. Only Shevardnadze was wearing a Soviet Slava watch. "For a start," he told his ministers, "let's turn all these over to charity."

The first measures he took in combatting corruption were later adopted by Andropov, who shifted them to an all-union setting virtually unchanged: the same sequence in removing ministers and high Party officials, and even the same number—about twenty during the first months of the purge. It was plain that the Georgian scenario—detailed, with real-life obstacles, slipups, and happenstances—suited Andropov better than the neat, unblotched scenario for the police coup in Azerbaijan. Both Shevardnadze and Andropov, during their first months in power, gave prime importance to workers on the ideological front, whose task was to explain the country's new political line and "implant it in the consciousness" of the masses. One of Shevardnadze's first steps was to name a new Central Committee secretary for ideological work, and a new editor-in-chief of the main newspaper, *Zarya Vostoka* (Red Sky in the East). Similarly, Andropov would effect an immediate purge of his ideological department, replacing the Central Committee's secretary for propaganda and the editor-in-chief of *Izvestia*.

And Andropov's phase-two actions coincided, down to the smallest details, with those of the Georgian Party boss. (Andropov was enchanted by the effectiveness and inventiveness displayed in the Georgian version of a police state.) The devices the two men used in common include publicizing the firing of Party officials, and cautiously sowing dissension between "the common man" and the nomenklatura (the "new class," in Milovan Djilas's phrase), which had usurped power and privilege in the country. It was the Ministry of Trade—the traditional hotbed of corruption, bribery, and illegal operations—that was hardest hit during the first phase of the purges in

Georgia. The dismissals affected the entire ministry, ranging from the minister himself and his deputies to a dozen executives. Along with them, the manager of Tbilisi's largest department store was fired. The reason for the store's shortage of basic foodstuffs was promptly discovered: instead of being delivered to the store, those foodstuffs were going to the black market. Also, in lieu of decent cafeterias for the workers, posh restaurants for top officials had been built at government expense. In the same way, Andropov would later close down a subsidized cafeteria in the Central Committee building where CC staffers could enjoy scarce delicacies at reduced prices. And he prosecuted Yuri Sokolov, the manager of Moscow's best food emporium, because he was furnishing the tables of high Party officials with sturgeon, caviar, and French cognac, among other things.

But there was one way in which Shevardnadze outdid both his predecessor, Aliyev, and his successor, Andropov. In his campaign against the violators of "socialist legality," he made use of the most far-reaching of the mass media: television. Every evening, when we were in Tbilisi, we saw the streets emptying and people hurrying out of movie houses, restaurants, and stadiums so as to be home at the appointed hour. That was the hour when a mustachioed security officer would appear on the screen with exposés that might affect even those people then seated in front of the TV set who did not yet know that they had been found out by the law and its loyal servant, Eduard Shevardnadze.

In this way, public exposure was given to thousands of cases of corruption, the theft of government property, embezzlement, speculation, and black-market operations involving people from all walks of life. They ranged from top Party officials (including Shevardnadze's own deputy), two judges of the Supreme Court of Georgia, and even the chief of the regular Georgian police, to plant managers, doctors, engineers and cabdrivers. In five years of continuous purges, more than thirty thousand people were arrested, half of whom were Communist Party members. Another forty thousand were dismissed from their posts. In 1977 alone, seven thousand people lost their jobs.

Shevardnadze reduced the span—already short—between prison and freedom in Georgia. There was no one who did not have a near or distant relative, a friend or close acquaintance, who had served a prison term. Among the Georgians, doing time in prison is nothing to be ashamed of; and Shevardnadze added another touch to it: martyr-

dom. He imprisoned people convicted of bribery, graft, and nepotism—charges whose juridical meaning was simply not understandable to most of his compatriots, because corruption had penetrated
every nook and cranny of human and economic relations, and bound
things into a whole. The people of Tbilisi kept shaking their heads
over the disparities between the crime and the punishment. "Just
imagine! He wrote out a false work order for a thousand rubles, and
got twelve years for it. Is that just? He's a war hero, head of the
construction project, and such a lovely man!"

Hatred of the TV security officer became universal and implacable. He was hated as a man of straw—as a pseudonym for
Shevardnadze.

It is known that there were at least two attempts on Shevardnadze's life. In one case, a bomb failed to explode. In another, his
personal chauffeur—ordered by the Georgian Mafia to "save Georgia"
by doing a deed of honor—faltered at the last moment and, instead of
shooting Shevardnadze, put a bullet into his own head. And there
were frequent fires, which arsonists usually timed to coincide with
Soviet holidays or formal sessions of the Communist Party of Georgia.
Hatred toward Georgia's Party boss—especially among the small pro-
prietors, whose black-market operations had been badly hurt under
Shevardnadze—waxed intense. On April 12, 1976, a bomb exploded in
front of the building occupied by the Georgian SSR Council of Ministers. According to some reports, it was intended for Shevardnadze
personally.

But the most striking symbol of that hatred was the burning of the
Paliashvili Theater of Opera and Ballet. The building, located in
downtown Tbilisi, caught fire at midday on May 9, a few hours before
the scheduled arrival there of Shevardnadze, heading up the Party
elite, to celebrate the anniversary of the victory over Germany; and the
fire raged all day and all night. Then, one after another, planted
bombs began to explode: in a film studio, in an agricultural institute,
in a stadium, at an aircraft plant, and even in a children's department
store. Plainly, the republic was getting out from under the control of
its top cop.

Brezhnev's worst fears about Shevardnadze and his brutal police
methods had been confirmed. The latter's extreme measures, and his
constantly experimental style, were destroying the understanding between the Kremlin and its satraps in the republics, which was based

on evasive compromise, mutual benefits, mutual deception, and—thanks to these—relative stability.

It cost Andropov a very great effort to persuade Brezhnev—and not only Brezhnev but the entire Politburo—to continue the Georgian experiment. His arguments are not hard to reconstruct. Once again he invoked the shade of the disgraced former leader of Georgia, now living in lonely retirement as if he were a widower in Tbilisi while his wife was still living in the Ukraine. And Mzhavanadze, with his voluntarism in governing and his long-standing practice of indulging corruption, bribery, capitalist instincts, and nationalistic yearnings, was held responsible for all the present troubles, conflicts, and ideological deviations in Georgia. Using psychological pressure, Andropov translated the general secretary's doubts and fears about the critical situation in Georgia into indignation against those subversive elements, with their nationalistic leanings and petty bourgeois consciousness, who were deliberately obstructing that enthusiast of the Soviet empire, Eduard Shevardnadze. And according to rumors circulating in Tbilisi, Andropov advised the latter, by way of diverting suspicion from himself, to deliver at the Twenty-fifth Party Congress in Moscow an especially loyal speech—"socialist in content and nationalist in form," reportedly joked Andropov, using the imperial-Communist cliché Stalin was so fond of.

Let us recall that a few years later Andropov would give this same advice to another "republican" protégé, Geidar Aliyev; and that Aliyev followed that advice at the Twenty-sixth Party Congress, surpassing the all-union quota for flattering a Kremlin vozhd.

With Shevardnadze, it was different. In saying things sweet to the ears of Brezhnev, he stirred up a storm of indignation in Georgia. From the speakers' platform at the Moscow congress, he declared for all the world to hear that for Georgia the sun rose not in the East, as for every place else in the world, but in the North—in Moscow. One of Shevardnadze's closest friends, a man high in Party and government circles, told us that he shuddered when he heard (on the radio) that slavish, obsequious metaphor, which in Georgia fell upon ears that were only too sensitive. It was sharply hurtful to nationalistic feelings, and exploded in the Georgians' hearts like those bombs that were exploding from time to time in the center of Tbilisi.

The rest of Shevardnadze's reign was marked by traits of inertia and passivity; and his compatriots got the impression that he had tarried too long in his post. Not having been assassinated or dismissed, and not having died of a heart attack, he was now doing through momentum what only a short time before he had been doing out of inspiration.

Obviously, he himself realized the cause of his failure. The fact is that illegal businesses in Georgia, from private distilleries to under-the-counter sales in shops—that black-market capitalism he had combatted with all his vigor and tireless inventiveness—filled in gaps left by the state. The state's weakness favored private initiative. Shevardnadze proved to be a poor dentist: instead of the decayed tooth, he pulled out a healthy one, although it had grown in the wrong place—illegally. And yet he really can't be blamed. A decayed tooth is something that Georgia has in common with Russia; but no one would have let Shevardnadze pull it out. The Tbilisi satrap was tied hand and foot because of the Moscow administration's sluggishness, idleness, paralysis, and centralized government. In short, Shevardnadze never managed, in his republic, to replace the laws of the jungle with bureaucratic circulars.

After several years of continuous purges and replacements of the republic's leadership, the Georgian reformer came to realize, as Aliyev had in Azerbaijan, the strict limits of a police regime. But there was a difference between the two. Aliyev, knowing no doubts and believing in decrees, had gone at his republic like a tank. And out of an instinct of self-preservation, everyone had either made way for him or gone deeply underground, until there was a new change of leadership and the political experiment came to an end. Unlike the rigid Aliyev, however, the Georgian secretary had tried to expand the narrow limits of the police regime and seek new, more flexible methods of governing the republic and running its economy. But except for a relatively successful experiment in agriculture, those attempts were mostly failures. Merely in order to preserve what had been gained by forcible means over a period of several years, Shevardnadze had to carry out new (and, in general, continuous) purges. So there were more purges: in the ministries, the prosecutor's office, regional and municipal committees, the regular police, the KGB, and lower down—at all professional levels. (The most recent wave of purges—the ninth—hit Georgia in May 1983, when about three hundred high Party and government officials were dismissed, some of them being put on trial. Among them were the ministers of trade, finance, and industry, who

Andropov in Hungary in 1956

Soviet Ambassador Yuri V. Andropov. (Wide World Photos)

The short-lived triumph of the Hungarian revolution: the lopped-off head of an overthrown statue of Stalin. (UPI Photo)

Central Committee secretary for supervision of ruling Communist parties

Andropov (circled), *arriving in Budapest eight years after the Hungarian revolution (1964). In the foreground, with raised hand among the well-wishers, is Khrushchev.* (UPI Photo)

A few months later, after the fall of Khrushchev: Andropov between two Communist leaders, Chinese Premier Zhou En-lai and Soviet Premier Aleksei Kosygin. Far left, Pham Van Dong of North Vietnam. (UPI Photo)

A Lucky Ticket: The KGB

The headquarters of the Committee of State Security in Moscow. This is also the location of the famous Lubyanka Prison, where tens of thousands of political prisoners have been tortured and killed. Before the building stands a monument to Felix Dzerzhinsky, the founder of the secret police, in whose honor the square was named. (© 1980 Vladimir Sichov from Black Star)

The new master of the building, Yuri Andropov, chairman of the KGB beginning in 1967. (Sipa Press from Black Star)

Neo-Stalinism in the USSR:

a trend that takes in not only the military and the secret police but the common people as well

In the ancient city of Suzdal, a man with a portrait of Stalin tattooed on his chest. (©1980 Vladimir Sichov from Black Star)

A painting by Soviet artist Mikhail Savitsky, which was shown at an official exhibit and reproduced in a major Soviet newspaper. It shows a German officer and his helper, wearing a striped prisoner's uniform with the Star of David on his chest, smiling conspiratorially at each other across a heap of Christian children's corpses. The symbolic conclusion to be drawn from this painting is that in the death camps the Jews were not the victims but the murderers. (NYT Pictures)

Andropov Smiles at a Joke by Brezhnev (1975)

Foreground, *Andrei Gromyko, minister of foreign affairs.* (© 1982 Sipa Press from Black Star)

Andropov's Caucasian Rehearsals

General Geidar Aliyev (above), head of the Azerbaijani KGB, and General Eduard Shevardnadze, Georgian minister of internal affairs, who, aided by Andropov, carried out Chekist coups d'etat in and became the leaders of their respective republics—the former in 1969 and the latter in 1972. A few days after Andropov's self-appointment as general secretary in 1982, one of the "putchists," Aliyev, was called to Moscow, brought into the Politburo, and named first deputy chairman of the USSR Council of Ministers. (Top, Wide World Photos; bottom, UPI Photo)

The Triumvirate—

*Leonid Brezhnev, Aleksei Kosygin, and Nikolai
Podgorny—that succeeded Khrushchev in the "Little
October" of 1964 and fell apart, as a result of
Andropov's intrigues, after the disgrace of Podgorny in
the spring of 1977. The photograph was taken in 1976
at the Vnukovo Airport in Moscow.* In the
background: *Minister of Defense Dmitri Ustinov and
KGB Chairman Yuri Andropov* (smiling). (UPI
Photo)

Andropov's Crushing of Dissent

The Soviet émigré General Petr Grigorenko holding a photograph of himself in uniform. Because of his activities in defense of human rights, he was demoted to enlisted status, deprived of his general's pension, confined in an insane asylum, and (after his departure from the USSR) deprived of his Soviet citizenship. (UPI Photo)

An arrest on a Moscow street. Any political protest is instantly dealt with. (© 1983 Vladimir Sichov from Black Star)

This New York Times *front-page photograph of the authors, Vladimir Solovyov and Elena Klepikova (May 4, 1977), was accompanied by an article about them and how they established, for the first time in Soviet history, an independent news agency:* The Solovyov-Klepikova Press. (David K. Shipler/NYT Pictures)

The Ceremonial Leader

While the Western press kept insisting that all the power was held by Brezhnev, during his last years, he was physically incapable of governing, as one can judge from photographs. After his speech in East Berlin, the exhausted Brezhnev is carried from the speaker's platform by an aide and the East German President, Erich Honecker (October 1979). (UPI Photo)

The Funeral of the Chief Party Ideologue, Mikhail Suslov, on January 29, 1982

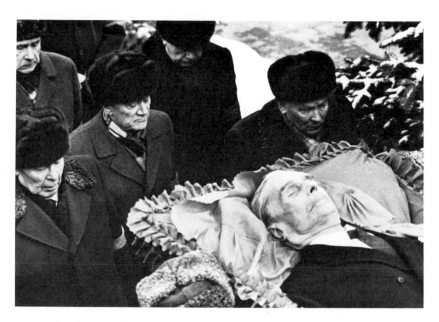

On the same day, Andropov arrested the friends of Brezhnev's daughter and launched his palace coup, which brought him to power a few months later, while Brezhnev was still alive. Of the five men following Suslov's coffin: Kirilenko (fourth from left), Brezhnev's closest aide, would be eliminated from political life by Andropov immediately after Suslov's funeral, and Brezhnev himself (far left) would die nine and a half months later. The other mourners: Gromyko, Tikhonov, and Chernenko.
(Wide World Photos)

Andropov at the May Day Parade in 1982, after seizing power.
(© Sipa Press from Black Star)

The Fate of Chiefs of the Secret Police in the USSR

Genrikh Yagoda: executed in 1938.
(Wide World Photos)

Nikolai Yezhov: executed in 1939.
(Wide World Photos)

Lavrenty Beria:
executed in 1953.
(Wide World Photos)

Alexander Shelepin: fell into
disgrace and political oblivion
in the seventies. (UPI Photo)

Yuri Andropov: in 1982 after
fifteen years' service with the
KGB, he became the fifth
Soviet leader. (© Sipa
Press from Black Star)

Andropov's Entourage

KGB Chairman Victor Chebrikov (right)
and Minister of Internal Affairs Vitaly
Fedorchuk. (Time magazine)

Mikhail Gorbachev, a secretary of the
Central Committee and a member of the
Politburo, Andropov's landsman and close
friend for many years. (UPI Photo)

Former Leningrad Party boss Romanov—
Andropov's rival in the Brezhnev era and his
co-worker in the Andropov era. (Wide World
Photos)

Andropov's military advisors: General of the
Army Aleksei Epishev, chief of the armed
forces political administration and the main
architect of the blitzkrieg in Afghanistan;
Marshal Victor Kulikov, commander-in-chief
of the Warsaw Pact forces, the chief overseer
of Poland, and the blackmailer of the Polish
leaders; Marshal Nikolai Ogarkov, chief of
the general staff, an adept of the theory that a
preemptive atomic strike would be
advantageous. (UPI Photo)

Two of Andropov's protégés: his son Igor
(left), an official in the Ministry of Foreign
Affairs; and chess grandmaster Anatoly
Karpov, who became world champion and
twice successfully defended his title against the
defector Victor Korchnoi—with the help of the
KGB. (UPI Photo)

The Polish Crisis in the Soviet Empire

The historical and geographical tragedy of Poland: between the Germans and the Russians. The dictator of Poland, General Wojciech Jaruzelski, between Soviet Marshal Kulikov and the East German minister of defense, General Hoffman, during military exercises of the Warsaw Pact forces (1981). (© 1981 Sipa Press from Black Star)

Andropov with the leaders of the Warsaw Pact countries. His protégé during the Hungarian revolution, Janos Kadar; the Bulgarian leader Todor Zhivkov, whose daughter, the moving spirit of Bulgarian nationalism, died suddenly at the age of thirty-eight; Andropov; the Soviet puppets Gustav Husak of Czechoslovakia and Erich Honecker of East Germany; the dissidents—Rumanian President Nicolai Ceausescu and General Jaruzelski, the savior of Poland (1983). (Black Star)

(© 1983 Sipa Press from Black Star)

were fired for the second and third times, respectively. Since this most recent cataclysm took place after Andropov had become general secretary, it must be construed as a demonstration by Shevardnadze of his loyalty to his former patron and co-worker, as a clamorous bid for attention in the hope that he, like Aliyev, will be called to Moscow by Andropov.) This was the vicious circle of a police regime. Once it had, by coercive means, squeezed out a maximum of energy potential from people in an extremely short time, that regime required their replacement by new, fresh cadres and a new cycle of forcible measures.

Such are the inevitable limits—the extreme range—of a police-type regime: a short creative period, then a new purge and a new application of force. Purges are justified, according to Shevardnadze, by the age-old human capacity to adjust to new circumstances—even such harsh ones as those produced by a continuing police-type experiment. In the words of his minister of internal affairs: "Regrouping, carefully camouflaging themselves, resorting to more refined methods, and switching from those sectors of the economy where they have traditionally operated to new ones, the plunderers [of socialist property] are going on with their dirty work."

Alas, there can be no surprises here—no genuine revolution. The barbed-wire fence of a police state cannot be expanded. And Andropov, who after coming to power followed in the footsteps of his protégés in the provinces, will inevitably run up against that same fence, unless he opts for more radical means: a dictatorship *à la Stalin*.

As for Shevardnadze, Andropov once again did him a bad turn. Since the outset of the police coup in Georgia, the latter had been insisting on the stepped-up Russification of the republic. He did so partly in order to please Brezhnev, who took a guarded attitude toward Shevardnadze, and partly because he himself was a true believer in empire and considered the claims and prejudices of small peoples as evils that had to be rooted out. Also, he had directly applied to Georgia the pattern used in Azerbaijan, where Marxist-Leninist propaganda and the Russification imposed by police methods had not provoked either the burning of government buildings or mass demonstrations. And when he proposed—through Shevardnadze—that the Azerbaijani model of forcible Russification be used in Georgia, the flaw in his unbending imperialist mode of thought once again became evident.

The Azerbaijani language, which originally was written in Arabic characters, was in 1925 forcibly switched to the Latin alphabet; and in 1939 it was switched to the Cyrillic. After such radical operations, it has lost some of its native expressiveness. But things are different in Georgia, as became plain when Andropov adopted a policy of total discrimination against the Georgian language. He did so out of sheer ignorance, not even having the faintest idea that he was the most recent in a long series of conquerors who had tried unsuccessfully to overcome, or at least influence, the Georgian language. Among his predecessors were the emperors of Byzantium, the Persian shahs, the Khazar and Arab caliphs, the Turkish sultans, and the Mongol khans.

So it was that in March 1978, when nationalistic feelings were running high, Andropov issued an order to Shevardnadze to delete, from a draft constitution for Georgia, a paragraph specifying that Georgian was the official language of the republic. Given Georgia's historical background, this was a very crude, vulgar lapse—a typical trick played by a political intriguer with no understanding of the real state of affairs. So blind was he to the world around him, and so boundless was his imperialist scorn toward the ethnic problems in one of the empire's republics, that he *really* figured the Georgians wouldn't notice this slight omission in their constitution—one that would transform Georgia, *de jure*, into a Russian colony.

Doing what he could, and trying to please Moscow, Shevardnadze had earlier ordered that more Russian lessons be given in Georgian schools, and made it mandatory that all scholarly dissertations written in Georgian be simultaneously submitted in Russian. Things got to the point of absurdity: a dissertation on Georgian translations of Lope de Vega's works had itself to be translated into Russian. In justifying this requirement, the Georgian leader quoted Andropov's pronouncement that the Russian language, for the peoples of the USSR, is the same as the English language for the peoples of the world.

In these matters one can only sympathize with Shevardnadze. He was not an ideal functionary, a quasi-automatic executor of orders, such as Aliyev—and such as he was perceived, by analogy with Aliyev, by his powerful patron, Andropov. The neat scenario for a police coup in a Soviet republic that Aliyev had presented to Andropov was, in Georgia, besmirched by ethnic idiosyncrasies. The national background on which the political pattern was imposed was too deep and rich in its coloration not to distort that pattern drastically.

Unlike Andropov, Shevardnadze knew that in Georgia, totally dependent on Russia both economically and politically, the only remaining weapon of independence was the Georgian language—a source of national pride and a symbol of the Georgian people's ethnic survival during a great many centuries of foreign conquests and subjugations. The Georgian language has so successfully resisted all outside influences that the works of the great Georgian poet Rustavelli, which date from the twelfth century, can be read in the original by students in the lower grades of Georgian schools.

Events took a turn which it was not difficult for Shevardnadze, the scapegoat in this case, to predict. Hundreds of demonstrators—most of them students from Tbilisi University—gathered in front of the Central Committee building bearing placards with slogans demanding the restoration of the Georgian language. From the balcony, Shevardnadze called down to them in a tone of biblical rhetoric: "My children, what are you doing?" The response was curses and shouts: "We're not your children! Go to Moscow, where both your children and your parents are!"

Andropov's crude mistake badly compromised Shevardnadze in the eyes of his compatriots; and this time, too, everyone realized that he had been compelled by Moscow to make such an antinationalist move. But the incident made it plain how totally dependent the republic's leader was on Moscow; and this deeply wounded the pride of the Georgians.

The next day, on personal orders from Brezhnev and Suslov, the deleted paragraph was restored to the text of the new constitution: "The official language of the Georgian Soviet Socialist Republic is the Georgian language." This sentence coincides almost completely with the text of the Georgian constitution of 1937.

But the Kremlin's concession only whetted the edge of Georgian passions and Georgian problems; and it brought Georgia into the front ranks among the Soviet republics in their struggle against the Russian language. Right on the heels of the Georgians, other Caucasian peoples—the Armenians and even the Azerbaijanis—earned the right (after street demonstrations) to have their languages constitutionally recognized as the official languages of their republics. The struggle was both for the empire and against it—for national independence; and this was understood by both sides in this historic battle of languages, which took place in the seventies in the Caucasian republics of the USSR.

As for Georgia, Andropov's tactical blunder gave rise there to a process which contravenes all the laws of the "fraternal" republics' living together under the imperial roof: Georgification instead of Russification. Ambitious parents now prefer to send their children to Georgian schools rather than Russian ones. Not knowing Russian is no longer an insurmountable barrier to a career. And even the local Russians, who account for 12.3 percent of the population of Tbilisi, have for the first time been faced with the choice of either learning Georgian or going back to Russia. The number of Russians who consider Georgian to be their second language has risen from 10.5 percent in 1970 to 15.5 percent in 1979. Such are the unpredictable and fantastic results to which an ignorance of national traits and historical traditions can lead. Upon attaining the supreme power, however, Andropov promptly revived his long-nourished imperial idea of fusing more than 100 nations and ethnic groups into a single Soviet nation, a Soviet melting pot. And as the first means of achieving that top-priority goal of the empire, he would resort to "extraordinary measures" to step up the study of the Russian language in republic schools—something characterized in the Politburo's official bulletin as "an objective necessity and requirement for every citizen." But it was not just the ideological goals of consolidating the empire that stimulated the coercive Russification of the national republics: the empire's military goals were also a major factor. Marshal Nikolai Ogarkov, Chief of the General Staff, declared that the lack of a single, Russian-language medium of exchange among the draftees brought into the Soviet Armed Forces (numbering some 5 million, more than half of whom are non-Russians) was a serious obstacle to the training and military effectiveness of those forces.

Let us, however, be fair to Andropov. In one respect that was very important for Georgia, he came to Shevardnadze's aid; and the two of them began a close, secret, and fruitful collaboration. Although neither of the two gendarmes was a specialist in agriculture, the power structure in the Soviet Union is so inert that the initiative for reform—even in the most specific sector of the national economy—must come from the country's leader. Thus it was with Khrushchev, who in fact became the USSR's chief agronomist and personally tried—by means of impetuous reforms—to drag agriculture out of the swamp into which it had sunk thanks to another "agronomist," Stalin, with his "revolutionary" idea of collectivization. And such is the case with

Andropov, who is now transferring his experience in reforms from the Georgian rough draft to the fair copy for Russia as a whole. In April 1983 he announced that the administration of agriculture would be reorganized in accordance with the model he and Shevardnadze had tested in Georgia.

What had happened was that Shevardnadze, as soon as he became head of the republic, set about looking for ways to increase agricultural production—in which Georgia, despite its very rich natural resources, ranked fifteenth (i.e., last) in the USSR in 1972. He calculated that merely from the sale of mandarin oranges grown on his plot, a Georgian private trader made about fifty thousand rubles a year. Also, that the overall income of private traders from the sale of carnations, chrysanthemums, citrus fruits, tomatoes, walnuts, and almonds on the markets of Moscow, Leningrad, and other big cities amounted to three hundred million rubles. Only what was left over (if anything) from private marketing was delivered to the state by the Georgian peasants.

Shevardnadze decided to put an end to such arbitrary "planning" of agriculture. He set up a system of exit passes and roadblocks on all highways leading out of Georgia. And in a few years he had sharply reduced that profitable trade so deeply ingrained among the Georgians.

Ultimately, however, he reached the limits of police-type methods in combatting the capitalist instincts of the Georgian peasants. No longer able to haul their produce overland, they displayed marvels of inventiveness and began to ship out their citrus, flowers, walnuts, and bay leaf on freighters, seagoing barges with hoisting cranes, and chartered cargo planes.

It was at this point that Shevardnadze, driven to desperation in his battle against the private traders, was helped by Andropov. The latter proposed trying out, in one region of Georgia, an agricultural experiment that had been successfully carried out, in the early fifties, in a small agricultural cooperative in Hungary, and then extended—also successfully—to the whole country.

Ambassador Andropov's visits to the Hungarian kolkhozes had not been a waste of time. Hungary remained in his memory as a model of a well-organized economy and of public services, among the socialist countries. Although he had been on trips to Hungary after the fifties, and had observed more progressive methods of raising the productivity of agriculture and livestock breeding, in 1973, when he proposed the Hungarian methods for Georgia, what he had in mind were the practices introduced at Hungary's first experimental agricultural co-operative, the Nadudvar Red Star Agricultural Cooperative. And without making the slightest changes—his favorite way of putting plans into action—he applied those practices to a Georgian kolkhoz.

Such was the origin of the so-called Abasha experiment in Georgia, named after a region in the western part of the country—one of the most economically backward and hopeless regions—where in 1973 a new incentive-based system of payment (in the form of a share of the overall crop yield) was introduced.

We shall not enumerate all the stages in the Abasha experiment, which was later extended to other regions of western Georgia, in one of which it accounted for an astounding increase in the grape harvest over a period of several years. But it is significant that unlike Shevard-nadze's other campaigns, which were widely publicized, the Abasha experiment was kept under wraps. There was not even any announce-ment of the beginning of the experiment.

Andropov was being extremely cautious, waiting for concrete re-sults from adapting the Hungarian methods to the soil of Georgia. And he was placing great hopes in this experiment. He was aware—as was every last inhabitant of the Soviet Union—of the critical state of Soviet agriculture, especially as regards grain production. The situa-tion was so desperate, with a dangerous tendency to get even worse, that finally the authorities stopped publishing figures on grain harvests altogether. He was also aware that Brezhnev, with his instinctive fear of any reforms, even the most urgent, preferred a situation of political and economic stagnation. So that he had dealt with the pressing prob-lem of supplying the country with grain in his typically opportunistic and evasive way: instead of making long-term investments in Soviet agriculture, he was making purchases—massive and regular, from year to year—of grain from abroad.

Such an irresponsible and essentially absurd way of dealing with the problem, which aggravated it to the point of catastrophe, struck Andropov as devastating for the nation's future, since it made for the Soviet Union's increasing dependence on grain-exporting countries, and especially on the United States. The Soviet Union was becoming vulnerable just at that point where Andropov, as head of the KGB, was trying to make it defensible and strong. And this had a painful effect on his well-nurtured ambitions for the empire.

As we know, Andropov is fond of plans that look to the future. So that when he had installed his own man in Georgia and planned the agricultural experiment based on Hungarian practices, he was already hoping, ambitiously, to contribute his widow's mite to solving a problem that seemed quite hopeless. That is why he was so cautious about the initiative he had taken in Georgia: he was afraid that Brezhnev would react prematurely to it.

When the Abasha experiment, a direct copy of the Hungarian model, proved successful in western Georgia, with its favorable subtropical climate, Shevardnadze naturally proposed extending the scope of the experiment to the whole republic. But he was restrained by Andropov, who did not yet have enough clout in the Politburo to sanction the drastic restructuring of Georgia's agriculture on the basis of the Hungarian model without risking both his own career and the experiment itself, which he intended—if he should ever come to power—to apply throughout the vast expanses of the Soviet Union. He was also well aware that Brezhnev disliked both of his provincial protégés: Geidar Aliyev and (especially) Eduard Shevardnadze. (It was not until November 1978—in view of his evident services to the motherland, and with Andropov's direct support—that Shevardnadze was approved by Brezhnev as candidate-member of the Politburo.) Brezhnev's persisting distrust of Shevardnadze was another reason why Andropov decided not to publicize the success of the agricultural reforms in Georgia.

But the situation changed drastically in about 1981, when Andropov had gained enough clout in the Politburo that he could take his own initiative in Georgia without worrying about "the opinion of the comrades." Shevardnadze promptly applied Hungarian methods in the most vulnerable area of Georgia's agriculture: livestock breeding. At a plenum of the Georgian Central Committee he confidently declared: "The first steps in assimilating the experience of the Hungarian People's Republic in the sphere of cooperation between the state and private sectors have yielded very good results." A Georgian delegation was sent to Hungary to make an on-the-spot study of the system of cooperation between the two sectors. An active exchange of experience was initiated between Hungarian and Georgian livestock breeders, soil engineers, and Party leaders, including a visit to Georgia by Hungary's minister and deputy minister of agriculture. At that time Georgia was the most experimental part of the Soviet empire. Also, that was the period of active collaboration between Shevardnadze and Andropov, who is now planning a complete overhaul of the administration of agriculture in the USSR. That phase of the feverish adaptation and fitting of the Hungarian model to Georgian conditions—before it was put to use throughout Georgia—concluded with Shevardnadze's sentimental pilgrimage to that same Nadudvar Red Star Agricultural Cooperative in Hungary that Soviet Ambassador Yuri Andropov had visited in the fifties, and from where, in 1973, he got his idea for the Abasha experiment.

After returning to Georgia, Shevardnadze, at a regular congress of the Georgian Communist Party (in January 1981), announced that during the next five-year plan period the republic's agriculture would be oriented toward the Abasha model. Also, he appointed the secretary of the Abasha region the Georgian minister of agriculture.

When, in the spring of 1983, Andropov (who was already general secretary) began to think about radically restructuring the leadership of Soviet agriculture and proposed several specific steps—in particular, consolidating the ministries in charge of individual branches of agriculture—he was borrowing directly from the Georgian experience: the merger of small auxiliary ministries into the Georgian State Committee of Agricultural Production. The Georgian experience was directly transferred to the administration of the kolkhoz system of the entire Soviet Union.

On this point, one cannot but have certain doubts as to the aptness of such direct applications. If the Hungarian recipe was absolutely right for Georgia's need, as Shevardnadze claims, it by no means follows that the Georgian model is just right for Russia. But Yuri Andropov, judging from all his previous actions, will develop Soviet agriculture by means of a direct adaptation of the Georgian experiment. With his "methodical ambition," with his capacity for planning and thinking in long-range terms, he was obliged for a long time to lie in waiting, to wait things out, reconnoitering and then retreating again. The main stage was occupied; another show was going on there; and he was not allowed to come onstage. So he was compelled, all that time, to confine himself to "chamber rehearsals" before stepping out onto the main stage. Or, more accurately, before seizing it and occupying it.

Thus Andropov, in line with his accumulative method of governing, began to acquire republics within the Soviet Union through his protégés, who were former KGB officers. And by the end of the seventies he was better informed as to the country's general political and economic situation than not only Brezhnev but the entire Politburo.

He tried more than once to expand his acquisitions within the Soviet Union. It is quite plain that he made an attempt on the third Caucasian republic, Armenia. Using the Armenian branches of the KGB and MVD (Ministry of Internal Affairs), he laid the groundwork for a police coup patterned after those in Georgia and Azerbaijan. And when, in late 1973, Erevan's central newspaper published an article exposing—with unheard-of directness and candor—"moral decay," Armenia's high crime rate, and the flourishing of graft in the republic, it meant the beginning of a campaign to oust the old leadership in Armenia. But Brezhnev stoutly opposed it.

Andropov made his attempt on Armenia in order to round out his plan for "the conquest of the Caucasus"—all three Caucasian republics. But he failed with Armenia. And that republic, the only one in the Caucasus where his plan didn't work out, has long chafed the pedant in him: his strong need to tie up loose ends, his life-long penchant for ticking off items (in the bureaucratic manner) when a measure has been carried out.

For that matter, the two republics sufficed. In them the scenario for a police coup under the guise of a campaign against corruption had been elaborated to the point of perfection, with refinement of detail and "redundancy." All that remained was to mount a production on the all-union level.

The most valuable lesson Andropov learned from his Caucasian rehearsals was his discovery of an all-purpose weapon for eliminating his political opponents. Backed by the resources of the KGB, he could now use the charge of corruption—to which any Party functionary is vulnerable—as a pretext for getting rid of his political rivals, just as his protégés, Aliyev and Shevardnadze, had done in their own republics.

But unlike them, he had no highly placed protector. He would have to act strictly at his own risk.

5

The Crushing of Dissent and the Campaign Against Détente

Georgia and Azerbaijan, in each of which Andropov had installed one of his people as Party boss, while at the same time testing methods whereby the secret police could seize power and govern, were like two microcosms obeying the same laws as the macrocosm of which they are a part. And yet, for all his success there, his "works and days" in the Moscow of the early seventies were proceeding sluggishly and not at all in accord with his vigor and powers of concentration. While formally giving his activities broad scope, the Kremlin was in fact doing everything possible to limit them, narrowing Andropov's functions and hence his opportunities. In 1973, to be sure, he was elected to the Politburo (along with the ministers of defense and foreign affairs). It was the first time since the shooting of Lavrenty Beria that the Kremlin chiefs had decided to bring a KGB chief into the supreme ruling body on equal terms with themselves; and it showed just how much he was now inspiring their trust, and how much they now needed him. Then a year later, when Andropov turned sixty, he was awarded (as is *de rigueur* for a member of the Politburo) a gold medal of Hero of Socialist Labor, and the Order of Lenin. On June 24, 1974, at a grand ceremony in the Kremlin, both decorations were pinned on Andropov's chest by Nikolai Podgorny, chairman of the Presidium of the USSR Supreme Soviet. As he did so, Podgorny said: "For more than seven years now, you have headed up the Committee of State Security of the USSR Council of Ministers. I am sure I speak for all of us members of the Politburo when I say that your work as head of the Committee has met the Party's requirements."

Therein lay an important contradiction: while meeting the Party's requirements, Andropov had by no means been satisfying his own ambitious demands. He was impatient, yet knew how to wait. He knew how to put together a big victory out of a series of little ones. He knew how to build up his forces by small increments, in cases where another man would have launched an immediate, all-out attack. He was working for the future; and to hasten its coming would mean to lose it entirely. It was a time of deep underground dwelling for our hero—deeper than at any time before or after. Not that he was idle. To the contrary, he even came to grow fond of the underground, secret nature of his work—so much so, that later he preferred it to any overt activity. This could not but have left an imprint on his psyche. His long-range calculations and improbable plans got so far ahead of reality that he saw reality as an obstacle on his path that had to be removed. Even when, finally, he surfaced as leader of his country, he had difficulty in recognizing a reality that he had learned about, up until then, only through secret dispatches and denunciations. His eyes had grown used to the dark; and like an owl, he was blinded by daylight.

In the early 1970s, thanks to initiatives taken by West German Chancellor Willy Brandt and U.S. Secretary of State Henry Kissinger, the Kremlin agreed to an easing of tensions in relations with the West. The warm winds of détente had much the same destructive effect on the KGB as on a snowman. That organization, which had gained new strength after the occupation of Czechoslovakia, was obliged by the conditions of international détente to be restrained, if not actually idle, within the boundaries of the Soviet Union.

With amazing rapidity, this was borne in upon a few dozen Moscow intellectuals who, under the shield of détente and the Helsinki agreement between East and West, launched a human-rights movement—apparently assuming that the KGB's torpor was a permanent condition, like the paralysis of old age. Hence a certain romantic heedlessness in the dissidents' pantomime, which ended tragically a few years later. Dissent in the USSR was definitively crushed after the election of President Carter, who, in disowning détente, deprived the Soviet dissidents of their only shield against Yuri Andropov's all-powerful organization. They were the children of détente, and were buried under its ruins. But before that happened, in order to offset the temporary idling that had been imposed upon the KGB at the height of détente in the early and mid-seventies, it was allowed to step up—very sharply—its operations abroad.

Along with his zeal for the job and his high ambitions, Andropov brought something else to his work at the KGB: new, modern, professional methods. In part, he was helped in this by his close collaboration with Harold S. (Kim) Philby, an officer in the British intelligence service and simultaneously a mole for the KGB, who defected to the Soviet Union a few years before Andropov became chief of the secret police. It was to Philby that Andropov owed the Westernization of the KGB, and perhaps his own Westernization as well. Just how great was Philby's contribution to Soviet espionage in English-speaking countries can be judged from the noticeable decline in its quality after he went into retirement. Kim Philby was not an irreplaceable man. But he was an extraordinary one, highly gifted; and that is a rare thing in any bureaucratic system—not just in the KGB. There are reports of a personal friendship between Philby and Andropov, but we have no way of verifying them. Nor is that so important. What matters is that the Englishman Philby was a personal advisor to the chairman of the Committee of State Security—something that was reflected in the KGB's work abroad.

And that organization was in need of immediate reforms in order to bring its foreign mechanism into line with world standards. The Soviet Union could afford to lag behind the West in agriculture, medicine, quality of clothing and footwear, and electronic equipment—even in military technology—but not in the mechanics of espionage, thanks to which it was to catch up with the West in those areas where it was lagging behind. For example, the electronic technology that the Soviet Union could not itself produce could be stolen from its rivals; and it was usually easier and cheaper that way. Under Andropov, industrial and technological espionage was brought to a level unprecedented in the USSR. The chief of the Los Angeles branch office of the FBI, Edgar Best, wittily remarked that the Americans are actually carrying on a scientific race among themselves: "We invent, and they steal."

Andropov's ubiquitous agents cleverly took advantage of the openness of the Western democracies—the fact that in those countries scientific information is available to any outsider. And Andropov's spies were first-rate professional scrutinizers. Making a clean break with earlier times, he chose for his foreign teams the most talented graduates of the Moscow and Leningrad colleges and universities, who had a good command of foreign languages, and even decent manners. Employment with the KGB was attractive because of the high pay, trips abroad, and a promising future. What Andropov needed was not professional secret policemen but professional diplomats, journalists, doctors, scientists, and engineers—agents from other fields of knowledge. They were the best collectors of the political and scientific information freely circulating in the free world. Virtually all Soviet citizens abroad, including tourists, are under orders from the KGB.

As for classified information, it was bought through intermediate firms not directly connected with the USSR, or through hired agents.

Andropov shifted the recruitment of spies from an ideological level to a strictly financial one. The ideological system of recruitment that had been used since the thirties, whereby people became Soviet spies not for the sake of money but in the name of high ideals (for example, the brilliant Cantabridgians Donald Maclean, Guy Burgess, Anthony Blount, and Kim Philby himself) was totally exhausted. The Soviet Union had lost its ideological attractiveness. In the West, the left was sometimes even more sharply critical of the USSR than was the right, especially in connection with violations of human rights, for which the KGB was blamed. As a basically cynical man without any ideology, Andropov preferred to deal with people like himself: ideology made an agent less reliable than did money.

Marxist ideology was still playing a certain role in organizing insurgent movements in Asia, Africa, Latin America, and among the Palestinians. But even in those areas it was rather a kind of camouflage: the main thing was the military aid that the Soviet Union provided to the insurgents, either itself or through a man of straw (Cuba, East Germany, or Vietnam) Under Andropov, not only did the network of worldwide terrorism grow but its activities became more coordinated and international in character. Side by side with Palestinians, Germans, Japanese, and Italians underwent training and took part in terrorist actions. Italian members of the "Red Brigades" were given military training in a Palestinian camp in Lebanon; Cubans helped the Basque separatists; and Germans helped the Irish Republican Army. The KGB set up schools for terrorists in the Soviet Union. By the late 1970s the USSR had become a regular nursery of worldwide terrorism, with the Palestinians (whom the KGB supported directly) as the privileged nurslings. Then, in their own camps in Lebanon, Libya, and other Arab countries, Palestinians shared what they had learned with their brothers-in-arms from other countries and continents, regardless of ideological leanings. The extreme right-wing

terrorist Mehmet Ali Agca, who was assigned to kill the Pope, underwent training in an extreme left-wing Palestinian camp.

Andropov attributed prime importance to "bringing up" terrorists. He of course realized that few of them would rise to a position of
leadership in their countries; but in any case they served as destabiliz-
ing factors in Africa, Asia, Latin America, and the Middle East. In the
summer of 1982 Palestinian graduates of KGB schools, armed to the
teeth, fought off the Israeli army as no regular army from any Arab
country had ever done. And even Israel's victory over them was in part
a Pyrrhic one, since the large number of deaths among the noncom-
batant Palestinians brought about a "mutation" of world public opinion. With the exception of right-wing circles, public opinion turned
against the Israelis, with a richochet effect on Israel's ally, the United
States.

Local terrorists performed an important function not only in the
underdeveloped countries but in Italy, Great Britain, and Spain,
where they weakened democracy. Everywhere, they inspired fear and
revulsion—something which, from Andropov's point of view, made
them useful. And their actions in certain countries of Central America—justified both in essence and in the eyes of world public opinion
by the ferocity and sadism of the military juntas ruling there—caused
turmoil in the United States's backyard. They served as a kind of
diversionary maneuver that the White House inevitably fell for, especially when the president was a right-winger. And finally, since
murder was the trade of these KGB trainees, they could be used as hit
men quite apart from any ideology.

But Andropov's paramount enemy on the international scene was
still détente, which was cramping the KGB's movements on the
domestic front and hurting its position in the alignment of Soviet
political forces. His campaign against détente was at the same time a
campaign against its proponents, both among the Kremlin chiefs and
abroad. One of the first blows he struck was aimed at Willy Brandt,
the architect of "Ostpolitik." In 1974 one Günther Guillaume, a member of Brandt's personal staff, was exposed as an East German spy, and
the chancellor of West Germany had to resign. His successor, Helmut
Schmidt, was more restrained in his feelings about Eastern Europe,
and hence more pro-American. This was at the same time a very
strong blow against Brezhnev, as a proponent of détente with the
West. If one seriously weighs all the pros and cons, there is no doubt

that Willy Brandt was more useful to the Soviet Union than Günther Guillaume. If Brezhnev had had his way, he would have preferred not to have "his man" on the staff of the West German chancellor.

Here we have to bring in a conversation between one of the authors of this book and a KGB agent by the name of Boris Pavlovich Chudinov. It was set forth in detail in an article by Vladimir Solovyov published in the *Partisan Review* in 1982. In what follows, we quote only that part of it having to do with Günther Guillaume. We pick it up at the point where Chudinov has just said that the PLO was one of the KGB's subsidiaries.

"Do you mean the KGB had a hand in the Munich massacre?"

"Well, I think it's safe to say that nobody really wanted to kill them. If the Israelis had been more willing to talk, everything would have turned out all right, as I see it. Of course, the Palestinians can't be controlled right down to a T. They're like a genie. Once you let him out of the bottle. . . ."

"But isn't the KGB afraid its people will be exposed? After all, not long ago Günther Guillaume of Willy Brandt's staff was exposed as a spy for East Germany."

Chudinov smiled ironically. "Don't feel sorry for Guillaume. We ourselves expose people like him—or we help to expose them. For us, his exposure was a thousand times more important than the work he did."

Then, satisfied with the impression he had made on me, he added, "And you think we're nothing but fools."

Today, it is hard for us to understand why Andropov's employee was so frank. Maybe he was counting on getting his interlocutor to be equally frank, since that was a standard psychological device of the KGB. Nor can one rule out the possibility (although it is slight) that Chudinov was lying. The KGB has a way of obtaining by means of rumors what it does not really possess. But in this particular case, the function of the rumor is quite incomprehensible. One can perhaps understand why the KGB had to expose its own spy. But why talk about that self-exposure if in fact it didn't take place? On the other hand, placed in the context of all the KGB's work in the seventies, that version looks completely convincing. Moreover, to all appearances, Andropov and his East German helpers were concentrating special efforts on West Germany—even after détente had been dealt a blow by the Carter administration. (Andropov, incidentally, had nothing to do with that blow: for him, it was heaven-sent.)

Early in 1978 the Hamburg weekly, *Der Spiegel*, published "The Manifesto of the First Organized Opposition in the GDR [German Democratic Republic]," dated October 1977. The GDR authorities declared that the document was a forgery—the Soviet bloc countries' traditional device for disowning dissident materials anonymously appearing in the West. The "Manifesto" was sharper in tone, and in the opinions it offered, than any of the documents that had previously reached West Germany from East Germany. Along with anti-Soviet declarations, it clearly sounded a note of German nationalism and revanchist sentiments—not only a bugaboo of official Soviet propaganda but a real fear felt by the Soviet people, in whose memory the tragedy of World War II was still very much alive.

There were heated disputes about that "Manifesto" in the West German press. Someone claimed its author was the singer Birman, who had just been expelled from the GDR. But Birman flatly denied it, saying he did not write German so wretchedly as the author of the manifesto. Someone else maintained it had been written by an East German official of middle or even high rank. But that was all the less likely, since even middle status was too high to risk by putting together such a document and sending it to the West. The most credible explanation was the one that came from official circles in Bonn: that the document had been smuggled in by East German Stalinists or the GDR security service on orders from the KGB so as to hamper the establishment of bilateral relations between the two German governments. And Herbert Wener, one of the leaders of West Germany's Social Democratic Party, flatly declared that the document was a deliberate provocation, regardless of who was responsible for it.

The one responsible for it was the one who had something to gain from it. To this we add only that no East European intelligence service can take any kind of action in the international arena without prior sanction from the KGB. In most cases they act on direct instructions from Moscow and serve, not their own countries, but the whole empire; or, more precisely, the parent state.

These actions by Andropov no longer met "the Party's requirements," to reintroduce the expression used by Podgorny when he pinned those decorations on Andropov's chest. To the contrary, such actions were undertaken in order to outflank the requirements of the Party; and they were in direct contradiction to its policy of détente.

But one must understand Andropov, too: he had no other way out. He had none from the viewpoint of his political career, because in a period when tensions between East and West were being eased, he was being squeezed out by other officials with a single advantage over him: they did not represent an organization which, in its very structure and purpose, contravened the spirit and letter of détente. (For the KGB, détente was a death threat, whereas the cold war had been its nutrient medium—its forage reserve.) Nor did he have a way out from the viewpont of the empire, whose tasks his organization understood and carried out better than any other. Détente had to be destroyed, because it was helping to break down the sinews—provided by the military, the secret police, and the censorship—that held the empire together. And dissent, in that empire, was beginning to enjoy impunity. For any arrest, one had to get special permission from the Politburo. Any KGB action now involved keeping an eye on the West, taking its reaction into account and making complex timetable calculations so that an arrest, a house-search, or even simple expulsions from the Writers' Union would not (God forbid!) coincide with a meeting between Brezhnev and Nixon, Giscard d'Estaing, or Helmut Schmidt. Détente even offended Andropov's personal tastes. Being an ascetic and a devotee of "clean living," he chafed at Brezhnev's drinking bouts with foreign leaders at the Kremlin and at his dacha; and at the sumptuous gifts that Brezhnev received (mostly new makes of foreign cars: he had acquired a whole collection of them), and that he himself gave unstintingly. More and more often, he remembered the Caucasus: it was because of just such high living that the Party bosses of Georgia and Azerbaijan had been dismissed and replaced by Eduard Shevardnadze and Geidar Aliyev. True, this had been done with his help and backing, whereas he himself had no one to look to for help.

But help did come to him, and from where he might least have expected it. In America, Jimmy Carter was elected President. And as his national security advisor, Carter chose Zbigniew Brzezinski, with his blind hatred of Russia (which Andropov ascribed to his Polish origins and Polish complexes), his defiantly outspoken manner, and his crude bluntness. In the context of détente, Andropov and his organization needed enemies more than they needed friends; and if the former had not existed, they would have had to invent them. But now they had a real enemy—and one who was artless, outspoken, and garrulous, in complete contrast to the secretive, closemouthed, furtive Andropov. It was especially gratifying to work with such an enemy after dealing with the cunning, shifty, elusive Kissinger, whom Andropov respected but was a bit afraid of. (After Andropov had become the leader of the USSR, his minions, wanting to flatter the boss when talking to foreign journalists, compared him to Kissinger.) Brzezinski was all the more useful in that, for a man as exact in his calculations as Andropov, it was easy to forecast all his anti-Soviet fulminations, and plan future KGB action accordingly.

From the very outset, however, the big stumbling block between Andropov and Brzezinski was the question of the Soviet Union's living up to the Helsinki agreement on human rights. And although it was not a struggle among equals, since Andropov's opponent was weak and unskillful, the former fought the duel brilliantly. And his victory in it was decisive in another of his struggles: that for power in the Kremlin.

The new American administration's outspoken defense of human rights in the USSR promptly produced results quite the opposite of those intended. In response to Carter's rhetoric on that subject, the audience he accorded to the former Soviet political prisoner Vladimir Bukovsky, and the telegram he defiantly sent to Academician Andrei Sakharov, leader of the Moscow dissidents, Andropov, combining the two methods of *wilde Dressur* and *zahme Dressur*, put a few dozen dissidents behind bars and expelled the same number of them from the country. In short, he got rid of about all the dissidents there were. There couldn't have been more of them, because the dissident movement in the USSR is rather a Western myth than a Russian reality. The West (above all, America) was indulging in wishful thinking. And a handful of Russian political romantics, truth seekers, and persons eager for fame, headed up by the Russian Don Quixote, Academician Sakharov, taking advantage of the Kremlin's policy of détente and the temporary restraints put on the secret police, tried to endow that myth with the traits of reality. For that purpose they naturally had to redirect their activities completely. They were counting, above all, on a response in the United States and Western Europe and not in Russia, where there could have been none—not, at any rate, among the native Russian population. But to call upon a totalitarian empire to become democratic, as Jimmy Carter did early in his presidency, is completely absurd, because for the empire, democracy means its immediate collapse. In other words, the U.S. president was calling upon the Soviet Union to commit suicide.

So that in response to the American demagogy about human rights, the empire's instinct of self-preservation was triggered; and its leaders had recourse to the services of its most reliable organ, the Committee of State Security. It was just what Andropov had been waiting for. Not once in the quarter century since Stalin's death had the KGB reaped such a rich harvest. During the first few months of Carter's presidency they arrested Anatoly Shcharansky, Mykola Rudenko, Alexander Ginzburg, Yuri Orlov, Zviad Gamsakhurdia, Mirab Kostava, Oleksa Tikhy. . . . As it moved from sheaf to sheaf with its sickle, the KGB put all of its strength into its work—able, for the first time in many years, to throw caution to the winds.

Today, when even that Potemkinesque dissent has ceased to exist in Russia, having been rooted out by Andropov, one is struck by the discrepancy between the deeds of the dissidents (virtually nil) and the reaction to them: on the one hand, from the KGB, and on the other, from Western public opinion, which got unexpected support from the Carter administration. If America's blown-up view of the scarcely visible sprouts of opposition in the USSR was based on an associative preconception (a totalitarian society was being measured in terms of democratic concepts), Andropov's blown-up view of the internal opposition was produced by reflection—chiefly of what was said in the American press, whose opinion was confirmed (and, as it were, officially sanctioned) by Carter's campaign in defense of human rights.

It is hard to say how sincere Carter and Brzezinski were in representing the few people grouped around Academician Sakharov as seriously challenging the Soviet system. If they were sincere, it was out of ignorance. As a matter of official duty, Andropov could not permit himself such ignorance. He made a sound evaluation of the wretched possibilities for dissident activity in the USSR even during the period of détente, when the KGB was being kept on a leash. On September 9, 1977, in a speech honoring the memory of Felix Dzerzhinsky, the founder of the Soviet political police, he characterized the dissidents as follows:

. . . certain people alienated from our society have set out on a path of anti-Soviet activity. They violate the laws, they supply the West with libelous information, they spread false rumors, and they try to organize various anti-

Soviet sorties. . . . These renegades have no foothold, and can have none within our country. . . . The existence of the so-called dissidents has become possible only because the enemies of socialism have plugged the Western press into this matter, along with diplomatic, intelligence, and other special services. It is no longer a secret to anyone that "dissent" has become a profession unto itself that pays off very well in foreign currency and other handouts—something that differs very little from the way the imperialist special services remunerate their agents.

. . . we are trying to help those who have erred. We are trying to get them to change their minds, to dispel their illusions. But we must act differently in those cases when some of the so-called dissidents begin to violate Soviet laws by their actions. There are still a very few such people among us, just as there are, unfortunately, thieves, grafters, speculators, and other regular criminals. Both groups are damaging our society, and hence must be penalized in full accordance with the requirements of the Soviet laws.

Among the audience in the Bolshoi Theater, where Andropov delivered his speech, were all the Kremlin leaders, headed up by Brezhnev. But one may assume that Andropov's secret reports to Brezhnev were quite different. In accordance with laws operative in totalitarian states like the USSR, and brilliantly described by George Orwell in his novel *1984*, words spoken officially are always to be understood in their opposite sense. Since Orwell's time, however, the totalitarian system in the Soviet Union has become yet more complex—so much so, that an official lie is often closer to the truth than are secret and intimate communications. In the tradition of official propaganda, Andropov was supposed to distort the picture of dissent in the USSR. And that is just what Brezhnev understood: that Andropov was playing down the importance of dissent—all the more so, since in his private reports to Brezhnev, dissent was presented as something very threatening. And Brezhnev may well have been sorry that way back when, right after the occupation of Czechoslovakia, he didn't heed Andropov's advice and order the arrest of the suspect citizens on the blacklist that Andropov had providently drawn up. In confidential talks with Brezhnev, by way of confirming his secret evaluation of dissent as undermining the very foundations of the Soviet regime (and hence of Brezhnev's power, personally), Andropov had cited comments on the Soviet dissidents made by American officials and in the Western press—to which, naturally, Brezhnev gave more credence than he did to Soviet propaganda. Thus the Western myth of opposition in the USSR became the justification for expanding the KGB's functions in combatting sedition.

Meantime, the Soviet dissidents underwent a really tragic metamorphosis: they were transformed from live human beings into a football that was kicked around hard by both sides, until it was worn out and had to be replaced by a new one—first Afghanistan, then Poland. The two or three dozen Soviet dissidents arrested soon after the inauguration of the thirty-ninth president of the United States were used in a visual lesson in Russian history taught personally by Yuri Vladimirovich Andropov and especially intended for Carter (totally ignorant of the subject) in response to his liberal pantomime. And on the blackboard were live human beings: Mykola Rudenko, Yuri Orlov, Anatoly Shcharansky. . . .

This is reminiscent of the old story about the famous Italian artist who had been asked by an Eastern potentate to come and work at his court. One day the two of them got into a dispute because the potentate had doubts as to the anatomical accuracy with which the artist had painted a lopped-off head. In order to prove that he was right, the tyrant—without giving the matter a second thought—ordered that a slave he brought before him and, as the consternated artist looked on, cut off the slave's head. Then he asked: "See? Who was right?"

President Carter was a man whose goals were immediate, not long-range ones. Like an actor, he placed more importance on the resonance of his words than on their consequences. It seemed to him at first that he could reeducate the Soviet leaders—the illusion of a missionary preaching to savages. It was an illusion not only because the Soviet gerontocrats were too old and too vain to learn (not to mention being reeducated); and not only because behind their backs, watching over the empire, stood the calculating, crafty, and inflexible Andropov; but primarily because in fact Carter was trying to reeducate the entire Russian people—a task that had proven too much even for such native geniuses as Peter the Great, Leo Tolstoy, and Vladimir Lenin.

Carter seems to have had what used to be called a "Napoleonic complex," the only difference being that his missionary undertaking was not a military one but strictly peaceful and limited to moral aims. It should be recalled that Napoleon was convinced that his Russian campaign would be successful since he was counting on support from the serfs, to whom he had promised freedom. But he paid dearly for his psychological error: the serfs rose up in arms to defend the tyranny under which they lived, because they themselves had created it. (In this they differed from, for example, the Poles, who went over en masse to the side of the liberating conqueror.)

A slave can be liberated only by himself—when he himself wants it. To free slaves by coercion is impossible.

Other peoples can and should be defended against Russia. But this does not apply to the Russian people, who do not ask for such defense, and do not need it. One cannot defend anything against itself, be it an individual or an entire country.

Most likely Carter had not the slightest expectation that the KGB would react so swiftly and rapaciously to his liberal demagogy on human rights. It was as if that was all Andropov had been waiting for—a few gestures by the U.S. president toward the Soviet Union— as a pretext and justification for a hard crackdown within the country. The ten-minute audience granted to Vladimir Bukovsky and the telegram to Sakharov were of course only theatrics, in which the president was the actor and Zbigniew Brzezinski was the director. It is amazing that the latter should have been so grossly mistaken about a country to the study of which he had devoted his whole life. Apart from everything else, he underrated his Soviet counterpart. Because Andropov's status in the Soviet hierarchy in 1977 was analogous to Kissinger's under Nixon or Brzezinski's under Carter, but considerably more promising than theirs.

Apparently Western observers failed to notice that Andropov, toward the end of his service with the KGB, already possessed incredible powers. That no doubt explains why, as recently as a year before Brezhnev's death, they almost never mentioned Andropov among his most likely successors. And even when Andropov had become general secretary of the Communist Party and was receiving foreign guests after Brezhnev's funeral, U.S. Vice-President George Bush, in an attempt to ease the formality of the occasion, said jokingly, "I feel I already know you, since we served in similar positions." Andropov simply did not react to this, since for him a comparison—even if jocular—between the position of KGB chief and that of CIA chief (which Bush once held) was an inapt denigration of his own previous role.

Unfortunately, we have no way of knowing whether our hero has ever read G. K. Chesterton's novel *The Man Who Was Thursday*. But even if he hasn't, the English writer's fascinating detective-story plot is the kind of thing that is inevitable as a method of any secret-police force, and especially of the KGB. The novel tells of an underground revolutionary organization in England, all of whose members had most unusual cover names: the days of the week. "Thursday," the main character, is sent by the police to infiltrate the organization. His mission is to gain the trust of the other members and render their activity harmless. To his surprise he discovers that another member of the organization is an agent of Scotland Yard. Then he finds out the same thing about a second member, a third, and a fourth, until finally it turns out that all of the members, including the mysterious leader called "Sunday," are police spies. Having realized that it was inevitable that a subversive organization would come into being, Scotland Yard had preferred to create that organization itself.

In Russia such a novel could not have been written, if only because its plot would not have seemed paradoxical. To the contrary, it would have resembled a real-life story. Could it be that Chesterton took that plot from the usual, routine practice of the Russian police? After all, many revolutionary actions were engineered by the Okhrana, the tsarist secret police. One of the first attempts to combine revolution with police action was undertaken in the late nineteenth century by Colonel Sudeikin, head of the national criminal investigation department, who fostered the revolutionary movement with the help of his agent Degayev, a member of the People's Will Party. Sudeikin was trying in that way to frighten the tsar and set up a police regime in Russia, with himself as dictator. But his bold scheme was brought to a sudden end when he was shot by the revolutionary and provocateur Degayev, whose revolutionary sentiments had apparently gotten the upper hand over his zeal for police work. In the very beginning of the twentieth century, one Zubatov, chief of the Special Section of that police force, engineered the founding of Russia's first trade unions, which were thoroughly infiltrated by police agents. These were the first cells of "police socialism." In 1905 Father Gapon, with the knowledge of the police—and possibly on instructions from them—organized a mass demonstration against the government at the Winter Palace in Petersburg. The demonstrators were fired on by troops, and the event went down in history as Bloody Sunday. To take another case: it is still not known why, in 1911, the student Dmitri Bogrov assassinated Prime Minister Stolypin in a Kiev theater. Did he do it on orders from the

Okhrana, whose agent he was? On orders from the Social Revolutionary Party, of which he was a member? Or on his own initiative? (When
asked why he had killed Stolypin and not the tsar, who was standing
nearby, Bogrov—a Jew—replied that he was afraid he might provoke a
pogrom.) Again, one of the seven leaders of the Bolshevik Party
before World War I, and a Bolshevik deputy in the state Duma, was
the police agent Roman Malinovsky, who was exposed and shot after
the revolution. The question is: Was he the only police agent among
the Bolshevik leaders? It has been theorized that the burning of the
police files immediately after the February revolution of 1917 was the
work of revolutionaries afraid of being exposed as double agents. It is
thought that Stalin had especially good reasons for such fears.

After seizing power, the Bolsheviks naturally put to good use the
know-how of their predecessors—including (and above all) the know-
how of the political police. In his book *Russia Under the Old Regime*,
Richard Pipes has shown how much the Bolsheviks learned from their
former persecutors. The Bolsheviks' notion of what government
should be was a mirror image of the tsarist regime. But it was an
intensified one, because that regime had shown them its worst side:
the police apparatus. When they came to power, they replicated that
worst aspect of the tsarist regime, elevating the police apparatus to the
state level. But there was a difference. On the basis of their experience
in prisons and as oppositionists, the Bolsheviks had become familiar
with all the flaws and defects of that apparatus—defects that had
enabled them to overcome it. And when they became Russia's rulers,
they got rid of those defects, so that under Stalin the police machinery
came close to absolute perfection.

In those days "creative" activity became the big thing in the security services, upstaging everything else. Secret organizations and
subversive plots were created *after* the arrest of the "plotters," who,
before their arrest, had known nothing of the plots' existence. They
were conjured up during interrogations, within prison walls, under
torture, or by the strength of suasion, as was the case with Nikolai
Zalmanovich Rubashov, the very plausible main character in Arthur
Koestler's novel *Darkness at Noon*. This was theater completely de-
tached from reality, with an absurdist aesthetic. There was one director but a huge cast of actors, and they all played the same role: *an
enemy of the people*.

Of course, Andropov could not restore a reign of terror on the

Stalinist scale; but he undoubtedly used the traditional, tried-and-true methods of the Russian secret police. Hence one may easily suppose not only the existence of provocateurs among the dissidents but that their number is greater than has so far been revealed, or perhaps ever will be revealed. If the improbable happens and there is another revolution in Russia, the first thing the "revolutionaries" will do is to destroy the building on Dzerzhinsky Square with its files and dossiers on informers. After all, exposing domestic KGB agents is exclusively the job of that same KGB when "the Center" decides to switch the role of "our man" from that of provocateur to that of a witness for the prosecution or of a tattletale in the newspapers. This happened recently with the dissident Orthodox priest Father Dudko, who not only repented of what he had done but slandered his former friends and followers. And it happened with Sanya Lipavsky, a Jewish "refusenik" and dissident who had been the roommate of Anatoly Shcharansky: he exposed Shcharansky in court and in the Soviet press. But the one-shot role of exposer is less useful than the permanent role of spy and provocateur; and this permits the assumption that there are more unexposed KGB agents among the dissidents than exposed ones.

The story of Sanya Lipavsky, dissident, provocateur, and double agent for the CIA and the KGB, is also intriguing in that it offers an ambiguous picture in lieu of the usual, strictly rhetorical illustration of the eternal "Jesus-Judas" theme.

Soviet reality skillfully transmogrifies that crudely drawn illustration so that Judas can be imagined in the role of Jesus, and even vice versa. Actually, if the person in prison were not Anatoly Shcharansky but the prosecution's witness against him, Sanya Lipavsky, the latter would be a hero and a martyr because Jesuses are born but Judases are made. And today they do not become Judases for thirty pieces of silver, as in the unsophisticated Judeo-Roman world: Andropov's methods were incomparably more refined and harsh. Sanya Lipavsky's father had been convicted of financial manipulations and sentenced to death. The KGB gave the son a chance to save his father by betraying his friend, who in any case would have been convicted of espionage, even if Sanya Lipavsky had not testified against him and written a letter to *Izvestia*. That jesuitical distortion of the choice troubles our minds even today. We still don't know what choice we would have made if we had been in that situation. We therefore leave it up to the reader to get out of that dilemma himself, remembering only that under the conditions Andropov imposed, suicide offered no way out: it would have meant death for the father and prison for the friend.

Our intention here is not to vindicate a Judas but to express compassion in the case of a forced betrayal.

Both young men—Anatoly Shcharansky and Sanya Lipavsky—were originally Jewish "refuseniks," but an extreme situation drove one into close collaboration with the KGB, and the other into a sharp confrontation with it. Both are infinitely to be pitied, because they were threatened by a sinister fate personified—in its two aspects, military and civilian—by the organization which at the time was headed by our hero. Both were guinea pigs in an experimental tragedy composed in the building on Dzerzhinsky Square.

Let us give due credit to the imagination of the man who was boss in that building. In combatting dissent, he cultivated his mind to the point where real dissent struck him as insufficient, so that along with it he created fictive forms. (For example, the openly anti-Semitic and national-Bolshevist magazine, *Mnogaya leta* [Many Years],* faked up as a dissident publication, was actually printed in the building on Dzerzhinsky Square.) Not only that, but Andropov tried to add doses of criminality to real dissent. Drugs, foreign currency, and weapons were planted in the homes of dissidents and Jewish "refuseniks," and then "discovered" when those homes were searched. It was important to him to represent the Soviet regime's ideological opponents as regular criminals: drug addicts, currency speculators, traitors, terrorists, and recidivists. This was already coming close to Stalin's methods of having the secret police create crimes.

In early 1977, in a Moscow subway car, there was an explosion that killed several passengers. Almost immediately afterward, foreign correspondents in Moscow were given two versions of the incident. The KGB agent Victor Louis, an English journalist but a Soviet citizen, laid the blame for the explosion squarely on the dissidents; while Academician Sakharov blamed it on the KGB. Of course one cannot rule out the possibility that the explosion was due to the carelessness of a laboratory technician from a research institute in Chernogolovka, near Moscow, who was carrying explosives on the subway in violation of safety regulations. (We are here giving one version of the incident.)

Mnogaya leta (Church Slavonic) is also the title of a piece of music (composed by Bortnyansky) used in the Sacred Pontifical Liturgy of the Russian Orthodox Church. (Translator's note.)

But in the Soviet Union, what with the sharp political polarization between the regime's critics and its chief guardian, Andropov, there was no room for accidents. They were outside the law. The dissidents and the authorities, it would seem, were competing with each other in giving reality an ideological tincture, each using his own. Andropov, who through Victor Louis declared the dissidents were responsible for the explosion, had no clear proof of that. But neither did Academician Sakharov have any direct evidence: he could not prove that the explosion was the work of Andropov's people. The difference was, however, that Andropov was in a position to seize the opportunity and involve Sakharov's supporters in the case, whereas Sakharov had no such power. And once again, as in the cases of the "airplane people" and Anatoly Shcharansky, the Kremlin chiefs curbed Andropov's zeal for police work. He had to relinquish his plan—already worked out and (as usual) finely detailed—to represent the dissidents as terrorists and get them convicted under the corresponding article of the criminal code. Finally, three Armenians—none of them a dissident or (of course) a KGB agent—were charged with having set off the explosion, convicted, and executed. They were tried behind closed doors, which raises the presumption that they had nothing to do with the explosion but were simply being used as scapegoats. But the crime had to be pinned on *somebody*, otherwise the omnipotent KGB might be suspected of incompetence.

Basically Andropov was obliged to love his dissident enemies if only out of a feeling of gratitude. Thanks to them, he built up his prestige to a point where it was easy for him to overcome all his Politburo rivals when the time came for a decisive struggle for the supreme power in the Kremlin. Any sprouts of dissent—even the tiniest—confirmed the *raison d'être* of his agency; and each new sprout added to the KGB's importance. The growth of Andropov's prestige was directly proportional to the growth of dissent in the country. Hence the KGB had an interest, on the one hand, in suppressing the opposition and, on the other hand, in exaggerating dissent and the damage it was causing.

That is why Andropov, after crushing real dissent, began to pin the label of dissent even on things which, a short time before—in the Khrushchev era and the first phase of Brezhnev's rule—would have been quite acceptable as the kind of public activity sanctioned by the authorities. These included routine complaints, public initiatives, or literary experimentation (e.g., the fuss raised about the politically innocent and artistically feeble miscellany, *Metropol*). Andropov was putting behind bars, or confining in psychiatric hospitals, even people who sent a critical analysis of the economy to *Pravda*, or founded a group to campaign for peace, or published a feminist magazine. If it had not been for these complainers, seekers after literary fame, or social pathfinders, he would have had to create dissidents out of totally loyal and even devoted citizens of the USSR, since by the late seventies the real dissidents had been wiped out.

The paradoxical and melancholy result of what the Moscow dissidents did resides in the fact that through their activities they stimulated political repressions instead of reducing them. If Mephistopheles said that he was a force that desired evil but wrought good, we have before us a contrary example: a goodness which, not desiring it and not even knowing anything about it, wreaks evil—an even greater evil than the one it was trying to root out.

It is not up to us to tell the story of today's Gulag Archipelago. We are concerned only with the mite that Andropov contributed to its development—or, more accurately, its restoration. Usually the treatment of political prisoners in the last years of Brezhnev's rule, when Andropov was in charge of such matters, is compared with the Stalin era. And Andropov, when measured against Stalin, may in fact appear to be a liberal. But that comparison is not valid, since it skips over the Khrushchev era. What we must do is to compare juxtaposed things; otherwise we will not be able properly to evaluate Andropov's innovations in his campaign against dissent.

First of all, he lengthened the period of imprisonment before trial (in special cases, it was unlimited), thereby giving himself and his agents time to do a more thorough job of falsifying the charges against the prisoner so as to make them more plausible.

With each new arrest he broadened the scope of the KGB's activities, doing away with the immunity that dissidents had enjoyed because of belonging to an elite profession, holding a high post, or being famous throughout the Soviet Union and even the world. It looked as if he would not arrest Anatoly Shcharansky, because he was being defended by powerful Jewish organizations all over the world; Father Gleb Yakunin, because he was a priest; the physicist Yuri Orlov, because he was an associate member of the Armenian Academy of Sciences; and so on. But he arrested all of them, thereby demonstrating that all without exception were vulnerable and defenseless vis-à-vis the KGB, regardless of their previous status and present fame. The last person from whom Andropov took away the shield of his former services to the country and his present world fame was Nobel Peace Laureate Academician Andrei Sakharov. The measure taken against him, however—administrative exile to the Volga city of Gorky—was relatively mild. For this, though, Sakharov is obliged not to Andropov but to Brezhnev, who was more sensitive to shifts in world public opinion vis-à-vis Russia. Andropov, as always, had insisted on taking harsher measures, if only by way of exemplary punishment.

It was not Andropov who first thought up the idea of declaring a dissident insane: that method of combatting sedition had been used in Russia well before the Revolution. But it was he who endowed it with broad scope on the state level, and scientific methodicalness. Under him there was a sharp increase in the number of special psychiatric hospitals that had prison status and were widely used in the campaign against "malcontents." In 1964, when General Petr Grigorenko was put in a psychiatric hospital for his human-rights activities, there were two such hospitals; by the end of Andropov's tenure as KGB chief there were more than thirty. To these must be added those psychiatric hospitals that were used in suppressing not dissidents but ordinary "complainers" or citizens with a critical cast of mind. According to the most modest estimates, about a thousand mentally healthy people have been put in insane asylums for their convictions. (Among them was the Pole Lech Walesa, a Donets coal miner named Vladimir Klebanov, who founded the first free trade union in the USSR. What happened to him subsequently is not known, though most likely he is still in an insane asylum.) According to information from Moscow sources, in one such prison-type hospital—the Chernyakhovsk Psychiatric Hospital, where General Grigorenko was confined several years ago—the prisoners rioted in 1981, seizing medical personnel as hostages and protesting against forcible treatment with large doses of aminazine, haloperidol, and other drugs with a deteriorating effect on the intelligence and the will. The riot lasted for four days, and was put down brutally.

All those who tried to protest against the use of psychiatry as a repressive measure were arrested. They included the mathematicians Vyacheslav Bakhtin and Alexander Lavut, the computer specialist

Irina Grivnina, the radiologist Leonard Ternovsky, the blue-collar worker Felix Serebrov, the paramedic Alexander Podrabinek, and even the psychiatrist Anatoly Koryagin, who was sentenced to seven years in prison and five years of internal exile for trying to save a dissident from the "loony bin."

Directly imitating the Stalinist method, Andropov began to arrest the relatives of prisoners. Raisa Rudenko, whose husband Mykola was already serving a seven-year term for human rights activities, was sentenced to prison in Kiev. And in Moscow the entire family of the biologist Sergei Kovalev was in prison: himself, his son Ivan, and his daughter-in-law Tatiana Osipova.

Another device of Stalin's that Andropov brought up-to-date was to arrest the same person a second time, and even a third and fourth time. Among the "repeaters" were the Georgian Zviad Gamsakhurdia; the Ukrainians Tikhy and Lukyanenko; the Lithuanians Petkus, Niklus, and Gajauskas; and the Armenian Airikian. The Russian writer Anatoly Marchenko, who had already spent a total of fifteen years in prison and exile, was sentenced a fifth time—to the same fifteen-year term that he had already served out: ten years in prison and five years of exile. All these people were imprisoned not for a new "crime" but for loyalty to their beliefs. And some prisoners are doomed never to get out of incarceration. When their term is up they are tried again, right there in prison, and sentenced on the same charges to a new term, sometimes even longer than the earlier one. Today, not a single political prisoner has anymore confidence that he will ever be freed, or even sent into internal exile. In many cases, because of the prisoner's age and state of health, second terms mean imprisonment for life, or even a death sentence.

Naturally, during the fifteen years when Andropov was head of the KGB, the conditions under which political prisoners were confined in prisons and penal camps grew worse. There is evidence of a refined sadism in the treatment of prisoners. Thus on December 28, 1978, the Ukrainian writer and film director Gely Snegirev died under torture involving the use of recently developed drugs.

Finally, a quarter century after Stalin's death, Andropov revived the practice of political murders camouflaged as gangland hits, automobile accidents, or suicides—but so transparently camouflaged that no one had any doubts as to whose handiwork it actually was. The

KGB, however, left no direct clues; and as the saying goes, "If you're not caught, you're not a thief."

As always, Andropov liked to try out and rehearse "new" methods in one of the union republics. If they proved successful, he would shift them first to the Moscow stage and then to the worldwide one, where he experienced a misfire at the time of the attempt on the Pope's life.

This time (in the early seventies), the place chosen for the tryout was the Ukraine, where the brutality of the KGB's methods was compounded, first, by the savageness of the local mores and, second, by the personal brutality of Vitaly Fedorchuk, who in 1970 became chief of the Ukrainian KGB.

A professional Chekist who had begun his career in "the organs" when he was nineteen, at the height of the Great Terror, Fedorchuk took the work in hand straightaway. On November 28, 1970, in the little town of Vasilkovo, not far from Kiev, the painter Alla Gorskaya (on whom the KGB had been keeping an eye) was brutally murdered. That mysterious murder marked the beginning of a whole series of similar reprisals against individuals regarded by the authorities as objectionable. Another painter, Rostislav Paletsky, had his throat slit in broad daylight in a village near Odessa. And yet another nonconformist painter, Vladimir Kondrashin, was found hanged from the girders of a bridge, with traces of torture on the corpse. Father Gorgula, a priest who had "disagreed" with the authorities, was burned alive in his own home, along with his wife. Their fellow villagers, going through the charred ruins, found scorched ropes on the corpses. Another priest from the Western Ukraine, O. E. Kotik, was drowned in a well. The brother of the poet and political prisoner Mikhail Osadchy was murdered under mysterious circumstances. Before the very eyes of his admirers, the famous Ukrainian composer Vladimir Ivasyuk was forcibly put into a KGB car and taken off to an unknown destination. A month later his corpse—bearing the marks of cruel torture— was found hanging from a tree in the woods surrounding the government officials' dachas, which is guarded by special KGB squads.

The Ukrainian rehearsal of "wet jobs"* was no less successful than the "campaign against corruption" in the Caucasus; and both methods were shifted to Moscow, where, in 1982, Andropov's protégés showed

---

*KGB slang for "murders." (Translator's note.)

up. Geidar Aliyev became a member of the Politburo, and the first deputy of the Chairman of the USSR Council of Ministers. As to Vitaly Fedorchuk, he at first replaced Andropov as head of the KGB for six months, after which he replaced Andropov's personal enemy, Shchelokov, as minister of internal affairs.

In Moscow the political murders were camouflaged in a more complex way than in the Ukraine; yet at the same time that camouflage was deliberately transparent.

After the defection of UN Undersecretary General Arkady Shevchenko, his wife was forcibly taken from New York to Moscow, from where it was soon reported that she had committed suicide. Two mutually exclusive versions—one saying she had died by poison, the other, by strangulation—were issued at the same time, so that it would be easier to surmise the real reason for her death. This was not only the punishment of a "traitor" but a plain lesson for other Soviet citizens working abroad.

A tragic death finally overtook the once-popular Soviet film star Zoya Fedorova. Stalin had put her behind bars for treason; or, more precisely, for her wartime affair with an American naval officer, Captain Jack Tate, by whom she had a daughter named Victoria in honor of VE Day, when the lovers parted. Following Stalin's death and her release from a penal camp, Zoya Fedorova, taking advantage of détente, managed to locate Tate, who by then was an admiral. And after a long battle with the KGB, she sent her daughter to America. Victoria was just as beautiful as her mother had once been, although she did not have the same talent as an actress. Nonetheless, she played the role of a dissident Leningrad poetess in a sharply anti-Soviet television film. Some time later it was reported from Moscow that Zoya Fedorova had died from a bullet wound in the head. As in the case of Arkady Shevchenko's wife, the authorities put out two contradictory versions of her death—one saying that she had died from a heart attack, and the next saying she had been killed by a burglar—again emphasizing the implausibility of both, especially the latter. Why implausible? Because in the Soviet Union a burglar may be armed with a knife, an axe, or a crowbar, but not with a gun, since there is no place where he can get one. Victoria Fedorova and her American husband are convinced that the murder was premeditated and politically motivated. And once again, this was not just punishment (for

Victoria) but a warning to other émigrés not to take part in anti-Soviet political activity.

There are enough other "wet jobs" in which the KGB undoubtedly had a part. One can hardly, for example, put down to chance the death of one man from the provinces who came to Moscow to see Academician Sakharov "to get the truth," and vanished after leaving Sakharov's apartment building. A few days later his body was found on a railroad embankment: he had been thrown off a suburban train. It was a vivid lesson for other seekers after truth and justice.

In Moscow we lived near the "Airport" subway station, in a district where there is a complex of "writers' buildings"—a hotbed of sedition, from the KGB's viewpoint. And in fact our neighbors included such "suspect" writers as Vladimir Voinovich, Vasily Aksyonov, Vladimir Kornilov, and Lev Kopelev. On the evening of April 26, 1976, Konstantin Bogatyrev, a well-known Moscow translator and a close friend of Academician Sakharov, was murdered right in front of the door to his apartment, which was in the building next to ours. The killing had been done very professionally; there were no indications of burglary; and all attempts at investigating the crime were blocked.

At Bogatyrev's funeral, Vladimir Voinovich said: "Kostya's murder was one more attempt to frighten our intelligentsia. Under Stalin, Bogatyrev was sentenced to death. The supreme penalty was commuted to a term of twenty-five years. Stalin died, and Bogatyrev served only five years. Not long ago we, his friends, celebrated with him the end of that twenty-five-year term he was supposed to serve. But it was the first sentence that was actually carried out: the death sentence. They killed Kostya. And we recognize that hand—that writing is familiar to us."

After that murder the atmosphere of fear that hung over our apartment buildings and over all of Moscow's intelligentsia grew thicker. The place that was supposed to be most secure—one's own apartment—became the most frightening place of all. Even today, for us there is no more dangerous passage than those few steps we took when, after coming out of the brightly lighted elevator, we crossed the dimly lit landing to reach our own door. . . .

To us (and here we are permitting ourselves a brief autobiographical digression) it seemed not only humiliating but impossible to live in such an atmosphere. So we founded the first independent news agency in Soviet history: the Solovyov-Klepikova Press. Our undertaking found support among American and West European correspondents, and we began to supply the world press with free information about the Soviet Union. It didn't last long: the authorities demanded that we leave the country immediately. (Before we founded the agency, when we were simply the married couple Vladimir Solovyov and Elena Klepikova, our request for permission to emigrate was flatly rejected.)

Here in America we dug up the issue of the *New York Times* dated May 4, 1977, which had a photograph of us on the front page, and there we read: "Each person has his norm, his quota of fear, just as each person can sleep only so many hours, then wakes up. I have had my quota of fear. I have used it all up."

Such were the words spoken by one of us, as accurately translated by the then Moscow correspondent of the *Times*, David Shipler. We remember that on the following day the Voice of America broadcast that article in Russian, and that the phrase about the "quota of fear" had a rousing effect on some of the radio audience. But one of our acquaintances did say, "That's true. Fear does have its limits, and it goes away. But only for a time—until a new fear comes along. And then everything starts all over again."

We had had wit on our side, but our acquaintance proved to be right. Andropov has managed to restore to the Soviet Union an atmosphere of fear close to that of the Stalin era, although not on the same huge scale (for the time being). But then he doesn't need it. What with the deep, subconscious reserves of fear implanted in "Soviet man" by the Stalin era, a few hundred arrests and a few dozen murders suffice to make that fear surface again and flood the whole country.

The Kremlin chieftains placed a high value on Andropov's success in rooting out all sprouts of dissent and bringing the country back from the Khrushchevian "Thaw" closer to the very cold days of Stalin. On August 31, 1979, in the Kremlin, a special government award was conferred upon him: the Order of the October Revolution. But this time it was not (as had been the case five years before) Nikolai Viktorovich Podgorny, chairman of the USSR Supreme Soviet, who pinned the decoration on Andropov's chest; it was Leonid Ilich Brezhnev, now chairman of the USSR Supreme Soviet. Because not long before that, Podgorny had fallen into disfavor and lost his post as head of state, along with all his other Party and government posts. The troika consisting of Brezhnev, Kosygin, and Podgorny that had overthrown Khrushchev in October 1964 had fallen apart. An irreversible process whereby the aged Party leadership was being replaced by military and secret-police leaders was already underway in the Kremlin. And it was being directed by Andropov. Having disposed of the liberals, he was now turning against the partocrats. And there was no way he could stop: he was full of energy and schemes.

6

Andropov in the Politburo: At Home Among Strangers, a Stranger at Home

He knew human folly like the back of his hand . . .
— W. H. AUDEN, "Epitaph on a Tyrant"

When Andropov was first brought into the Politburo, none of its members figured he was of much importance. Until almost the end of the seventies, he was not taken seriously, as someone on the same level with the elite group within the Politburo: as a potential rival or competitor. His chances as a political heir were rated no more highly than those of the "second class" members of that ruling body: in particular, the *minoritaires*, such as the Kazakh Kunayev, or the Latvian Pelshe. Willy-nilly, Andropov belonged to the lower category of "chiefs," and that for two reasons. First, because he was a new arrival—from the KGB. Second, and more specifically, because during the quarter century since Beria had been executed, the top partocrats had grown unaccustomed to having a chief of the secret police take a direct part in ruling the country. For them, he was somewhat of an errand boy.

Moreover, in the Politburo Andropov was a loner: he had no cronies there, and no protectors. Nor did he belong to any of the factions which formed and then fell apart in the course of the infighting, weakening each other and maintaining the mobile equilibrium for forces in the Kremlin. True, he was often commended by Mikhail Suslov, the jealous guardian of Party morale, for his industry, modesty, and "comradely openness." And it was Suslov who supported Andropov's relentless crusade against corruption on the Party level in Azerbaijan and Georgia. But when, in the late seventies, under the guise of a similar campaign against corruption, Andropov began to move in on the Russian partocrats (not yet those in Moscow, but others: Party officials in the oblasts and elsewhere outside of Moscow), Suslov was put on his guard. By then, however, it was too late to take preventive steps against "the exposer" himself.

For that matter, Andropov did not mind being a loner. Indeed, it was a condition he had sought out, figuring that in view of his long-range plans it was safer, for the time being, to remain in the background, overshadowed by his Party comrades. In general he was good at protective mimicry in any environment although it cost him considerable effort. And in the Politburo what his performance displayed was not ambition but modesty, practicality, and vigor. In certain matters he was perhaps only too vigorous; but that aroused no one's suspicions. Everyone could see that the KGB chief was zealous and sometimes overstepped the bounds of his authority. But that was a naïve and quite harmless trait typical of a novice in political infighting on a high level. And the mighty partocrats knew from their own experience that a top post is not attained by zeal alone. He managed, in a subtle way, to play up to his colleagues in the Politburo, taking into account their "rank," whims, and vanity, and minimizing his own, too specific KGB coloration. For example, every time he needed to talk with Gromyko—whose favor he was trying to win and keep—instead of inviting him to KGB headquarters or meeting with him on neutral ground, he himself went to the MID. Among his Party colleagues, he was perhaps a bit too much of a Uriah Heep; but these gestures on the part of the KGB chief were very flattering to them.

But there was another trait which worked to put him at a disadvantage among his Party colleagues (including Brezhnev), and which, given the sharp rivalry among Politburo members with respect to personal achievements, was often brought out against him, and wounded him deeply. In terms of formal training, he was the most ignorant man among them: none of the others had had such a paltry education.

He was born one month before the outbreak of World War I (at the railroad settlement of Nagutskaya in the Stavropolsky Territory, just north of the Caucasus), so that he came of age in the thirties, when a genuine cultural revolution was sweeping the country. The national economy had been rebuilt; and the number of students on the college level—most of them from worker and peasant families—had increased fivefold since 1913. It was a time when there was an acute need for people with advanced technical training; and Lenin's urgent appeal, now revived, to "Learn, learn, and keep learning!" resounded in all parts of the country. Among those who enthusiastically responded to it were all of Andropov's future colleagues in the Politburo, even those who were by then no longer young. Dmitri Ustinov, for example, graduated from the Leningrad Institute of Military Mechanical Engineering; and Aleksei Kosygin was a graduate of the Leningrad Institute of the Textile Industry. Nikolai Podgorny, like Andropov, was at first a Komsomol leader; but unlike Andropov, he held down that job while at the same time continuing his studies. In 1926 he graduated from a "workers' college," and in 1931 from the Kiev Technological Institute of the Foodstuffs Industry. Even the Kazakh Kunayev, who came from an even more remote and outlying republic than Andropov's native Stavropolsky Territory, proved responsive to the beck and call of the times, and in 1936 got his engineer's diploma from the Moscow Institute of Nonferrous Metals and Gold. In that same decade Nikolai Tikhonov took a degree at the Dnepropetrovsk Metallurgical Institute, where he had been a fellow student of Brezhnev's and of the latter's future wife, Victoria. Even Nikita Khrushchev (under whom Andropov made his Hungarian début), although he was not of an age to respond directly to this urgent Leninist call, found in that slogan something endlessly appealing to his inquisitive nature. (He did, in fact, graduate from a "workers' college" in the Donets Basin and, later, from the Industrial Academy in Moscow. But he was always painfully aware of how inadequate that nominal education was; and he kept trying to "round it out" wherever he could—especially in the field of agricultural science.) This is not to mention such pillars of learning in the Politburo as Arvid Pelshe, historian and associate member of the Latvian Academy of Sciences; Mikhail Suslov, alumnus of a whole series of institutions of learning (the Prechistensky Workers' College, the Institute of the National Economy, the Institute of Economics); or, finally, Andrei Gromyko, Doctor of Economic Sciences with a fluent command of English—something that has always been an unattainable dream for Andropov, both in his youth and in his old age.

In the enthusiasm of workers and students in the early thirties, in the craving for knowledge displayed by young people from the remote rural areas of illiterate Russia (like Gromyko, Suslov, and Pelshe)—in all that, one could hear a pure note of historical necessity, progress, justice, and the elimination of Russia's economic backwardness: a note later distorted by Stalin's ideological hypocrisy.

In the years that followed (even decades later), a higher education (or the lack of one) affected the individuality of a Soviet person to a greater degree than can be imagined by a person of the free world who has access to a regular flow of information, both general and specialized, that he can assimilate without going to a college or university. In the USSR information is just as restricted—just as much of a privilege for the elite—as are all the other good things in life; and it is incomparably more accessible to a student than to a nonstudent. And the impression left by one's student years is one that lasts throughout the life of a Soviet person, determining what he reads, what kind of friends he has, and his outlook in general.

But this call of the times, which in the thirties was literally sounded throughout the country via loudspeakers, for some strange reason did not reach the ears of Yuri Andropov. Either that, or he didn't heed it, which is more likely. Although he had joined the Komsomol, he never finished high school. When he was sixteen—at a time when his future Party compeers were students at technical schools or institutions of higher learning—he did the opposite of what they did. They went north, to the center of knowledge and technical progress. But he went south, to the Caucasian Autonomous Republic of Ossetia, where in the little town of Mozdok he worked as a telegraph operator. The next stages in his murky job history (which he himself has obscured) are as follows. For a while he was an apprentice film projectionist, wandering along through villages on the Volga with a portable projector, showing movies for country people. Then, for a year, he was a crew member on a Volga steamship. Finally, in 1932, chance brought him to Rybinsk, a city on the Volga, where he enrolled in a river transport tekhnikum (the lowest level of vocational school in the USSR). But he couldn't cope with the tekhnikum's very limited curriculum, and switched to a job as "exempted secretary" of the local Komsomol, meaning that he was exempted from continuing his studies. At that time the job of exempted secretary at a tekhnikum was rather an unusual and unstable one. The usual thing was to combine

Komsomol work with one's studies, as most of Andropov's coevals did.

Another young man who was a student in Rybinsk during those
same years was Andrei Kirilenko. He was enrolled, however, not at a
vocational school but at an aeronautics institute (such institutes were
very much in vogue at the time, because of the rapid expansion of
aircraft construction), from which he later graduated with high marks.
(Afterward he worked as an aeronautics engineer.) In those years
Kirilenko knew Andropov—knew him as a dropout and budding
Komsomol functionary. One can imagine his astonishment when,
many years later, he again met up with that marginal character at the
highest Party level. And one can also imagine, quite easily, Andropov's inferiority complex because of Kirilenko's professional career, which by the standards of the time had been brilliant. In short,
Andropov had accounts to settle with Kirilenko of which the latter
had no inkling. And he settled those accounts (including his youthful
humiliations) many years later by getting Kirilenko removed from the
Politburo.

Andropov's career in the Komsomol, begun at the Rybinsk
tekhnikum, offered no great future. And he would have had to drudge
along there indefinitely, had it not been for Stalin's devastating
purges. As a result of those purges, the local Komsomol leadership
was completely wiped out in 1937; and in 1938, much to his own
surprise, Andropov was named first secretary of the Komsomol in the
Yaroslavl Oblast, which included the city of Rybinsk. If his natural
gifts were against him, circumstances were working for him. In due
course it would be a prerequisite to obtaining a high Party post, even
on the oblast level, that one have a diploma from an institute, or an
advanced Party education. Konstantin Chernenko, for example, who
was about the same age as Andropov, took a degree from the Kishinev
Teachers' College when he was forty-two, although he already had a
diploma from the Advanced Party School of the Central Committee—
all of which he managed to do at the same time he did Komsomol and
Party work.

But Andropov was a slow learner. He had such a singular incapacity for any kind of study that his Party sponsors had literally to
push him from one school to another, because of the educational
requirements for high Party officials. And yet he never graduated
from the university in Petrozavodsk (where he had gone with a strong

recommendation from his benevolent patron Otto Kuusinen), or, later, from the Central Committee's Advanced Party School in Moscow, although he must have tried hard *not* to get through that school, because great indulgence was shown to Party officials.

It is quite possible that Andropov's low educational level—as compared to that of his Party comrades—was among the causes of his slow advancement. He was too provincial and dull witted for Moscow. And it was only thanks to Kuusinen's personal efforts that he found himself in Moscow (along with the former), where he would have had to spend long years as a Party drudge (as he had in the Komsomol) if the Hungarian opportunity had not turned up, and along with it, the Hungarian revolution. It was only then that our hero was able to emerge in the full splendor of his mastery of intrigue. And he could rightly say that from then on, everything he accomplished in his life he owed only to himself.

Actually, he talked a bit differently, but he said essentially the same thing. One of our Moscow acquaintances—a former Soviet spy in the Middle East, and now a teacher of Arabic at a KGB school—told us that Andropov's favorite saying was a line from Mayakovsky: "We didn't learn our dialectics from Hegel."

That line is familiar to every Soviet schoolchild. But in order to make it more understandable to foreign readers (for whom this book about Andropov was written), we quote it in the context of the lines preceding it:

> . . . we didn't have to read to figure out
> what camp to join, what camp to fight in.
> We didn't learn our dialectics from Hegel.

The life Andropov himself had lived exemplified the opposition of practice to theory, actual, direct experience to the "book learning" that came so hard to him. Nor was this the first time, in the Kremlin, that a quasi illiterate had vanquished educated men. The same thing happened with Stalin, who had been expelled from a theological seminary for his bad grades, although his Soviet biographers claimed it was for revolutionary activity. His Party comrades, virtually all of whom he later annihilated, were hated by Stalin for (among other things) their education, their knowledge of foreign languages, and the fact that he, because of his ignorance, could never take part in their theoretical discussions. He scornfully called all of them "eggheads." As for Andropov, when he became KGB chief, his feelings of inferiority about education were manifested in a more complex way than Stalin's.

It was under Andropov that the KGB people became involved in an intensive creative process: mythmaking. They concocted and promptly publicized KGB legends, circulating rumors and entertaining stories which built up an idealized image of that punitive organization. Toward the end of the sixties, pop literature and (especially) the movies and television were taken over by the modern-day state policeman, demonstrating his mental superiority over the enemy, whoever he was: a CIA agent abroad or an enemy at home. The Soviet secret agent Stirlitz (in the popular TV series "Seventeen Moments of Spring"), after making his way into a Nazi headquarters, overcame the enemy not by crudely forceful means, and not by crafty manipulations with pistols and other kinds of concealed weapons, like the charming thug James Bond, but by strictly intellectual devices.

This patriotic image was fostered by Andropov himself, and reflected his ideal notion of the KGB as the "brains" of the Soviet Union, and of his employees as intellectual supermen with the highest IQs and the greatest efficiency in the country. The origin and development of that image in Andropov's mind have a long prehistory, dating back to the darksome days of his boyhood, when the young Yura gathered cartridge shells from the railroad crossties near the station of Nagutskaya in the Northern Caucasus during the civil war. Later, during World War II, when the Party sent the Komsomol activist Yura Andropov into Karelia to organize partisan bands behind the enemy lines, the fleshed-out image of the Soviet reconnaissance scout would preserve all the loftiness of the provincial boy's dream. Here, from that potent dream were now emerging the familiar traits of the TV films of the late sixties about the work of Soviet agents behind the enemy lines in wartime. Andropov was very fond of those TV series, which reflected in idealized form the particular kind of military experience he had gone through as a young man. We have taken our information on Andropov's underground work during the war from his official biography, although we have some grounds for doubting the accuracy of that information, since the biography does not mention a single military or postwar decoration given to Andropov—such decorations usually being awarded to all veterans as a matter of routine on military anniversaries. If the official biography corresponds to reality, Andropov should have been given at least ten or more decorations: certainly the medal to A Partisan in the Patriotic War (First or Second Class), for the Victory over Germany, and a couple of anniversary decorations, along with one or two like The Red Star, The Red Banner, Glory, or The Patriotic War, and possibly even higher awards. Andropov's lack of military decorations strangely contradicts the official biographer's statement as to his part in organizing partisan detachments behind the enemy lines. It seems most probable that what we are dealing with here is a biography tailored to Andropov's desiderata. For Andropov's generation, taking part in the war was just as much of a sine qua non as was, for the preceding generation of leaders, taking part in the Revolution or meetings with Lenin, which likewise were often ascribed to Kremlin leaders without adequate substantiation.

In an indirect way, all those valorous TV heroes, that endless and rather monotonous succession of intellectual Chekists, relived Andropov's own life story: from the underground organizing of partisan detachments through the secret mission to suppress the Hungarian revolution to, finally, top-level secret work as head of the political police. In the imagination of the dreamer from Dzerzhinsky Square, it seemed that the whole of that life he had conscientiously devoted to secret work was parcelled out to individual characters: Major Pronin, Colonel Stirlitz, and the other brilliant intelligence agents he saw on the TV screen were like little Andropovs, his different pseudonyms. In their persons he cherished his own image, dreamed up during his obscure Komsomol youth. He looked at himself from the outside, mentally conquering his countless enemies on both sides of the Soviet border. There was good reason why those TV series and detective stories about the dangerous work of Soviet intelligence agents started coming out immediately after Andropov's appointment to the KGB. It was propaganda not only for the organization he headed but for himself.

It is noteworthy that the scripts for these films and TV series were written either by KGB people themselves (e.g., Andropov's first deputy, Semyon Tsvigun) or by "hired writers" on orders from the KGB.

But toward the end of his service in the KGB, Major Pronin and Colonel Stirlitz no longer sufficed for Andropov. His ambition was no longer satisfied by secret power and his alter egos in books and on television. He grew impatient, because he was coming to power at too venerable an age, being much older than his predecessors had been when they acceded to power. In short, the author himself wanted to step out onto the stage under his own name.

Such was the making of the Andropov presented to the world in 1982—a man who surpassed all the Pronins and Stirlitzes lumped into one. He was a refined intellectual, an indulgent liberal who knew foreign languages and was at home with all of European culture. (That he was head of a punitive organization only added another touch of color to this brilliant bouquet of virtues.) But even that was not enough: more and more facets of the rare diamond were polished. While spreading abroad the tall tale of his knowing English, for consumption at home (where no one dared employ criticism to set reasonable limits to his fantasy), he offered the even more bizarre image of a future Kremlin chief who read Montaigne in the original before dropping off to sleep.

This was his revenge for his humiliation, for his wounded pride, for the fact that he had not stood out among his Politburo colleagues, with their stubborn reluctance to rate him as a worthy competitor in the power struggle; for the fact that they had kept throwing his poor education up at him; for his backwoods youth so barren of promise; for affronts layered one stratum on another, until finally they formed a kind of tableland—for all this he could settle accounts with them only when he had grown old. It was his revenge for having had to travel such a long, long road to power—the longest ever travelled by a future Kremlin vozhd; for those endless years spent underground; for the fact that he had been shortchanged by God and underrated by men. By means of this splendid image of an enlightened potentate, exotic and lacking in verisimilitude against the background of the Kremlin ikon screen, the ignorant lad, slow to develop but with the fertile imagination of a provincial, rid himself of the complexes that had grown overripe in his old age.

The Andropov of 1982 was just as much of a pseudonym as Pronin and Stirlitz, because the real Andropov remained unknown. The real Andropov was simpler, coarser, cruder, and more ignorant. The real Andropov knew Montaigne only by hearsay. Not only had he never read him in French, he hadn't read him in the fine Russian translation of the *Essays* published during the Khrushchevian "Thaw." The real Andropov had not even read Machiavelli, whom he might have taken as his mentor. As with dialectics, so with respect to his own first-rate Machiavellianism. Andropov could rightfully say that he had not learned the science of political intrigue and crafty scheming from Machiavelli but had come by it on his own, through experience that was sometimes rough. The atmosphere in the Kremlin was not favorable to the *dolce vita.*

One of the chief difficulties, for him, had to do with camouflage: the problem of protective coloration. Always preoccupied, outside of politics and intrigues he was a man whose human qualities were hard to grasp, being secretive and stonily taciturn—a classic example of *"omnia mea mecum porto."* Outwardly he was usually gloomy and aloof; and if he did not look like a wolf, as in most of his official photographs, then he looked just like an owl. Even that mechanical smile of politeness for which he was known in Hungary appeared ever less frequently on his face, and ever less apropos, until finally it vanished altogether: the conditioned reflex had ceased to function. And that physiognomic breach of etiquette might have hindered his career. "Only look up clear; to alter favour ever is to fear": that rule was operative not only in the courts of the Scottish thanes of Duncan's time but among the Kremlin partocrats in Brezhnev's time. Brezhnev himself, Andropov's downstairs neighbor, was a crude sensualist in his daily life and pleasures, while Andropov was more austere, squeamish, and undemonstrative. At first it was hard for him to take Brezhnev's vulgar familiarity and jovial expansiveness (to which he had to reply in kind), with his uncouth habits of back slapping and shoulder slapping in the new, locker-room manner. "Go to it, Yurka!" he would exclaim, when Andropov was leaving after having paid him an official visit.

Incidentally, this vulgar practice of clapping (not to say hitting) someone on the shoulder was something that Brezhnev had picked up from President Gerald Ford in 1976 at their first meeting (arranged by Henry Kissinger) at the Vladivostok Airport. When Brezhnev, for starters, had said a few complimentary words about Kissinger, Ford showed his own approval of the secretary of state by clapping him on the shoulder really hard—to Brezhnev's great astonishment and delight. Nor was this free-swinging style the only thing Brezhnev picked up from the freshman president of the United States: he also got his wolf-skin coat, after first having asked to try it on. (This unseemly practice of asking foreigners for things that have caught one's fancy—whether it be Ford's fur coat or a watch obtained from a Kissinger aide several years earlier—offended Andropov's imperial pride.)

What Andropov found particularly unbearable during the first phase of that period when he lived in the same building as Brezhnev was that the latter, unlike himself, did not draw a strict line between official business and home life. As a neighbor, he was obtrusive (partly with a view to a crude kind of surveillance), sentimental, boastful, and frank, while at the same time demanding frankness; whereas Andropov preferred to keep his own impressions to himself. That the two should bump into each other in the elevator or at the front entrance, discuss trifles as fellow tenants, and even exchange family visits—all these things were inevitable. Of course Brezhnev was not a cantankerous dictator like Stalin, who had made his "Party comrades" drink with him, laugh with him, suffer (as he did) from insomnia throughout the night, and satisfy all his despotic whims: in short, to adapt themselves to the tempo and weird coloration of his own life. Still, Brezhnev demanded comradely cohesion, sincerity, and proofs of "fidelity to the Party line," not only on the job but at home. And in this sense it was hard for Andropov, at first, to "reply in kind."

And in fact, the atmospheres in the two homes differed sharply. In the Andropov family it was more balanced, more modern, without bearing any personal imprint. In the other, there was the unbuttoned, loud, convivial life-style of the Brezhnev household, with its heavy, odorous Ukrainian meals and the inevitable vodka; and with the entire family's fondness for luxuries of the flashier variety, ranging from country homes with swimming pools and billiard rooms, from Mercedes-Benzes and Rolls-Royces to amber knickknacks and gold pendents, some of them gifts from the satraps of union republics. As for Andropov, his notion of luxury was tantamount to the highest degree of comfort—the most suitable conditions for relaxing after work. It was only in this sense that he was attracted by certain articles commonly used in the West which reduce household cares to a minimum.

At this point, by way of defining Andropov's tastes more precisely, we must again mention Hungary, which left an indelible impression on him, both in the sense of economic profitability (as against the economic decline in the Soviet parent state), and in the sense of an ideal of domestic and social well-being. It was while serving as ambassador in Hungary that Andropov—a man with unpolished manners who had spent most of his life in the Russian backwoods doing fictive Komsomol work—learned decent manners and even a certain secondhand elegance. Like any complex-ridden nouveau riche with only a smattering of education and no real upbringing who lands in "high society," Andropov placed a high value on his acquired *politesse* and *bon ton*, and was secretly proud of them.

In Andropov's family the intellectual veneer and overemphasized modernity were of course borrowed traits—imitative and not in keeping with the plebeian tastes of the head of the family. The image of the powerful intellectual—something Andropov never was, either in terms of his educational level or his natural inclinations—was firmly implanted in the household. And that unnatural, forced family atmosphere had a painful effect on his children—especially on his daughter Irina, whose sensitivity was more refined than her father's.

Andropov's obvious inferiority complex had its effect on his parental vanity, as is often the case. In contrast to his own wretched youth, *his* children were to get the highest and best education in the country. Brezhnev, on the contrary, was so satisfied with his childhood in Dnepropetrovsk and the fact that he had come from "a typical worker family" that he had his children educated in the same way, according to his ideal model. That is, they were educated in the old way, not on a level with modern standards, but with those extra privileges deriving from his high political status.

This explains why, in terms of culture and education, there was such a vast difference between Brezhnev's daughter Galina and Andropov's daughter Irina, as though the two were from totally different eras. Galina Brezhneva—vulgar, with crude makeup—found her kicks and amusements in the fast lane, with her dubious hangers-on and lovers from the world of the circus, her absurdly high-and-mighty ways, her fondness for antiquated luxury, and her comical efforts to play the role of a social "lioness" in the elite Party salons of Moscow. In eloquent contrast to her, Irina Andropova had taken music lessons since childhood, then became an assiduous student in the humanities department of Moscow University during its most liberal phase (attending the seminars of the gifted literary critic Vladimir Turbin) and a passionate adept of the famous (though erstwhile disgraced) literary historian with religious leanings, Mikhail Bakhtin—whose name Galina Brezhneva did not of course know even by hearsay.

For Andropov, however, fatherhood was neither a passion nor a foible; and he did not deeply concern himself with the life and up-bringing of his children. Family life did not provide the latitude he needed to satisfy his boundless ambition and vengeful passions. But it did suffice in one respect: he could project onto his family certain painful complexes that went back to his youthful years of failures and ignorance. If his daughter Irina had got a higher and, by Soviet stan-dards, "elegant" education, his son Igor, at his father's insistence (it is hardly likely that his son had any choice in the matter), was obliged to become a graduate of Moscow's most elite institution of higher learn-ing, MIMO (the Moscow Institute of International Relations). There he finally learned, to the great satisfaction of his father, the English language: that same English language that the elder Andropov had never learned—not merely because he lacked the opportunity to do so, but by reason of his singular inaptitude for foreign languages, just as for any kind of systematic study. And his future reputation (fabricated by himself) as a polyglot—English, sixteenth-century French, Hun-garian, Finnish, German—was something he acquired by proxy be-cause of his son's linguistic achievements, regarding them as family property.

To come back, however, to 26 Kutuzovsky Prospekt, we must say straight out that at first it was hard for Andropov—given his ascetic tastes—to socialize with his higher (although downstairs) neighbor and immediate superior. But in the end he solved the problem of protective coloration brilliantly. Not only did he gear himself to Brezhnev's crudely whimsical nature: he transformed the disadvan-tage of having to live in the same building as Brezhnev into an ad-vantage for himself. He himself began to keep an eye on Brezhnev, scrupulously studying all his domestic habits and human foibles.

This tactic had the result that, little by little, he wormed his way into the complete confidence of Brezhnev. And since in his domestic life Brezhnev was wide open and even ostentatious (while Andropov was secretive and devious), Andropov gradually came to know all the little secrets of the Brezhnev family. Among them: the whole family's fondness (ruinous, as the future would show) for circus spectacles and connections with circus people, including two that Galina Brezhneva had previously married; and the fact that Brezhnev's son Yuri was addicted to the universal Russian vice of alcoholism—something that was blinked at by his fellow employees at the Ministry of Foreign

Trade where, thanks to his father's patronage, he held the post of deputy minister. He also learned things about Brezhnev's cronies and protégés scattered throughout the boundless expanse of the USSR, ranging from Vasily Mzhavanadze, the Party boss of Georgia (whom Andropov managed to remove from his post with the aid of "his man in Tbilisi"), to the first secretary of the vast Krasnodarsky Territory, Sergei Medunov, the next target of Andropov's punitive campaign to undermine the authority and power of his garrulous downstairs neighbor.

Besides Brezhnev, however, there were at least ten other members of the Politburo that had to be watched closely.

Andropov was not counted among Brezhnev's potential heirs, but he kept close track of each new claimant to the Kremlin Party throne. Some of the possible pretenders took themselves out of the competition because they were cautious, lacked fighting instincts, or had already satisfied their ambitions. Among these were Andrei Gromyko, the professional diplomat, and Victor Grishin, the Moscow Party secretary, who moreover was always sickly. Both had previously let it be known—by means of the Masonic signs used in that milieu—that they were withdrawing from the intense power struggle going on behind Brezhnev's back. The field of battle was given over to two hostile factions: the "Dnepropetrovsk Mafia," which included Brezhnev's "landsmen," comrades-in-arms, and protégés; and the so-called Leningrad troika—Suslov, Kosygin, and Romanov. Although Suslov was not a native of Leningrad, there was much that drew him close to the two Leningraders (at first to Kosygin, then to Romanov): their modesty, strictness, and adherence to Party principles, which contrasted sharply with the fawning ways and provincial amateurism brought into the Politburo by Brezhnev's "boys" from Dnepropetrovsk. An antagonism between the two kinds of national character also played a role here. And in this "stylistic" opposition, the Leningrader Kosygin was for Suslov quintessentially Russian in his ways, as against Brezhnev's bravura Ukrainian style, with his fondness for magnificent display, his "royal" hunting trips, and grand receptions for foreigners. There had been persistent rumors about the antipathy between Brezhnev and Kosygin since the day when the two of them replaced Khrushchev in his two posts as Party boss and head of the government. Kosygin, humorless and misanthropic, who always wore a sullen expression of dissatisfaction, and was extremely modest and unaffected in social intercourse, preferred to remain offstage. When he went to Leningrad to visit his parents' graves, he would use only one limousine—not five or more, like Brezhnev on his trips. And when he reached the cemetery, he would dismiss his bodyguards and stay there alone. Unlike Brezhnev, who neglected the entire Soviet economy, Kosygin tried to introduce economic reforms. They were blocked by Brezhnev and Company, even though his economic advisor, Leonid Kantorovich, had won a Nobel Prize for his theoretical rationale for those reforms. Kosygin's strict and businesslike ways were bound to hold appeal for Suslov, devoted as he was to ideological purity and orthodox communism, though he had no militaristic or police leanings. Gradually the two of them joined forces in opposing Brezhnev's cronies in the Politburo, who fawned upon the general secretary—contravening Lenin's ethic for intra-Party relations, which was upheld by both Suslov and Kosygin.

Neither Kosygin nor Suslov took part in the struggle for Brezhnev's succession. They were automatically put out of the running: *de jure*, because of their positions; and *de facto*, because of their age. (The former was three years older than Brezhnev, and the latter, four.) Kosygin could not lay claim to any higher post, since he was already prime minister and had (without any evident ambition) shared the supreme power with Brezhnev for a long time. It is quite possible that power, with the Brezhnevian coloration it had been taking on more and more, was distasteful to Kosygin. Thus he tried to retire in protest against the occupation of Czechoslovakia, having voted in the Politburo against that action. Nor, as we have said, was Suslov suitable as Brezhnev's heir. Throughout his long career, he had relished the role of gray eminence behind palace coups and shake-ups. He was regarded as the Party's chief theoretician, and was patronage boss for the high Party and government posts.

But if neither Kosygin nor Suslov could lay claim to the supreme power, Romanov, the protégé of both, had very good grounds for so doing. First of all, since he was relatively young, he stood out against the background of the antiquated Politburo. (In 1979 he was fifty-six—the youngest member.) Again, he found favor with Kosygin and Suslov because of his self-effacing ways and the purposefulness he had evinced in his post as Party boss of Leningrad. No doubt he had taken into account the sad experience of his predecessor, Vasily Tolstikov, who had behaved in Leningrad with the arrogance of the high and mighty—a compound of a Levantine satrap and a Roman proconsul. This cost him his job; and he was sent into honorary exile as ambassador to China. For a long time after Tolstikov's removal, Leningrad remained without a first secretary. Then Suslov came from Moscow and "swore in" Grigori Romanov, violating the Party hierarchy and bypassing more likely candidates.

Romanov was at pains not to set himself above others. He lived in a modest apartment, which was regularly inundated because of broken plumbing in the apartment above his, whose occupant was a friend of ours. When he became secretary for Leningrad, marble steps were installed at the entrance of the building, and a strip of carpet was laid, extending up to his floor. Otherwise, there were no visible signs of his privileged position among the other tenants in the building. He forbade journalists to mention his name in reporting those official ceremonies in which he was obliged to take part by virtue of his office. His modesty was a kind of farsightedness: he was loyal to Brezhnev; yet at the same time he was doubly the creature of his sponsor Suslov and his fellow townsman Kosygin. Because of his name, he was the subject of many jokes. In one of them it was predicted that he would restore the three-hundred-year-old Romanov dynasty to the throne. The last thing Romanov could be suspected of, however, was nostalgia and yearnings for a restoration. Judging from the stern methods he used in governing Leningrad, he was more suited to be Brezhnev's heir and a restorer of Stalinism. His political position was close to that of Andropov. But the Kremlin power struggle temporarily drove the potential allies into opposing camps.

Then Suslov and Kosygin pulled off something that had not been done for a long time in the personnel practice of the Politburo: they made the Party boss of Leningrad a full member of that august body. (Romanov's predecessor, for example, had not been deemed worthy of that high honor, although he very much aspired to it.) But their next move was made too openly: they started to groom their Leningrad protégé as the future ruler of the country.

When, in November 1978, an American delegation headed by Senator Ribicoff arrived in Moscow, it was received in the Kremlin by Kosygin and Romanov—something most extraordinary. Kosygin, of course, had sometimes taken a hand in foreign affairs—not just in internal economic matters. Thus he travelled to Canada, where he was attacked by a Hungarian émigré with strong nationalistic feelings. He met with Lyndon Johnson during a period of tension in relations between the United States and the Soviet Union. And he even went to Peking, where at the airport he talked with Zhou Enlai for several hours in an attempt to settle the border conflict and cool off the hostility between the two countries. But in the mid-seventies Brezhnev took all this away from him. He himself was fond of summit meetings. Détente, trips abroad, receiving guests—all these things flattered his imperial vanity. And Kosygin, a practical man quite devoid of vanity, relinquished those functions quite willingly.

So that Kosygin's receiving the American senators, with Romanov taking part, was an extraordinary event. It was an attempt by the aging prime minister to turn his post over to Romanov with the full approval and sanction of Suslov, the patronage boss for the Kremlin. Incidentally, the American senators were shocked by Romanov's coarseness, the abruptness with which he interrupted the interpreter, his impoliteness in talking with Ribicoff, and his total ignorance of foreign affairs. But then Romanov wasn't thinking of the American senators. He was trying—perhaps trying too hard—to win brownie points with his sponsor Kosygin in this, his first international meeting at such a high level.

That meeting with the American delegation proved to be a turning point for Romanov, but not in a sense favorable to him. It became plain that his highly placed sponsors were grooming him either for the post of prime minister, to replace Kosygin, or for the Central Committee Secretariat, to replace Brezhnev. It became so obvious that Western journalists starting writing about him as very likely to succeed Brezhnev—as a man on the way up. Moreover, even if he had not taken part in that (awkward) episode with the American senators, he would have stood out as an obvious candidate for the succession, since all other candidates could be ruled out on the basis of age, ethnic background, or lack of powerful sponsorship.

Once again, enter our hero—the man whom, in 1979, the entire Western press persistently regarded as a "dark horse" in the race for power in the Kremlin. But Andropov had different ideas about himself—totally different—although up to that point he had confined his participation in the power struggle to stirring up strife (in a quiet, underhanded way) between the opposed factions, so that they would destroy each other. When he learned (chiefly from the foreign press) that Romanov had been chosen as the successor, he sounded the alarm. Although he himself had set his sights on the succession, he was one of the oldsters in the Politburo; and that old-age syndrome was very painful to him. Because of Romanov's invulnerability in that respect, he exaggerated Romanov's chances as Brezhnev's heir.

Also, he knew that in the Khrushchev era there had been a precedent established when Frol Kozlov, first secretary for Leningrad, became Number Two man in the Kremlin: a Politburo member and the Central Committee secretary supervising the KGB. But then came the scandal involving the Soviet spy Oleg Penkovsky, a high-ranking intelligence officer, who transmitted secret information to the West directly from his official automobile while driving along the central streets of Moscow. Kozlov's KGB subordinates repeatedly took bearings, with radio direction-finders, on the signals being transmitted from his car; and they reported this to Frol Kozlov. But he was deaf to their reports; he didn't believe them; he didn't manifest due vigilance. When Khrushchev finally found out about the whole thing, he waxed so furious that at a Politburo session he threw a marble paperweight at Kozlov. His missed. But on that same day Kozlov had a heart attack. The papers announced that he had not appeared at a recent parade on November 7 "owing to illness"—an illness from which he soon died.

Still, the precedent existed; and Andropov had reason to fear it would be repeated.

He also detested those endless jokes about Romanov's belonging to the royal house of the Romanovs: they, too, even if indirectly, confirmed the claim of the Leningrad Party boss to the Kremlin throne. So Andropov decided to try out that inapt joke in the real-life circumstances of Grigori Romanov.

The occasion was this: Romanov's daughter had decided to get married. Naturally, she could not have imagined that the head of the KGB would take such a passionate interest in such a strictly family affair as a wedding. Just as naturally, the affair was arranged not by Romanov (who was divorced from his daughter's mother) but by his bodyguard, an entire detachment of KGB agents. As a man accustomed to an unpretentious life, Romanov was surprised, when he arrived at the banquet in honor of his daughter, to notice that the tables were laid with elegant porcelain ware. It was something that he, not being a specialist in porcelain, could not assay at its true worth. He was basically an ignorant man, and could not distinguish between chinaware produced five years before by a Leningrad factory and the porcelain crafted two hundred years ago, in Petersburg, for Her Highness the Empress Catherine II. And he was even less able to surmise that a setback in his political career was concealed in that same elegant dinner service laid out on the banquet tables at his daughter's wedding.

He took his seat at a table, and the banquet began. When the gaiety was at its height, and the guests were three sheets to the wind, one of the KGB officials (a personal acquaintance of Romanov's) dashed a teacup to the floor, following an ancient (and long-since forgotten) Russian custom: a way of wishing happiness for the young couple. His example was followed by the other guests. And soon the floor was littered with fragments of porcelain—much to the displeasure of Romanov, who, although he didn't even suspect just what kind of porcelain that was, had an instinctive apprehension (like a true Leningrader) about riotous goings-on. And besides, he didn't like to see property wasted.

And least of all could he link up the well-known joke about him as the direct heir to the Romanovs' throne with that dinner service, which, as was ascertained the morning after the wedding, had belonged to a member of the royal house of the Romanovs; namely, Catherine the Great. It had been borrowed directly from the Hermitage for the family festivities of Leningrad Party boss Romanov. The curator of the Hermitage, Boris Piotrovsky (whom his co-workers had nicknamed "How Can I Serve You" because of his fawning upon higher authorities) had, on orders from the KGB, made the priceless dinner service available without demurring. It had not, however, been taken from a museum exhibit, as was reported in some American newspapers, but from the vaults of the Hermitage. Catherine the Great's dinner service comprised thousands of pieces and there were usually no more than a hundred on exhibit. (Incidental note: Boris Piotrovsky, on his sixtieth birthday in 1972, did not get the honor he so fervently longed for: Hero of Socialist Labor. But on his seventieth birthday he did get it—owing, among other things, to the prompt services he rendered on the eve of Romanov's daughter's wedding.)

Andropov did his best to see that information about Romanov's aristocratic affectations reached both the Kremlin and foreign countries. In both places Romanov was removed from the agenda as the most likely heir of Brezhnev; and he was declared to be the *enfant terrible* of the Politburo. The reaction in the Kremlin, however, proved to be somewhat different from what Andropov had planned. At first, everyone was indignant at such "porcelain arrogance" on the part of Romanov. Brezhnev, for example, kept in his office a porcelain vase with his own portrait on it—the most he could allow himself. And Suslov, that moral purist, promptly gave Romanov a Party reprimand. And yet something in this whole affair troubled him. In any case, Romanov managed somehow to defend himself and explain things: he was not expelled from the Politburo. Here again, Andropov was undone by his insensitivity to nuances—to the actual makeup of human character. His aim was to smear Romanov in the eyes of his Party comrades. But he didn't think out his means really thoroughly. The result was that he tried to pin on Romanov, a man of coarse tastes and a simple way of living, aristocratic habits and a kind of high life that were unthinkable—unthinkable not only against the background of Romanov's own life but against that of Leningrad, where this whole bravura episode took place. Because Leningrad is a city that has been frightened over and over again; a city whose complexion is bureaucratically gray, and which is permeated by the KGB; a city buttoned up tight and implacable when it comes to protocol.

Lord knows Romanov was innocent in that affair, and everything testifies in his favor, including his basic ignorance. He could not have demanded Catherine the Great's dinner service from the Hermitage, because he didn't know for sure that there was such a collection in the Hermitage, not to mention its being in vaults. For him, a porcelain dinner service kept in a display case at a museum, a landscape by Monet, or a death mask of Tutankhamen were all the same: everything contained in the boring concept of museum—a place where, from time to time, he took official delegations of foreigners.

The episode that Andropov tried to pin on Romanov was far-fetched—a caricature of Romanov. But even though Romanov remained in the Politburo, Andropov got what he wanted: Romanov was not transferred to Moscow; and he was out of the running as a successor of Brezhnev, or even of Kosygin. Romanov showed up in Moscow several years later, when Andropov was already in power, and when the ideological consentients had ceased to be political rivals. Andropov had an acute need for proponents of his neo-Stalinist policy—people like Fedorchuk, Aliyev, and Romanov. Each of them had proven his efficiency by ruling harshly and sternly in his own domain: Fedorchuk in the Ukraine, Aliyev in Azerbaijan, and Romanov in

Leningrad. Romanov, moreover, had a special advantage over the rest of Andropov's protégés, because of his unfortunate experience with Catherine the Great's dinner service. That advantage may be most succinctly characterized by the Russian saying that has the literal meaning of: "For one horsewhipped man, you'll get the value of two unwhipped men." The fact that Romanov had been horsewhipped was a reliable pledge of his slavish loyalty to Andropov. From the viewpoint of Kremlin etiquette, which is based on servility, his undeserved whipping served him well.

Still and all, Romanov came out of it relatively well. The fate of all the other potential heirs of Brezhnev was either sad or irreversibly tragic. Since in the Soviet Union there is no direct succession it is only natural that the successor is not named at a session of the Politburo. Even Brezhnev had to be very cautious in getting close to anyone from his immediate retinue, because that disturbed the balance of power in the Kremlin. Announcements as to who were Brezhnev's "official" heirs were given out only in the Western press, with detailed lists of their qualifications and chances for success. The grounds for the ordination of an heir might be the most trivial, purely situational; e.g., who stood closest to Brezhnev during a grand ceremony. And yet the "official" announcement in the Western newspapers as to who was to succeed Brezhnev usually played a fateful role in what happened to that person. And in the worst case, it amounted to a death sentence.

One of the first to be heralded in the Western press as Brezhnev's heir was the late (and now totally forgotten) Fyodor Kulakov, who in 1978 was (after Romanov) the youngest member of the Politburo, and was in charge of agriculture. But he died—suddenly and under mysterious circumstances—at the age of sixty. According to one of the quasi-official versions of Kulakov's sudden death, he committed suicide by slitting the veins of his wrists because he had failed in his efforts to cope with the deplorable state of Soviet agriculture. Other versions, of course, are not ruled out. In any case, Kulakov's professional duties as regards agriculture were promptly handed over to Mikhail Gorbachev, Andropov's only creature in the Politburo, and his landsman from the Stavropolsky Territory. Once in Moscow, Gorbachev set a record for climbing the Party ladder—one that was later equalled by another protégé of Andropov's, Aliyev. In 1979, at the age of forty-eight—which made him almost a child when compared to the Politburo members' average age of seventy—Gorbachev became a candidate-member of that body; and within a year he was a full member.

There was yet another of Brezhnev's heirs who came to a tragic end. Petr Masherov was a Byelorussian and a candidate-member of the Politburo. But the Western newspapers had given him high marks for his ability to solve economic problems and to discuss foreign policy with foreigners, so he joined the ranks of the "official" heirs of Brezhnev. But he didn't stay there long: in the autumn of 1980 he was killed in an automobile "accident." If we bear in mind that Soviet leaders, as well as the Party secretaries of republics, travel in bulletproof Chaika limousines, preceded and followed by black Volgas carrying guards, and often escorted by squads on motorcycles, along a road that has been cleared in advance and across which not even a cat can run—not to mention a dump truck or bulldozer that might have collided with Masherov's limousine—the official version of an automobile "accident" seems altogether too far beyond probability. For that matter, the fact that Brezhnev's potential heir had fallen into disgrace even before his death was confirmed by the top partocrats themselves: not one of them attended the funeral services for him.

In view of the sad fate that befell each and every candidate elected abroad to succeed Brezhnev, we would advise Western correspondents, out of purely humanitarian considerations, to stop their public guessing. For that matter, it is a vain and idle way to spend one's time: not once since their profession has existed have the Kremlinologists guessed correctly who the future leader would be.

Andropov gradually acquired more power and influence in the Politburo, eliminating or weakening his opponents—not, however, in direct competition with them but by a simpler, more elementary method. According to Rousseau's well-known theory, every society is held together by a social contract. After the death of Stalin, which put an end to his death-dealing orgies throughout the country and at all levels of Party leadership, Khrushchev's Politburo adopted a basic moral code requiring that all of its members follow the commandment "Thou shalt not kill." The inner rules of Brezhnev's Politburo were based on more democratic and comradely principles; because Brezhnev's government, unlike Khrushchev's, was devoid of any extremes of voluntarism. Brezhnev might abuse the impressive outer trappings of power, but all decisions on the state level were taken by the Polit-

buro members jointly. Only those who showed signs of political voluntarism and ideological radicalism were removed from the top echelon.
But such removals did not come about as the result of personal intrigues, plots, or the undermining of power—not until 1977, when
Andropov intervened in that process. According to the Brezhnev rules
of intra-Party relations, expulsion from the Politburo was not accompanied by exile, imprisonment, or—*a fortiori*—death. To the contrary,
a former member was assured of a high pension, a comfortable apartment, and an honorable old age—without, however, being accorded
the honors of a state burial beside the Kremlin Wall in Red Square.

But if a Politburo member behaved decently and followed the
general rules based on the contract which was in effect during a quarter century and acquired almost legislative force in the Brezhnev era,
he was assured of the permanence of his official status (usually until
his death), nonintervention in his personal life, and of course personal
security. Andropov was the only one to break that social contract, that
mutual guarantee of power. And since he did it covertly, without
informing the other Politburo members, they, still being bound by
that contract, continued to fulfill it and were therefore completely
defenseless against Andropov's intrigues.

The Alliance with the Military and the Invasion of Afghanistan on Christmas Eve 1979

7

The secret of Brezhnev's political longevity (eighteen years at the helm) lies in the fact that for him—unlike his predecessor, Khrushchev—power was more important than ideas. He had no qualms about sacrificing the latter to the former.

Such were his tactics up until the mid-seventies: after overcoming a political rival personally, he would yield to him ideologically, making a compromise with his views. Thus, after getting rid of the most ferocious Stalinists in the Politburo, Brezhnev himself was steadily altering the course of the Ship of State in the direction of Stalinism. But he would do it more smoothly than his "radical" rivals had intended it should be done. So it was that his "little counterrevolutions" in the first half of his reign—roughly, one every two or three years—were at the same time gradual transformations of the regime. Of the "fallen angels," at least three had insisted on abruptly turning the clock back to the Stalin era. It was from that era that Alexander Shelepin had derived his police-state model, Dmitri Polyansky his chauvinistic one, and Petr Shelest his dictatorial one.

By the end of the seventies, of the seven Politburo members who had voted to send troops into Czechoslovakia ten years before, only one remained: Brezhnev. The difference between him and the Stalinists was rather a situational than an ideological one: the responsibilities of power restrained his natural inclinations; and the bureaucrat in him got the upper hand (to some degree) over the Stalinist. It is easy to imagine what the Soviet Union's policy would have been if the Stalinists—who, unlike Brezhnev, had remained unbureaucratized and irresponsible—had managed to keep their footing at the top of the Kremlin hill. And yet the Stalinists' defeat by the centrists (with

Brezhnev at their head) was possible only because the latter were steadily becoming more Stalinist. Such was the paradoxical nature of the Kremlin's shifting compromise in the seventies: the right-wing extremists were dislodged from the top leadership; yet on the other hand, the top leadership moved steadily toward the right. It was as if it were undergoing an inevitable degeneration. The cellular tissue of the entire state organism was degenerating, as in a case of cancer, when healthy cells give way to metastasis.

> The victor, after his victory, ends up vanquished.
> And the vanquished ends up victorious.

Brezhnev's counterrevolutions continued, with the same frequency, into the late seventies and early eighties; but beginning with the expulsion of Podgorny in 1977, they had a purely personal character, not an ideological one. The Stalinization of the country's political course went on at its own pace. But the fall from favor of Podgorny, Mazurov, and Kirilenko had nothing to do with it: it was strictly the result of a power struggle. The final outcome was that by the autumn of 1982, out of all the members of that old Politburo which in the autumn of 1964 had carried out a coup and overthrown Khrushchev, only one remained: Brezhnev himself. (Formally, Andrei Kirilenko was still a member. But Andropov no longer allowed him to attend sessions of the Politburo, from which he was definitively expelled right after Brezhnev's death.) Of course many of Brezhnev's former comrades-in-arms had died with their boots on (e.g., Kosygin and Suslov); but most of them were overtaken by political death long before they died physically. Brezhnev's bustling attempts, toward the end of his life, to bring his old buddies from Dnepropetrovsk (Tikhonov) or Moldavia (Chernenko) into the Politburo to replace members who had been expelled did not mean that he was seeking a successor. Rather, he was trying to save himself from the political solitude that was usually followed by a political death.

As KGB chairman, Andropov took an active part in the struggle between Brezhnev and those who were challenging his power, although he did so rather as one who executes policy than as a policy maker. This state of affairs, however, lasted only until 1977. At that point the situation changed radically, and Andropov became the inciter of Brezhnev's counterrevolutions. Previously, Brezhnev had told Andropov who was to be punished and who was to be spared. But now it was Andropov who, in an exchange of roles, advised Brezhnev as to which of his confreres was suspect and should be expelled from the Kremlin paradise. At the time, various ailments—heart attacks, leukemia, emphysema, gout, and other illnesses of old age—had taken their toll on Brezhnev and further weakened his power. The defector Arkady Shevchenko, former UN undersecretary general, who had a personal meeting with Brezhnev in 1977, said that at that time he was ". . . a complete invalid, in fact a living corpse, quite incapable of exercising control. Even his memory was failing him." And yet various factions of the Kremlin establishment still had need of that frail and helpless old man, because none of them felt strong enough to seize the power from his hands.

In order to make that old man, enfeebled not only physically and politically but mentally, aware of his (Andropov's) indispensability, the chief of the secret police had to fabricate anti-Brezhnev plots where there were none—a device he took directly from Stalin's arsenal. It was important to him to sow dissension among former colleagues and comrades-in-arms, discovering in them potential—that is to say, future—enemies. The first one to be victimized by this subversive tactic was Nikolai Viktorovich Podgorny. The powerless Brezhnev's struggle against Andropov's enemies—under the guise of a struggle by Andropov against Brezhnev's enemies—began with Podgorny.

Podgorny was a member not only of the Politburo but of the ruling triumvirate. Formally he was Number Three man in the state (after Brezhnev and Kosygin), which he officially headed as chairman of the Presidium of the USSR Supreme Soviet. He was not ambitious enough to challenge Brezhnev when the latter was at the height of his physical and political powers. But when Brezhnev in fact went out of action and Podgorny learned that Andropov was on his side, he made up his mind that his hour had come. In lectures on the international situation given behind closed doors at research institutes, instructors from the Central Committee began to criticize, quite outspokenly, Brezhnev's overly liberal policy of détente. It is hard to say with any accuracy whether this was done on orders from Podgorny or at Andropov's instigation.

At any rate, in the spring of 1977 Podgorny set off on a long trip through various African countries. Judging from the sudden changes in the itinerary, the fact that some of the visits had not been planned in advance, and the arrogance and self-assurance of the distinguished traveller, his trip was an impromptu, independent one inspired by a whim. That's the way the fully empowered leader of a country travels, but not the third-ranking member of a country's triumvirate: that trip focused the whole world's attention upon him for the first time. On the wings of victory, he returned to Moscow, where he had left things in the reliable hands of the chief of the secret police, who was not merely his supporter but his prompter and advisor. (In all likelihood, without Andropov's assurances he would not have decided to take such a trip, which was not much in keeping with his character and his age of seventy-four.) He was coming back to the capital as a victor, but he actually got back as one vanquished. Promptly upon his return, he was stripped of all his Party and government posts. True, in exchange for them he was given a lesson. But in his situation that kind of knowledge was quite useless, since he could not even share it with anyone else—not to mention use it himself. Podgorny was the first of the Kremlin leaders to discover to his own cost Andropov's strength and perfidy.

After Podgorny's fall, the question arose as to who should inherit his post as chairman of the Presidium of the USSR Supreme Soviet—a post which, in the Soviet hierarchy, is nominal and decorative, conferring upon its holder not so much real power as a heavy load of ritualistic and bothersome duties. Usually it is awarded for past services and not with any promise for the future. Most often it is a pensioner's job, given to a partocrat who isn't suitable for anything else, but whom (for various reasons) it isn't convenient to put out to pasture. The men who, at one time or another, have held that post—Sverdlov, Kalinin, Shvernik, Voroshilov, Mikoyan—either were never among the real Kremlin chiefs, or were no longer among them when they were named to that post. Podgorny was one of the few exceptions. Another was Brezhnev, who held the post from 1960 to 1964. But for all that, both of these most influential chairmen of the Presidium of the USSR Supreme Soviet ranked (at best) third in the Kremlin hierarchy.

After fourteen years of service under Brezhnev, Andropov had thoroughly studied his chief's character—including his weaknesses. Much as he loved power, Brezhnev had always preferred its outward show to the thing itself. His ideal was to be not a general secretary but a tsar: on the throne, with a crown on his head and a sceptre and orb in his hands. Just how important this emblazonry was to him can be judged from the fact that the first thing he did when he came to power was to effect a statutory change of his own title. Instead of the Khrushchevian, democratic "first secretary," meaning *primus inter pares*, there was a reversion to Stalin's terminology: "general secretary." Formally, however, Brezhnev was neither chief of state nor even prime minister (like Stalin or Khrushchev). And he did not get his share of honors abroad, since the title of "general secretary" was a Party title and not a governmental one; that is, it was recognized only within the Soviet empire. In accordance with diplomatic protocol, congratulatory telegrams from foreign leaders were not addressed to him, and it was not he who signed important international documents. There were even problems with welcoming salutes on visits abroad. This had always disturbed him. But in his old age, when for him power had been totally transformed from reality into a baby's rattle, his vanity knew no bounds. So that he even wept (which, by the way, he was doing more and more often) when Andropov suggested to him that he take over Podgorny's post, thereby simplifying diplomatic etiquette and concentrating in his own hands both Party and governmental power.

If Brezhnev was motivated by an old man's vanity (aided by an old man's feeblemindedness) when he accepted the KGB chief's advice, Andropov, by contrast, was acting on the basis of a far-reaching plan that he had carefully prepared. First of all, even though Brezhnev remained general secretary of the Party, in taking the honorary, pensioner's post of chairman of the Presidium of the USSR Supreme Soviet, he was succeeding to his own subordinate and regressing to his own past, when he had held that post under Khrushchev. These were merely nuances, of course. But when added together, they gave the feeling—even offered the prospect—of the sick leader's gradual fading from the political scene. Most important, however, was the fact—clearly realized by Andropov but not even suspected by Brezhnev—that the former triumvirate had served as a kind of protoplasm for the nucleus of the Brezhnev regime. When that triumvirate fell apart, the general secretary lost his protective medium. Now there was nothing Brezhnev could do but depend entirely on Andropov to protect his regime—all the more so since Premier Kosygin, too, had dropped out of the triumvirate, having been on his deathbed since late 1979. Thus instead of the mighty triumvirate, all that now stood in Andropov's path to power was a weak old man and a few of his colleagues—

insignificant men who were about as old as Brezhnev himself was.

Unfortunately, we have no information to account for the sudden disgrace, in November 1978, of First Deputy Premier Kirill Mazurov, a Politburo member who was of the same age as Andropov, whom many people saw as the heir of Brezhnev, or at least of Kosygin. But one thing is beyond doubt: there was no ideological quarrel between him and Brezhnev. And since by that time all personal dossiers on Politburo members were in the keeping of the KGB chief—who, while bearing the responsibility for their protection, also had them tailed and kept track of their every move and every single telephone call—it is most likely that Mazurov's disgrace was provoked by Andropov himself. And in October 1980, Mazurov's protégé and landsman, Petr Masherov, Party boss of Byelorussia, was killed under mysterious circumstances. Three weeks after his death, Nikolai Tikhonov, Brezhnev's co-worker and friend (their friendship dated back to the Dnepropetrovsk days), who still spoke with a heavy Ukrainian accent, was named prime minister to replace the dying Kosygin. He was a year and a half older than Brezhnev—one reason why he presented no threat to the latter's power. For that same reason, Tikhonov—unlike Mazurov, Masherov, or Romanov—was not a rival of Andropov's, either. The suggestion that Tikhonov be appointed as Kosygin's successor came from Andropov. Naturally, Brezhnev accepted it not only with enthusiasm but with appreciation. It would have been rather awkward if he himself had taken yet another old friend in tow and pulled him up to the top. He had already done that with enough of them.

Tikhonov's candidacy was supported by one more Dnepropetrovskian, Andrei Kirilenko, who, in Brezhnev's absence (whether the chief was on a trip, or for reasons of illness, which were becoming more frequent), carried out his functions as general secretary. Brezhnev, Kirilenko, and Tikhonov, along with Konstantin Chernenko, formed the Dnepropetrovsk Mafia in the Politburo. Andropov did more than a little to strengthen it. He definitely preferred it to the "Leningrad" and "Byelorussian" factions, since he was familiar with its Achilles' heel, which with each passing year made that group weaker and more vulnerable. For the fact was that by 1982, when the decisive, hand-to-hand fighting for power began, the average age of the men in Brezhnev's inner circle was seventy-five—five years more than the average for the Politburo, which likewise was not distinguished for its youthfulness.

The Politburo was more and more coming to resemble the council of elders of some primitive tribe. All access to it for Party functionaries who were forty, fifty, or even sixty years old was sealed off. Outside observers ascribe that entire situation to Brezhnev's instinct for self-preservation. But it is most unlikely that this gerontocratic principle could have occurred to him, given his waning consciousness. From 1977 on, Brezhnev was quite unable to carry out his political functions, not to mention setting up a complex system of fortifications around his throne. Responsibility for order in the palace and the tranquility of the patriarch rested with Andropov as head of the secret police. Whatever suspicions Brezhnev entertained were due only to Andropov's prompting. It was within his power to make the sick old man suspicious to the point of paranoia, although Brezhnev had been free of such complexes from early youth to ripe old age. But now, because of his physical frailty, it was easy to frighten him with what was going on behind his back, especially in his absence. It was Andropov who fabricated plots, and it was Andropov who exposed them. He made use of insinuations; and he implanted a fear for the future in the consciousness of the Kremlin oldsters, filling their old age with disquiet and suspicion. The main target of all Andropov's intrigues was Brezhnev himself, whom the atmosphere of suspicion and fear created by his chief gendarme must have reminded him of his political youth, because there had been nothing like it in the Kremlin since the time of Stalin. The Stalin era was Andropov's chief arsenal. He could make ready use of the secret KGB files—a priceless handbook in a power struggle. Everything Andropov did in those days was done both from a sense of duty and out of a fondness for intrigue, combined with the secret (but ever more discernible) aim of reaching the very summit of power. Like the idea of the nucleus and the protoplasm, the idea of an age qualification for getting a ticket of admission into the Kremlin was Andropov's personal invention. It suffices to mention that Brezhnev's first deputies were the following: for the Party, Andrei Kirilenko, two and a half months older than Brezhnev; and for the Presidium of the USSR Supreme Soviet, Vasily Kuznetsov, who was six years older; while the first deputy premier under Tikhonov (who was a year and a half older than Brezhnev) was Ivan Arkhipov, Brezhnev's coeval.

It was not a matter of accident that the only person exempted from the "age rule" was Andropov's devotee, Mikhail Gorbachev, who was elected at age forty-nine a full member of the Politburo—no doubt as a counterpoise to Romanov, who at the time was Andropov's *bête noire*. With the election of Gorbachev, the "plus" that the fifty-six-year-old Romanov had enjoyed in terms of age was promptly cancelled out. The gist of the matter was that for the sixty-five-year-old pretender to the throne, Andropov, the "young men" were much more dangerous than the seventy-three-year-old Brezhnev, who had occupied that throne for almost fifteen years.

Except for Gorbachev and Minister of Foreign Affairs Gromyko, there was no one in the Politburo who was close to Andropov. He maintained correct relations with all the members, but did not join any faction. By the end of the seventies, however, that was no longer very important. While the "Dnepropetrovsk Mafia" was enjoying its majority in that Party organization, the real power was rapidly shifting from the building on Old Square, which housed the Central Committee, to the one on Dzerzhinsky Square, from which Andropov was directing a plot against the partocrats/gerontocrats. All that was left to them were their titles and their habituation to the titles, while reality was taking on a completely new shape. It was hard to understand anything. Everything now had a double meaning, the old one and a new one; and only the future would show which of them would hold up the better. Just who and what were those KGB agents Andropov assigned to the Politburo members? Were they bodyguards or custodial guards? A guard of honor, or a grim guard detail set to keep watch over prisoners? And perhaps all the Politburo members were already under house arrest but didn't know it for sure and only vaguely surmised it. Some Muscovites called that period one of dual sovereignty, others called it one of anarchy. The poet Yevtushenko went around Moscow lamenting to all and sundry that now he had no one of whom he could ask a favor, or with whom he could lodge a complaint, because he didn't know who, at the moment, had the real power in the country. It was obvious to everyone that Brezhnev didn't have it; and it looked as if the Politburo, too, was out of things.

Nonetheless, in May 1982, shortly before the curtain fell on the ostensible Brezhnev era, Andropov left his post at the KGB and appointed himself acting general secretary of the Central Committee under the still-living Brezhnev. It might seem that there was no longer any need for this formal change of position: Andropov could have continued to run the country from Dzerzhinsky Square. But being an arrogator and usurper who had, from the viewpoint of Party custom, circumvented the Kremlin hierarchy, he was trying with this move from the one building to the other to legitimize his somewhat unusual (but so very natural) seizure of power. Sooner or later the head of the secret police would succeed in carrying out a police coup in a police state!

By way of contrast, we shall quote the conclusion drawn by John Barron in his *KGB*—a book that no doubt provided great gratification to the chief of that organization as a science-fiction novel having only a slight bearing on reality, and hence as proof that the KGB is able to keep its secrets and remain impenetrable even for Western specialists on the subject. (The author refers to information he received from the CIA, the FBI, the Pentagon's Counterintelligence Department, and West European intelligence services.) But the conclusions that Barron's research led him to—"The political controls are so strong and pervasive that the KGB will probably never break its leash and turn against its Party masters"—was refuted by Andropov personally.

True, it has been hypothesized that Andropov came to power thanks to a long-standing alliance with Dmitri Ustinov, minister of defense and a Politburo member. That hypothesis belongs in the same category as the rumors Andropov spread about himself, although it is supposed to have originated with Roy Medvedev, the only Moscow dissident with legal status and immunity against prosecution. It cropped up right after Andropov's accession to power, and was intended—like his move to Old Square—to camouflage his police coup, if only as a more presentable one: a military coup. This is rather a Western model than a Russian one, and "Western" not in a narrowly geographical sense but in a broader, political meaning of the word. That is why it includes not only such historical examples as Napoleon's "18th Brumaire" but such contemporary ones as the military coups in Greece, Chile, Pakistan, Argentina, Turkey, and Poland, where the army has held political power—unlike the Soviet Union, where that power was taken from it by the KGB. It was precisely for this reason that such a military coup did not take place in the USSR, while a police coup *was* carried out. Incidentally, it was the first successful police coup, unsuccessful ones having been attempted by Beria and Shelepin. As for military coups, not a single one has been attempted in all the sixty-six years of Soviet history: not by Zhukov, although he was accused of Bonapartism; not by Tukhachevsky, although he was executed as a plotter (on the basis of a false charge); and not even by Leon Trotsky, the founder of the Red army and its favorite, when Stalin began to squeeze him out of the Soviet leadership right after the death of Lenin. And today's Soviet armed forces are quite incapable of any independent actions, since they are permeated from top to bottom with KGB agents.

To come back to Dmitri Ustinov: neither in terms of his age or his character was he capable of any plots. Just as Brezhnev, toward the end of the seventies, became merely a symbol of Party and governmental power, so the aged minister of defense was strictly a figurehead. Andropov's chief sources of support in the armed forces (or, to put it more accurately, "his people" there) were Marshal Nikolai Ogarkov, chief of the General Staff; Marshal Victor Kulikov, commander-in-chief of the Warsaw Pact Forces; General Ivan Shkadov, personnel chief of the Armed Forces; and General Epishev, chief of the Armed Forces Political Administration, whom we have already met. All four had made their military careers thanks to close collaboration, in their early years of service, with the "organs" of state security. (For that matter, there is no other way to make a career in the armed forces in peacetime.) In order neither to underrate nor overrate their roles, it would be most accurate to call them Andropov's military advisors. Together with him, they planned a military operation—unprecedented since the death of Stalin—which in all respects it was more advantageous to carry out behind the screen of Brezhnev's fictive government. And so, when Brezhnev—sick and almost mentally incompetent but still transportable—was taken to Vienna to sign the SALT II agreement jointly with Carter, one member of that military troika, General Epishev, went on Andropov's instructions to Afghanistan to make on-the-spot preparations for the occupation of that country. Quite apart from everything else, Andropov was counting on the blitzkrieg in Afghanistan to neutralize the efforts being made both in the West and among the Kremlin leaders to revive détente—something hateful to him and, from his viewpoint, disastrous for the empire.

Afghanistan was in every way an undoubted success for Andropov—the result of long, thorough planning. He skillfully stirred up hostility between the two factions of the Afghan Communist Party, which had come to power after the April revolution of 1978, likewise carried out with direct help from the KGB. The majority or "Khalq" faction was headed by Noor Mohammed Taraki and Hafizullah Amin, and the minority or "Parcham" faction by Babrak Karmal. The differences between them were not so much ideological as personal. Taraki was a typical Party functionary, Amin's ideological bent was toward China, and Karmal was the most pro-Moscow of the three. (It was through Karmal that Andropov maintained liaison with the Afghan Communists.) From time to time the quarrels between the factions heated up to the point of becoming military skirmishes, with killed and wounded on both sides. Ultimately it was Amin, the man at the farthest political remove from Moscow, who gained the most influence in the government; and he saw to it that Babrak Karmal was sent into honorary exile as ambassador to Czechoslovakia, a long way from Kabul. Under the presidency of Taraki, Amin took over the post of prime minister.

Andropov was aware that Amin had lived for a time in the United States, and had even got a university education there. Karmal, for his part, flatly declared that Amin was a CIA agent. In principle, it didn't matter to Andropov whether Amin was a CIA agent or not; but he knew very well that he was *not* a KGB agent, while Karmal was one. So it was decided to get rid of Amin. On his way back to Kabul from a conference of nonaligned nations in Havana, Taraki made a stopover in Moscow and even discussed with Karmal the distribution of ministerial portfolios in the new government after Amin's overthrow. But Amin learned of the plot against him. Upon his return from Moscow, Taraki was arrested; and a few days later he was strangled in prison. Karmal was saved by his honorary exile. Amin summoned him back to Kabul, but the crafty Karmal refused to obey this order, which was at the same time a death sentence.

This temporary setback got Andropov even more worked up. All during 1979 he was busy with preparations of international scope for the occupation of Afghanistan. In February U.S. Ambassador Adolph Dubs was killed in Kabul—under very strange circumstances, and in the presence of four KGB agents. The Carter government accused the Russians of having had a hand in it, and cut its diplomatic staff in Kabul down to a minimum. Anti-American demonstrations erupted in several Moslem countries. (Judging from their coordination, they were organized by the KGB.) The biggest of these were held in front of the U.S. embassies in Pakistan and Iran, countries bordering on

Afghanistan. Ultimately the embassy in Teheran was seized by Iranian leftists with clearly discernible ties to Moscow. The tenacity with which they kept the Americans prisoner, while yet showing restraint in their treatment of them—both of these things indicate that the operation was carried out under the direction of the KGB. But the most amazing thing was the date on which the American hostages were seized: November 4, 1979, exactly one year before the next presidential election in the United States, with the obvious intention (one that the future showed was well based) of making the matter of the hostages a key issue in the electoral campaign. The Iranian leftists were in no way concerned with American presidential elections. Andropov, though, had a vital interest in them. Nor was that interest merely a personal hobby of Andropov's: it was a rather solid tradition in the Kremlin. Thus Khrushchev, in his memoirs, tells of how, during his meeting with John Kennedy in Vienna in 1961, he asked the president the rather impudent question: "And do you know that we voted for you?"

"How?" asked the very surprised Kennedy.

"By not freeing the American pilot before the elections."

He was talking about Francis Gary Powers, the pilot of the U-2 spy plane shot down over Soviet territory. At a session of the Politburo, Khrushchev had said: "If we free the pilot, it will be to Nixon's advantage."

Khrushchev was of course exaggerating, out of naïveté, his role in the election of an American president. If any of the Soviet leaders has so far managed to take part in an American election—and with a swing vote to cast—it has been Andropov alone. Just as, in 1960, it was up to Khrushchev to release or not release the American pilot before the presidential election in America, so twenty years later it was up to Andropov to free or not to free the American hostages before November 4, 1980. Now, however, the matter had become really decisive: it was up to Andropov, personally, who would become the fortieth U.S. president. And the way he placed his bet was a direct result of the situation in the fall of 1980, when the Soviet empire was undergoing an acute crisis because of the events in Poland. Carter's reelection would have meant four more years in the White House for Zbigniew Brzezinski, whom Andropov regarded as one of the three Poles most dangerous to Moscow. So the problem of the American election was considered along with that of eliminating all three of those Poles:

Zbigniew Brzezinski, Lech Walesa, and Karol Wojtyla, who on October 16, 1978, was elected Pope. (Andropov apparently figured that Brzezinski had had a direct hand in that election, with a view to alienating Poland from Moscow.) The KGB chief's almost maniacal concentration on these three Poles prevented him from rendering harmless, while there was yet time, a fourth Pole who turned out to be the most dangerous to the KGB, and the most invulnerable. But all that lay ahead. Meantime, in November 1979, Andropov still didn't know whom he should bet on in the American election, or how he would play the trump card he held. What was important to him at that time was to paralyze U.S. actions in the international arena, especially in the Moslem world; and he managed to do it through the seizure of the U.S. embassy in Teheran.

Now Andropov had to wait for favorable domestic conditions; in particular, for several Politburo members to be removed from political life, either temporarily or for good, by illness. He didn't have long to wait, because old age is already an illness. By the end of the year, both of the formally recognized leaders, General Secretary Brezhnev and Premier Kosygin, were *hors de combat*; and the condition of both was so grave that the doctors had little hope for their recovery. (Yet another rumor of Brezhnev's death had arisen in Moscow; but this one was closer to reality than any of the previous rumors.) Arvid Pelshe and Andrei Kirilenko were also ill; and Suslov was undergoing an operation. So it was that the decision to send a "limited contingent" of Soviet troops into Afghanistan to render "international aid" to the Afghan Communists was made privately among Andropov, Gromyko, Gorbachev, and the military troika of Epishev-Kulikov-Ogarkov, plus their obedient servant, Ustinov. Chernenko, Grishin, and Tikhonov were notified *post factum* of the decision that had been made; and there was nothing they could do but agree with it. The majority of the Politburo members—the five patients in the "Kremlyovka" (a VIP hospital) and the three out-of-towners (the Leningrader, Romanov; the Ukrainian, Shcherbitsky; and the Kazakh, Kunayev)—did not learn of the occupation of Afghanistan until they read about it in the newspapers.

In accordance with the Hungarian model, the new president of Afghanistan, Babrak Karmal, was brought into Kabul in a Soviet tank. All of the previous leaders, headed by Hafizullah Amin, were shot when the presidential palace was seized.

The reaction throughout the rest of the world was more clamorous than effective. Thanks to the partial embargo on American grain shipments to Russia, the USSR discovered other sources of grain in Latin America, so that the effect of the embargo was not only neutralized but rebounded from the consumers to the producers: the American farmers. And Carter's declaration of a boycott against the Moscow Olympics did not prevent the games from being held—the only way in which it could have been justified. What it did do was (1) spare Andropov needless trouble from the presence in the USSR of several hundred thousand American athletes and tourists (Harrison Salisbury rightly called that boycott "a boon for the KGB") and (2) increase to the point of excess the number of medals won by the Russians, thereby strengthening the propagandistic effect of the Olympic games on the Soviet public. (Here again, as with the grain embargo, the losers were the Americans—this time not farmers but athletes.) In sum, thanks to both of these American sanctions, Andropov knew exactly what the next Soviet invasion would cost, if things came to that. And the price set by Carter was one the Soviet empire could well afford.

Also useful to the Soviet Union, in the final analysis, was the optimistic to-do in the American press about the Afghan rebels' extraordinary successes in combatting the occupying troops. Actually, the poorly armed, uncoordinated, and mutually hostile groups of *mujaheddin* were virtually incapable of offering any real resistance to the superpower's "limited contingent," which numbered one hundred thousand and was equipped with the latest in technology. Nonetheless, raptures over the rebels' fantastic feats left little room for sympathy with the Afghan refugees (about three million—one-fifth of the country's population) or indignation at Soviet genocide. While these crudely drawn pictures of romantic heroics were being presented in the American press and on American television, the Soviet occupiers—as though taking advantage of a smoke screen provided by the enemy—were doing some rapid construction work on the territory they had seized. (Needless to say, they first drove out the native inhabitants.) They built big military air bases: one in Shindand and another in the Vakhan Pass, a narrow valley 150 miles long leading into China. They built a strategically important railroad from their own border to Kabul; they threw a bridge across the Amu-Darya River, on the frontier; and they moved troops close to Pakistan to cut

Afghanistan off from the rest of the world.

In its turn, the optimistic exaggeration of events in Afghanistan brought the American press to the point of out-and-out hyperbole: Afghanistan was Russia's Vietnam. Apart, however, from the natural and understandable urge to wish one's own misfortunes upon one's enemy, there was no basis for that comparison.

The war in South Vietnam was waged by North Vietnam with the help of two great powers, China and the USSR, which assured their client state of a constant supply of weapons via land, sea, and air. In Afghanistan there were not two Afghanistans but only one. And it was occupied by Soviet forces, opposed by a dozen mutually hostile rebel groups receiving worldwide moral support but almost no military support.

Even more important, though, is the difference between the Soviet Union and America. In the USSR there is no public opinion, no free press, no opposition. There are no pacifists, no draft dodgers, no liberals—not even a Daniel Ellsberg. There is only fear, which welds together this anachronistic empire, swollen with space. So that even if the Soviet Union, during a ten-year occupation of Afghanistan, were to lose fifty-eight thousand soldiers, as America did in Vietnam, that would (1) not become known to the Soviet public; (2) not provoke mass protests; (3) not compel the Russians to leave Afghanistan, or even to make concessions to the rebels, or hold talks with them. As compared to democracies, totalitarian states are much less sensitive not only to public opinion but to losses of human life. What is Afghanistan, when in World War II the Soviet Union lost twenty million people, and at least as many perished during Stalin's Great Terror?

The Western democracies' high sensitivity to the loss of human life is an admirable trait in all respects but one, the military, where it is an Achilles' heel. Among many examples of the Soviet indifference to casualties, we, as former Leningraders, shall cite the one closest to us. What other country but the USSR would have continued to hang on to its second largest city when almost its entire population had died as the result of a nine-hundred-day siege?

Thus the Soviet Union can well afford not only the international price but the actual cost of Afghanistan, including the losses in lives and military equipment (which are of course far less then those reported in the American press). This is the payment being made for a network of military bases directed against China. Because Afghanistan has no other strategic value than its proximity to China; and the one hundred thousand troops stationed there are nothing more nor less than reinforcements for the million troops on the Soviet-Chinese border.

Andropov and his military advisors attributed special importance to the Vakhan Pass, the great route from West to East and East to West, which crosses the roof of the world, the Pamirs, at a height of seven thousand meters. It was through the Vakhan Pass that the hordes commanded by Genghis Kahn's grandsons broke through into Persia and southern Europe in the thirteenth century. And in that same century Marco Polo peaceably crossed that same pass in the opposite direction, on his way to discover China for Europe. Afghanistan came by that appendix of land quite by chance. In the late nineteenth century the British decided to use it as a barrier against the Russians, who had come close up against British possessions when they seized neighboring Tadzhikistan. One hundred years later that stretch of no-man's-land, measuring twenty thousand square kilometers, became a bone of contention between the Russians and the Chinese. From the viewpoint of both countries, those barren valleys high up in the mountains, with their nomadic Kirghiz tribes, offered a tremendous strategic advantage to the side possessing them as a launching area for an attack on the enemy. In Moscow it was being claimed (whether sincerely or not is another question) that Maoists from a group called "The Eternal Flame" were driving the Kirghiz out of their pasturelands and gradually occupying the Vakhan valleys. Andropov even showed Gromyko and Ustinov documents taken from Chinese partisans indicating that with the approval of the Afghan president and CIA agent, Hafizullah Amin, joint detachments of Chinese and American troops were to enter Afghanistan through the Vakhan Pass. Those documents served as an *ultima ratio* for the Kremlin chiefs who were physically in a condition to discuss the plan for the occupation of Afghanistan—as they did later for Brezhnev, when he had somewhat recovered. And yet the argument Andropov used in this case was the same old kind he had used in the Czechoslovak and Hungarian crises; e.g., the Red army beat the Bundeswehr to the punch by just a few hours. This time, though, he laid it on even thicker. After the invasion of Afghanistan, he told the Politburo members that the Soviet troops had suffered their greatest casualties in the Vakhan, when a detachment of paratroopers dropped there met up with desperate resistance from seven hundred Chinese of the "Eternal Flame" group. (We have had no way of checking on the authenticity of that report.)

In annexing the Vakhan, the USSR posed a threat to the nearby (only fifty miles away) road from China to Pakistan through a pass in the Karakorum chain of mountains. That road had been built by the Chinese, and they regard it as of great strategic importance. At the same time, the Soviet Union began to squeeze China out of Indochina. To that end, it skillfully provoked Vietnam's anti-Chinese imperialism—the Vietnamese invasion of Laos and Cambodia, and the war on the Chinese-Vietnamese border. Also, it launched a rapprochement with India, with which it now had a common border, thanks to annexation of the Vakhan. This patent strategy of encircling China threw still more light on the reason for the Soviet invasion of Afghanistan.

For that matter, in the Kremlin no great effort was made to conceal that reason. The only Western politician who in January 1980, right after the Soviet blitzkrieg in Afghanistan, managed to see Brezhnev upon his discharge from the Kremlin hospital was Jacques Chaban-Delmas, president of the French National Assembly. All during their talk Brezhnev kept switching the topic of conversation from Afghanistan to China. (By that time he had fully accepted Andropov's view of the military action carried out by the empire in his own absence.) He told Chaban-Delmas: "Believe me, after the destruction of Chinese nuclear sites by our missiles, there won't be much time for the Americans to choose between the defense of their Chinese allies and peaceful coexistence with us."

Several times, as if by reflex, Brezhnev repeated that the Soviet Union would not tolerate the West's supplying atomic weapons to China. That, he warned, would compel the USSR to make a preventive strike against China, and the United States would have very little time in which to make its choice.

In the light of all that, it is not even worthwhile to refute the two detective-story theories most commonly encountered in the American press, which chalk up the blitzkrieg of Afghanistan to the Russians' eagerness (1) to seize the oil fields of the Arabian Peninsula, thereby cutting off sources indispensable to the West or (2) to gain access to the warm-water and ice-free ports of the Indian Ocean.

Of course, along with the main reason for the invasion of Afghanistan, there were others that cannot be ruled out, although they were necessarily tied in with that main reason. For example, the necessity for a proving ground for the constant training of the army under natural conditions, so that it would not grow stale and lose its fighting spirit. For that matter, it was not just the army but the whole country that needed to have its fighting spirit boosted. It was not just by chance that one week after the occupation of Afghanistan, one of the major Moscow newspapers published an article by the well-known Russophile writer Valentin Rasputin, full of historical allusions and containing a warning in a militaristic vein: "Is Fate not bringing closer to us the time when we shall again go forth onto the Field of Kulikovo to defend Russian soil and Russian blood?"

It should be recalled that the Battle of Kulikovo (against the Tatars) is ranked in Russian history as one of the most important—on a level with Borodino in the war against Napoleon, and Stalingrad in the war against Hitler. It is regarded not as a battle between states but as one between races and continents. It took place six hundred years ago; but the Russians feel that sooner or later it will have to be fought again—perhaps in the near future.

As for Chaban-Delmas, promptly after his hour-and-a-half talk with Brezhnev, he flew back to Paris, cancelling his plans for further travels in the Soviet Union by way of protesting Academician Andrei Sakharov's expulsion from Moscow—something Andropov had effected under cover of the action in Afghanistan. With the arrest or emigration of his comrades-in-arms, Sakharov had long since become a living anachronism against a background of the hardening, by the secret police, of the country's foreign and domestic policy. Now the dissident movement, undone by Andropov, was deprived even of its symbolic significance. For all the lack of equivalence between the invasion of Afghanistan and Andrei Sakharov's exile to Gorky, both events were links in the same chain. Put together, they meant that the Soviet Union was definitively divorcing itself from the policy of détente.

Andropov's attack was going ahead on all fronts; he was sweeping away all obstacles in his path. But he would soon be faced with a very severe test: six months after the rape of Afghanistan, the Soviet Union lost Poland. In the summer of 1980, in the Gdansk shipyards on the shore of the Baltic Sea, a strike broke out—a strike that would lead to the fall of the pro-Soviet regime in Poland.

8

The Dnepropetrovsk Mafia and the Defeat in Poland

> Poland cannot be shot, and she cannot be hanged;
> consequently, nothing lasting or conclusive can be done by
> force. Whenever there is a war or agitation in Russia, Poland
> will rise up against us, so that there will have to be one
> Russian sentry for every Pole.
> — PRINCE PETR VYAZEMSKY,
>   diary entry for September 14,
>   1831, during an anti-Russian
>   uprising in Poland

> Will no one rid me of this turbulent priest?
> — HENRY II OF ENGLAND, on
>   Thomas à Becket, Archbishop
>   of Canterbury

A schemer with an unbridled imagination, Andropov hated reality: it was his worst enemy. He would have preferred not to notice reality at all—especially since physically he was almost insensible to it, and became more and more so as the years passed. Even in his younger days, however, he had been rather ascetic as regards all of the five senses. And as he approached old age, one of them began to fail him: his vision was going. It is said that God compensates blind people by giving them more acute hearing. To Andropov God gave a more acute inner vision: he saw things that did not exist, and failed to notice others that did. He was mentally farsighted and physically nearsighted. With hundreds of plans in his head, he often didn't notice things that were right in front of his eyes.

Andropov's office was on the third floor, at the point of juncture between two buildings: one had belonged, before the revolution, to the All-Russian Insurance Company; the other had been built after World War II by German POWs and Soviet political prisoners. Despite its location, Andropov's office gave him the feeling that he was in

an underground bunker from where he was directing all the operations on the face of the earth. The feeling of being "underground" was
largely a result of the layout of his office, which was hermetically
sealed off from the rest of the world—connected with it only by a
battery of secure telephones. The windows, made of bulletproof glass,
were also provided with iron shutters. The shutters could be raised by
pushing on a button concealed behind the curtain; but he almost never
did that, preferring a world he himself had created to one created
without his participation. Next to the office was a bedroom with an
adjoining bathroom. He often spent the night there; and he even came
to prefer his office on Dzerzhinsky Square to his barren apartment on
Kutuzovsky Prospekt, where he had as downstairs neighbor his chief,
Leonid Ilich Brezhnev.

Brezhnev was the particular reality that his "false imagination" (to
borrow an expression from Plato's *Timaeus*) was skipping over: triumph in Afghanistan had blinded him to the outer world. The man
Andropov had almost totally ignored, as if he were a living corpse, had
unexpectedly begun to recover somewhat in the spring of 1980.

Brezhnev might be cited as an example of Soviet medicine's undoubted success in the field of geriatrics: slowly but surely the antiquated Soviet vozhd was coming back to life and, at the same time, to
limited political activity. It was as if, through his stubborn longevity—
despite the sporadic rumors of his death, and even in defiance of
them—the seventy-three-year-old Brezhnev had decided to show the
world (*and* his chief of secret police) the truth of the old Russian
saying "A man who is buried before his time will live longer." By
resuming his ceremonial functions, he strengthened the position of the
Dnepropetrovsk group, which had weakened during his illness. Andropov had underrated the possibilities of modern medicine and,
along with them, the combined strength of the political enemies he
had nudged out of power. The triumph won in Afghanistan by Andropov and his military advisors had, conversely, helped to strengthen
the Dnepropetrovsk Mafia in the face of the common enemy. It was a
time of unstable equilibrium in Moscow, when neither Andropov nor
the Dnepropetrovskians dared make a resolute move. It was already
too late to dismiss Andropov without jeopardizing the entire shaky
pyramid of Kremlin power; and Andropov did not yet dare to attempt
a palace coup. The enemies made little sorties against each other
(sometimes expending all their efforts on them), because any retreat

might have proved fatal. In this situation secondary matters took on primary importance. An example was the clash, in that same year of 1980, over Sergei Medunov, Party secretary of the Krasnodarsky Territory, an old friend and creature of Brezhnev's.

Andropov tried to do with Medunov the same thing that he had done in 1972 with another of Brezhnev's friends, Vasily Mzhavanadze: to remove him from his post as Party secretary publicly, using the press in bringing charges of corruption against him. But in this case the target was less accessible to Andropov. Although the Krasnodarsky Territory borders on Georgia, where Andropov had achieved success, it is part of the Russian Republic, so that Medunov had closer ties with Moscow in addition to Brezhnev's personal protection. The operation was a kind of experiment at undermining Brezhnev, but by proxy—through his protégé. Andropov had thought it out some years before, thoroughly and methodically adjusting all its details. Perhaps that is why it can be retraced in a documentary manner, if one is not lazy about gathering up all the scattered links and bringing them together into a whole.

Almost every summer during the seventies, Andropov used to take his vacation in his homeland, the Stavropolsky Territory, which borders on the Krasnodarsky Territory. In the former, near Kislovodsk, there is a sanatorium for the Party elite called Krasnye Kamni. At Stavropol, Andropov would be met as usual by Mikhail Gorbachev, then first secretary of the Stavropolsky Territory. On the way from the airport to the resort, Gorbachev would complain to his influential friend about his neighbor and counterpart, Medunov, with whom he was competing in terms of all indexes, economic and cultural. But there could be no fair competition, because Medunov was under no one's authority but Brezhnev's, and the latter was not inclined to "present bills" to his own people, regarding it as a breach of the code of friendship. In the Krasnodarsky Territory, and especially in the famous resort city of Sochi, graft and other kinds of corruption in Party and government organizations had attained an almost official status. One had to pay a bribe in order to buy a car, get an apartment, a promotion, or even a hotel room. There wasn't a single system that would function without bribery. Gorbachev had gradually put together a thick dossier on Medunov; and after completing his regular course of treatment at Krasnye Kamni, Andropov tried to exploit it. An organized stream of "letters from the workers" with complaints about the local leadership began to flow from the Krasnodarsky Territory into the Central Committee, the KGB, and the Moscow newspapers. Finally, in December 1978, *Pravda* itself printed several such letters. The result was a Party-administrative reprimand. It was directed, however, not against Medunov but against the editor of *Pravda* for having dared print the complaints of the Krasnodarians.

Andropov then abandoned his head-on attack against Medunov as unrealistic and undertook a flanking movement—again making use of the Moscow press. He bethought himself of one of his ideological "hairy mongrels" from the Russian Party, Sergei Semanov, a neo-Stalinist by conviction. At the time, Semanov was editor-in-chief of the monthly *Chelovek i zakon* (Man and the Law), directly tied in with the KGB. On orders from Andropov, he published an article criticizing high officials of the Krasnodarsky Territory, including Medunov. By the standards of the Soviet hierarchy, this was an unheard-of thing to do; and Semanov had done so only because he was confident of Andropov's support. But Brezhnev's backing of Medunov proved to be stronger, and Semanov was promptly fired. True, Andropov mitigated the punishment as best he could: Semanov was given a modest job on the editorial staff of the nonpolitical journal *Bibliofil*.

Since Medunov had not yet proved vulnerable, thanks to his protection in the Kremlin, Andropov had to resort to a backup version of "Operation Get-Rid-of-Medunov." Hence the sudden prominence of the valiant city prosecutor of Sochi—a town which, in the prosecutor's opinion, was riddled with graft and corruption in general. On secret instructions from Andropov, the prosecutor tried to arraign several of the city's high Party officials. But he would soon learn the limits of his own power, and that of his highly placed protector. When he brought charges against the mayor, accusing him of having taken bribes of three thousand rubles on every apartment rented, it was not Sochi's mayor who was removed from office but its prosecutor. Not only that, but he was expelled from the Party; his home was searched; and he himself was put under house arrest. He had been transformed from a truth-seeking prosecutor into a "prosecutee."

Having seen that his zealous underling had failed in trying to combat corruption in Sochi, and taken due note of the unlimited power that Medunov enjoyed in his own fief, Andropov started hitting below the belt. That is, he had recourse to a device that Brezhnev and the rest of the Politburo regarded as strictly prohibited—although

Andropov would use it several times more in his struggle against the Kremlin gerontocrats. What he did was to make it possible for information about corruption in Sochi and the abuse of power throughout the Krasnodarsky Territory to be leaked to the Western press.

Brezhnev did not like to see his dirty linen washed in public—particularly when that public included Western correspondents. Andropov, however, saw no basic difference between the empire's dirty linen and its clean linen. He did not share Brezhnev's old-fashioned, petty-bourgeois scruples. Here again was a point of extreme divergence. The other Politburo members, along with the entire Central Committee, followed the old Party ethic with respect to the USSR's reputation abroad; but Andropov violated that ethic without any hesitation, so that those who stuck to it became vulnerable to his machinations. In this case he had wanted to use the strongest medicine against Brezhnev: the general secretary would learn about the scandals in the Krasnodarsky Territory from the Western newspapers.

That same tireless prosecutor from Sochi, who had escaped from house arrest with the help of Andropov's people, surfaced in the summer of 1980 in Moscow. Through a front man, he got in touch with a Western correspondent, to whom he recounted all his mishaps in trying to prosecute Sochi's high Party officials for graft. Andropov had carefully briefed him for this meeting. But once again there was a slipup—probably because Andropov, as always, had neglected real-life nuances and the details of verisimilitude. The correspondent decided the whole thing was a canard, and did not write a story about it. Then Andropov, vigorous and methodical to the highest degree, mobilized all his domestic resources. Proofs gathered during many years of investigation were brought to bear on the mayor of Sochi, Medunov's direct subordinate. In November 1980 he was arrested, convicted, and sentenced to thirteen years for graft and other kinds of corruption—following the model that had been widely used in Azerbaijan and Georgia, next door to the Krasnodarsky Territory. Ultimately the story about Sochi found its way into the Western press and got back to Russia via the BBC and the Voice of America.

But even with all that, Medunov held firm: Brezhnev was still able to defend his friend and protégé. Moreover, he dismissed a first deputy premier of the Russian Republic, Vitaly Vorotnikov, who had supported Andropov in his long, relentless campaign against Medunov, and sent him into "honorary exile" as ambassador to Cuba.

The final accounting, however, was in Andropov's favor. Gorbachev, his Stavropol friend and landsman, was in the Kremlin; a Party princeling from Sochi was in prison; and Medunov, although still at large, had a badly besmirched reputation. As for Brezhnev, he clung to Medunov as to a last straw. He realized that to retreat now would be even more dangerous than in the case of Georgian Party boss Vasily Mzhavanadze, whom he had served up as a meal for Andropov—something he now regretted. That had been a mistake, because power is manifested not only in one's ability to put one's people in important and lucrative posts but in the ability to defend them in case of need.

The Kremlin gerontocrats' instinct of self-preservation now came into play: the entire Dnepropetrovsk Mafia, headed by Brezhnev, "stonewalled" for Medunov. Even Suslov, that orthodox champion of revolutionary austerity and against petty-bourgeois excesses, joined forces with them. Medunov himself was no longer important or necessary to anyone: not to Brezhnev, not to Suslov, and not even to Andropov, who had nothing against him personally. This was a struggle for power under the guise of a campaign against corruption, and one round in that fight had had the code name "Medunov." The fact that Medunov, frightened almost to death, was still hanging on to his position, testified to Brezhnev's strength.

But when, less than two years later, Brezhnev proved unable to defend his in-law Tsvigun, his friend Kirilenko, or even his own daughter, Galina, against Andropov's intrigues, Medunov was toppled—once and for all. In July 1982 *Pravda* printed a brief item saying that he had been "relieved of his post, owing to a transfer to other work"—the bureaucratic formula used when a Party official has fallen into disgrace. His place was taken by Vitaly Vorotnikov, whom Andropov urgently recalled from Havana, and whom, a year later, he made a candidate-member of the Politburo as a reward for his loyalty. By that time Andropov had no more need of Medunov—not even as a victim. But he was used to carrying things through to the very end, leaving nothing to be tidied up. In this case it was a kind of formal obligation toward a plan he had nurtured for several years—a plan which was labor consuming and multi-staged, with complex ramifications, and which now required the final bureaucratic dotting of the *i*'s and crossing of the *t*'s for our hero's inner satisfaction. It was also a form of revenge for his defeat when he took on the Dnepropetrovsk Mafia in 1980.

At that time, however, the main field of battle between them was Poland. Andropov was in a position to win there, because Eastern Europe was his fief; and in both of the earlier battles fought in that fief—in Hungary in 1956 and Czechoslovakia in 1968—he had been victorious. But as befitted a pedant, he insisted on following a time-tested model in dealing with the Polish question, completely ignoring the uniqueness of the situation there, its radical difference from the situations in Hungary and Czechoslovakia and, most important, the difference between Poland itself and any other Warsaw Pact country.

Back before the end of World War II, some Polish Communists requested of Stalin that Poland be made a part of the USSR as a union republic, like Estonia, Latvia, and Lithuania—countries which, like Poland, had been part of the tsarist empire and, like Poland, had cut loose from it right after the revolution.

Stalin's answer to the Polish comrades was a flat refusal.

Stalin's reason for his refusal was the same as the reason for the request: both sides wanted someone else to pull the chestnuts out of the fire for them. The Polish Communists would have preferred to have Poland be governed directly from Moscow without having to depend on their own resources. But Stalin preferred to have order in Poland restored by Poles, remembering from history how much the Russians were hated there. Governing Poland had always been equally hard, whether it was a part of the Russian empire on a par with other satellites, or had autonomous constitutional status. Since the late eighteenth century, Polish uprisings had been a fixture of Russian history. In a certain sense this was a vicious historical circle. One may even risk saying that the Polish uprising and the Russian suppressions of them were equally Sisyphean. This was a war in which there was not, and could not have been, any victor. The perdurable motto of the Polish patriots, "Poland has not perished!" kept running up against the perdurable instinct of self-preservation of the Russians' empire—first the tsarist one, then the Soviet one. In comparison with the Poles' permanent revolution against the Russians, the Hungarian events of 1956 and the Czechoslovak events of 1968 were children's games. Neither the Hungarians nor the Czechoslovaks had any historical hatred toward the Russians. They had expended their quota of hatred on the

Austrians and the Germans, and whatever hostility they felt toward the Russians was something acquired.

Among the European peoples subjugated by Russia, it is only with the Poles that the Russians have been engaged, for several centuries running, in a stubborn struggle for political supremacy. In the late sixteenth and early seventeenth centuries, Russia and Poland had equal chances of creating a great empire. (Poland may even have had a better chance, given the Lublin Union with Lithuania, the formation of the Rzeczpospolita, the imperial ambitions of Stefan Batory, and success in competing with the Russians over the Ukraine, up to and including the occupation of the Russian throne by the Polish puppet, the False Dmitri, given out to be the son of Ivan the Terrible.) On their narrow historical path, these two peoples could not have passed each other by peaceably: for each, it was a question of either getting the upper hand, or yielding; of becoming an empire, or a colony. In other words, Russia had no other choice than to become an empire. Otherwise, it would have become a province of Poland.

In the historical perspective, it is quite possible that the Poles came out better; for an empire is the kind of burden under which even giants stoop. More important, today the threat to Polish independence on the part of Russia is less than the threat to the very existence of the Russian empire posed by peoples it has subjugated or humiliated. So that each Polish revolt raises two questions: not only whether there will or will not be an independent Poland, but whether the Russian empire will or will not be. That is understood in both Moscow and Warsaw. The Russian Damoclean sword which has been hanging over Poland for almost two centuries is, from the Russian viewpoint, a defensive weapon.

That such is the case can be judged from the first step that Andropov took—or managed to get taken—right after the strike broke out in the Gdansk shipyards in the summer of 1980. The Soviet Union was cut off from all news about Poland. All foreign radio stations broadcasting in Russian—The Voice of America, the *Deutsche Welle*, and the BBC—were totally jammed. In order to get a good idea of that, an accurate metaphor is required. It was as if the Soviet Union had put up a Berlin Wall all along its perimeter (thousands of miles long) so as to block any free information about the Polish events from getting into the country. Just as in ancient times bearers of bad tidings were executed, so Andropov, not yet having found a way of dealing with the Polish crisis, first of all took out his wrath on the news about it. (For that matter, the Polish crisis merely served as an occasion for such a measure: the jamming was continued after General Jaruzelski had established his military regime in Poland, and it continues to this day.)

On the desk of the KGB chairman, however, reliable news reports from Poland kept piling up—each one more disquieting than the last. Lech Walesa and his comrades had gained official recognition of their free trade unions; the earlier Polish leadership had fallen; throughout the country, people were demanding an end to censorship, economic reforms, free elections, and even a review of Poland's obligations under the Warsaw Pact. What was taking place was a natural passing of the power from the enfeebled hands of Party bureaucrats into ever-stronger hands of the worker-revolutionaries. It was exactly that kind of revolutionary situation for which Lenin gave the classic formulation: "The lower orders no longer want to live in the old way, and the upper classes can't."

It was enough to drive the Kremlin to desperation. On the Politburo's agenda the question as to whether military means should be used to set things right in Poland became more and more urgent. Moscow kept raining down threats, one after another, to intervene and use force to put an end to the "counterrevolution" in Poland. But the Poles weren't frightened by words and hints, and the Kremlin couldn't make up its mind to use force. Andropov found himself among a minority in the Politburo. The Dnepropetrovsk faction, headed by Brezhnev, preferred (as always) to take a wait-and-see position, hoping that everything would somehow shape up by itself, and that the Polish revolution would finally peter out. Their chief argument ran as follows: unlike Czechoslovakia and Hungary, Poland (except for the sea) was hemmed in on all sides by Warsaw Pact countries. There was no direction in which Poland could escape. Its geographical position made it a Soviet satellite. Andropov objected (and in this his military advisors gave him their full support) that it was precisely because of its intermediate geographical position that anarchic and anti-Soviet Poland was cutting off the Warsaw Pact's military communication lines, including the most important one: that between the Soviet Union and East Germany. In response to that, Brezhnev agreed to step up Warsaw Pact maneuvers in Poland and around it, testing the reliability of communications lines and, at the same time, black-mailing and frightening the constantly changing Polish leadership.

Andropov did not even have anyone he could count on in Poland. He would have tried to put his money on his former colleague, General Mieczyslaw Moczar. But in a Poland overtaken by a whirl-wind revolution, Moczar couldn't make a career because of the fact that when he was minister of internal affairs he had carried out an anti-Semitic campaign in 1968 resulting in the expulsion of most of Poland's last Jews, some of whom were former inmates of Nazi con-centration camps who had survived by a miracle. Both by nature and because of his job, Andropov was distrustful. He did not trust Rus-sians, his own people; and for him all Poles without exception were suspect. But the three he regarded as the most threatening of all—Lech Walesa, the Polish Pope, and Zbigniew Brzezinski—had to be got out of the way, not as an alternative to a military action but as a precondition, because it would be easier to cope with a leaderless country.

Andropov felt, furthermore, that the most dangerous of the three, and the primary source of the Polish evil, was Brzezinski, who in 1977, quite the other way around, had been useful to Andropov because of his defiant human-rights campaign. In 1980, however, he became a serious threat, with the election of the Polish Pope and the outbreak of the crisis in Poland. Moreover, Andropov now ascribed the entire anti-Soviet campaign of Carter's administration to the Polish feelings of his national security advisor. Andropov found many indications, both latent and overt, that he was right. Among the latter was a photograph that had been published in much of the world's press. It showed Brzezinski, looking bellicose and holding a machine gun, while around him stood Afghan rebels whom he was teaching how to fight the Russians. And one might label as covert what was reported by an American who had accompanied Brzezinski on a trip to China; namely, that at the Great Wall of China, "Zbig" picked up a handful of stones and threw them toward Russia. It seems that even the Chi-nese were dismayed by such an open display of political passions, although they smiled politely.

Articles about the "Polishness" of Brzezinski's attitudes toward Russia began to appear in the Soviet press. On January 30, 1980, *Literaturnaya gazeta* published a long article on him: on his origins and his views. Among other things, it was mentioned that Brzezinski regarded Soviet foreign policy as a continuation of tsarist policy. Only a few years before, the Soviet press would unfailingly have followed that up with a denial. But this time no such thing happened. Instead—and this was completely amazing—an official Soviet newspaper printed a quotation from an anti-Soviet émigré paper in which it was said that Brzezinski was motivated by "a blind hatred of Russia." The conflict had been shifted from the political plane to the ethnic one: the Poles' traditional hatred of Russians.

Even earlier, right after the election of Karol Wojtyla as Pope in October 1978, Andropov had instructed Special Service #1 of the KGB's First Main Administration to make an analysis of how the new Pope was elected. Those who drew up the document for Andropov (a copy of it was pilfered by a foreign intelligence agency) concluded that Brzezinski and another American Pole, John Cardinal Krol of Philadelphia, had pressured the American cardinals—when they attended the consistory held in the Vatican following the sudden death of John Paul I—to insist on the election of Karol Wojtyla as Pope. The ultimate aim of that election (said those who drafted the document) was part and parcel of the Polish revolt and, consequently, of Poland's breaking loose from Moscow. Later events—the Pope's triumphal visit to Poland in the summer of 1979, and the founding of free trade unions and their support by the Polish spiritual leader—directly confirmed (from Andropov's viewpoint) the information, conclusions, and recommendations in that report. Zbigniew Brzezinski, with his Polish complexes and anti-Russian feelings, was directly responsible for all that was now happening in his native land. So that he might prove to be the main obstacle on the Red army's path into Poland when Andropov finally managed to talk his Kremlin colleagues into direct intervention in Polish affairs. And that he *would* manage, Andropov had no doubts. He remembered Khrushchev's vacillation about Hungary, and Brezhnev's vacillation about Czechoslovakia: sooner or later the empire's instinct of self-preservation would get the upper hand over any doubts.

Two and a half years after the events described above (in the spring of 1983), when Andropov was already general secretary of the Communist Party, the daily paper *Zycie Warszawy* (Warsaw Life), citing its Washington correspondent as the source, reprinted from a leftist Madrid paper a "top secret" memorandum from Zbigniew Brzezinski

to President Carter. It set forth in detail the operations plan for elect-
ing the Polish cardinal to the papacy, and for the further destabiliza-
tion of Poland, resulting in "Poland's switchover from the Communist
camp into the capitalist one." Not only the style and content of that
memorandum but its itinerary (typical of Soviet disinformation tactics)—from a left-wing Madrid paper via Washington to one of the
major Polish papers—betrays the hand of the KGB, which concocted
and circulated that forgery.

What really matters, however, is not that the memorandum was a
forgery, but that the KGB supplied its own version of the Polish
Pope's election: under the covert direction of Zbigniew Brzezinski,
with an anti-Soviet aim. This means that Andropov believed in that
version in 1978, in 1980, and later, when he became leader of the
Soviet Union; and that he still believes in it today. Instead of refuting
the "Bulgarian connection," that forgery indirectly confirms it, betraying Moscow's alarm over the Polish Pope and his role as fomenter
of the events in Poland, and especially over the background figure of
Russia's archenemy, who set all this Polish machinery in motion, and
who is still controlling it from overseas in his fight against the Russians: Zbigniew Brzezinski.

And so Carter, who had formerly been useful to Moscow in all
respects—even in combination with Brzezinski—had now become
dangerous to it in connection with the events in Poland, which by
November 1980 had taken on a plainly anti-Soviet character, despite
the camouflage and caution of Lech Walesa and his moderate friends
in the Solidarity movement. For Andropov the camouflage and caution were even more suspect than openness and radicalism: unlike the
Kremlin gerontocrats, headed up by Brezhnev, he would not let himself be tranquilized by promises and hedging. He had no need of
excursions into the history of Russo-Polish relations. He knew the way
things would go in Poland, on the basis of what had happened in
Hungary and Czechoslovakia. Poland had to be reconquered. There
was no getting away from that, no matter what it cost—even if it cost
Russia more than Hungary and Czechoslovakia had. Andropov's calculation was simple. It was based on an arithmetic summation of the
results that followed the suppression of Hungary and Czechoslovakia:
one year of foreign obstruction and twelve years of internal stability in
the Soviet empire.

If it had not been for Poland, Andropov would have backed Carter.

The American hostages would have been freed before November 4, 1980; Carter's indecisive diplomatic tactics would have been justified; and the Americans, in one big surge of patriotism, would have elected Carter to a second term. But that didn't happen, because Andropov was removing all obstacles that might hinder the Red army on its way into Poland. What mattered to him was not who would be in the White House but who would *not* be there: Zbigniew Brzezinski.

If, in a paradoxical way, Andropov was obliged to Carter (with his human-rights campaign) for strengthening the KGB's position and, in the final analysis, for the KGB chief's victories over his rivals and his accession to power, in a no less paradoxical way Ronald Reagan is obliged to Andropov for his victory in the 1980 election. The issue of the hostages was the hottest one at the time; and if they had been freed before the election, its outcome might have been quite different.

Now Andropov had to make haste. It would have been hard to imagine a more convenient moment in international relations for an invasion of Poland than the transitional period in the White House, when the top officials of the outgoing administration were giving up their jobs, and the new ones had not yet taken over. Andropov and his military advisors decided to replicate the experiment they had made in Afghanistan and, without waiting for the Politburo's sanction, to act at their own risk once again. The jump-off for the operation was set for early December, when Brezhnev was to leave on an official visit to India, accompanied by his ceremonial retinue. Andropov immediately put his military advisor, Commander-in-Chief of the Warsaw Treaty Organization Forces Victor Kulikov, in direct charge of the Polish operation. Reservists were called up for service in the armed forces—not for three weeks, as was usual for routine training maneuvers, but for six weeks. A continuous stream of vehicles carrying Soviet troops moved along all roads leading to the Polish border. At the very border, in spite of the freezing cold, five crack divisions were positioned under field conditions—in tents, dugouts, and trenches—a situation that was supposed to last for a few days at the most.

The troops were put on Red Alert. An unprecedented anti-Polish campaign was launched in the Soviet press; and its tone left no doubt that it was intended to accompany an invasion of Poland by Soviet troops.

On the night of December 4 the Central Committee of the Polish Workers' Party issued a statement beginning with the words: "Citizens, the fate of the nation and the country is hanging by a thread."

That same night Radio Warsaw announced an extraordinary session of the Polish Defense Committee called by War Minister General Wojciech Jaruzelski to discuss "the problems faced by the army in the situation that has developed." Never before had that potent but secret organ of power announced its sessions; and it had never issued any statements.

A catastrophe seemed inevitable: the Soviet forces had been ordered to advance. There was a moment when it looked as if the Red army was already moving in on Poland, and some TV commentators reported that army units had begun to cross the Polish border. There had been no more dangerous point of time in Polish history since the Wehrmacht had attacked the country on September 1, 1939.

What saved Poland (this time) from occupation, Russia from shame, and mankind (possibly) from World War III? Who brought the galloping steed to a halt when he had already put one hoof over the abyss? Why were TASS's morning bulletins on the counterrevolution in Poland, which were supposed to supply the ideological grounds for its occupation, suddenly withdrawn from the daytime and evening news? What made the Kremlin, at the very last moment, backpedal and cancel the order to advance?

Politicians and journalists have tried to guess what it was that stopped the Russians from sending their troops into Poland to suppress the continuing revolution. Was it Western public opinion? A fear of economic, diplomatic, and political countermeasures from America and its allies? Or fear of the Pope, who is supposed to have sent a letter to Brezhnev threatening to return to his homeland in order to head up resistance to the aggressor?

Undoubtedly, these things played an auxiliary role, along with the main reason. But by themselves they could not—either separately, or in their totality—have held back the Red army. It was stopped by General Jaruzelski's warning that in case of a Soviet invasion, he would order his troops to fight. In December 1980 the Polish leaders told Brezhnev the same thing that Wladyslaw Gomulka had told Khrushchev fourteen years before, in October 1956, thereby saving Poland from the fate that overtook Hungary two weeks later. And once again, what was at stake was nothing more nor less than a Soviet-Polish war, its outcome an X factor.

The history of Russo-Polish wars includes, over a period of several centuries in a row, some defeats that were very painful to the Russians, among them the Poles' capture of Moscow early in the seventeenth century and, closer to our own time, their seizure of Minsk and Kiev in the Soviet-Polish war of 1920, plus the Red army's humiliating defeat near Warsaw. The Russians' traditional *military fear* of the Poles was not the least of the reasons for the catastrophe in the Katyn Forest, where Stalin had ten thousand Polish officers killed. And was not that fear also one of the reasons for the Russians' nonintervention (actually, their betrayal of the Poles) in August 1944, when officers of the Red army, on the east bank of the Vistula, watched through field glasses as the Germans, on the other bank, rained down death and destruction on insurgent Warsaw?

In order to take Czechoslovakia in 1968, the Soviet Union had to send in 600,000 troops. The Russians figured they needed that many to be on the safe side, although the Czechoslovak army did not fire a single shot in response to the Soviet marauding. The Polish army is the largest in Eastern Europe: 317,500 troops, not counting the police and security forces. And unlike the Czechoslovak army, it is patriotic, nationalistic, and full of fighting spirit. If the Polish cavalry ("the best in Europe," as the Poles naïvely boasted) even tried to oppose the Wehrmacht's tanks, that is all the more reason to expect resistance in our time, when the Polish army is equipped with the same Soviet rockets, tanks, and aircraft as the "fraternal" army of the potential aggressors. The only difference in armanent between the two forces is the atomic weapon, which the Russians have and the Poles do not. But at the time, its use against Poland was ruled out, since for the moment the Russians had not even decided to use it in a preventive strike against their preeminent enemy, China. (This despite a very strong temptation, because in that global confrontation time is plainly not on the side of the Russians.)

As for the number of Soviet troops that might have been sent in to pacify the unruly Poles, the Russians' possibilities were limited—if only because of the fact that they were fighting a war in Afghanistan at that time, and because one-fourth of the Soviet army was being held in a condition of combat readiness on the Chinese border. (One of the jokes being told in Moscow in those days linked Russia's two worst enemies: "Why are Russian soldiers studying Polish?" "Because the Chinese troops won't stop until they hear it spoken.")

The greatest number of troops that the Russian dared send into

Poland was that same six hundred thousand that had been sent in to crush the Prague Spring. The war probably would have been one between numerically equal forces. Because Poland, threatened by no one but Russia, would have been able to commit its entire regular army to combat; and it would certainly have been bolstered by volunteers and partisans. Qualitatively, the Polish army would have had a distinct advantage over the Red army, since along with Soviet weapons it would have had a huge psychological arsenal: the Poles' historical hatred of the Russians, resentment over lost territory, and a thirst for revenge (for the Katyn Forest massacre, to name only one thing). Then, too, the war would have been fought on its own soil; and troops fight harder when defending their own country than when attacking another. One should not forget the fierce winter of 1939–40, when little Finland, with a population one-ninth that of Poland, heroically defended itself against the Russian invaders. (According to Khrushchev, the "Winter War" cost Russia one million casualties, while costing the Finns twenty-four thousand.) One should also imagine the Russian soldier, possessed by doubts and fears, and acting only with the muzzle of a machine carbine at his back (the special KGB units in the army).

Of course, one cannot rule out the question as to who would have been the more resolute: the Poles in defending their own country, or the Russians in defending their empire? No good answer to that question could be found, particularly in the Kremlin; so that among the Politburo members, a sensible pragmatism got the upper hand over unbridled fantasy. This was a contretemps for Andropov—but, he no doubt hoped, a temporary one. At that time the Polish revolution was entering a new phase—one of anarchy in the streets and a political power vacuum. Andropov now placed his main bet on that situation. Anarchy would supposedly corrode the Polish nation to the point where it would be incapable of military resistance to Moscow. The only role left to it would be that of a kamikaze, which would have suited Andropov just fine.

Anyone looking through the Soviet papers for 1981 is struck by the fact that the most sinister threats from the Kremlin came during those brief periods of social and political calm in Poland: what Andropov feared above all was political harmony among the Poles. In order to block it, he made use of the Soviet mass media, ascribing to Solidarity's leaders words they had never uttered and actions they had never performed. For him it was important to radicalize the Polish worker movement, to provoke even greater political polarization in that country, to bring civic passions up to the boiling point, to split Poland asunder and render it feeble and defenseless in the face of Soviet aggression. Meantime, the question as to whether to eliminate or neutralize the leaders of the Polish resistance—Stefan Cardinal Wyszynski, Pope John Paul II, and Lech Walesa—was left undecided.

As a person who paid little heed to the limitations of reality, Andropov had failed to allow for yet another possibility: the appearance in Poland of a man who would see the situation there just as he (Andropov) did but would draw opposite conclusions, because he was guided by Poland's interests and not Russia's. The Polish anarchy, in which Andropov placed his chief hope for the empire, was regarded by that man as the chief danger to his own country. For all his fertile imagination, Andropov's mode of thought was crude and bureaucratic. While he was preoccupied with enemies among the Polish clerics and labor leaders, Russia's most dangerous adversary in Poland was gathering strength in the segment regarded by the Kremlin as the most reliable: the Polish Army, which came under the general command of the Warsaw Pact forces. In February 1981 General Wojciech Jaruzelski became prime minister, while keeping his portfolio as minister of defense; and in October he was elected first secretary of the ruling party, while retaining both of his other posts. The case was unprecedented in Eastern Europe. Andropov would have realized all its sinister implications for Russia if he had so much as taken the time to look into the Polish laws, under which the Polish Defense Committee consists of three persons: the first secretary of the Party, the chairman of the Council of Ministers, and the minister of defense. Now the entire Polish Defense Committee consisted of one man: Wojciech Jaruzelski. In addition to taking into his own hands a record number of command posts, General Jaruzelski militarized both the government cabinet and the Party's Politburo in the course of 1981, bringing into both bodies generals who were loyal to him. Also, he organized special military detachments to combat corruption and anarchy; he retained in military service some forty thousand soldiers scheduled for discharge; and finally, he restored the military cult of the Polish heroes, Tadeusz Kosciuszko and Jozef Pilsudski, despite the fact that they were thrice-damned enemies of Russia. (Or was it precisely because of that?)

All these things were direct preparations for a Polish "18th Bru-maire," which in fact took place on the night of December 13, 1981—just as unexpectedly for Russian observers as for Western ones. Jaru-zelski had planned his military coup well. And if the Russians had been his sponsors, as the majority of American experts believe, it would not have been necessary for Andropov to get Zbigniew Brzezin-ski out of the way by taking part in the American election on Reagan's side, or to make careful preparations for attempts on the life of the Pope and the leader of Solidarity.

There is a Russian saying, "Brave before a lamb, but a lamb before the brave." In his power struggle against the Kremlin gerontocrats, Andropov had perfected his talent for scheming, but at the same time he had simplified his thinking. Intellectually, the Polish general was head and shoulders above him, and our hero could not surmise his designs.

Andropov had made a good showing against the Kremlin back-ground. But what he was measuring himself against was at such a low level (a bunch of oldsters) that ultimately he became unused to free competition; and both the background and the milieu began to have a negative influence on him, dulling his sharpness, for which there was no real need in that situation. Here another saying is apropos: *"Au royaume des aveugles les borgnes sont rois."* (In the kingdom of the blind, one-eyed people are kings.) That is the main reason for Andropov's being a winner in Moscow and a loser in Poland.

In "the kingdom of the blind" he also had to beat a temporary retreat in early March 1981 at the Twenty-sixth Party Congress. He brought several of his deputies into the Central Committee; but he did not manage to make Geidar Aliyev, his Azerbaijani protégé, a member of the Politburo and thereby strengthen his own position in that anachronistic organ of power.

The Dnepropetrovsk Mafia, although no longer in a position to dismiss Andropov, tied him hand and foot. The invasion of Afghani-stan, in which he took pride as a personal success, was held against him: he had exceeded his authority and violated Party discipline. The campaign against him was led by Andrei Kirilenko, his antagonist since youth, when both had lived in the same Volga town, Rybinsk. Kirilenko insisted that Andropov be removed from his post as KGB chairman, while keeping his membership in the Politburo. Andropov managed to intercept this conversation between Brezhnev and Kirilenko; and for the moment he even forgot about Poland as he summoned up all his energy and skill at intrigue to ward off the blow that was about to fall on him. Although it was risky, he was ready, in case of extreme need, to carry out a coup and take the power into his own hands. Apparently Brezhnev realized this. Or, more accurately, Andropov let him know it quite unequivocally. Instead of dismissing Andropov from his post as KGB chairman, it was decided to give more power to his first deputy, Brezhnev's relative-in-law, General Semyon Tsvigun.

The year 1981 was, throughout, one of dual sovereignty. Or, to put it another way, one of a struggle between two squares: Red Square, the traditional center of Soviet power, and Dzerzhinsky Square, the new focus of power. Between the two there was less and less communication and more and more conflict. This was most obvious when it came to the Polish question, in which the two factions—Brezhnev's and Andropov's—crossed swords.

A constant stream of Soviet visitors flowed into Poland. Brezhnev sent secretaries and members of the Politburo and Central Committee, and Andropov sent military men—above all, Marshal Kulikov. Andropov managed to get his man Mieczyslaw Moczar back into the Polish Politburo. Although he didn't stay there long—when the ballots were cast at the July congress of the Polish Workers' Party, he didn't even make it into the Central Committee—Moczar was apparently responsible for Poland's again seeking out the tried-and-true scapegoat for the disasters that had befallen that country: the Jews. Anti-Semitic articles, leaflets, pamphlets, and graffiti on buildings declared the Jews were responsible for the activities of the free trade unions.

This all sounded rather strange, since Moczar had driven the last Jews out of Poland. (Out of the ten million members of Solidarity, it was hard to scrape up a few dozen Jews.) It is likely that Moczar and the chauvinistic group "Grünewald" were merely being used as tools in this belated and inapt wave of anti-Semitism, and that it was being directed—on the basis of the earlier Czechoslovak model—by Andropov, who, as always, was seeing the phenomena of East European dissent in general terms. He was ignoring the specifically Polish nature of the dissent in that country, and was apparently too busy to notice that there were almost no Jews left there. In view of that widely known fact, it would hardly have occurred to a Pole to blame the Jews for such a purely Polish phenomenon as Solidarity. The leaders of both the free trade unions and the Polish Communists sharply repudiated the anti-Semitic attacks, regarding them—quite correctly—as the work of provocateurs.

They were also preparatory measures. In late March, shortly after the start of the campaign against the absent Polish Jews, the Soviet Union began again to concentrate troops on the Polish border. At the same time, Soviet, Polish, and other East European forces carried out joint exercises on Polish territory. It is hard to say with certainty whether this was a real threat or just ordinary blackmail. But whatever it was, Moscow's military preparations did not, this time, reach the same dangerous apogee as in early December 1980.

In April the Kremlin power struggle unexpectedly came out in the open at the Sixteenth Congress of the Communist Party of Czechoslovakia, where an unaccountable thing happened—an incident noticed by all the Western observers, and not explained by any of them. In the course of a seventy-nine-page speech at that congress, the Czechoslovak leader, Gustav Husak, flatly declared that "antisocialist forces in Poland, supported and incited by foreign enemies of socialism, are trying to carry out a counterrevolution in that fraternal country." Reminding his audience of Brezhnev's so-called doctrine of limited sovereignty, which had served to justify the Soviet invasion of Czechoslovakia in 1968, Husak ominously warned that "the defense of the socialist system is the common concern of the states of the socialist community."

This was a preamble to a military action in Poland, and was understood as such by everyone who heard the Czechoslovak leader's speech.

The next day, however, the delegates to the congress were addressed by a guest from Moscow: Leonid Ilich Brezhnev, who had actually been brought to Prague in an ambulance plane, so sick and feeble had he become. Unlike the usual marathon speeches, Brezhnev's welcoming speech was eleven pages long and took only twenty-two minutes. What amazed everyone, though, was not its brevity but its conciliatory, moderate tone vis-à-vis Poland—especially as compared with the main speaker's head-on attack on that country.

Why was Husak more of a papist than the pope? There can be only one reason for that: as Andropov's protégé and direct subordinate, he was acting on orders that came straight from the KGB chief. Brezhnev, on the other hand, in spite of the ailments that were besetting him, had been sent to Prague to defend the more moderate viewpoint of the Dnepropetrovsk faction.

Almost immediately after Brezhnev's speech, TASS announced the suspension of the military maneuvers in and around Poland, which might at any moment have turned into armed aggression.

The next month Andropov suffered yet another setback. On May 13, 1981, in St. Peter's Square in Rome, the Turkish terrorist Mehmet Ali Agca fired several shots at the Polish spiritual leader, Pope John Paul II. Although badly wounded, the Pope was not killed.

The attempt on the Pope's life created a worldwide sensation. But it produced its greatest impression in the Kremlin, on Andropov's colleagues and rivals in the Politburo: one of his worst failures on the international scene had become one of his biggest successes at home. It took the American journalists and Italian investigators months to discover that the right-wing Turkish terrorist's motives had nothing to do with fanaticism or ideology but were strictly mercenary. His compatriot Bekir Celenk had promised him $1.25 million for the murder of the Roman Pontiff—something in which Celenk, a businessman and smuggler who was acting on orders from his Bulgarian bosses, had no interest. The latter would likewise have been indifferent to the Pope's fate except for the fact that *their* bosses, operating out of Dzerzhinsky Square in Moscow, had something to gain from the Pontiff's death. But for that—which in Rome and Washington demanded thorough investigation—experience, intuition, and fear sufficed in the Kremlin: "Obviousness is diminished by proofs," as Seneca said. Brezhnev was not let in on Andropov's plan. Because if he had been, then judging from all his earlier, relatively pragmatic policies, he would never have approved it. It was precisely for such a reason that he had no advance knowledge of it.

On the other hand, Andropov could not but have known of it. In the line of official duty, because of his earlier professionalization in East European affairs, and, finally, out of personal inspiration, he was the chief planner of the pacification of Poland, in spite of all the monkey wrenches thrown into the machinery by his Party colleagues from Brezhnev's Dnepropetrovsk cohort. Both in December 1980 and in March-April 1981, he had failed secretly to prepare for an invasion of Poland, so as to present the indecisive Kremlin oldsters with a *fait accompli*. Hence he did not consider it necessary to increase the number of those privy to his plot against John Paul II. The Kremlin gerontocrats were, in fact, presented with a *fait accompli*; and the turmoil in their camp was even greater than that in the Vatican. Now none of them had any more doubts as to just what kind of man was among them. From their viewpoint this was a resolute return to the Stalin era, with its intrigues, craftiness, murders, and fear. None of them had any concern for the Pope: they were thinking only of themselves and of their total defenselessness before that enigmatic man with the ambiguous smile on his thin lips and the nearsighted eyes behind his thick glasses. If he had tried to have the Pope killed, he would not hesitate to do the same thing to any of them who got in his way. Thus the shots fired in St. Peter's Square—which, thanks to a miracle and the skill of the Italian doctors, did not prove fatal to the Pope—did become fatal for the Kremlin gerontocrats. Beginning on May 13, 1981, the Stalinist terror returned to the Kremlin. To sum up, Mehmet Ali Agca's failure in Rome sufficed, nonetheless, for Andropov's triumph in Moscow. Because for a future tyrant, there is no better weapon than terror.

The consequences of that terror had their effect on the age-old customs of the Kremlin within two weeks after the incident in Rome. On May 25, in violation of previous protocol, Brezhnev was brought to the building on Dzerzhinsky Square for a conference of the Committee of State Security (KGB). Neither Brezhnev himself nor any of his predecessors—not even Stalin—had ever dared cross the threshold of that building, the most sinister in Moscow, and perhaps in the whole world. On this occasion Andropov behaved like a zealous host, but he made no effort to conceal his triumph. His gloating smile never left his lips as he showed Brezhnev—already sufficiently frightened—the historical sights of his castle. It was like the account given by the renowned French writer and traveller, the Marquis de Custine, who got the permission of Emperor Nicholas I to visit the Shlisselburg Fortress, a notorious prison: once he got there, he was overcome by the fear that he would never again be set free.

The Soviet newspapers published brief items on Brezhnev's visit to the KGB headquarters, thereby stressing the new importance of that organization and its enigmatic chief in the ruling hierarchy.

Unfortunately, we do not know whether Brezhnev, in the course of his unusual visit to the headquarters of the secret police, asked its chief about the attempted assassination in St. Peter's Square. Most likely he didn't, because such a question would have demanded a great deal of courage.

One other person who, besides Brezhnev, could not have had advance knowledge of the plan for an attempt on the life of the Pope was Todor Zhivkov, the leader of the country ordered to carry out that plan. Here in America there is a tendency to exaggerate Bulgaria's loyalty to its imperial patron. In any case, in the late seventies that country began to show signs of separatist and pro-Western tendencies associated with the name of Todor Zhivkov's daughter Ludmilla, who by that time had become a member of the Politburo and one of the most influential Bulgarian leaders. But that trend was suddenly broken off. Stanko Todorov, a close friend of Todor Zhivkov's and a supporter of his daughter, was replaced as prime minister by the Soviet puppet Grisha Filipov. (Filipov was born in the Ukraine and was a graduate of Moscow University.) Shortly thereafter, in March 1981, came a report of the sudden death of the thirty-eight-year-old Ludmilla Zhivkova—due, according to the official version, to overwork. Whereupon the seventy-year-old Bulgarian leader disappeared from the political scene for a long time, reappearing only at Brezhnev's funeral.

Ludmilla Zhivkova's tragic death, which occurred only two months before the attempt on the Pope's life, came two and a half years after the mysterious "umbrella incidents." In the first of these, a Bulgarian political émigré named Vladimir Kostov who was living in Paris, was found to have been seriously poisoned after being jabbed by someone's umbrella. Ten days later, in London, another Bulgarian political émigré, Georgi Markov, died a few days after a stranger had "chanced" to jab him with the point of his umbrella in Waterloo Station. When he heard about the death of his compatriot, Kostov (who by this time had recovered) went for a medical examination and X rays. It was discovered that a miniaturized platinum ball about the size of a pinhead, containing a virulent poison, had been fitted into the point of the umbrella. Chemical analysis showed that the poison was ricin, a substance extracted from castor oil, one ounce of which is enough to kill ninety thousand people. According to Western intelligence agencies, experiments with ricin are being intensively carried out in Hungary and Czechoslovakia.

Yet another Bulgarian political émigré, Vladimir Simeonov, died in London that same year under mysterious circumstances. When a correspondent asked the Bulgarian embassy in London to comment on all these strange incidents, he was told he had read too many novels by Agatha Christie.

Actually, according to the Bulgarian defectors Stefan Svirdlev and Iordan Mantarov, both former officers of the *Derzhavna Sigurnost* (the Bulgarian secret police), agents of that organization often take no less risks than some of Agatha Christie's characters. Unlike the latter, however, they usually come out unscathed. In all the above incidents, one can discern the signature of the Derzhavna Sigurnost, described by the writer Georgi Markov (later killed by its agents at Waterloo station) as "nothing other than the strong arm of the KGB in our country." (The Derzhavna Sigurnost was in fact founded by the Soviet occupation authorities in 1944.)

It was the Sigurnost that Andropov put in charge of "wet jobs," although the murder of Markov and the attempted murder of Kostov were probably done on the Sigurnost's own initiative. At the same time, however, they provided good training for international operations ordered by the Soviet Union. So that Andropov winked at the Sigurnost's reprisals against its own dissidents: he had always been fond of rehearsals in vassal republics and countries. And he trusted Bulgaria—insofar as his "distrustful" trade allowed him to trust anyone. The Sigurnost was headed up by his protégé, Dimiter Stoyanov, who had been trained at the KGB's Advanced Intelligence School in Moscow, had worked for the KGB abroad, and was now apparently being groomed as Todor Zhivkov's successor, following the recent Caucasian-Moscow model.

This book is being written concurrently with the investigation being conducted in Rome by Judge Ilario Martella; and it is quite possible that the trial in Italy of Sergei Antonov, the Bulgarian accomplice in the attempt on the Pope's life, will coincide with the publication of this book about Yuri Andropov. It would be absurd for us, therefore, to try and substitute our conjectures for the work of the Italian investigators—especially since, despite all the attention that incident has received in the world press, it is not essential to this biography. If the Vatican were a more democratic institution, and Popes were elected not for life but for a fixed term, Andropov would have tried to eliminate that "turbulent priest," Christ's vicar, by peaceful means—without resorting to help from Turks and Bulgarians. After all, no one shot at Zbigniew Brzezinski, even though

Andropov regarded him as the invisible source of the Polish evil. True, it looks as if there was also a Bulgarian-Turkish-Italian plot against the life of Lech Walesa. But again, this was because Walesa—although his was an elective position—had contrived to become Poland's labor leader (as the Pope was its spiritual leader) in a sense that was symbolic rather than merely official.

In terms of its ramifications, Andropov's scheme to eliminate the three Polish leaders at one fell swoop and thereby deprive the Polish revolution of its helmsmen can be regarded as, if not perhaps ingenious, then in any case grandiose, almost fantastic. Because of the last-named attribute, it could not wholly succeed: such an ideal scheme demanded equally ideal execution—something impossible in the real world. And once again, it was reality that got in the way of Andropov's calculations.

The noteworthy fact, though, is the sharp difference between Andropov's and Stalin's views of the Roman Pontiff. Stalin doubted the Pope's power, and even repeated (quite venomously) Napoleon's question: "How many divisions does the Pope have?" By contrast, Andropov realized that in certain situations one man can take the place of a whole army. He himself had done that when, during several days in Budapest, he had—at the risk of his own life—represented the Red army while making ready for its arrival. Unlike the Roman Pontiff, he was then operating covertly. But as head of the secret police he sensed a clandestine anti-Soviet plot behind every public speech the Pope made, whether or not there really was such a conspiracy. It was his métier to discover plots, and when none really existed, he used his imagination to create them where they rightly should have been, according to his notions and suspicions. Had it not been for Andropov's imagination, Mehmet Ali Agca would not have shot at John Paul II. Instead, he would have gone on serving out his term in a Turkish prison for the murder of the liberal journalist Abdi Ipekci. But on the night of November 23, 1979, he made his improbable escape from that prison so as to carry out (after eighteen months of training with the Bulgars and Palestinians) the orders of the future Soviet vozhd.

At the time, it must have seemed to Andropov that he had cleverly and completely covered his tracks. That a Turkish fanatic from the fascist organization called "The Gray Wolves" should be working for the KGB was simply beyond belief. And in any case, the trail from Dzerzhinsky Square to St. Peter's Square was so long, with so many quirky turns and so many straw men along it, that there was no possibility of retracing it, even if a genius in search of the truth had set out to do so. Finally, and most important: Andropov's fingerprints would not be found on Mehmet Ali Agca's pistol.

But while Andropov had gained more power in the Kremlin because of the incident in St. Peter's Square, he had not progressed by so much as an inch in settling the Polish crisis. True, Stefan Cardinal Wyszynski had died of cancer that summer. But both Lech Walesa and Pope John Paul II were still alive; and they were obstacles in the Red army's path into Poland, although not the main obstacle. The main one was the Polish army. With each passing day, however, Poland was sinking ever more deeply into the abyss of anarchy, so that the army's resistance was becoming increasingly doubtful.

While Suslov, Grishin, Ogarkov, and Kulikov were making plane trips to Warsaw (Kulikov, indeed, hardly ever left Warsaw), Andropov did not make one single visit to Poland. He preferred having everything done by the hands of others—Turks, Bulgarians, Russians, but in any case someone else—so that his own hands might remain spotless should he accede to power; and that accession seemed very near at hand and almost inevitable. He was not afraid of a bloodbath in Poland: not merely because he could blame it on Brezhnev but because he felt that a bloodbath was an affordable price for tranquility in the empire.

As was said before, there was one flaw in his calculations about Poland. He had not yet realized that along with himself another man—a Pole—was looking at the Polish situation in connection with the quarrels in the Kremlin. And if at first that Pole did not even figure in Andropov's plans, since for him all Poles were equally suspect and there had to be "one Russian sentry" for each of them, General Jaruzelski, in his own plans, placed a good deal of importance on Andropov as Poland's chief enemy and the man most likely to succeed Brezhnev. In that lay the distinct superiority of Jaruzelski's schemes over Andropov's. The latter was watching Poland as a whole, without seeing either the concrete differences between Poland on the one hand and Hungary and Czechoslovakia on the other, or the differences between one Pole and another. But Jaruzelski, through his dark glasses, closely scrutinized the faces of the Russian visitors, surmising that the Kremlin's top specialist on Eastern Europe was staying back in Moscow all the time and setting a trap for Poland. For Jaruzelski it was essential to forestall Andropov at any cost; and the attempt on the Pope's life made him even more resolute: he realized that Andropov would stop at nothing to pacify Poland. So on Sunday, December 13, 1981, when the Soviet threats were coming thick and fast, and it was no longer possible to tell blackmail from reality, General Jaruzelski carried out a palace coup in Poland. He suspended all civil liberties, banned all activity by both Solidarity and the Communist Party, and took all the power into his own hands.

"It is very regrettable that in such cases human nature is obliged to resort to force. But on the other hand, it cannot be denied that this is the highest tribute to truth and justice." Those words of José Ortega y Gasset apply with full force to the Polish general. In paying the highest tribute to truth and justice, he saved his country from a foreign occupation, thereby avoiding a bloody war. He did something that neither the two East European schismatics, Imre Nagy of Hungary and Alexander Dubcek of Czechoslovakia, nor their conformist successors, Janos Kadar and Gustav Husak, had been able to do for their countries.

Jaruzelski's actions were so unequivocal that one can only be amazed at the epithets—not only belittling but, above all, unjust—conferred on him by influential but shortsighted Americans: epithets ranging from "a Russian puppet" (*New York Times* columnist William Safire) to "a Russian general in a Polish uniform" (Secretary of Defense Caspar Weinberger). With his first decree the dictator of Poland closed the Polish borders—that country, of course, being bordered only by the Soviet Union and its satellites—and banned any foreign aircraft from landing on Polish airfields. That is to say, he blocked the very possibility of a Soviet invasion—probably at the very last moment.

He established martial law with the aid of police, security troops, and special units to combat anarchy and corruption, while the entire army of more than three hundred thousand troops was kept in reserve in a state of combat readiness to provide against foreign intervention. Dozens of Party conservatives, headed by former Polish leader Edward Gierek, were arrested. General Moczar, Andropov's representative in Poland, was not even taken into the ruling Military Council. And within a short time—after his attempts, on orders from Andropov and in accordance with the Andropov model, to charge General Jaruzelski with corruption—he was completely eliminated from

Polish political life. The Central Committee and local Party organizations—indeed, most organizations headed by Communists—were put
out of action. On radio and television the Polish national anthem was
played instead of the "Internationale." For the first time, the red and
white national banner was hoisted alongside the red flag atop the
Central Committee building. Even in the proclamation of martial law,
and in later official mentions, Jaruzelski was referred to as a general
and the prime minister; while, very significantly, no mention was
made of his title as first secretary of the Party—the highest one by
Moscow standards. A month after the coup a new paper—the organ of
Jaruzelski's military regime—began to appear in Warsaw, supple-
menting (and partially opposing) the Party newspaper, *Trybuna ludu*.
Symbolically, that paper was named *Rzeczpospolita*, which in literal
translation means "republic." But in historical terms it means much
more: it was the name of the Polish state from the time of the Lublin
Union of 1569 until Poland vanished from the map in 1775, when it
was partitioned by Austria, Prussia, and Russia. Invoking that parallel
was an act of pride and desperate boldness.

All this might have been seen as a façade if Poland were not now
headed by military men for whom, on the contrary, the façade facing
toward the east—toward that suspect Mecca, Moscow—was their *pro
forma* membership in the Communist Party. (Incidentally, Poland's
prewar dictator, Marshal Pilsudski, had a similar façade: in his youth,
he was a Socialist.)

General Jaruzelski had managed to do the very thing that Solidarity's farthest-out extremists had unsuccessfully called for: to eliminate from the nation's political life those Communists for whom
loyalty to the Party card meant more than loyalty to Poland.

What with all the emotional reaction to the military coup in Poland, few people noticed that the man who initiated the coup was
fighting on two fronts at the same time—against Polish anarchy and
Russian might. He was combatting Polish anarchy in order to neutralize Russian might. In other words, he was fighting to create a strong
Poland capable of opposing Russia on its own. Because in that conflict, inevitable for reasons of geography, no one else could help his
country—not America, not Western Europe, and not even the Vatican, with a Polish Pope at its head. From far away across the ocean, it
was easy and safe to try and guess whether the Red Army would or
would not invade Poland, just as in old Russia, a crowd of commoners

watching a beheading would try to guess whether the head would fall to the left or to the right. But things were different in Poland, especially for the military men who bore the heavy responsibility for the nation's sovereignty.

The military took power into their own hands only after they had become convinced that Solidarity was unable to carry out its own program of reforms without jeopardizing the very existence of Poland. Solidarity turned out to be a political interlude—or, to put it in sports terminology, a pinch hitter. It had managed to throw the old regime off balance, but it couldn't replace it. In destroying the prestige of the Party, Solidarity cleared the way for the army. With the military coup of December 13, 1981, the army declared itself responsible for the fate of the republic. The Polish revolution had passed from the hands of the workers into those of the military men.

Such is the nature of revolutions; their scope is international: they develop in a zigzag pattern, retrogressing and even undoing their own master pattern en route. And such is the eternal antithesis of revolution, its gigantic pendulum swinging from anarchy to dictatorship.

(In spite of its military dictatorship, Poland remains the freest country in Eastern Europe. Antigovernment demonstrations, a free church, and official recognition of the workers' right to strike—these things are quite impossible in any other country of Eastern Europe.)

By making his tragic choice between Poland's freedom and its independence—by transforming the country into an armed camp in a condition of combat readiness—General Jaruzelski deprived the Kremlin of any choice, putting an end to its Hamletesque doubt and internal debates. As things now stood, an attack on Poland would mean the beginning of a war. And how long it would last, or how it would end, nobody knew, or knows.

So it is that although *Time* magazine chose Lech Walesa as its Man of the Year for 1981, and displayed on its cover his portrait as hero and martyr (sketched in the best traditions of socialist realism), the real hero of the year was another Pole, the antihero of the Polish revolution—the man who actually saved it and continued it.

Jaruzelski's military coup came as a complete surprise to the Kremlin. And it was the greatest defeat Yuri Andropov had ever suffered: the Polish general had forestalled him and outperformed him. The weapons that Andropov had used to gain victories in Moscow, Budapest, and Prague proved worthless in Poland.

Andropov's Ultimatum

9

Vogue la galère!

On December 19, 1981, the seventy-fifth birthday of Leonid Ilich Brezhnev was commemorated with great ceremony in the Kremlin. It was fated to be the last birthday celebration of his life.

It is hard to say just to what extent the Kremlin vozhd was conscious of what was going on around him. Sick and feeble after several strokes and heart attacks, with poorly controlled bodily movements, a stumbling gait, taut, immobile facial muscles, stammering and incoherent speech, and heavy, irregular breathing, he made a painful impression. His birthdays were the last source of comfort for this old man fallen into his second childhood. The year before, in order not to cast a pall over his birthday, it had even been necessary to postpone for several days the news of Premier Kosygin's death, which had occurred on the very eve of the scheduled celebration. Brezhnev grew sentimental and wept at the mention of his own name, while being presented with gifts and decorations. On his seventy-fifth birthday there were especially many of the latter: in addition to Soviet decorations, he was awarded the highest orders of the people's democracies, brought to him by their leaders. Thus when the president of Afghanistan, Babrak Karmal, pinned the Afghan Order of Freedom to his chest, the old man from the Kremlin embraced the grateful satrap, kissed him three times, and broke into tears.

Did Brezhnev notice that among the decorations he was awarded that day, there was none from Poland? And did he notice the absence, among his guests, of the Polish dictator Wojciech Jaruzelski, who just a week before had carried out a military coup? Of course Jaruzelski had no time for birthday parties: he had plenty to do at home. Still, it was a serious violation of the Kremlin's Levantine protocol. And if he himself couldn't come, he could at least have sent a decoration.

But not only was this a more liberal era than that of Stalin, the people in the Kremlin had little time to worry about Jaruzelski; because behind the façade of paeans and congratulations to the senile old man festooned with decorations and other regalia, a power struggle was entering its decisive phase. Actually, the situation in Russia was no less tense (if not even more so) than that in Poland, although the Russian drama, unlike the Polish one, was being played out not in the streets but in offices; and the birthday party in the Kremlin gave an added stimulus to its action.

As for Brezhnev himself, he took almost no part in that power struggle because of his failing health. It is most likely that he didn't even notice the absence of Wojciech Jaruzelski at his birthday fête. To the contrary, the presence of the proud Polish general, with his ramrod-stiff back and his very dark glasses, would have struck a dissonant note at the festivities. It would no doubt have been (to use the Russian expression) like a spoonful of tar in that barrel of honey that the Soviet chieftain was tasting for the last time.

Significantly, it was that very occasion which marked the beginning of the misadventures that dogged Brezhnev for the rest of his life. For however useful the moribund leader was as a screen for Andropov's complex maneuvers, toward the end the KGB chief began to show signs of impatience, and radically changed his tactics. While continuing to vie with Brezhnev's official heirs, he launched a campaign against the leader himself. When Brezhnev finally died, Muscovites joked that Andropov hadn't replaced his pacemaker battery in time. One thing, however, is clear: Andropov had begun to dig his predecessor's grave even before he died. And the first shovelful was dug on Brezhnev's last birthday.

In Leningrad a magazine for young people, dealing with both literary and political subjects, is published under the title of *Aurora*. It is named not after the Greek goddess of the dawn but after the cruiser which, during the night of October 25, 1917, fired several blank shots at the Winter Palace, where at the time the provisional government was in session. In so doing, it signalled the beginning of a new era: the next morning the Bolsheviks seized power in Russia.

In late 1981 that same magazine, with its proud revolutionary name and more-than-reliable reputation, printed in its December issue, which was devoted to Brezhnev's seventy-fifth birthday and adorned with his portrait on the cover, an out-and-out lampoon of him appropriately titled "Birthday Speech," and even symbolically appearing on page 75! This was something unexampled in the censored Soviet press.

The subject of this comic sketch was an anonymous but easily recognizable old man who "to everyone's amazement, isn't even thinking about dying." Its author was Victor Golyavkin of Leningrad, well known for his absurdist writings. Openly parodying the frequent rumors of Brezhnev's death, he wrote: "The day before yesterday, I heard that he had died, and I freely admit that I was filled with joy and pride. But my joy was premature. I hope, however, that we won't have to wait for long. He won't disappoint us. We all believe in him so! Let's hope that he completes the work that he still has in hand, and gladdens our hearts as soon as possible."

Incidentally, in this satirical sketch the old man's profession was given as that of a writer—something which in no way contravened Brezhnev's image. To the contrary, it was a subtle send-up of a certain trait in the official panegyrics of Brezhnev which in recent years had taken on a hyperbolic and even indecent character. Three volumes of his memoirs had been published, in many languages and in printings of millions. They had been recommended for reading even by schoolchildren; and their author had been given the highest literary award, the Lenin Prize, which is more or less like the Goncourt in France or the Pulitzer in America. Rave reviews about the trilogy and its lofty literary qualities began to appear in newspapers and magazines; and one critic even called Brezhnev "one of the world's most widely read authors." In these very panegyrics there was an element of hidden irony which easily disclosed itself to readers and remained unnoticed only by those who wrote them and by the complacent object of their praises. So that the premature obituary of Brezhnev published in *Aurora* as a whole, and the choice of the subject's profession in particular, were kept strictly within the bounds of parody.

It is interesting that even Stalin, who in his lifetime was elevated to the rank of a god by official propaganda, was never called a great writer, although in his case there were much better grounds for it. In his youth Iosif Dzhugashvili (Stalin) had written and published poems in Georgian; and one of them appeared as the opening selection in a textbook used to teach the Georgian language to students in the lower grades—a book published during his lifetime. (Georgians who are now over forty years old still know it by heart.) In 1949, when the nation was preparing to celebrate the seventieth birthday of "the father of peoples," a well-known translator was called to the Kremlin and instructed, in strict secrecy, to translate into Russian a book of Stalin's youthful poems, working from literal versions that had been made in advance. The translator carried out the task with which he had been honored, and received a triple fee for his work. But somehow the book of Iosif Stalin's poems never was published. Perhaps someone had sense enough to realize that the image of the god would be tarnished by attributing to him the doubtful glory of a poet, thus making him vulnerable in literary matters. Even more likely, Stalin himself restrained both his extravagant flatterers and his own literary vanity— something he certainly had in his youth. (In Georgia one can hear many amusing stories about it.) When all was said and done, the role of a Russian vozhd was more to his taste than the fickle fate of a Georgian poet.

This time, however, there was no one to stop the overzealous flatterers who were compromising Brezhnev with their adulation. He himself, it would seem, was incapable of foreseeing the side effects of all that hallelujah-shouting. And Andropov, who *was* capable of such foresight, knew that those side effects would serve his own interests; so that instead of putting a stop to the absurd panegyrics, he encouraged them. But for him, that was not enough. He therefore authorized, or more likely even suggested (not personally, of course, but through front men, with the help of his subordinates), the exposure in print of the ludicrous and ironic position into which the hallelujah shouters had put the aged Kremlin vozhd and writer. Yes, that vozhd-writer who wanted at all costs to avoid dying, despite the constant rumors of his death and even express wishes for it, including one in print that appeared on his seventy-fifth birthday in the Leningrad magazine.

One of the coauthors of this book, Elena Klepikova, worked in the editorial offices of that magazine for more than five years and is well acquainted with Gleb Goryshin, who was its editor-in-chief when the anti-Brezhnev sketch was published. Although by virtue of his ideological leanings he is an adept of the neo-Stalinist and national-chauvinist movement (actively supported by the KGB), and although the members of that movement considered Brezhnev as almost a liberal, criticized him for détente with the West and too much permissiveness within the country, and were impatiently awaiting his departure from the political stage, Goryshin would never have dared print in his magazine a malicious lampoon on the top Soviet leader without prior permission from above. This is confirmed by the relatively light punishment handed out to him: he was removed from his position as editor-in-chief; but he was not expelled from the Writers' Union, and he kept his Party card. It is worth remembering that under Stalin he would have been shot for such a thing. And under Khrushchev, or under Brezhnev when the latter was still functioning normally and independently, he would not only have been expelled from the Party and the Writers' Union but would probably have been imprisoned for anti-Soviet propaganda—along with the author of the sketch and several of the magazine's staffers. For that matter, under Stalin—and even under Khrushchev or Brezhnev, when the latter still wielded real power—such a thing simply could not happen, and never did happen. Thus the very fact that such a lampoon of the Kremlin's top leader appeared in the state-controlled press was a sure sign that the power of Brezhnev and his entourage was on the wane, a result of an increase in the power of their cynical and crafty rival.

It was not by chance that the place chosen for such a risky adventure was Leningrad. The most reactionary Soviet city—the proving ground of the KGB, where all its undertakings and experiments are pioneered—it is under the complete control of the secret police. It is a capital city in terms of architecture, and a province in terms of politics. And that's what it is called: "the capital of the Soviet provinces." The absence of foreign correspondents and diplomats makes Leningrad the fief of the KGB organs, where they can do whatever they want. The KGB's usual tactic is to try out a new procedure in Leningrad, and then shift it to Moscow. (Or not shift it, in case of failure.) It was in Leningrad in 1963 that for the first time in the post-Stalinist era a writer—it happened to be Joseph Brodsky—was arrested, although he was later released under the pressure of public opinion. It was here that, in 1970, the widely publicized trial of the "airplane people" was held. It was here that, some months before the treason trial of Anatoly Shcharansky, a Jew, another Jew by the name of Leonid Lyubman was tried on a similar charge, and sentenced to fifteen years. And it was here that Andropov first tested out the method of discrediting political rivals through their children. (The rival in question was Grigori Romanov, Party boss of Leningrad.)

Leningrad became the city of first drafts, of rough sketches, of informal rehearsals before shifting the more successful of them to the larger stage of Moscow. It was the ideal place for publishing the anti-

Brezhnev sketch. And that marked the beginning of Andropov's final, decisive attack on the aged Kremlin vozhd.

It is most likely that Brezhnev never even learned about the nasty gift presented to him on his birthday by the city generally regarded as the cradle of the revolution, since the Kremlin camarilla spared its ailing protector any unpleasant news that might unexpectedly hasten a fatal dénouement. In any case, thanks to the scandal that had broken out, Victor Golyavkin's merry tale achieved widespread fame. Those copies of *Aurora* that had not been confiscated were promptly bought up. The regular price of the magazine was thirty kopecks, but the December issue was selling on the black market for twenty-five rubles. Also, people were passing on typescripts and photocopies of the lampoon—something especially strange, since photocopying machines are a rarity in the Soviet Union, and the right to use them is strictly limited by such agencies as the KGB.

The rest of the action took place in Moscow, where events followed each other almost without a break, in a quickening tempo unheard-of since the death of Stalin and the shooting of Beria. The Leningrad episode served as a prologue to the Moscow drama of a palace revolution that was carefully planned in advance. Which is why it could be squeezed into the space of a few months, from Brezhnev's birthday in late December 1981 to late May 1982, when the dramatic plot had in fact worked itself out, and its author took over the position of second secretary of the Party's Central Committee—actually, that of an all-powerful regent at a time when the great chief was politically and physically feeble. In a certain sense Leningrad had again served as the cradle of a revolution—a palace revolution carried out by the head of the secret police.

As befits a nation's top cop, Andropov long remained in the shadows, mixing up the cards of the Western Kremlinologists, who in any case have no special prophetic talents and have a hard time catching on to the Byzantine style of cloakroom intrigues at the Kremlin. In the group photographs distributed by TASS—taken during Brezhnev's birthday party in St. George's Hall in the Kremlin, during a formal session in the Kremlin's Palace of Congresses, or when a high-ranking foreign guest was being greeted at Sheremetevo Airport—Andropov is always somewhere behind or off to the side. In just the same way, a painter of the Renaissance, when portraying a well-known historical subject, might include his self-portrait in the form of a minor figure in the background. Another reason why the author of the drama produced on the Kremlin stage in early 1982 remained invisible was that the audience's attention was given over to the last movements of the dying main character.

It is now our task to reconstruct that author's intention in the light of the epilogue, since no one can think up something that another person cannot surmise. Here is how the major events unfolded after Brezhnev's birthday and the presentation of Leningrad's gift to the Kremlin's chief tenant.

Exactly one month later, on January 19, 1982, General Semyon Kuzmich Tsvigun, Yuri Andropov's first deputy at the KGB and the husband of Mme Brezhnev's sister, was found in his office shot in the head. Six days later Mikhail Suslov, the chief Party ideologue and patronage boss for the highest positions in the country, who was the behind-the-scenes engineer of Khrushchev's overthrow in 1964 and from whose hands Brezhnev received the supreme power, unexpectedly died of a heart attack. Such a gift from the "gray eminence" was the least likely thing Andropov could have counted on. Ideologically orthodox, Suslov had preferred to keep any and all Bonapartes at a good distance from the supreme power—especially a Bonaparte from the secret police.

Before Suslov's body was lowered into its grave in the Kremlin wall not far from the grave of Stalin, under whom that tallest and thinnest of the Politburo members had begun his career, Brezhnev, supported by two assistants, breathing heavily, and speaking somewhat incoherently, bade his eternal farewell to his patron: "In taking leave of our comrade, I want to say to him: 'Sleep in peace, dear friend. You lived a great and glorious life.' "

That wish was not to be fulfilled. Immediately after Suslov's death, a gigantic purge of the Party and state apparatus was carried out, and several thousand of Suslov's protégés were swept out of office. Among them was the chairman of Soviet Trade Unions, Aleksei Shibayev, who had been especially close to Suslov. And on the very day of the funeral (January 29), when all the Kremlin gerontocrats were in Red Square, came the arrest of Boris Buryatia, a singer with the Bolshoi Opera, whose professional name was Boris Tsygan (Boris the Gypsy), and who was known throughout Moscow for the rich ornaments he affected, from a sable coat and diamond stickpin to a green Mercedes. A search of his apartment revealed a cache of diamonds which he said belonged not to him but to his lover, Galina Churbanova. Her name was also mentioned by another man arrested immediately after Boris Tsygan: Anatoly Kolevatov, director of the State Circus, in whose apartment $200,000 in hard currency was found, along with more than $1 million in diamonds and other jewelry. Both were in fact close friends of Galina Churbanova, and had been since the time when she was married to her first husband, an animal trainer with the circus. Now she was married to Lieutenant General Yuri Churbanov, first deputy minister of the USSR Ministry of Internal Affairs (MVD). But the most important thing about Galina was that she was the daughter of Leonid Ilich Brezhnev, and her passion for antique jewelry was known to everyone in Moscow.

One must give due credit to Brezhnev for his ability to scent things out. He had taken into account the possibility of a coup d'état, and seeing that the basic danger lay in the two parallel ministries, each of which had its own troops in Moscow, the MVD and the KGB, he had set up a complex system of protection against both ministries, which had the function of safeguarding his regime but were also capable of encroaching on it. The very division of the police into regular (MVD) and secret (KGB), and the corresponding separation of powers between them, weakened both organizations. In order to strengthen that parallelism and equalize the two ministries, Brezhnev increased the friction between them, both personal and departmental. For example, he simultaneously promoted both Andropov and Shchelokov (head of the MVD) to the rank of general of the army; and the two decrees of the Presidium of the Supreme Soviet on the promotions were published side by side in the major Soviet newspapers in September 1976. Not only that, but he assigned both men living quarters in his own apartment house on Kutuzovsky Prospekt, giving one the apartment above his and the other the apartment beneath, which enabled him to keep both ministers constantly in his field of vision.

This equalization was in many respects unjust. The secret police, working both within the country and abroad, fulfilled incomparably more complex and important functions than the regular police, who basically dealt with ordinary criminals, alcoholics, and violators of traffic regulations. Personally, moreover, KGB Chairman Yuri Andropov felt himself to be distinctly superior to Minister of Internal Affairs Nikolai Shchelokov intellectually, psychologically, and even in terms of his family. In the last-named respect, fate itself played a spiteful trick on the covert pretender to the Russian throne. Not only had his son and Shchelokov's son studied at the same privileged educational institutions and specialized in the English language and English-speaking countries, but they were namesakes. There was, however, a marked difference of ability between them—no less than between their fathers. Igor Andropov was (and is) purposeful, hardworking, and had an excellent command of English. It was not only his father's influence but his own doggedness that enabled him to hold down a position in the Institute of the U.S.A. and Canada and in the Ministry of Foreign Affairs, and to take frequent trips abroad. By contrast, Igor Shchelokov was perhaps the most spoiled and dissolute of the Kremlin leaders' children. He regularly arrived at the institute where he was a student in a Mercedes given to him by his father. He hosted noisy orgies at his father's dacha. And he did disgustingly poor work in his studies, especially in English. But this did not stop him from being sent off to the Soviet embassy in Australia for an "internship" during his last year of study—a very rare case in the history of Soviet student life.

One does not have to be a psychologist to realize how this humiliating "equalization" must have irritated the future Soviet leader, all the more so since he realized that it was directed against him personally, and not against Shchelokov, who was none too clever and had no great ambitions. At the same time, it served as a kind of negative inspiration for Andropov: the obstacles tempered his will and put a sharp edge on his aspirations. In any case, the first thing he did after coming to power was promptly to fire his unworthy and artificially created rival from his position as head of the MVD and expel him from the Central Committee. As his replacement (as though wreaking vengeance on the rival ministry), he named one of his own aides, Colonel General Vitaly Fedorchuk, former chief of the Ukrainian KGB, who was notorious for his stern temper. With this appointment Andropov destroyed the unrealistic parallelism, stressing the KGB's predominance in this pairing, and the subordinate position of the regular police.

Long before Brezhnev's death, however, the KGB and its chief had managed to win two significant victories and move upward. In

1973 Yuri Andropov became a member of the Politburo along with two other ministers, while Shchelokov did not become a member. But the other victory was more important. On the grounds that the regular police (MVD) were not coping with the nationwide graft and corruption, that function was transferred to the KGB. This truly revolutionary move was destined to play a decisive role in Andropov's struggle for power. As head of the KGB, he was on the receiving end of all complaints about high Soviet functionaries abusing their official positions. Among these functionaries were his direct rivals in the Politburo; and he put together a thick dossier on each of them (or else on his co-workers, relatives, or friends)—something which, at any moment, he could set in motion or use for blackmail. The KGB headquarters on Dzerzhinsky Square became the center of a gigantic spiderweb spun by the skillful master which easily spread inside the medieval walls of the Kremlin. For a certain length of time, Brezhnev supported (or was obliged to support) his chief gendarme's efforts to combat corruption in high places, until he realized that the huge network the latter had spun was threatening his own cobweb-like dominions.

Brezhnev made an attempt to restore control over the KGB and at the same time, just in case, to strengthen control over the MVD—the former being really dangerous to him, and the latter potentially so. As first deputies to Andropov and Shchelokov, respectively, he named two of his in-laws: Semyon Tsvigun, the husband of his wife's sister, and Yuri Churbanov, his daughter's husband. They both had double loyalties: directly to their chiefs, but primarily to their relative-in-law and patron. Semyon Kuzmich Tsvigun's loyalty to Leonid Ilich Brezhnev cost him his life.

The version of Tsvigun's suicide put out by the KGB and credulously picked up by Western correspondents in Moscow—i.e., that he killed himself because he was ordered to stop the investigation of the diamond affair, in which Brezhnev's daughter was involved—does not stand up to criticism. First, because people don't commit suicide over things like that. Second, because in terms of his psychological makeup, a Soviet official of that rank and that age (sixty-four) is least of all inclined toward suicide—which is why there has not been one such case among them during the postwar years. Third, because by virtue of his individual character traits, Tsvigun was not a potential suicide. He was an even-tempered police bureaucrat who had begun his career during the war as a member of SMERSh, and who combined his work in the KGB with writing. (Under his own name he published several mediocre novels about the Great Patriotic War, as the Russo-German phase of World War II is known in the Soviet Union. Under the pseudonym "S. Dneprov," he wrote the screenplays, based on those novels, for a "combat series" of films that was popular in the USSR. And under another pseudonym, "S. Mishin," he is listed as a KGB consultant in the credits for films about the heroes of the secret police.) But the most important thing is that since Tsvigun was an in-law and protégé of Brezhnev, and since, unlike Andropov, he did not hold a position high enough that he could dare to challenge his mighty patron, he had no interest to be served in continuing an investigation which might to some degree besmirch the reputation of Brezhnev (upon whom he was totally dependent) and destabilize his own position. Indeed, the only thing that he could do was to obstruct that investigation insofar as he was able to, seeking help from Brezhnev himself and his clique, or from Suslov and his apparatus. Which in fact was what he tried to do.

As for the official obituary of Tsvigun, which was ostentatiously signed by Andropov and all the top KGB officers, but not by Brezhnev, one can only wonder at the naïveté of the Western journalists in Moscow. They accepted the KGB's explanation of this event at its face value: as a sign of the state police's solidarity with its comrade, who had perished through no fault of his own, and whom Brezhnev had anathematized, during his life and even posthumously. But in fact the signature of the KGB chief was out-and-out camouflage, while the absence of Brezhnev's signature testified to what was perhaps the most courageous act in his lifetime. He had flatly refused to sanction, posthumously, the murder of his in-law, comrade-in-arms, and old friend.

But what actually did happen in the interval between Brezhnev's birthday and the murder of Tsvigun?

Andropov had launched his "circus operation" back in December 1981, during the week following Brezhnev's birthday. On December 27 a collection of jewelry that had once belonged to a family of Russian aristocrats was stolen from the apartment of the famous lion tamer, Irina Bugrimova. Since Anatoly Kolevatov, the director of the State Circus, and the opera singer Boris Tsygan, in whose homes the jewels were later found, could not possibly be suspected of burglary, one could only suppose that the jewels had been stolen from Bugrimova and then planted in the homes of Galina Brezhneva-Churbanova's friends by Andropov's agents, with a political aim that could easily be discerned. The handiwork was so crude—and it was so literally reminiscent of the case involving the ring worn by the wife of Georgian Party boss Mzhavanadze, which cost him his career—that no one was left with any doubt as to who was the target of Andropov's "circus affair."

But the investigation suddenly came to a halt—something that can be explained only by the intervention of forces even more influential (for the time being) than Andropov. And those forces could have been activated only by Semyon Tsvigun, whom Brezhnev had assigned to Andropov to spy on him. Tsvigun easily surmised where the blow about to be delivered by his service chief would fall, and took countermeasures—not so much out of gratitude to his patron as out of an instinct of self-preservation, since he knew that in the event of Brezhnev's fall, he himself would not last even one day.

For Andropov, however, there was no longer any place to which he could retreat: he would either win everything or lose everything. In mid-January 1982 Andropov was closer to defeat than to victory; and had it not been for the successive deaths of Semyon Tsvigun and Mikhail Suslov, he would have suffered the ill-starred fate of Shelepin, whose path to power was blocked by the partocrats at the very last moment.

It is said that the support of Minister of Defense Dmitri Ustinov was decisive in Andropov's victory. But Ustinov supported him only later, when it was no longer the fate of Andropov but that of Ustinov himself which depended on that support. Of course the alliance between the armed forces and the KGB was important to Andropov's career. But that was more true in its earlier stage, when during the Christmas season of 1979 the two ministries carried out the blitz of Afghanistan.

It is worth recalling that none of the Ministry of Defense's troops are stationed in Moscow, so that in the struggle for power, Ustinov was a general without an army. And he would not have dared to act against Suslov, whose Party authority was incontrovertible, and whose people held the apparatus of the Central Committee in thrall. (For the "gray eminence" was in charge not only of a dead ideology but of living key personnel.) And then there was Brezhnev's alter ego, Semyon Tsvigun, who was tying Andropov hand and foot. That is why, in order to become a claimant to Brezhnev's throne, Andropov was obliged (in accordance with the unwritten but strict Party etiquette) to move first from the KGB to the Secretariat of the Central Committee. But this meant being deprived of the chief instrument of his power, the secret police, which would automatically have come under the control of Brezhnev's protégé Tsvigun. Andropov's promotion would have been the beginning of the end for him, and Brezhnev's power would have been inherited by someone from the Dnepropetrovsk Mafia. Not only did he have no room for retreat, but it was too late.

At this point we get into the kind of situation that is better coped with by a John le Carré. Our own journalistic investigation, however, requires us only to note this: what destroyed General Semyon Tsvigun was the fact that he overrated the possibilities of his sponsor and in-law, and underrated his immediate superior in command. And he may, at the same time, have overrated his own possibilities. In any case, the investigation of the diamond affair, which he had brought to a halt for almost a month, again got underway at full speed after his death and that of Suslov. Galina Brezhneva-Churbanova was called in for questioning. People who saw her at the time say that Galina, a society lady who was usually full of self-confidence, looked like a whipped dog, and that once she lamented, "Now it's all over for them," meaning not only her opera and circus friends and lovers but all of her own regal family.

The nature of the investigation was obvious: Galina Brezhneva-Churbanova's friends would be indicted for graft, corruption, and illegal currency operations. For example, Anatoly Kolevatov, who was in charge of eighty circus troops, ice extravaganzas, and travelling zoos (about twenty thousand persons, including six thousand actors), had taken bribes in hard currency from each actor for setting up foreign tours. Shortly before, several high officials in the Caucasus and central Asia who had been tried on similar charges had been shot. These people belonged to the "red bourgeoisie," the "new class" in the classless Soviet society that includes at least a quarter of a million people. So why, out of all this superstructure apparatus, were only a few people from Brezhnev's immediate entourage chosen for this show trial? There can be no two opinions here: the idea was to undermine the general secretary himself.

It is obvious that in his campaign against Brezhnev and his clique, Andropov made good use of both of his Caucasian "rough drafts." But in so acting, he followed the method of deduction, not induction. For example, he knew in advance what he was looking for and what he would find at the homes of Anatoly Kolevatov and Boris Tsygan. He knew that ultimately he would manage to garner the scattered pieces of the Russian aristocrats' family jewels, even if he had to order a search in the apartment of his downstairs neighbor at 26 Kutuzovsky Prospekt, and that the museum's jewel collection would serve him in his ascent toward the top. Brezhnev himself was a clever intriguer, which is why he had remained in power for so long; but now his physical frailty had made him feeble politically. Moreover, his rival was using devices too subtle for his crude mind to grasp, even when he still enjoyed full physical strength. Here are two reasons why the KGB intriguer overcame the bureaucratic intriguer.

The Dnepropetrovsk Mafia had kept Brezhnev in power too long, believing in his invulnerability—and, thanks to him, in its own. Only Andropov knew that Brezhnev was not only mortal but vulnerable. Moreover, it was within Andropov's power to step up the degree of that vulnerability, and hence to make his entire Kremlin retinue more vulnerable. The most dangerous of Brezhnev's devotees was the Ukrainian Andrei Kirilenko, a secretary of the Central Committee. True, Brezhnev's wanting to expand his "kitchen cabinet" had the result that yet another Ukrainian, Konstantin Chernenko, made his appearance among those few who were at once members of the Politburo and of the Secretariat. But instead of strengthening Brezhnev's power base, this expansion made it shakier. A fight over Brezhnev's succession broke out between Chernenko and Kirilenko. Andropov had reasons for adding fuel to that fire, and the means of doing so. On this occasion the KGB chief followed the example and practice of Brezhnev, who had played him (Andropov) off against Shchelokov, trying in that way to neutralize both. But Andropov knew from his own experience how this game of playing one man off against another usually ends. Sooner or later, in the duel between Kirilenko and Chernenko, one of them would get the upper hand. And the one with the best chance of winning was Kirilenko, an old wolf in Party intrigues. The device that Andropov had already tested on Grigori Romanov and Leonid Brezhnev—discrediting one's opponent through his children—could be applied to Kirilenko. But in this case there was a need for something more potent than broken cups from Catherine the Great's dinner service, or stolen jewelry once worn by one of her favorites.

The political career of Andrei Kirilenko came to an end when a member of his family requested political asylum in England. That event was so unlikely, bearing in mind that Kirilenko himself was on the threshold of supreme power in Russia, while the defector was already a high-ranking official, that not to suspect artificially created conditions for that defection would be just too naïve, even for an academic investigator. Although Kirilenko was still listed (*pro forma*) as a secretary of the Central Committee and a member of the Politburo, he disappeared from the public's field of vision. His portrait is no longer displayed on the streets during holidays; and one does not even find his signature under official obituaries alongside the signatures of his former, more successful (for the time being) Kremlin colleagues. His disgrace was total and definitive. At the same time, rumors were being spread about his terminal illness. Disinformation is not only the KGB's stock-in-trade but its hobby and passion—so much so, that it is not always possible to understand right away the aim that agency is pursuing in disseminating this or that falsehood. It is just the same as the difference between theft and kleptomania.

The road to power had finally been cleared: none of Andropov's opponents or rivals was left. Suslov was in his grave, Kirilenko was in disgrace, and Romanov was still in Leningrad with a besmirched reputation. Both the Kazakh Kunayev and the Ukrainian Shcherbitsky had been put at a safe remove from the epicenter of the power struggle and were in their own respective republics, thousands of kilometers away. The Moscow Party boss, Victor Grishin, had no hunger for more power. Pelshe, at age eighty-three, and Tikhonov, at seventy-six, were too old to succeed Brezhnev; and Mikhail Gorbachev, fifty-one, was on the contrary too young and inexperienced, besides which he was a creature of Andropov. Minister of Defense Dmitri Ustinov and Foreign Minister Andrei Gromyko (who had held that post for a quarter century) were both too narrowly professional for the job of general secretary. As for Konstantin Chernenko, it was only in the eyes of Western correspondents that he looked like a possible successor to Brezhnev. He was too simpleminded and unsophisticated to succeed Brezhnev, or even to contend against Andropov for the succession. Even a simple process of elimination showed Andropov to be the only one worthy of becoming the leader of the Soviet state. And that was just what the KGB chief had figured. He wanted the West itself to see him as Brezhnev's heir and, through

Russian-language broadcasts from Western radio stations, to make the Soviet public ready to accept the next Kremlin chieftain.

Andropov has more than once used the press of the free world for his own purposes, and he will do so in the future. This time, however, he made a serious slip: he overrated the ability of the Western Kremlinologists—especially the American ones. In February, March, and April 1982, when in fact the reins of power were already in Andropov's hands, his chances in the power struggle were being rated as minimal, merely because there had never been a time in Soviet history—or, one might add, in the entire thousand-year-old history of Russia—when a head of the secret police became head of the state. As if only what has happened in the past will happen in the future!

This is not the place to comment ironically on the predictions made by the Kremlinologists at that time, although they cast doubt on Western observers' understanding of the political and ideological power structure in the USSR. But the fact is that Andropov, as befitted the head of the secret police, preferred to stay off to one side, in the shadows, figuring that his secret weapon was more reliable than ritualistic shifts in Brezhnev's retinue. The mole dug his secret tunnel to the top of the Kremlin hill, and surfaced for the first time only after he had completed all the dirty work. On April 22, to the great surprise of Western observers, Yuri Andropov appeared as the main speaker at the ceremonies devoted to the 112th anniversary of Lenin's birth. With the exception of the absent Kirilenko, all the other members of the Politburo, headed by Brezhnev, listened to him docilely. By that time the power struggle was already over. Andropov presented his ultimatum to his former rivals, and there was nothing more they could do but accept it; they were all only too well aware of the fate of Tsvigun, Kirilenko, and even Brezhnev himself, whose daughter had turned out to be mixed up in the jewelry caper. On May 24 the frightened members of the Central Committee "elected" Andropov second secretary; and to succeed himself as KGB chief, Andropov named Vitaly Fedorchuk, "the butcher of the Ukraine." Andropov realized that this was a temporary appointment for a few months only, until the final departure of Brezhnev, when he (Andropov) would transfer Fedorchuk to the MVD, where his brutal style would be more appropriate. But for the moment he had particular need of Fedorchuk in order to spread fear in Moscow and prevent any encroachment on his own authority as all-powerful regent.

Andropov's shift to the Secretariat of the Central Committee, while he retained control of the secret police, essentially marked the completion of a coup d'état whose most intensive and risky phase had come during the early months of 1982. This is the only explanation for the ease and rapidity with which the KGB chief, only a few hours after Brezhnev's death, became head of the Party. As Hamlet said in a similar situation, "The funeral baked meats did coldly furnish forth the marriage tables." But while Brezhnev was still alive—even though he was virtually sidetracked from power and his actions were blocked by Andropov—the latter had to decide what to do with him. Meantime, the noose of the investigation involving the diamonds was tightening around Galina Brezhneva-Churbanova. At this point her father was presented with an ultimatum: either shameful expulsion from the Kremlin, or honorable retirement. One can imagine the tragedy of a feeble old man with a waning consciousness for whom power was more like a toy than anything else. But like the other members of the Politburo, he no longer had any choice but to accept the ultimatum. He could now expect anything at all from his former top cop.

Not relying on his "patient," Andropov himself took the steps required to hasten, by any means, Brezhnev's departure from the political stage. Here again, as in the incident involving *Aurora*, the oft-tested alliance between the KGB and the propaganda apparatus came in handy; although this time Andropov's manipulation of the Soviet media was more complex and sophisticated. Unexpectedly, Brezhnev's image in the Soviet press—and especially on the television screen—changed radically, becoming more realistic, to a degree that was rare in the Soviet press. Brezhnev was shown as he actually was.

Up until only a short time before, the TV cameras had shyly turned aside, showing the viewers an audience or a crowd of welcomers, whenever something embarrassing happened with Brezhnev. And such things were happening with him more and more often: he stumbled, he walked in the wrong direction, he began to speak quite incoherently. During a visit to India, the interpreter became completely confused. He didn't know what he was supposed to interpret until one of Brezhnev's assistants handed him a previously prepared text. Then, paying no attention to the old man's mumbling, he translated all of Brezhnev's speech from the printed version. But that image of the senile old man—one to which Western TV viewers had already become accustomed—was unknown to the Soviet viewers. The true image of the Kremlin gerontocrat had been carefully concealed from them.

The tale is told of an oriental potentate who was blind in one eye, and who ordered the execution of two artists—one because he had portrayed his defect, and the other because he had concealed it. But he richly rewarded a third artist, who had painted him in profile.

So Brezhnev's portrait had been shown by Soviet propaganda "in profile": when he managed to take a normal step or utter a normal word. Live broadcasts of any ceremonies in which Brezhnev took part were strictly prohibited. And for newsreels or TV news programs, a careful selection was made of frames in which the Soviet potentate looked more or less decent. When the general secretary made a four-hour speech at the Twenty-sixth Party Congress, the television and radio broadcast only the first six minutes of the speech as read by Brezhnev. Then, after a brief pause "for technical reasons," he was replaced by an announcer who read all the rest of the speech.

But now everything had been changed, and Brezhnev was being presented to the Soviet public as he really was. The TV cameras no longer hid anything. To the contrary, it even seemed that, as if correcting the former varnished image of Brezhnev, the cameramen were now choosing frames that compromised him.

That television campaign to discredit the Kremlin patriarch had been launched as early as February, when the amazed TV audience was able to view—filmed in detail, and even with a certain degree of relish—Brezhnev's hysterics at the funeral of General Konstantin Grushevoi, political commander of the Moscow Military District, with whom he had served in World War II. And one could understand Brezhnev: this was his third loss in two weeks. (The other two were his in-law Tsvigun and his patron, Suslov.) He was losing his closest friends, and along with them his power base. The same period witnessed the first arrests of his daughter's friends. The rug was being pulled from under his feet. Brezhnev was weeping not only for his buddy but over his own lot, which by now was not an enviable one.

On September 26 in Baku, the capital of Azerbaijan, whose all-powerful master was Andropov's man Geidar Aliyev, something very unusual happened to Brezhnev—especially unusual because it was witnessed, in all its details, by millions of TV viewers. In lieu of Brezhnev's previously prepared speech, someone had palmed off on him a totally different text, which he had quite unsuspectingly begun to read to the assembled Azerbaijani Party stalwarts. Not only that, but the TV cameras simultaneously showed the flurry and hurried consultations among Brezhnev's assistants on the rostrum, and picked up one of them as he rushed up to Brezhnev to give him the right text. Even if we assume that the goof with the speech was accidental, it is very hard to write off as mere chance the TV cameras' emphasis on everything that happened on the rostrum. But the fact that neither of these things was accidental was confirmed by Brezhnev himself, who easily surmised what had happened. Setting aside the text that had been palmed off on him, he smiled and said: "It's not my fault, comrades. I have to start from the beginning." And then, calmly and even with dignity, he read the forty-minute greeting to the Azerbaijani Communists.

But he no longer had the strength to struggle against those who were persistently tarnishing his image, and that process was in high gear. Although in fact he often fell ill, the number of times he did so was doubled and tripled by rumor. And he heroically bore up under the very heavy work schedule that Andropov arranged for him—a schedule that even a healthy man would have had a hard time keeping, with weekly (and sometimes even more frequent) trips and speeches. He could not have failed to derive Andropov's intentions: for the latter, Brezhnev's natural death was preferable to his forced retirement.

When Brezhnev was returning from a trip to Tashkent, he had a stroke in the airplane. The ceremonial greeting at the Sheremetevo Airport had to be cancelled. An ambulance took him from the airplane to the hospital—a new occasion for rumors of his death.

That much was unofficial. Officially, TASS continued to distribute photographs of Brezhnev throughout the world, but now they were of a different kind: informal and intimate. Brezhnev surrounded by the many members of his household, including his wife, whom the Soviet public had never seen before. (The position of First Lady does not exist in the Soviet Union.) Brezhnev with his little granddaughter on his lap. Brezhnev with the baby carriage in which his great-granddaughter is sleeping. Brezhnev under a parasol on the shore of the Black Sea, wearing a pajama-like outfit and slippers, and holding a newspaper. These are typical images of the Soviet senior citizen in retirement—the grandpa. Never before had Soviet propaganda portrayed in that way a Kremlin vozhd. It was a deliberate diminution of

Brezhnev's image, designed to accustom Soviet and foreign public opinion to the idea of his impending departure. It must have become obvious to everyone that such a man was no longer capable of governing the country. And such was indeed the case.

An attitude reminiscent of an American election slogan, "Anybody but Brezhnev!" was inevitably formed. It was against this background—ideal for any successor to Brezhnev—that the apocrypha about the future Soviet leader arose. Their source was the same as that of the compromising rumors about Brezhnev.

10

Andropov's
Double Self-Portrait:
At Home and Abroad

Enter Rumour, painted full of tongues.
— SHAKESPEARE, *Henry IV*,
Part 2

In all probability, there is no better way to show yourself off to advantage than to be photographed with the Leaning Tower of Pisa as a background, thereby emphasizing your own stability. The rumors about Brezhnev and Andropov that arose in 1982 were interrelated, but by way of contrast. And in being set off against each other, they emphasized those traits of the all-powerful regent that were no longer possessed—or never had been possessed—by the old man of the Kremlin who, although formally still at the helm of the state, was for all practical purposes no longer governing it: intelligence, decisiveness, cleverness, culture, pro-Westernism—even a knowledge of the English language. True, rumors about Andropov had attended his entire career as head of the secret police. But it was precisely in the summer of 1982, immediately after the KGB palace revolution engineered by Andropov, that they were most actively bruited about. And they reached their culmination at the end of the year, after Brezhnev's death and Andropov's self-appointment to the office of general secretary of the Communist Party of the Soviet Union. Later one of Andropov's spokesmen, Georgi Arbatov, director of the Institute of the U.S.A. and Canada and a member of the Central Committee, would cynically acknowledge that such a campaign to create an image of Andropov for Western eyes had in fact been waged. Naturally, however, he denied that Andropov had organized or instigated it. "The buildup of Andropov was by spontaneous sources," he told the American journalist Joseph Kraft. "It was not his work. It was the work of volunteers."

[238]

But Kraft's piece in the *New Yorker*, dealing with the gossip about Andropov that he picked up in Moscow, testifies (quite without the author's intention) to the exact opposite. It shows not only that those bits of gossip were concerted but that his trip itself—the appointments and talks he had in Moscow, and even their sequence and the impressions he carried away with him—had been contrived in advance and staged by a skillful (although invisible) director behind the scenes. Incidentally, this was not the first time that the KGB has had recourse to help from Western correspondents—not only without their permission, but even without their knowledge. Kraft served the KGB as one of their many inadvertent Western mouthpieces: an American Aaron for a Soviet Moses.

In this connection one should not forget the feedback to the Soviet Union of unofficial information obtained from there. That information is fed back in the form of items from the Western press broadcast by radio stations with Russian-language programs. The KGB's manipulation of these channels for passing on quasi-official information to the Soviet public is a matter that merits special attention. This is all the more true in that the KGB is capable of completely jamming some broadcasts or, on the contrary, of creating ideal listening conditions for others, depending on their subjects and whether they are harmful to the Soviet listener, or "useful."

Kraft's itinerary through Moscow, laid out by the KGB, was so arranged as to assure future Soviet listeners that the Andropov era would not be a continuation of the Brezhnev era by sheer momentum, while at the same time allaying any fears on the part of Western readers that it would mark a return to Stalinism. The version suggested to Kraft by the guides assigned to him featured Lenin, the founder of the Soviet Union, as a model for its new leader.

Indeed, almost all of Andropov's traits, as depicted by Kraft's numerous interviewees, fully coincide with Lenin's canonical traits: modesty, simplicity, efficiency, practicality, a dislike of slogans, a passionate enthusiasm for politics, and knowledge of a foreign language (perhaps even more than one). And the first thing Kraft heard from Roy Medvedev, the only surviving Moscow dissident, was that Andropov's paternal grandmother was Jewish. This is a slightly displaced reflection of the fact—officially concealed but at the same time universally known in the USSR—that Lenin's maternal grandfather was Jewish.

Kraft's "Letter from Moscow" ends with an account of how he was taken to the Moscow Art Theater to see a play about Lenin—one so keenly perceptive and true to life that it was licensed only after having been previewed by the Politburo, headed by Brezhnev, a few months before the latter's death. On the occasion when Kraft saw the play, accompanied by two admirers of Andropov, the privileged audience consisted mostly of Central Committee members and deputies of the Supreme Soviet, whose joint session, marking the sixtieth anniversary of the founding of the Union of Soviet Socialist Republics, was to open two days later. The enthusiastic response to the play on the part of these high officials (including the guides assigned to Kraft) also had an effect on the American journalist's impression (despite some critical remarks about Lenin), and hence on the impression gained by his readers, who could not have failed to note the traits shared by the Lenin of the play produced at the Moscow Art Theater and the Andropov in the play mounted for Kraft, the readers of the *New Yorker*, and the listeners to the Voice of America, by an invisible director.

It is quite natural that among the people Kraft talked with in Moscow, not a single one would utter—if only for the sake of plausibility—so much as one critical word about the former head of the secret police. This was not only because the *raconteurs* were afraid of the main character in their stories but also because all of them, without exception, belonged to the privileged caste of Soviet society. They included a privileged physicist, a privileged journalist (with easy access to Andropov), a privileged economist, a privileged "Americanist" (Andropov's son Igor worked at his institute under his direct supervision), a privileged poet, a privileged director (an actor in his theatrical company is married to Andropov's daughter Irina), and even a dissident, who—let it be said with no reproach to him—is privileged by comparison with those dissidents who have been expelled from the country, internally exiled, or imprisoned.

Just as swiftly as he came to power a few hours after the death of his predecessor, the new master of Russia set a unique national record in a field that is undoubtedly important to him. In all the sixty-five years of Soviet history there has never been another vozhd in the Kremlin about whom so many rumors have been spread during his first few days in power. Even the launching of the cult of Stalin required a waiting period of quite a few years after his advent to power, not to mention Khrushchev and Brezhnev. Most likely this new record can be ascribed to the fact that the cult of Andropov had its beginnings while Brezhnev was still on the scene, in May 1982—yet one more indication that a palace coup was carried out in Moscow just at that time. Again, while Brezhnev served as a kind of negative background for the upcoming Soviet leader, the latter's heroic prototype was Lenin. And since the seclusion and secretiveness of Kremlin life was hence in no way diminished, the source of the afore-mentioned rumors must be sought in the organization that Andropov formerly headed up, the KGB, which perfected its art of "disinforma-tion," bringing it up to the point of virtuosity, just at the time when he was in charge.

The very style of these manufactured rumors—the legends about the liberal, intellectual future leader of Russia supposedly being com-pelled to conceal his positive traits and, instead, to display and even intensify his negative ones in order to remain in power—points to a goal which is at least threefold. First, to achieve by means of rumors that which their subject (who is at the same time the sower of them) does not in fact possess, or else possesses to a much lesser degree. Second, to conceal behind their façade a reality that plainly differs from the image created by the rumors. Third, on the contrary, to disown the image of Andropov that emerged from his Hungarian and police experience, making it appear to be a mask he was compelled to wear. In other words, the closet liberal, intellectual, and "Wester-nizer" had to pretend to be just as much of a monster, and perhaps even more of one, than his Kremlin superiors and colleagues, so as not to seem suspect to them and be exposed.

In his *New York Times* tribute to Andropov, Harrison Salisbury tells a story associated with his own novel *The Gates of Hell*, whose characters include a dissident writer—a kind of centaur, half Solzheni-tsyn and half Sakharov—and Andropov himself, who sympathizes with the artist fallen into disfavor but as a matter of duty must expel him from the country. One of Salisbury's Soviet acquaintances who had read the novel asked the American author: "What are you trying to do to Andropov?"

"What do you mean?"

"Well, you present him as a human being. You're going to ruin his standing in the Politburo."

Underlying all these rumors is the rather low opinion that the KGB and its former chief have of their Western clients, the consumers of Soviet rumors for export—an opinion that is in part justified, as we have seen. After all, neither Salisbury nor Kraft nor any of the other retailers of the myth about the liberal Andropov even paid attention to the fact that Andropov's fear that his liberal character might be disclosed contradicted his own persistent efforts to create a liberal reputation for himself. But the most important contradiction is the one between the rumors about Andropov and his specific acts as head of the KGB and as ambassador to Hungary at the time of the anti-Russian uprising there. This is true even though the newly revived Hungarian gossip about Andropov soft-pedals his direct participation in suppressing the uprising, while stressing his liberal support of Janos Kadar's economic reforms.

In general, looking for a liberal in the Kremlin—not to mention one who headed up the secret police longer than any of his predecessors and is responsible for Russia's gradual return to Stalinism—merely because he supposedly speaks English, likes American jazz, and drinks scotch instead of vodka, is an even more futile undertaking than that of Diogenes as he walked along the streets of Corinth with a lantern in the daytime. What the whole thing amounts to is that the rumors the KGB is spreading about Andropov's liberalism have fallen on the fertile soil of Western wishful thinking. So it is not surprising that their dissemination is in no way hindered by the fact that Yuri Andropov, after replacing Brezhnev as the Soviet leader, has not lifted a finger to substantiate those rumors with deeds. Nor has it been necessary for him to do so: rumors always exist independently of life's realities.

Among the rumors supposedly compromising Andropov in the eyes of other Politburo members is the report that he is one-fourth (or even one-half) Jewish. Roy Medvedev says unequivocally that this hindered him in his struggle for power. But this rumor can be neither confirmed nor refuted. Etymological analysis of the name "Andropov" shows that he is most likely from a family of Russianized Greeks, and that the original name of his father's forebears was Andropoulos; but that of course doesn't rule out his being one-quarter Jewish. However, while Greek origins (like any other: Ukrainian, Tatar, Armenian) may not play a decisive role in one's political career in the USSR, to have Jewish blood is a sign of being unreliable and socially unacceptable, especially given the total anti-Semitism that now obtains in high Party circles. It is an obstacle on the path to the summits of power, even in a leader who in all other respects is ideal by Soviet standards. The issue of Jewishness is a universal means of compromising an opponent or dissociating oneself from an evil. As we have seen before, the Russian nationalists blame the Jews for all Russia's calamities since the revolution. The Georgians, trying to dissociate themselves from Beria (who was from a small Caucasian tribe called Mingrelians), claim that he was a Jew. On the other hand, the Soviet authorities carefully conceal the fact that Lenin was one-fourth Jewish, fearing that its disclosure might tarnish the image of the founding father. And so on. Andropov himself made use of this universal means when, among the other rumors compromising Brezhnev, he put out one to the effect that Brezhnev's wife was Jewish. The issue, however, proved to be a boomerang, coming back to wound the one who had used it. And yet the import of the rumor about Andropov's Jewishness is ambivalent. On the one hand, it compromises him. But on the other, it makes his image more complex, and not merely by analogy with Lenin. In a man heading up the secret police, the chief weapon employed in pursuing a policy of undisguised and often harsh anti-Semitism, one-fourth part Jewish blood is an especially piquant trait, symbolically suggesting the secret affinity between the hangman and his victims. And yet this is most likely a rumor intended for the foreign market, since unlike the U.S. president, Andropov does not have any dependence on a Jewish lobby or Jewish voters.

Are there any foundations for this rumor? None whatsoever. Given the conditions that exist among the Kremlin elite, where anti-Semitism is one of the basic principles, even one-fourth part Jewish blood would have blocked Andropov from being appointed head of the secret police, not to mention becoming the top Soviet leader. By its very nature, this rumor betrays jesuitic tendencies in the man who is its subject, and who himself floated it. There have been cases where Jews, concealing their Jewishness, have become violent anti-Semites. But for a person who is anti-Semitic (if not by nature, then in practice) to pretend to be a Jew is much more amazing.

Among all these rumors, there are of course some that are based on the truth. Thus Vladimir Turbin, the well-known literary critic and professor at Moscow University, told us that at one of his seminars on Russian literature he recounted to his students the sad fate of the old Russian literary historian, Mikhail Bakhtin, the author of brilliant studies of Dostoyevsky and Rabelais. For some thirty years he had been in disfavor. In the late twenties he had been exiled to Kazakhstan for six years because he had been a member of a study group in which religious and philosophical questions were discussed. When his term of exile was up, he settled in Saransk, capital of the Mordovian Autonomous Republic. In the sixties his star again began to rise in Moscow literary circles. But he couldn't move back to Moscow because of the strict internal passport regulations.

Among Turbin's students was Irina Andropova. With Andropov's help, the old and ailing Bakhtin not only got a Moscow residence permit and an apartment in the writers' housing complex on Krasnoarmeiskaya Street* but was accommodated for a year in the so-called *Kremlevka*, a special hospital for high-ranking Soviet leaders. (Granted, he was assigned to a second-rate ward reserved for distinguished guests from the Third World in case they should fall ill.) In 1975, a few months before Bakhtin's death, one of the authors of this book (Vladimir Solovyov) was a guest at his home, and Bakhtin fully confirmed Turbin's account.

In spite of their parents' attempts to dissuade them, both Irina Andropova and her brother Igor wanted careers as actors. But at their tryouts at the Taganka Theater, both of them failed. Yuri Lyubimov, the artistic director, rejected them without knowing whose children they were. Later, Andropov felt obliged to Lyubimov for the latter's decision. He had wanted a different kind of career for both his children, and in the case of Igor his hopes were realized: Igor followed in his father's footsteps, and made a political career for himself.

As for Irina, her dream of a life in the theater was realized indirectly: she married Alexander Filipov, an actor at the Taganka. Thanks to this matrimonial link, the Taganka—aesthetically the most avant-garde theater in the Soviet Union, and politically a gadfly which had been in constant conflict with the authorities—received unexpected support from the head of the secret police. Both sides grasped the paradoxical nature of this link, but both profited from it. Through the good graces of Yuri Andropov, Yuri Lyubimov was able to produce several shows with a political bite to them. And Yuri Andropov, thanks to Yuri Lyubimov, strengthened his reputation as a liberal—a reputation which, for the head of punitive organs, had been rather ambiguous.

*It is also called "the Pink Ghetto," because the buildings are in fact made of pink brick, and the majority of the writers who live there are Jewish.

What does all this testify to? To Andropov's fondness for art? To his paternal love, for the sake of which he risked neglecting his official obligations? Or to the fondness that tyrants have not only for executions but for clemency, since in clemency the power of the omnipotent man is displayed more vividly—both for him and for his victims? That is why the object of a tyrant's clemency is also his victim, although with a minus sign—a victim who for the moment has avoided the sacrificial altar. (Incidentally, after coming to power Andropov promptly demanded a sacrifice of Lyubimov. As we have already mentioned, he banned a Lyubimov production based on Pushkin's chronicle play, *Boris Godunov*, dealing with a power struggle in the Kremlin in the late sixteenth and early seventeenth centuries which differed little from the struggle that Andropov had waged in the same place several centuries later. So it was that in Andropov, the real gendarme got the upper hand over the fictive liberal.)

One evening at a theatrical banquet, which Andropov was attending because of his daughter's ties with the theater, he started to clink glasses with an actor sitting across the table from him. Noticing that the actor was hesitating, Andropov smiled and said, "I advise you to do it. Don't forget that the KGB has a long arm."

That joke reveals the character of a man who not only uses his power but takes pleasure in it, relishes it. Recalling the frightful reputation of the secret police in the USSR, it's very hard to make oneself smile at it. Under the old Russian definition, that joke belongs in the category of "gendarme humor."

Andropov was clever enough to realize that the very reputation of the organization he headed up made an acquaintanceship with him, on the part of any intellectual, not only useful but intriguing. And such was in fact the case. We remember how Yevgeniy Yevtushenko, the former quasi-oppositionist poet who by that time was a quasi-official one, boasted to us that Andropov's telephone number was on the first page of his address book. On the evening of February 17, 1974, having learned that Solzhenitsyn had been expelled from the Soviet Union, Yevtushenko, after taking a few drinks to bolster his courage, dialed that number.

"How could you deprive the motherland of such a great talent?"

Andropov, detecting a note of drunkenness in the poet's voice, advised him to call later when he had slept it off.

More than a year before, in the spring of 1972, Yevtushenko had called that same number and obtained a private audience with its owner. Since Yevtushenko made no secret of that meeting and told not only us but many others about it, we see no reason why we should remain silent about it—as compared with other confidential, personal bits of testimony about Andropov which we have either kept undisclosed or have quoted without giving the source.

On that occasion both had need of such a meeting, although of course for different reasons. Yevtushenko wanted to get satisfaction for an offense committed against him. Upon his return from a junket abroad he had been, for the first time, subjected to a methodical search of several hours' duration by the customs agents, like an ordinary Soviet citizen, whereas he regarded himself (not without reason) as an extraordinary Soviet citizen. Not only that, but after the search he ascertained that several things were missing from his luggage: a few issues of *Playboy*, two or three bottles of medicine, and a dozen émigré publications. With this incident as his subject, he dashed off a poem full of outrage that he read to us. He had also read it, he said, to Andropov, to whom he complained about the customs agents. The gist of the poem was that the motherland, instead of greeting her poet with bouquets when he returned after having done a hard, patriotic job of work beyond her borders and among her enemies, had belittled and insulted him with unworthy suspicions. According to Yevtushenko, his complaint was promptly redressed. Andropov apologized for the misunderstanding, and promised that the items taken from him would be returned.

"The matter is settled," said Andropov. "Let's forget about it. We'd do better to talk about literature." And he smiled his famous smile—as enigmatic as that of the Mona Lisa.

At that point Yevtushenko realized that the search by the customs agents—something he had never before experienced upon returning from a junket abroad—was a special kind of invitation for a chat; and that its extravagant form had been determined by the means available to the KGB.

The friendly chat between the most successful Soviet poet and the most (as it turned out later) successful head of the secret police lasted for several hours. The part of the conversation that Yevtushenko himself rephrased for us had to do with a poet much less successful than himself, Joseph Brodsky, whose poems were under a total ban in the USSR.

"I wanted to talk with you about Brodsky," Andropov said. "Not about his talent, but his career as a poet. What is your notion of it? Can you see him having one under current conditions in our country?"

Stirred by the trust placed in him by the chairman of the Committee of State Security, Yevtushenko gave a direct, honest answer—or so it seemed to him at the time. But later, in talking with others, he often came back to that answer, trying to prove that he could not have answered any other way. It seemed as if something was gnawing at him—if not qualms of conscience, then certain doubts. Yevtushenko in fact played into the hands of his powerful interlocutor: his answer was the one that the latter expected to hear. Right then Andropov needed to shift the responsibility for the decision from his own shoulders to those of a friend and colleague of Brodsky's. And he did so with complete success.

Shaking his head, Yevtushenko told Andropov: "No, Yuri Vladimirovich, frankly speaking, I can't see Brodsky having a career in our country. He's a talented poet, but he'd be better off abroad."

Such was the way in which Joseph Brodsky's fate was decided. Perhaps it might have turned out to be the same even without Yevtushenko. But he took upon himself the responsibility of deciding whether the best Russian poet should live in his own country or be expelled from it.

"I have the same feeling," Andropov promptly agreed.

Yevtushenko, sensing that his position coincided with the official one, quickly added: "But at least give him a break on the bureaucratic formalities: the trips to the OVIR,* filling out questionnaires, waiting."

Andropov promised to "give him a break," and kept his word: Brodsky was expelled from the USSR within a few weeks.

Undoubtedly, Yevtushenko remembered the advice he had given at that time when, more than a year later, he called Andropov about Solzhenitsyn. That is why he found the courage to make the call. He was trying in that way to make up for his sin of pusillanimity and playing into the hands of the KGB chief in the matter of Brodsky.

Stalin, too, before destroying Mandelstam, decided to consult a prestigious writer, and telephoned Pasternak. Alas! Pasternak lost his

*Visa and Registration Office. (Translator's note.)

head and wasn't up to defending his colleague, thereby provoking Stalin's just (if hypocritical) reproach: "If I were a poet and a poet friend of mine got into trouble, I'd go into a frenzy to help him."

On the other hand, it is of course quite possible that Andropov enlisted the support of people like Yevgeniy Yevtushenko and Yuri Lyubimov with a long-range goal in mind: so that his idealized, contrived portrait would look more lifelike with the help of realistic traits and prestigious witnesses. After all, a half-truth always looks more like the truth than an out-and-out lie does.

At any rate, it was precisely in 1982—at first in the early summer, right after his palace coup, and then with new force after Brezhnev's death and Andropov's inauguration as general secretary—that all these rumors came in handy for presenting the new vozhd of the Kremlin to the public at home and abroad. Naturally, rumors based on reality proved to be in short supply; and others, totally unfounded, were floated. But Andropov's calculation was accurate: he knew how much the free press hungers after sensationalism. His job was to sow the seeds. And the soil in which he sowed them was such that even stones would have sprouted from it.

For example, on May 30, 1982, the *Washington Post* published a story about how Andropov would send his own car to fetch a dissident to his home for a friendly midnight chat, and then send him back to his own home in the same car. The midnight guest in question, now living in Israel, when finally contacted just before the *Post* was to go to press, flatly denied this account as pure invention. But this did not stop the article from being published. Its author mentioned the last-minute statement, but one got the impression that his denial was born out of fear. This, although it would seem that the source had nothing to be afraid of, since the account ascribed to him was strictly laudatory of Andropov.

Of course rumors disavowing the reputation that clung to Andropov because of his fifteen years' service with the secret police are mostly intended for Western ears, because for Russian ears such a reputation has a sweet sound. It is a sign of hope. The majority of Russians willingly see the former head of the secret police as a strong personality capable of finally establishing order in the country. Andropov's campaign against corruption has already enjoyed the support of the people, who view the Party bureaucrats as parasites; and the KGB's assault on dissidents, liberals, and Jews has left the people, in the best case, merely indifferent. Hence the fact that Andropov's self-portrait is a double one. Like Janus, it has two faces, each looking in a different direction: the stern, adamant image for domestic consumption; and the liberal, intellectual one for foreign consumption. Or, to modify the figure, for the West it was necessary to daub over the same image that had to be brought out vividly for the Russians. The inevitable contradictions involved led to repeated disavowals and disavowals of disavowals.

Such was the case, for example, with the rumors about Andropov's knowledge of English. They were very important from his viewpoint, since a knowledge of English implied that he regularly listened to the Voice of America in English, read American and English newspapers and magazines every day, and even had the habit of reading an American book when he relaxed, whether it was Jacqueline Susann's *Valley of the Dolls*, Richard Llewellyn's *How Green Was My Valley*, or Salisbury's *The Gates of Hell*. Another version had it that he listened to American jazz and pop songs, and that a distinctive feature of his apartment was a Japanese stereo system, together with an abundant collection of records: Glenn Miller, Chubby Checker, Frank Sinatra, Peggy Lee, Bob Eberly, et al. The American newspapers seemed to be vying with one another in paying compliments to the man who was at first the future, and soon afterward, the new ruler of Russia. The record was set by the paper that prides itself on its fame as "the most reliable source of information in the world": *The New York Times*. Harrison Salisbury, even forgetting about Lenin, who had a good command of Latin, English, and German, wrote that Andropov was the first Russian leader since Emperor Nicholas II to know English. What he said was used in a sensational subhead for his article: "Andropov Reads America, Fluently."

The source of most of the information about Andropov's Anglo-American tastes has been Vladimir Sakharov, a former Soviet diplomat and KGB agent who defected in 1971, and before that had been a friend of Igor Andropov and visited the KGB chief's apartment. It is not even a question as to how truthful his testimony is. (A comparison of his early reminiscences about himself with his later ones about Yuri Andropov shows that, somewhat lacking in imagination, he most likely attributed his own tastes to his schoolmate's father.) Much more interesting is the fact that all of the former KGB agent's information about his former chief (who was not his immediate superior in command) surfaced in the American and Western European press precisely in the summer of 1982, and proved adequate to fix the West's notion of Andropov as pro-Western in terms of his tastes and proclivities. His knowledge of English was his visiting card—his pass allowing free entry into the free world.

The only point on which there was disagreement was how and where Andropov had learned English. Some people said that when already old, he took private lessons in English twice a week. Others claimed that he had learned it as a young man, when in the North he had dealings with the crews of American and British ships in convoys bringing war matériel and foodstuffs for the Red army. But that image was demolished only a few days after Andropov became the fifth Soviet vozhd. At the funeral ceremonies for his predecessor, and during a special tête-à-tête with Vice-President Bush, Andropov uttered not a single word in English. He was not even able to read the document presented to him by the American delegation, but instead patiently listened as it was translated by the official Kremlin interpreter, Sukhodrev. Malcolm Toon, the former U.S. ambassador to Moscow, who met with Andropov several times, has confirmed that all their talks were in Russian. And Andropov's minions, in a hurry to correct this faux pas, have backpedalled. One of them, in a conversation with Joseph Kraft, said that he saw an English grammar on Andropov's desk.

Such was the path taken by Andropov in his de-Anglicization: from *Valley of the Dolls* to a schoolbook.

The only one of his Western traits that has been confirmed by numerous eyewitnesses (including people who drank with him at official diplomatic receptions) is his preference for scotch, bourbon, or rye over vodka. Needless to say, this has only to do with the Kremlin chief's gastronomical tastes and nothing to do with his political ones. For that matter, Andropov himself, in an interview with a correspondent of *Der Spiegel* in the spring of 1983, refuted the rumors about his fondness for foreign beverages. As the Soviet vozhd, he no longer has the last word in his choice of drinks, and must give preference to vodka, if only out of patriotic considerations: what Zeus could do as a bull is not permitted to Zeus himself.

Right on the heels of the testimony about Andropov given by one Soviet agent who had fled to the West came more from another agent who had defected, former KGB Major Vladimir Kuzichkin. He escaped to the West in June 1982; i.e., right after the palace coup was carried out in Moscow. We find his tale even more fantastic than that of his colleague and namesake, Vladimir Sakharov. He told Western intelligence agents and journalists what they wanted to hear; namely, that Afghanistan would be a Russian Vietnam. The fledgling defector had borrowed that syllogism from the American press, where it had quickly become a commonplace. In order to make it more convincing, he put it into the mouth of his former boss, a KGB general, who allegedly told his subordinate one night: "Afghanistan is our Vietnam. Look at what has happened. We began by simply backing a friendly regime; slowly we got more deeply involved; then we started manipulating the regime—sometimes using desperate measures—and now? Now we are bogged down in a war we cannot win and cannot abandon. It's ridiculous. A mess. And but for Brezhnev and company we would never have got into it in the first place." (Quoted in *Time* magazine, November 22, 1982.)

Given the strict subordination and total fear existing in the Soviet Union, especially in military and KGB circles, for a KGB general to make such risky admissions to a subordinate—one, moreover, who was considerably beneath him in rank—is virtually impossible. That would have cost him his career, and perhaps his life. The question is: Was that "nocturnal conversation" the result of a free flight of the KGB defector's fancy? Or was it put into his mouth by his former— and perhaps still his real—bosses? In any case, the most important thing in that message from Moscow *urbi et orbi* is the allegation that Yuri Andropov and his Committee of State Security repeatedly advised Brezhnev and the other oldsters in the Politburo not to get involved in Afghanistan, but that they paid no heed, with the result that the Soviet Union now has its own Vietnam. This rumor was all the more expedient in that neither Brezhnev nor his coevals in the Politburo were able, for any practical purpose, to refute it. In general, during the period of his nominal presence at the head of the state, the feeble Brezhnev was extraordinarily useful to Andropov. He could be blamed for any unpopular actions (unpopular either in the West or at home) of which Andropov was actually the initiator, or in which he had taken an active part.

But the time was coming near when the secret author of the Kremlin drama would finally have to appear before the audience in the glare of the footlights.

Among all the rumors that preceded it, Andropov's accession to power was awaited like the advent of a Messiah. In the Soviet Union people hoped (and a few feared) that a new Stalin would come and, with an iron hand, restore order and prestige to the empire. Abroad, people hoped that a new Khrushchev would come, and with him, a new "Thaw": that dissidents would be released from prisons and insane asylums, the troops would be withdrawn from Afghanistan, the economy would be decentralized on the Hungarian model, and a new era of détente with the West would set in. As the passage of time has shown us, the Soviet forecasts proved to be more accurate than the Western ones.

It looked as if those responsible for Andropov's image in the West had overplayed their hand, underrating the receptiveness of Western public opinion and its tendency toward wishful thinking. And that might have undesirable effects later, when Andropov became officially the leader of the Soviet Union and did not justify the hopes placed in him by the free world, and when there was no longer anyone he could hide behind. Replacing *Valley of the Dolls* with an English grammar had been relatively easy. But now a much harder job lay ahead: to damp down liberal hopes for a future Soviet tsar, explaining in advance why they couldn't be realized immediately after his accession. As befitted a former head of the secret police, Andropov trusted almost no one—especially at such a decisive moment in his political career. *A fortiori*, he could not entrust to anyone else a task of such complexity: to moderate Western expectations while yet preserving his liberal image. So he decided to do it himself.

In that same summer of 1982, being already in fact (although not officially) the head of the Soviet Union, Yuri Andropov visited several Eastern European satrapies on a whirlwind trip. Although the KGB was already in the reliable hands of his loyal minion, Vitaly Fedorchuk, and although the trip itself was kept strictly secret, Andropov did not want to be away from the capital for long. He left at night in a special aircraft, and by evening of the next day he was already back, having managed in a few hours to visit Budapest, Prague, and East Berlin, and meet with the local leaders schooled by his organization: Janos Kadar, Gustav Husak, and Erich Honecker. He bypassed three other Eastern European capitals: Bucharest, because the Rumanian dictator, Nikolai Ceausescu, had fallen away from Moscow back in the mid-sixties; Warsaw, because he didn't trust General Jaruzelski all that much, being of the opinion that the latter's military coup was by no means the choice most favorable to Russia; and Sofia, because he preferred for the moment not to advertise his "Bulgarian connection," the other end of which led to St. Peter's Square in Rome. Anyway, the meetings in Hungary, Czechoslovakia, and East Germany sufficed for his purposes. And while he had kept his trip strictly secret in Moscow, in the East European capitals he found it useful to publicize them. Not only the fact of his trip but the content of his talks with his viceroys was made public.

Andropov confidentially told Kadar, Husak, and Honecker that in view of Brezhnev's failing health and his incapacity to govern the country, the Politburo had already elected him, Andropov, as Brezhnev's successor; and that for all practical purposes he was already the head of the Soviet Union. This much of the "secret" information was true, if one only remembers how Andropov's "election" occurred.

The next thing Andropov had to tell his East European protégés was more or less an open secret, and was surprising only because it came from the *de facto* leader of the Soviet empire. Andropov told them that the Soviet economy was in a catastrophic state, and that the most urgent task facing him was to straighten out the situation on the home front. He intended to do this with the help of able and honest military and KGB officers not tainted with corruption, who would be sent out on assignments to manage industrial production.

"I need at least two years to pull the country back from the edge of an economic abyss," Andropov said. "Right now I must concern myself only with domestic matters. So what we need now is a period of international quiescence."

"And what about Afghanistan?" one of his East European interlocutors is supposed to have asked.

"We have a greater interest than anyone else in a peaceful solution of that problem. We can make concessions, but they must be concessions with honor. If we are assured that Afghanistan will remain within the Soviet sphere of influence, we are ready to begin a phaseout of our troops. But this, in turn, will demand great compliancy on the part of the West."

And then Andropov explained specifically why he had made his supposedly secret trip. "I still have many enemies in the Central Committee. As leader I am not yet strong enough to make unilateral concessions. The West must take the first steps. Only then will I be able to respond to them, and not right away at that."

In this way Andropov postponed keeping those promises which, by means of rumors and hints, he had made to the free world. From his point of view it was an important corrective: while refusing to make unilateral concessions, he had proposed that the West make them.

Meantime, much more important matters were awaiting him at home. Those matters were so important that he hardly paid any attention to the war in Lebanon, and left his loyal client Arafat and the latter's PLO to the whims of fate. In so doing, he untied Israel's hands, and the PLO was doomed. There is no doubt but what Begin and Sharon, in their calculations, allowed for the fact that at that time the Kremlin bigwigs were caught up in a power struggle to the exclusion of everything else. Also, it was important to Andropov to highlight the picture of the empire's decline under his predecessor; and the Palestinians' defeat by Israel was unquestionably a defeat by proxy of the Soviet Union.

At this juncture Andropov's enemies were making desperate efforts to overthrow the imposter who had violated the rules of the Party hierarchy. They even won a few small victories; but they were victories that could yield nothing more than moral satisfaction. It was a struggle of the Lilliputians against Gulliver.

Konstantin Chernenko managed to drag Brezhnev to the Moscow Art Theater to see a play that had been banned by Andropov. It was called *Thus Will We Win*, and dealt with Lenin's last days and the problem of political succession. (This same play, when later viewed by Kraft, was accompanied by a pro-Andropov community.) The drama was entirely couched in the Aesopian style so commonly used in the Soviet Union, and was saturated with political allusions and analogies—something facilitated by the fact that Lenin and Brezhnev had the same patronymic, Ilich. It was partly for this reason that *Thus Will We Win* had been banned by Andropov: he did not want to have Brezhnev compared with Lenin (what did they really have in common?) and himself with Stalin. (Later, however, he gladly made use of the same play for the analogy "Lenin-Andropov.") But in the meantime Brezhnev, accompanied by his huge retinue, had gone to see a closed preview of the play, and had given his permission for it to be performed publicly. It was not a question of the Kremlin leader's political tastes but of his aesthetic ones. He had always loved melodramas. And now, commiserating with the dying Lenin on the stage and comparing him to himself, the moribund Brezhnev wept throughout the play—something regarded as the highest stamp of approval.

It was that play, which has to do with the political testament Lenin dictated not long before his death, and that the usurper Stalin kept carefully concealed for almost three decades, that gave the anti-Andropov group the idea of getting a similar document from Brezhnev.

As is generally known, there is no juridical form for a political testament in the Soviet Union: the USSR is a totalitarian empire, not a monarchical one. It was therefore decided to make use of Brezhnev's memoirs, the last volume of which was being rapidly ghosted at the time, and which dealt with events verging on the present. In that volume words describing Brezhnev's comrades-in-arms were put into his mouth. Nor did the ghostwriters neglect Andropov, whom Brezhnev "valued highly for his comradely humility, humanity, and outstanding managerial qualities." But the most flattering phrases were reserved for Konstantin Chernenko. He was characterized as a man "able to convince others and find the correct organizational forms," and as "an adamant fighter, receptive to the opinions of his comrades but ruthless toward himself." What this in fact meant was that Brezhnev was declaring Konstantin Chernenko to be his political heir. But if even Lenin's word did not have legal force, Brezhnev's had even less. Nonetheless, Andropov decided to insure himself—just in case. On his instructions and under various pretexts, the censors held up the publication of the last part of Brezhnev's memoirs, which had already been set in type by the magazine *Novy Mir*. It did not appear until January 1983, after Brezhnev's death, by which time the desiderata it contained were no longer of any importance.

Finally it became clear to the anti-Andropov group headed by Brezhnev and Chernenko that all their victories had been Pyrrhic; that they were fighting a powerful enemy, and using a weapon to which he was not vulnerable. At that point they tried to counterattack Andropov with heavier weapons. Alas, they were weapons that he wielded more skillfully than did his feeble opponents.

At 2:00 P.M. on September 10, all telephone connections between the Soviet Union and the rest of the world, including the East European countries, were suddenly cut off. The next day, when they had been restored, Soviet officials attributed what had happened to technical troubles. Specifically, they said there had been a malfunction in the two computer systems that the USSR had bought from France for the Moscow Olympics and were now being used for international telephone hookups. But from a technical viewpoint, that explanation was nonsense: similar systems were in operation in many other countries, and were functioning perfectly. Moreover, it was very unlikely that both systems would break down at the same time. In any case, no one in Moscow was particularly concerned about the plausibility of the explanation.

What had actually happened in Moscow that day was that a counterrevolution had been attempted. An awareness of what had been going on around him had finally come to the physically feeble Brezhnev. If it had not exactly penetrated his consciousness, it had at any rate alerted what was left of his once-powerful instinct of self-preservation. On the other hand, it was clearly realized by those whose power and position totally depended on the moribund and disgraced leader; but they could no longer act in his name as they had before.

Brezhnev's official heir, Konstantin Chernenko, was their last hope. In the Andropov camp he was contemptuously called "the country bumpkin." It was an allusion to the simplemindedness evident in the high-boned face of the Siberian-born Ukrainian, and also to his bluntness and lack of cleverness in intrigues—especially as contrasted with Andropov's jesuitism. When foreigners talked about Brezhnev's political heir with Georgi Arbatov, who was betting on Andropov, Arbatov told them that as a Soviet leader, Chernenko was impossible and even indecent. Formally, however, Chernenko remained secretary of the Central Committee and the person with the most frequent access to Brezhnev.

Another of Andropov's enemies who was still in the game was Nikolai Shchelokov, minister of internal affairs, who had under his command the many units of regular police in the capital, and who had no less reason to hate his more successful counterpart than Andropov had to hate him. Not only that, but he figured (and he was not mistaken) that if Andropov came to power, the first one to go on the junk heap would be himself, Shchelokov.

But the real fomenters of this plot of the doomed were the Churbanovs: Yuri Churbanov and his wife, Galina Brezhneva-Churbanova. Yuri was first deputy of the Ministry of Internal Affairs, but in fact was handling the duties of Shchelokov, who was seventy-two years

old. And Galina, whom Andropov's men were now subjecting to interrogations in connection with the diamond affair, had great influence
over both her husband and her father, Leonid Ilich Brezhnev.

Time was running out for the plotters. They took as their model
Malenkov and Khrushchev's arrest of Lavrenty Beria, then head of
the organs of state security, a few months after Stalin's death. They
realized that each step they took would promptly become known to
Andropov; and they acted rather out of desperation than coolly. Early
in the morning of September 10 the minister of internal affairs, General of the Army Shchelokov, received Brezhnev's official authorization to arrest Andropov "in the interests of national security," and
ordered Lieutenant-General Churbanov to immediately carry out the
instructions of the general secretary of the Communist Party and the
chairman of the USSR Supreme Soviet. Churbanov simultaneously
dispatched two detachments of police: one to Andropov's apartment,
and the other to his office in the Central Committee building. Naturally, both came up against special KGB troops. The one that had
been sent to the Central Committee building on Old Square was dis-
armed by troops loyal to Andropov while it was still on its way there.
The other one did its job better. According to rumors that we have no
way of verifying, an exchange of fire was heard that morning at 26
Kutuzovsky Prospekt, where Brezhnev's apartment was sandwiched
between Andropov's above it and Shchelokov's below it. Ominous
rumors about dead and wounded—most likely exaggerated—spread
rapidly through Moscow. In many parts of the country (especially in
the provinces), as soon as people learned that telephone connections
had been cut, they started to panic. In a matter of hours all supplies of
matches, soap, toothpaste, flour, sugar, and salt were bought up. People stood waiting in long lines around the stores, and by evening the
shelves had been emptied. Some were saying that a war was about to
begin. As always happens in a country where information is stifled,
the people's imaginations outran and exaggerated the gossip from the
court.

It is difficult to re-create in every detail what happened in Moscow
on September 10, 1982. Andropov's path to power led through the
pitch-darkness of total secrecy. And by no means all of its quirky turns
can be clearly brought to light by analyzing well-known facts, the
information we have got from the USSR (often via secret channels)
about little-known facts, and guesses about those that are completely

unknown. Here and there, that path remains so shrouded in darkness that one might think it had been planned by a trailblazer who deliberately did not blaze his trail, or else left false traces. Only the future will be able to map Andropov's path to power accurately—provided the future is more sharp-sighted and astute than the present.

One thing, however, is clear: the trust that Andropov had placed in Colonel-General Vitaly Fedorchuk, whom he had appointed head of the secret police, was fully justified. As soon as he learned of the attempt at a counterrevolution, Fedorchuk cut off all telephone connections with the outside world, put the troops under him on Red Alert, established martial law in the capital, and put all instigators of the counterrevolution—including Brezhnev—under house arrest. Fedorchuk's was the key role in suppressing the counterrevolution. His reputation for brutality was in itself enough to terrify both his enemies and his subordinates. Apparently even Andropov, who had counted on him at the decisive moment in his struggle for power, had reason to fear him. For that reason, among others—and also because he wanted to root out sedition in the KGB's rival ministry, the MVD—after coming to power Andropov transferred Fedorchuk from the former ministry to the latter. "The Moor has done his duty; the Moor may go." Or, more precisely, he may move on to another department.

(Immediately after Brezhnev's death all of the plotters were exiled from Moscow to the most godforsaken parts of the empire, under the pretext that they were being transferred to new jobs.)

It was only natural that after the failed attempt at a counterrevolution, Andropov's position should become even stronger. Beginning in September there were increasing rumors about Brezhnev's impending retirement. Two things about these reports were amazing: they came from government sources, and they specified that Brezhnev would be retired with honor. (With the exception of Lenin, all former Soviet leaders had been in a state of official disgrace.) At the same time, the ailing Brezhnev's schedule of public appearances and speeches became more and more demanding—something that was plainly beyond his strength. It was during this period that one joke about Brezhnev enjoyed special popularity. It seems that he mounted the speakers' platform, took a prepared speech out of his pocket, and began to read, only to discover that it was his own obituary. Noticing the commotion in the audience, he paused and looked closely at the typescript. "Oh, damn! Once again I've put on Andropov's jacket instead of my own!"

In that same autumn the Moscow career of an Assyrian lady by the name of Dzhuna Davitashvili came to an abrupt end. She was a faith healer from Tbilisi who, by means of emanations of mysterious bio-energy, had practically dragged Brezhnev back from the grave on several occasions. Other oldsters from the Politburo had also availed themselves of her services, as had famous people from the worlds of science, art, and literature. She was very much in demand, and enjoyed a tremendous vogue. Even the newspapers began to print articles about the miracles she performed with sick people: curing ulcers, rejuvenating tissue, and charming away Parkinson's disease. People with venomous tongues, however, called her "Rasputin in a skirt" and, by analogy with the last years of Emperor Nicholas II's reign, prophesied the imminent fall of Brezhnev, since a miracle maker had already made her appearance in his court.

And then, unexpectedly, an end was put to Dzhuna's practice. What had happened was that Andropov himself finally came to believe in the hypnotic powers of that Eastern woman, and decided to deprive his ward of her therapeutic support. It was explained to Brezhnev that the sorceress's mysterious visits to him were giving rise to undesirable rumors and dubious analogies, and infecting the people with superstitions that ran counter to the foundations of Marxism-Leninism.

As Andropov had figured, the excommunication of Dzhuna had a painful psychological effect on Brezhnev. And her disgrace enabled the Moscow wits to extend the historical analogy. They reminded their listeners that Grishka Rasputin, the "Holy Devil," was murdered by the court camarilla two months before the abdication of the last Russian emperor.

Actually, Brezhnev had even less time to live.

November 7, the day when the sixty-fifth anniversary of the Great Russian Revolution was to be celebrated, was drawing near. The weather forecast was for extreme cold. Brezhnev's doctors categorically opposed his appearing on Lenin's Tomb to review the military parade. They wanted him to avoid hypothermia, which is especially dangerous for old people. But Andropov insisted that Brezhnev should appear, claiming that his absence on such a day would be wrongly interpreted by both the Soviet public and foreign observers. The demands of holiday protocol in the USSR were binding upon everyone, and were fulfilled to the letter. Andropov did everything he could to hasten the fateful dénouement.

II

A Farewell Glance from Lenin's Tomb; or, An Obituary of Brezhnev

> As I see it, the life of a jailer is not one whit better than that of a prisoner. — ASTOLPHE, MARQUIS DE CUSTINE, *Russia in 1839*

> He could have killed more than he could have fed
> but chose to do neither. By falling dead
> he leaves a vacuum and the black Rolls-Royce
> to one of the boys who will make the choice.
> — JOSEPH BRODSKY, "Epitaph for a Tyrant," 1982

On November 7, 1982, three days before his death, the doddering Soviet vozhd, supported on both sides by assistants and pausing on each step to get his breath, struggled up to the rostrum atop Lenin's Tomb, where he stood for several hours, holding up his benumbed hand in a gesture of welcome. It was ten degrees above zero, the old man's blood gave him no warmth, and the muscles on his swollen face seemed petrified. It was his farewell to all that had once belonged to him: Red Square, Moscow, Russia. One week later his comrades would make their way up to the top of that same tomb; and his successor, Yuri Vladimirovich Andropov, would open the memorial service for him. Then his coffin would be lowered into a grave beside the Kremlin Wall, between the tomb which was the eternal resting place of the founder of the worker-peasant state, Lenin, and the grave of his successor (actually, his betrayer), Stalin, the man under whom Brezhnev began his political career.

Earlier, overshadowed by leaders of the first rank, he had climbed up that mausoleum with Stalin. Later on, it was with Khrushchev, whom he had served loyally until the autumn of 1964, when he overthrew him and took his place as Party leader. After that, he made the climb as one of a triumvirate, along with Podgorny and Kosygin, with whom he at first shared the Khrushchev succession, until he ousted Podgorny (on the basis of a denunciation by Andropov) and Kosygin died—some three years later. In recent years he had stood atop the mausoleum essentially alone, although surrounded by his ceremonial suite, the Politburo. It was to one of the Politburo members, Andropov, that he had fully entrusted the protection of his throne against pretenders, since by reason of age he himself was no longer able to delve into Kremlin intrigues—something required not only for the seizure of power but its retention. Thanks to Andropov he was assured of several tranquil years. At the same time, however, he doomed himself to the horrible agony of his last year, when he was unable to defend not only his closest friends and confreres but even his own family against his high-ranking keeper. For there is nothing more dangerous to a dictator than his own bodyguard.

But then, was he ever really a dictator?

Outwardly, perhaps.

The phenomenon of Brezhnev's political longevity was astounding when compared with political careers in other countries, and even when viewed against the Russian background. During his rule there were changes—sometimes repeatedly—in the leadership of most countries in the world, both democratic and totalitarian. Those countries include France, Great Britain, West Germany, Italy, Yugoslavia, Poland, the papal state, Spain, China, India, Pakistan, Iran, Israel, Egypt, and even Uganda. In the United States alone there were five presidents during that period. As for his own country, although there had been Russian tsars and vozhds who had ruled longer than he, there had not been a single functioning leader who had lived to such an advanced age. In this, Brezhnev held the record. Emperor Nicholas II was executed at the age of fifty; Ivan the Terrible, Peter the Great, and Lenin all died about the age of fifty-three; Nicholas I died at fifty-nine; Alexander II was killed by a bomb six weeks before his sixty-third birthday; Catherine the Great died at age sixty-seven; and even Stalin, despite the traditional longevity of Georgians, hardly made it to the age of seventy-three.

During the time he was in power, Brezhnev outlived, either physically or politically, not only all his rivals but all his compeers and even his potential heirs. Now Andropov was the only rival, compeer, and heir; although in the very recent past, only a few years before, he had been none of any of these. He was a man from the outside; and only toward the end did he join the ranks of the pretenders to the Kremlin throne. But he brought up the rear of those ranks, with the status of an outsider. In what was literally the final stage of that tense power struggle, during the last year of Brezhnev's nominal presence at the head of the Party and the state, Andropov outstripped at least a dozen more likely candidates for the top job from Brezhnev's immediate entourage, and hit the tape first. The only difference between the Kremlin power struggle and a sports competition is that in the former the tape was a relative concept: one could not guess exactly where it was. But one could bring it closer. Because for a person whose path was blocked by an old man, what could be a better presumption of innocence than the old man's death—often predicted and, more than once, falsely announced? As for the present biographers of Andropov, they would like to believe that no matter how much the power struggle heated up in 1982, both Suslov and Brezhnev died natural deaths.

How amazingly history sometimes repeats itself, even after a short interval! It's as if someone beyond our field of vision and our understanding had found, for an event in the past, the right modern rhyme to join together the unfastened links of the historical chain. Just as Andropov was now weaving a plot around the ill and enfeebled Brezhnev, did not Stalin do the same to the dying Lenin? One after another, he ousted all of those close friends and confreres with whom Lenin had made the revolution—Trotsky, Zinoviev, Kamenev, Bukharin, Rykov—so as, in the late thirties, to destroy all of them physically, along with so many others. And the mighty Lenin, who had overcome all his political opponents during the brief (several months) period of Russian democracy, found himself totally impotent before the intrigues of such a crafty, if intellectually contemptible, enemy as Stalin.

There was even a vague rumor that Lenin had not died a natural death but had been poisoned by Stalin. Not long before his own death, Trotsky wrote an article for *Life* magazine titled "Did Stalin Poison Lenin?" In it he mentioned, among other things: the pharmacopoeia of poisons available to the Soviet secret police; Bukharin's remark that Stalin was "capable of anything"; and, finally, the very strange state-

ment that Stalin made at a session of the Politburo, in the presence of
Trotsky, Zinoviev, and Kamenev—a statement to the effect that in late
February 1923 Lenin had asked him for poison in case he should feel
another stroke coming on. Such a request was very unlikely. At the
time, Lenin and Stalin were quarrelling violently over a crude and
insulting conversation Stalin had had with Lenin's wife, Krupskaya.
Also, on January 4 Lenin had dictated a codicil to his political testament stressing the necessity of removing Stalin from the post of general secretary. Lenin could not have asked anything of Stalin; not
merely because he didn't trust him but also because he was no longer
associating with him. Again, suicide by means of poison is rather a
Levantine way of doing it, understandable to a Georgian like Stalin. If
Lenin had made up his mind to commit suicide, he would probably
have done it in one of the usual European ways. But he bore little
resemblance to a suicidal type—especially to a suicidal type who
would have discussed his possible suicide with anybody, and in particular, with his rabid enemy, Stalin. Stalin's statement at the Politburo session was pure invention. Its purpose must have been to divert
suspicion from him in case Lenin died, although actually it was *per se*
highly suspect.

Even more suspect was the telegram Stalin sent Trotsky (then in
the Caucasus) giving a false date for Lenin's funeral. When Trotsky
reached Moscow, the vozhd's body had already been embalmed and
the viscera cremated. And why did Stalin have a mausoleum built, and
have Lenin's remains put in a glass coffin—in flagrant contradiction of
Marxist materialism? Was it not so as to prevent, with the aid of that
archaic Eastern ritual, any attempts at exhumation, either by contem-
poraries or posterity?

Life refused to print Trotsky's article; but ten days before his
murder by one of Stalin's agents, it appeared in a Hearst publication,
Liberty magazine. The question most often asked by critics of
Trotsky's theory about the poisoning of Lenin was: Why did Trotsky
keep that secret until 1939? But the truth was that Trotsky did not
keep it: he simply didn't learn it until 1939. Stalin's strength lay in the
fact that in the early twenties none of his colleagues (including Lenin
and Trotsky) even had an inkling as to what he was capable of. His
statement that in 1923 Lenin had asked him for poison did not strike
Trotsky as suspect. But after the trials of the revolution's leaders in the
late thirties, and the Great Terror that accompanied them, he had

second thoughts about that statement, and related it to other events. Trotsky, with his intellectual's blindness toward Stalin, did not understand him until late in his own life; and then he took a new view of Lenin's death. It was in all respects a tardy suspicion.

As for Brezhnev, who only a few months before had wept as he watched the play in which the great Lenin lived out his last days in mortal fear of his rival and successor (and possible murderer as well), he could not but have sensed that ominous parallel as he stood freezing atop Lenin's Tomb on the morning of November 7, 1982.

With each passing year it became harder for him to mount those polished marble steps. (For some reason, no one had thought of installing an elevator or escalator, a steam heating system, seats, or even a toilet next to the rostrum, which also cost him great inconvenience— something he was afraid to admit to anyone.) And each time it seemed to him that this would be his last appearance here. Because he was very sick. Every step was hard for him, his jaw hung slack, and he was short of breath: like a fish on the ice, he would open his mouth wide, gasping for the cold air. The time came when he ceased to understand why anyone needed to drag him up there, half alive, and show him to the people, instead of putting him to bed and letting him have at least a little rest before he died. He glanced around at confreres of his own age and saw that for them, too, it was intolerable to stand there, as required by the inflexible protocol, before those thousands of troops and civilians moving in columns across Red Square like a gigantic caterpillar. And what if, suddenly, they should all be felled by simultaneous heart attacks, before the very eyes of the panic-stricken holiday crowd? Then, too, directly below them on both sides of Lenin's Tomb, stretching along the Kremlin Wall, was the graveyard of the great, where they were destined to be buried.

During those last years he bore "the fateful burden of power" with a heroic endurance that was sometimes reminiscent of Hans Christian Andersen's tin soldier, at other times of those very real Japanese soldiers who went on hiding in the jungles and resisting an invisible enemy, long after their country had surrendered to that enemy and had even become friendly with him. He had trouble realizing what was going on around him. At the meeting with Carter in Vienna, he managed to sign SALT II; but he was no longer strong enough to keep hold of his attaché case, and would have dropped it if an assistant had not come to his rescue. On his last visit to Bonn, he kept going off in the wrong direction. And at a dinner party in India, he dropped his knife, fork, and spoon; but he was hungry, so he began to take food with his fingers. At the Twenty-sixth Party Congress, the last one in his lifetime, he was supposed to deliver a speech several hours long; and he did—in a way. But the words kept piling up, one on top of another, and he often got off the track. It seemed to him that he was reading the speech, but he was really just opening his mouth to emit incoherent whistling sounds. After six minutes of this, the live TV broadcast (from the Kremlin's Palace of Congresses) had to be discontinued, and an announcer read almost all of the speech for him. Meantime, he stood there at the lectern, hanging on to it so he wouldn't fall, gasping for breath, whispering, and making those whistling sounds. Yet he seemed to think that he was reading the speech, and that everyone understood him.

Many jokes had been told about his political longevity; and immediately after the above incident, a new one began making the rounds. It seems there was a man who had asked to be frozen for one hundred years so that he could find out what new things would have happened in the world during that time. When he woke up in the year 2081 and turned on the television, he heard: "At the Fifty-first Party Congress, the regular report was delivered by General Secretary of the Communist Party of the Soviet Union Leonid Ilich Brezhnev. . . ." Thanks to him, even immortality had become a subject of banter.

It's not just that he wasn't a dictator: he never managed, even for a short time, to become the country's sole, fully empowered ruler. At first he governed along with the two other members of the triumvirate, Kosygin and Podgorny, under the ideological supervision of Mikhail Suslov. Then, when the triumvirate fell apart and he was supposedly the sole official vozhd, his health failed him. One heart attack followed another, he lost the use of his tongue, and his legs refused to obey him. During this time a deadly fight for power was beginning behind his back; but he was in no condition to intervene, on one side or the other. Finally, as so often happens in Eastern courts, the commander of the palace guard got the upper hand. (In accordance with his modern-day status, that commander had many other duties besides.)

That was Brezhnev's secret: he never personally ruled the country. But he didn't suffer from that, because he preferred the trappings of power to the thing itself.

The Brezhnev era has been called colorless; and so it actually was in comparison with more vivid bygone times like those of Stalin and Khrushchev. It was as if nature had run short of pigments, having used them all up on earlier eras.

Unlike Stalin and Khrushchev, Brezhnev was devoid of that striking individuality which, in a totalitarian state, is a sign of voluntarism. If we leave moral judgments aside, Stalin and Khrushchev represent two extremes in the way the Soviet Union is governed. Both were voluntarists, although their voluntarism was expressed in opposite ways: in massive political terror under the former, and liberal reforms under the latter. Stalin caused the Ship of State to list heavily, and almost heel over and sink in a gulf of blood; Khrushchev saved it by making it roll to the other side. Brezhnev's crew righted it, and brought it back into the main channel traditional for Russia: bureaucratic government without liberal or tyrannical extremes. Being a colorless apparatchik with no strong political convictions, he became a figure of shifting compromise between the different tendencies, both at the top level in the Kremlin and among the lower classes. (We must not forget that there is a *law of elemental democracy* operative in the Soviet Union.) Brezhnev's era lacked luster because he resisted his opponents' attempts to color it one definite hue: all at the same time, he opposed the extremism of the liberals and that of the neo-Stalinists. Naturally, the latter were more numerous, steadfast, and aggressive than the former; and Brezhnev's resistance to the liberals was more effective than his opposition to the Stalinists.

And yet the colorlessness of the Brezhnev era was illusory. It is merely that during the period in question, the regeneration of the regime was a latent process. And the more undiscernible those changes before Andropov took the place that had been Brezhnev's, the more clearly they came into view afterward. The lackluster Brezhnev era—one that seemed to be ideologically neutral and strictly bureaucratic—was actually a time of radical and irreversible changes in the very structure of the Soviet state; changes that reduced the chief of state's role to a decorative minimum by putting a new center of power—police power—in the forefront. It was the very colorlessness of Brezhnev's bureaucratic regime that prepared the way for the sudden fireworks of the police state that followed it. Again, thanks to Brezhnev's unfailing presence at parades and ceremonies, the police coup carried out by Andropov while the former was still the titular leader, remained invisible to outside observers, and was discovered by them only after the old vozhd had gone to his grave. The paradox lay in the fact that despite his sickliness Brezhnev managed to outlive the Brezhnev era—the one to which he had given his name but for which he was nothing more than a Potemkinesque façade. Behind that façade the foundations of a new regime were being laid—imperceptibly but solidly.

Brezhnev was a living bridge across which Russia passed from one epoch to another.

In his last years he in no sense played an active role but rather a passive one, serving as a kind of force point for his impatient heir. While in no way comparing him to Imre Nagy, Alexander Dubcek, or Andrei Sakharov in terms of his political activity, we nonetheless make bold to say that in those last years he, too, like them, was Andropov's victim. And as he stood atop Lenin's Tomb on November 7, 1982, he could not have failed to understand that. His farewell to Moscow on that day was not only sad but tragic.

Three days later, on the morning of November 10, after having had breakfast and read *Pravda*, he went into his bedroom, followed by the bodyguards Andropov had assigned to him. A few minutes later they returned to the living room and told Victoria Petrovna Brezhneva that her husband had suddenly died.

On the Way to a Police State: Power Without Ideology

12

Order leads to all the virtues.
But what leads to order?

— GEORG CHRISTOPH
LICHTENBERG, *Aphorisms*

On New Year's Eve 1982–83, as usual, a TV announcer addressed holiday greetings to the Soviet public, although this time the greetings were unusual: "Happy New Year, comrades! Happy New 1937!"

This is of course a joke, the Soviet people's only form of political expression. And like most jokes, this one was based on artistic hyperbole: the Andropov era was not yet approaching that of Stalin. But then the Stalin era did not begin in the year 1937, which with its orgy of terror marked the apogee of that era: it had begun thirteen years earlier. Andropov does not have that much time available to him. He became Party leader at a later time in life than did any other Soviet *vozhd*: ten years later than Khrushchev, eleven later than Brezhnev, twenty-one later than Lenin, and a full twenty-four later than Stalin. (Stalin's was the earliest début, which may be why he outdid the others.) Judging from Andropov's age (sixty-eight when he officially came to power) and his state of health, his tenure as leader will be at the utmost as long as Lenin's: six years, probably less. True, one must allow for the fact that he is not altogether a freshman, having become the all-powerful ruler while Brezhnev was still around, so that what happened right after the latter's death must be seen as a strictly *pro forma* inauguration. There was not, and could not have been, any struggle or vacillation among the Moscow partocrats, all the more so

[268]

among the legislators, since Andropov was backed by the secret police. The former KGB chief simply dictated his will to the docile Central Committee; and then to that completely fictive organization, the Soviet Parliament, and all it did was to make the *de facto de jure*. That is precisely why Andropov needed only a few months to accomplish what it took Brezhnev thirteen years to do, Khrushchev five years, and Stalin seventeen: to consolidate in his own hands the Party, government, and military power. The power struggle in the Kremlin had ended long before Brezhnev's death: on that cold, January day in 1982 when his brother-in-law, General Semyon Tsvigun, deputy chairman of the KGB, was found in his office with a bullet in his head. Now, none of Andropov's closest entourage would risk his life by infringing on the power of the Kremlin's new master, even though his physical strength began to fail him as early as the spring of 1983. The atmosphere of Stalinist terror that he is now trying to revive throughout the Soviet empire was first revived in the Kremlin itself, among the Party and government bosses. So his usurpation of the three top posts—general secretary of the Party, commander-in-chief, and president—is merely formalistic and a way of honoring the "decorative" tradition, nothing more.

So while Brezhnev was yet among the living and the Politburo had become an almshouse, the center of power had shifted from the Central Committee to the KGB, for which Andropov had obtained the status of "a state within a state," no longer subject to anyone but subjugating everything around it. That is why the last years of the Brezhnev era differ so sharply from its beginnings: the rise of détente, and its inglorious end; the bloom of dissent, and its stamping-out; the authorization and upsurge of Jewish emigration, and its waning; the relative restraint of Soviet expansionism, and its new phase, which began on Christmas Eve 1979 with the annexation of a neighboring state (Afghanistan). It was as if, during those last years, the country were being ruled by another man—not the one who had been its ruler during the preceding decade. Alas, that is not a figure of speech: such was in fact the case. So that to expect a change in the Kremlin's policy because of Andropov's self-appointment would be rather naïve, not to say absurd—like waiting for a train that has already left. The roots of the regime established in Moscow after Brezhnev's death are to be sought in the last phase of his illusory rule. They will be found in the period of his physical and political death agony (lasting for years and not months, as in the case of Tito or Franco), when, after wiping out all traces of the Khrushchevian "Thaw," the bureaucratic empire again began to turn into a police state, as in the days of Stalin. The empire's policy was not changed by General Secretary Andropov in November 1982: it was changed long before that by Andropov the regent.

He succeeded in doing something that could not even be managed by Beria, who toward the end of Stalin's life had also gathered colossal power into his own hands as head of state security. But for Beria circumstances were not so favorable as for Andropov. In those days the man at the top was not an enfeebled vozhd but a tyrant who was wide awake even at night. Also, that was a time when the people had been exhausted by Stalinism; whereas toward the close of the Brezhnev era they were becoming nostalgic for it. They saw it as a bitter but necessary and quick-acting medicine to be used against economic collapse, unruly Poland, troubles along the border with China, and many other things.

In that context Stalinism was more or less a symbol of a certain kind of rule, a pipe dream of resurrecting Stalin's methods but not the tyrant himself: Stalinism, but without Stalin, in the hope of avoiding the paranoiac excesses of that era. And then the cult of Stalin was a bad thing for the new ruler because it didn't leave room for a cult of himself—even if it was, as in Andropov's case, a cult of modesty in imitation of Lenin, emphasizing the parallel with him: "Modesty is more prideful than pride." Finally, it was not just a question of Stalin but of a whole band of Russian historical heroes who, with steady hands, had guided Russia to glory and greatness, leaving mountains of corpses behind:

> In every age, when things were going hard
> Our land was strictly governed by stern men
> Who loved it from the bottom of their hearts.
> Amid the crowd, rebels and enemies
> All crossed themselves when, on the block, chopped-off
> Heads vilely cursed the Tsar, "the little Father" . . .
> Only the centuries showed they were right.
> With their field-glasses, holding pipe in hand,
> Their legs encased in jackboots, combat boots,
> They stand there in the empire's history.

We have a special reason for quoting this paltry verse by Felix Chuyev in which Stalin ("holding pipe in hand") is definitely shifted from one historical category to another: from that of the Bolshevik revolutionaries to the class of autocratic tsars like Ivan the Terrible and Peter the Great, also alluded to here. We have quoted the poem as yet more evidence that Andropov was brought to power not only by a police coup but by the people's yearning for that strong man whom Russia's trying times demanded. It was a moment when the law of elemental democracy began to function with unusual efficacy. Andropov's accession was welcomed by others than just the police and military; e.g., some of the Moscow intellectuals, although their enthusiasm was expressed in either an allegorical or a deliberately obscure way.

Thus in early 1983 the popular Soviet poet Igor Shklyarevsky published in *Literaturnaya gazeta* a poem whose theme was phenological, but which was interpreted by keen-eyed Soviet readers as a political paean to the new Soviet vozhd. (It must be borne in mind that the Khrushchev era, as compared to Stalin's, was called the "Thaw," while Brezhnev's was equated with a process of decay.)

> The earth rings out! I love the purity
> Of cold spells. They intimidate decay.
> Your mind's alert, and drives all sloth away.
> You're more aware that you hold life in fee.

The alert leader, the political cold spell, the campaign against sloth and decay: Aesopian language is so widespread in Russia that it is used not only for satire but for panegyrics.

The position taken by Roy Medvedev, the only dissident to survive Andropov's purges, demands more serious attention. We shall call him an official dissenter, since even if he acts on his own initiative and not on direct orders from the authorities, the latter have an interest in that personal initiative. Otherwise there would be no way to explain their pathological "democratism" toward him. At the same time, his knowledge of cloakroom doings at the Kremlin puts beyond doubt his role as a liaison man between someone in the Kremlin and Western journalists in Moscow. The information from the Kremlin's "Deep Throat," passed on by Roy Medvedev to Western newspapers, comes back to Moscow via the Russian-language broadcasts of the Voice of

America, the BBC, and the *Deutsche Welle*. And during those broadcasts the powerful Soviet jammers are either switched off or functioning at a low-decibel level, lackadaisically. If we take this into account,
we cannot escape the conclusion that the information in question is
precisely what is advantageous to the present master of the Kremlin.
And not only now, but before, when he was contending with the
Brezhnev clique for the supreme power. (The premature rumors of
Brezhnev's death, and the circus affair—the *salto mortale*—involving
his daughter, were broadcast to the Soviet listeners without inter-
ference. In the face of such news, the KGB jammers remained defer-
entially mute.) So that what we have here is an unofficial source of
official information that is carefully chosen in accordance with its
usefulness to Andropov. Often such information is known to be false,
but the fact that it comes from a quasi-official source gives it a certain
credibility. This was the case, for example, with the reported suicide
of Semyon Tsvigun, Andropov's deputy at the KGB; with the version
of Andropov's coup as a KGB-military one carried out with the help of
Minister of Defense Ustinov; and the hypothesis that Andropov is half
Jewish. When Andropov was officially appointed general secretary,
Roy Medvedev made haste to welcome the new Soviet vozhd and
thereby overstepped the boundary of his quasi-dissident role,
thoughtlessly betraying it. The matter was quickly straightened out.
He was summoned to the USSR General Prosecutor's Office, where he
was given a "serious warning" about his activities. Naturally, the
world press was promptly informed of that, and Medvedev's reputation was fully restored, the *New York Times* even comparing him to
Abelard. Supposedly, in prematurely welcoming the new regime,
Medvedev had sold his soul to the devil, and instead of gratitude had
received a reprimand. But that is a false picture: the summons to the
prosecutor's office had no effect on the Soviet Abelard's subsequent
behavior, and none on the Soviet authorities' attitude toward him.

On the basis of the many interviews that Roy Medvedev has given
on the subject of Andropov, and the many articles he has written
about him, one naturally expected the publication of a book about the
new Soviet vozhd authored by Roy Medvedev; and it was easy to
surmise in advance that it would be a panegyric in the official vein. A
book containing his observations and judgments actually did appear,
but under the name of his twin brother, kindred spirit, and co-author,
Zhores Medvedev. It is hard for us to tell who is in fact the author of

this book, or why the Russian Goncourt brothers had to resort to such transparent literary camouflage. But then that is not the important thing.

The book is an omnium-gatherum of all the myths Andropov has spread about himself, ranging from his non-participation in putting down the Hungarian revolution of 1956 to his opposition to the invasion of Afghanistan on Christmas Eve 1979. Andropov is presented as a character right out of a fairy tale who remains pure as the driven snow no matter how dirty everything around him is. In places, the fulsome flattery and vindications make this book absurd, as in the following statement with its classic dangler: "After fifteen years of heading the KGB, nobody can prove his personal responsibility for excesses. . . ." So writes Medvedev in his full-dress portrait of Andropov.

In this fairy tale, as in many another, side by side with the angel is the Devil incarnate: Brezhnev—who initiated the suppression of dissent and the occupation of Afghanistan—to whom the liberal-intellectual opposition was headed up by the chairman of the KGB. In this case we are not concerned with Roy Medvedev personally (and this applies even more strongly to his literary pseudonym, "Zhores Medvedev") but with him as a source of information—with his credibility. In the final analysis, he may not even know whose mouthpiece he is. It may seem to him that he is manipulating the news he gets from the Kremlin, while in fact it is manipulating him. For that matter, a cruder version is not ruled out.

These, however, are merely extra resources. Andropov would have come to power without them: a half-million KGB agents sufficed. (Actually, there are of course many more of them than that. One would have to look at the latest Soviet census to find out exactly how many "employees" the KGB has. It could not keep control of such a huge country if it did not knit all Soviet citizens together with fear and compel each of them, from the lowest to the highest, to work for it.)

Here is another joke about the new Andropov era. "What do you think, Yuri Vladimirovich—will the Soviet people follow you?" "Yes, they will. Because if they don't follow me, they'll follow Brezhnev."

Today, for the first time in Soviet history, Moscow has a regime with no ideology—a regime that will transform the worker-peasant state founded by Lenin into a purely police state with no tincture of ideology or its anachronisms. Even Stalin used Communist ideology as a cover for his reign of terror. And Brezhnev needed its façade to cover up the naked reinforced concrete of his bureaucratic structure. But Andropov's accession to power put an end to that Orwellian masquerade: the new Soviet vozhd has expressed disdain for the former slogans, and flatly stated that "you cannot get things done by slogans alone." Power no longer pretends to be anything else: it is power as such. On that basis alone, one may expect that the regime will be harsher on the home front and more aggressive in foreign policy, although it will no doubt be more jesuitic in both areas.

It remains an open question whether the new regime, having discarded the camouflage of Communism, will resort to another ideology that has always been concomitant with police-state tendencies in Russian history: great-power nationalism. The fact that Andropov's closest colleagues include an Azerbaijani and a Ukrainian, while he himself is from a family of Russianized Greeks in the South, so far presents no obstacle to such a course. As is well known, Stalin and his henchman, Beria, were both Georgians; but that did not stop them from spreading chauvinistic propaganda throughout the country after the war. Up to now Andropov has not had recourse to that time-tested weapon of the Russian empire, although he always has, ready at hand, his former protéges from the Russian Party. This means that for the time being he is well-enough served by his police arsenal of direct, extra-ideological means of pressure, the surest and most universal of which is fear. Thus the joke about the New Year's greeting in which 1937 is substituted for 1983 can be regarded in two ways. It can be seen as premature; or as prophetic, made up for future use, the way one buys clothes for rapidly growing children. But that the tempo of change under Andropov will be faster than under any of his predecessors is already plain to see from its rapidity since the very beginning—if we arbitrarily take as the beginning the day of his inauguration as general secretary of the Communist Party of the Soviet Union: November 12, 1982. He has to hurry, because he doesn't even have a decade in which to do the job, like Khrushchev, not to mention Brezhnev's eighteen years and Stalin's twenty-nine. The power he now holds is not merely executive: it is also legislative, and it is supreme. Today both the making of decisions and their execution depends upon him, and him alone. Before, there was someone to restrain him. Will he now be able to restrain himself?

Leo Tolstoy once wrote in his diary that the human condition is one of flux, and that man holds all possibilities within himself. Accordingly, we feel no inclination to confuse morality and politics and present Andropov with a bill for his former activities. Having carried out his police coup and usurped the power (from earlier usurpers), will Andropov change? Will there be a change in his methods, his habits, his way of thinking, his style? Will his new position make him a bigger man? Or will he go on being the same gendarme with a KGB man's mentality and methods—methods that will be applied even more unrestrictedly since now he can permit himself things that, before, were denied him by others? To put it more directly: will he have the resources to become the leader of his country? Or will he continue to be its chief gendarme, but with unlimited powers?

Power changes a person, making him more responsible. Henry V of England changed when he became king. True, he was much younger than Yuri Andropov; and in order to change he had to make a clean break with those boon companions (headed by Falstaff) that he hung around with when he was still a prince. Andropov, by contrast, took in tow all his cronies from the KGB: Geidar Aliyev became a Politburo member and first deputy premier; Vitaly Fedorchuk was named minister of internal affairs; and Victor Chebrikov became KGB chairman. (When he was serving as Andropov's deputy, he would summon dissidents to his office and introduce himself as "Rebrikov.") The secret police served as Andropov's main source of supply—not only of methods but of key personnel. For that matter, it was a case of mutuality: no one is more familiar with the habits and traditions of the police than policemen themselves. Or again, those who, while holding a Party position, have shown that police work is their real forte. For example, the Leningrad Party boss, Grigori Romanov, whom Andropov called to Moscow and brought into the secretariat of the Central Committee.

Andropov's entourage represented a radical change from Brezhnev's. Gorbachev from Stavropol, Romanov from Leningrad, Fedorchuk from Kiev, and Aliyev from Baku: all were people from the outside who were not tainted with Moscow corruption, who had not yet put down roots in Moscow and had no connections there—political loners who were totally dependent on their patron. A skillful intriguer and conspirator, aging and growing physically weaker, Andropov did everything to prevent that which, thanks to himself, had happened to Brezhnev.

But that was only the beginning. In lieu of that "new class" of partocrats, already aged not only physically but politically, Andropov has been creating a new "new class"—people who came late to the table and are now hastening to make up for lost time. In order to give power to these new people, it was necessary—what with the scarcity of high Party-government posts and the perks that go along with them—to get rid of the old boys in short order. The first to fall was Brezhnev's myrmidon (who tried to block Andropov's path to power), Andrei Kirilenko, Brezhnev's closest aide and one-time official heir. He was followed by others.

Minister of Internal Affairs Nikolai Shchelokov, Brezhnev's closest associate since the Dnepropetrovsk days, was sent off to be chief of (regular) police at the construction site for the Siberian gas pipeline. (His son Igor was in Siberia, too, but as a prisoner—allegedly because of black-market operations. And Shchelokov's wife came to a violent end in April 1983. Rumor has it that she committed suicide, but we have no way of ascertaining the actual cause of her death.)

Having wreaked vengeance on one of his neighbors at 26 Kutuzovsky Prospekt, the vindictive Andropov had not forgotten the other, from whom he had wrenched the reins of power. And since Brezhnev was no longer there to be dealt with personally, he expelled his relatives from Moscow: Shchelokov's deputy and Brezhnev's son-in-law, Yuri Churbanov, was dispatched—along with Galina Brezhneva, his wife—beyond the Arctic Circle to become chief of police in Murmansk; and Brezhnev's son Yuri was removed from his post as deputy minister of foreign trade (supposedly for constant drunkenness) and sent in exile to Kazakhstan, where a long time ago, under Khrushchev, his father served as Party secretary.

Former Central Committee Secretary and Deputy Premier Konstantin Katushev was sent off as ambassador to Cuba. Yevgeniy Tyazhelnikov, a former Komsomol boss, was named ambassador and packed off to Rumania. And another former Komsomol boss, Sergei Pavlov, was exiled as ambassador to a totally godforsaken place, Mongolia. (It is interesting to note that under Andropov the area of "ambassadorial exile," geographically extending throughout the world, has been politically confined to the socialist camp: in Mongolia, Rumania, or Cuba, it is impossible to request political asylum, and there is no place to which one can flee.) This list could be extended indefinitely. Purges are going on at all levels of the Party-government apparatus. Ministers are being dismissed, Party bosses of oblasts are losing their posts. And all these places are being taken by the "iron young men," as Andropov's people are called in Moscow. No, Andropov is not a Henry V: his Falstaffs are rapidly replacing Brezhnev's people and taking over the highest positions in the state.

The main character in an old Soviet novel meets up with Lenin (whose pseudonym in the novel is "The Grand Inquisitor") and says to him: "You shifted people from the peanut gallery to the best orchestra seats, and from the best orchestra seats to the peanut gallery, and you call that a revolution!"

Those words apply even more strongly to Andropov than to Lenin. The campaign against corruption that he launched while Brezhnev was still alive was basically a political campaign against his rivals. It will end up (if it has not already ended up) in a simple transfer of power—and, along with it, of scarce victuals and other perks—from the old "new class" to the new "new class," in a game of musical chairs between the outsiders and the favorites of the ruling elite. One may even say, without doing violence to the truth, that the Central Committee of the Communist Party, while retaining its name, is gradually being transformed into the Central Committee of the Committee of State Security, both in terms of its structure and of its membership.

The chief charge brought against Brezhnev is incontrovertible. During the eighteen years of his rule, he exhausted the country—perhaps irreversibly. He brought agriculture, which was already unprofitable, to the point of final collapse; he made the national economy dependent upon foreign investments; he weakened the reins of government within the country; he loosened the bonds of Eastern Europe; he retreated before America in such a key area as the Middle East; and he reduced the Soviet Union to the role of a second-rate power. The rapidly changing Kremlin leadership is faced with a great many problems, both domestic and foreign; and they will be dealt with only by forcible or Machiavellian means, since those means are the only ones available to the former KGB chief. When a man is close to seventy, as is the case with Andropov, he can still change his work place but not his working habits.

Nor is it just a matter of age. The experiences undergone on the road to power leave an indelible impression on the person who finally attains it. The means that proved good for getting it now seem essential for keeping it. The power struggle becomes a way of governing. Thus Stalin, even when he had become an omnipotent tyrant, prolonged the power struggle, although he no longer had any rivals except in his own imagination. That acute observer Tacitus concluded that "of all the Roman rulers, Vespasian was the only one who, after becoming *princeps*, changed for the better."

The important thing, in citing the examples of Henry V and Vespasian, is not just that they were exceptions to the rule, or even that they came to power when younger than Andropov is. What counts most is the kind of life they led before: Vespasian's earlier years were given over to fighting wars, and Henry V's to carousing. But Andropov, before getting into the Kremlin through the back door, busied himself for three full decades (and perhaps for even longer) with intriguing. It sharpened his mind; but at the same time, it made for a shallow, vulgarized mode of thought. We must also bear in mind his very low level of education (low even when compared to that of his Kremlin colleagues), which is about the same as Stalin's was. That, combined with thirty years of underground activity, has produced a limited outlook, unsophisticated reactions, and a bluntness in his way of doing things. As a man who is in some ways gifted without being cultivated, with a notion of the limitations imposed on him by nature, his poor education, his kind of experience, and his milieu, Andropov obfuscates matters that would not seem to require any camouflage or deception. But from his point of view they are always required, in order to hide his simplicity under a mask of complexity. Therefore he covers up his tracks even when there is not, and cannot be, anyone in pursuit. His spreading of rumors about himself is not imposture but, in its own way, a game of hide-and-seek he is playing with himself. We are not even sure he realizes who he actually is. His knowledge of himself has been made indistinct by many years of masquerading—years when he seemed to be following the advice offered in a famous poem by Fyodor Tyutchev:

> Keep silence, conceal yourself, and hide
> Both your feelings and your dreams . . .

His dream ultimately came true, but his feelings went dead. French Foreign Minister Claude Cheysson, who met with Andropov in late February 1983, was struck by his dryness, woodenness, and lack of human reactivity. When journalists asked Cheysson if he regarded Andropov as a modern man, he replied, "Yes, he is a modernist in the sense of a computer, in the sense of precision of word and gesture."

By itself, the fact of having to deal with a "bionic man" in the Kremlin might not be all that bad. But in view of his advanced age and the restraint imposed on him during at least ten years before he came to power, that bionic man now has to hurry. He has to, if he is to accomplish those things that he long ago thought out, to the finest detail, when dwelling in that deep underground in which he was kept by the Kremlin bosses so long as they had the power to do so. The only passion he still has—one which, favored by circumstances, grew even stronger when in his old age he emerged onto the surface—is "impatience of the heart." Because politically, he had long been "an old maid," to use the folk phrase. Hence the hard line that he took right after his inauguration. He stamped out the last traces of dissent. And he set in motion a police campaign against sloth, absenteeism, lateness in coming to work, and drinking during working hours. Every day, now, the newspapers, radio, and TV report the harsh penalties handed out to grafters (including some on the ministerial level), anti-Soviet individuals, shirkers (people guilty of absenteeism), and drunkards. In the first months of Andropov's era the police carried out raids with the code name "Trawl," since their purpose was to catch shirkers unawares: in movie theaters, cafes, bars, stores, and even bathhouses. Thus on one occasion the police descended on the famous Sandunovsky Baths in Moscow, photographed everybody in the buff, and demanded that those naked people show their papers. Those who couldn't produce their papers were taken to the nearest police station. Among the people who were detained were dozens of "shirkers" whose photographs, in the nude, were sent to their places of employment.

Naturally, this kind of thing increases not only the power of the uniformed police but their freedom to deal with "perpetrators" according to their own whims. And that is something against which a person has no protection: in the full sense of the phrase, he is naked and defenseless before the police. Incidentally, the pay of the regular police—now headed by the professional KGB man Vitaly Fedorchuk—has been raised by 70 percent, which puts them on a par with KGB officers and makes them members of the new privileged class. (Of course it was only to be expected that when a new vozhd came into power, a new class would arise. Since there had already been a leninocracy, a stalinocracy, and a brezhnevocracy, which in its last years became a gerontocracy—Khrushchev didn't have enough time, or wasn't able, to create a khrushchevocracy—it was inevitable that an andropovocracy should arise, although it did so more swiftly than the other "cracies," and is growing more swiftly.) So it turned out that there was a critical shortage of policemen because the scope of their duties had been enlarged: beefed up patrols and more checking of people's papers. Today service in the police is on the same level as military service, and draftees will be called up for the police force just as for the armed forces.

The growth of the police apparatus means an enlargement of the state's functions. Instead of the decentralization expected by Western specialists on the USSR, and by the thinning ranks of Moscow liberals, a centralization is taking place. The state is arrogating ever more authority unto itself, depriving Soviet citizens of the very few rights they have. Of course, there is not an infinite number of forcible means; but they are still far from having been exhausted. The Andropov era has not yet entered a Stalinist phase, although Andropov has already inoculated the whole country with fear.

For example, officials have introduced a device for exerting psychological pressure, which is making people frantic. Traffic lights have been installed at the entrances to certain plants and factories: green means there's plenty of time, yellow means you have to hurry, and red means you're fired for being tardy. On that subject, there is a joke in the vein of "black humor" that we can't resist quoting, even though it's the third joke in this chapter. It seems that Ivan Ivanovich did not show up for work at 9:00 A.M. He didn't arrive by 9:30, and by 10:00 he still wasn't there. Finally, his wife called in and said he had died during the night. "Thank God!" his boss exclaimed with a sigh of relief. "I was getting so worried about him being late."

Another reason why we have made such an abundant use of jokes in this chapter is that we are not at all sure they will be able to survive, now that the screws are being turned ever tighter. They may be the last swallows of the free Soviet press, be it only a word-of-mouth press. As far back as October 1982, *Komsomolskaya pravda* published an article about jokes titled "A Whisper from Around the Corner." The gist of it was that there is only one step from political jokes to treason; and in the USSR, as we know, treason is regarded as the most heinous of crimes and entails the harshest of punishments, including death by shooting. That article, however, was aimed not only at tellers of jokes but at those who listen to them. It's hard to say how many master jokesters there are in Russia—whether there are tens or hundreds of thousands. But there are undoubtedly millions of joke lovers, since jokes provide the only safety valve in a police state. The article printed in *Komsomolskaya pravda* was written in the building on Dzerzhinsky Square; and the big question is: What was the author's purpose? Did he want to put an end to anti-Soviet jokes? Or was it his aim to use jokesters—and possibly joke lovers as well—to beef up the population of the Gulag Archipelago, which in the Stalin era supplied the country with unpaid labor? After all, the industrialization of the Soviet Union in the thirties, and the restoration of the war-ravaged economy in the last months of the war, was mostly the work of political prisoners. (During the postwar period they were supplemented by a large number of POWs.) If it had not been for the Gulag, America would be the only superpower in the world.

At this point we must note the sharp difference (not to say opposition) between the remedies for the Soviet economy prescribed by Western specialists on the subject, and the search for a way out of the economic blind alley now being conducted by Andropov, Aliyev, Fedorchuk, Romanov, and their cronies in the Kremlin. From their viewpoint the economic crisis is not due to the USSR's lack of democracy, decentralization, and a free market, as the Western Sovietologists think, but to Khrushchev's dismantling of the Stalinist apparatus of coercion, intimidation, and repression, which was the USSR's only stimulus to labor productivity. And in fact, while the annual growth of the GNP in the fifties was 6 percent, by the late seventies and early eighties it had fallen to 2 percent.

This, in its turn, has been (as they see it) the cause of the USSR's present lag in the arms race with the United States—especially in the quality of weaponry, which in modern warfare is decisive, as was shown in the dogfights between Israeli and Syrian pilots over the Bekaa Valley in the summer of 1982. Therefore, the return to Stalinist-type labor legislation has a twofold aim. First, to tighten up labor discipline under the threat of punishment. Second, to enlarge the very concept of crime—including alcoholism, petty hooliganism, parasitism, absenteeism, the theft of government property, bribery, nepotism, corruption, etc.—so as to increase the population of the Gulag;

that is, the quantity of forced, ùnpaid labor. And for this purpose, it doesn't hurt to find additional political reasons for putting people behind bars, since with the rooting out of dissent, the Gulag's political source of supply virtually dried up. It is easy, for example, to imagine how amply the Gulag would be supplied if that article in *Komsomolskaya pravda* about joke makers and joke lovers were taken as a signal for action. And that article was not the only one of its kind. Since Andropov's seizure of power, all of the newspapers and radio and TV stations have been waging a vigorous campaign against political deviations, any of which is now regarded as subversive and the work of foreign provocateurs. Exactly as in the theater of the absurd, "voluntary" Jewish committees are being created to combat Zionism. The newspapers are calling upon the public to send in denunciations; the number of political arrests is growing; and political prisoners are getting rougher treatment. Less than a year before his sentence was up, the physicist and well-known dissident Yuri Orlov had his skull fractured, with serious damage to the brain. It looks very much as if the present tempo of the return to Stalinism is even faster than that of Stalinism's rise after the death of Lenin. Are we again dealing here with the factor of the new Soviet leader's age—an age at which he has to make haste? Or is it easier to revive an already tested form of government than to create one from scratch?

One of the first matters Andropov took up, by way of restoring order in the empire, was that of the railroads: he promised the people that the trains would run on time. One recalls that they ran on time in Stalin's Russia and Mussolini's Italy. But there is more involved here than historical associations. (For Andropov, one can find parallels that are even more complex, if not more flattering, for example, calling him a Soviet Lycurgus.) Andropov came to power with the idea of restoring order, which in fact Russia has always been lacking in. But to blame everything on national customs alone is as naïve as blaming everything on the vices of a government. There is a saying among workingmen which, in lieu of a one-sided interpretation, offers a bilateral one: "They pretend to pay us, and we pretend to work." The unilateral violation of that principle is due to the fact that Andropov has no way of raising the Soviet standard of living, but has sufficient police-type means of raising labor productivity. This can be called by different names: the idyll of a police state, the illusion of a police state, the utopia of a police state. But naming a thing doesn't change it. The fact is that Andropov, unlike Khrushchev or Brezhnev, having a puritanical cast of mind and being a sworn enemy of all excesses, is trying to apply the principle of austerity and discipline throughout the Soviet Union. It is not merely that he is unfamiliar with other methods but that he finds them ineffective in combatting national customs. He is a policeman both in his working habits and as a result of a deliberate choice. He must certainly know Marx's classic phrase about Peter the Great: that he rooted out barbarism with barbarous methods. The whole question is: How much do modern police methods differ from barbarous ones?

Andropov's accession to the Kremlin marked the collapse of the earlier Soviet system of government by a triumvirate, with both collaboration and competition among its three sectors: the Party, the government, and the secret police. In earlier versions, very well rendered by George Orwell in *1984* and Arthur Koestler in *Darkness at Noon*, the Party, aided by the secret police, set up and ran the apparatus of a totalitarian state. But Andropov has led the "revolt of the machine," the secret police, against its creator, the Party. Because of that, both of the aforementioned novels—including the one that was anti-utopian and offered a description of the future (now the very near future: 1984)—have become dated and no longer serve as a master key to the present version of the Soviet empire. (A bit of incidental advice to journalists: be cautious in using these books as examples when it comes to the Soviet Union today.) Andropov's coup d'état laid bare police foundations of the Soviet state, when the Party itself became merely an appendage to it. The entire course of Russian history was leading up to that, because the secret-police apparatus is the best product of the Russians' political development. It is rather strange that this kind of thing didn't happen earlier: Beria's and Shelepin's failures were less natural than Andropov's success. (Incidentally, both of them, on their way to power, were eager for reforms which would have boiled down to the same prescription of an austere police state now being written out for a sick Russia by its resolute healer, Andropov.) But in the nineteenth century, and earlier, this natural transformation of a totalitarian state into a purely police state was blocked by the monarchy's rule of succession. The top gendarme, Count Benkendorf, could not succeed Emperor Nicholas I, because the emperor had a legitimate heir, his son Alexander.

In the twentieth century the lack of a fixed system of succession,

along with the recurrent coups d'état (Lenin, Stalin, Khrushchev, and
Brezhnev were all in fact usurpers), gave the head of the secret police
carte blanche for seizing power, regardless of his personal qualifications. Andropov came to power thanks rather to his position than to
his own talents. In any case, the latter would not have sufficed if he
had held any other post in the Soviet hierarchy. He would have been
outstripped by whoever was (instead of him) chairman of the Committee of State Security with 15 years tenure. Andropov's self-appointment must be seen in the context of Russian history as its natural
result—something to be expected.

It is precisely for that reason that the factor of the new Soviet
leader's age is rather subjective and cannot have any great influence on
the future course of events. If Andropov, during his first six months in
power, managed to replace so many of Brezhnev's people by his own,
the span of time God grants him (however brief) will suffice not only
to replace the rest, but to lay the foundations, and put up the first
floors, of a new police state in lieu of the Party-bureaucratic one. And
that new state will better meet the requirements of the multinational
empire, whose enemies are both inside of it and outside of it. The
Marquis de Custine compared the Russia of Nicholas I to a garrison.
But in order to function efficiently as an empire, it is better for Russia
to have, also, prison walls put up by the police. The fact is the empire's enemies are the source of its negative inspiration—the basis for
its political, police, and military consolidation. The empire's fear of
collapse brought Andropov to power—along with his ramified apparatus of coercion and his well-tested methods of using violence.

In conclusion, we want to mention a law that has been forgotten in
the West but is well understood in Russia: the impossibility, for an
empire, of a static state. It either collapses, or it expands and takes on
new strength so as not to collapse. In order to cope with the difficulties
resulting from previous conquests, the conquests must be continued,
so as to fulfill the tasks imposed on the empire's ruler by the empire
itself. Andropov was an inspired servant of the empire. And if it had
not been for the top Party people, he would have earned the title of
imperator, because the invasion of Afghanistan (initiated by him) testified to his historical approach to his own country, and to his sense of
responsibility toward its history. The empire can go on existing only
by continuing its imperial policy; that is, a policy of new conquests.
True, in Western Europe it is faced with a natural barrier: the threat of

World War III. It is not ruled out, however, that Andropov may try to restore "order" in Eastern Europe. He has already made his first attempts in this direction, but has run up against stiff resistance from the East European dissidents. The Rumanian, Nicolae Ceausescu, discovered a pro-Moscow plot and executed the conspirators, while the Pole, Wojciech Jaruzelski, has so far succeeded in blocking the divisive activity of pro-Moscow spies.

As for the Pope's visit to Poland this summer, instead of shaking the foundations of Jaruzelski's military dictatorship, as extremists of various persuasions had figured, it strengthened the patriotic foundations of his military dictatorship and his ability to oppose Soviet demands. Jaruzelski deliberately assented to the Pope's visit to Poland, no doubt surmising that the latter would stress a love of freedom in his sermons, and perhaps even agree to it in advance. John Paul II openly told Moscow things that his compatriot in a general's uniform could not say, in view of the role he had voluntarily taken on in that Polish spectacle, which was riskier for him than for anyone else. With the help of the Pope and the crowds (numbering in the millions) who accompanied him on his ceremonial progress through their common motherland, Jaruzelski demonstrated to Andropov and his Kremlin Mafia the unity of the Polish people, its love of freedom, and its readiness to oppose foreign invasion. And the fact that Andropov needed such a reminder at that time is evident from the aggressive tone taken toward Jaruzelski and his comrades-in-arms by Soviet journalists and officials on the eve of the Pope's visit. The notion, widespread in the Western press, that John Paul's pilgrimage to his *penates* was aimed against Jaruzelski personally, was superficial and overlooks many not immediately apparent factors, ranging from the long, secret talks between the Pope and General Jaruzelski (via Cardinal Glemp) which preceded that visit, to the education that the future Polish dictator got, before the war, at an elite Jesuit school—an education which in no small degree made for success and credibility in his role as a general with a soldier's mentality.

Finally, as a result of two secret meetings between these Polish patriots, Jaruzelski managed to gain the full support of the Pope, whereas the Vatican's former protégé, the leader of the disbanded Solidarity trade unions, lost it. During his supposedly religious pilgrimage, the Pope showed himself to be more of a wise politician than a zealous preacher, making a choice (difficult for one in his position) between rhetoric and pragmatism. His essentially moral support of General Jaruzelski, who had saved Poland from a Soviet occupation, provoked charges that he was immoral. We are living in a world of inside-out, beyond-the-looking-glass ideas; and even Lewis Carroll, with his Alice, would go astray and be bewildered among them.

The path of Russian expansionism toward the southeast must also be regarded as tempting, in view of its relative security and harmlessness, judging merely from the fact that the Soviet Union acquired Afghanistan at almost no cost. To this one must add the Russians' demographic fear of China—one that is the Soviet empire's chief political, historical, and military stimulus in the late twentieth century. The Soviet Union's growing aggressiveness in Asia is a kind of sublimation of that fear, which is being heated up by official and nationalistic propaganda to the point of hysteria. All this may have fatal consequences in the future.

What matters here is not Andropov himself but his heirs—and even more than that, what political heritage they will receive from him. It looks as if he will not leave them with empty hands. In his *Annals*, Tacitus has one of his characters make this despairing remark: "It is quite likely that I can last a few days longer until the death of the *princeps*. But how escape the youth of the one who will immediately take his place?"

Merely in terms of his physical condition, Andropov is doomed to be a leader *ad interim*. After vanquishing his Kremlin rivals one by one, he has found himself face to face with an enemy against whom all his arts of intrigue are powerless. He arrived at the Kremlin too late to remain there for very long. His strength is ebbing, and in his victory there is a dash of bitterness that prevents him from feeling himself to be a victor. This makes Andropov a tragicomic hero: he came stage front when the drama in which he had taken part was reaching its end.

All his strength was expended on the struggle for power and on the first months of his rule, when he set such a furious pace, forgetting his age and overrating his physical capacities. Already in the spring of 1983, he had to have help to get to a conference table or to his limousine. But once he sat down, his strength returned: Andropov seated was the opposite of Andropov walking. Western observers of course noticed his physical frailty and ascribed it to various diseases, ranging from nephritis to Parkinson's disease (because his hands trembled). And some of them even discerned in it the ironic hand of fate: six months after the death of Brezhnev, Andropov was in the same state that his predecessor had been for at least his last five years. At the time, Muscovites were even joking that now Andropov would have to bring back to the Kremlin the Assyrian faith healer Dzhuna Davitashvili, who on several occasions had snatched Brezhnev from the arms of death, for which she was sent away by Andropov. But now it was he who needed her.

That resemblance, however, was only an outward one; Andropov's mind was still functioning as clearly as before. And yet he was growing catastrophically blind because of diabetes, overexhaustion, and nervous stress. The main thing for him, now, was to get to his desk. But the all-powerful seated Andropov again became powerless when he stood up. "Darkness at noon" came over him personally, even sooner than it did over the empire he was ruling and turning back toward the Stalin era. His progressive blindness made him even more suspicious, and now he was totally dependent, physically, on his nearest aides. Henceforth, whenever he appeared in public, he was surrounded by his bodyguards. Gradually, they relegated his Party colleagues to the background. Wearing dark glasses, and flanked by bullyboys, he began to resemble a "godfather," the chief of an omnipotent Mafia of KGB men that had seized power in the country, replacing the Party Areopagus.

They are now faced with a good deal of work in order to transform the shaky empire into a police torture chamber. But at this point we enter the realm of guesswork. And as Paul Valéry once said, the Pythia cannot dictate a whole poem, only one line.

Notes

The idea for this book was first conceived two months after the "changing of the guard" in the Kremlin in November 1982; and two months later it was offered to the publisher. Such were the exigent conditions of the contract—conditions proposed by the authors themselves in order to seize the initiative from the book's main character, who was mobilizing all means at his command (and very remarkable means they were) to create his own image in the world press, following the well-known rule that history is written by the conquerors.

Naturally, the book could not have been written in such a short time if its authors had not been making a study of its subject and his entourage over a considerable period: about three and a half years, in fact. We did this in our capacity as political commentators for many American newspapers and magazines. Indeed, long before Brezhnev's death we predicted (in the *Los Angeles Times* and the *Antioch Review*) Andropov's accession to power, whereas the majority of other journalists and historians figured his chances were minimal because of his service with the secret police—although it was precisely the "KGB connection" that played the decisive role in his victory over his rivals.

Although our articles (sometimes written jointly, at other times not) have from time to time appeared in such periodicals as the *New York Times*, the *Washington Post*, the *Wall Street Journal*, the *Christian Science Monitor*, *Dissent*, *Midstream*, and a number of others, we feel a particular obligation toward certain editors who, by regularly publishing our commentaries, have stimulated our work. They have made it possible for us to prepare for the writing of this book and, on a more elementary level, to devote full time to literary, journalistic, and historical pursuits. Chief among them are: Sidney Goldberg, executive editor of the Independent News Alliance (an affiliate of United Features Syndicate), Robert Fogarty of the *Antioch Review*, William Phillips of the *Partisan Review*, Laurence Goldstein of the *Michigan Quarterly Review*, Gwinn Owens of the *Baltimore Evening Sun*, Helen Donovan of the *Boston Globe*, John Twohey and Lea McClain of the *Chicago Tribune*, Jack Smee of the *New York Daily News*, Tim Rutten and Steve Wasserman of the *Los Angeles Times*, Woody Hochswender of the *Los Angeles Herald Examiner*, Elvira Cochran of *Newsday*, Sandy Close and Frank Viviano of the *Pacific News Service*, and Linda Lewis of the *Seattle Post-Intelligencer*.

Acting in concert (although there was no arrangement among them), they gave us the feeling that our work was needed—something especially important for recent émigrés from the USSR, who had exchanged not merely one country for another but a totalitarian one for a democratic one, the Russian language for the English language, one continent for another, and (most important) one culture for another. This listing of these editors obviates the necessity of making special reference to this or that idea, observation, or fact which, before appearing in this book, had already figured in the articles we published in the aforementioned periodicals. This applies not only to our predictions about Kremlin affairs but, for example, to our evaluation of the situation in Poland, which differed sharply from the majority of those published in the American press.

We have used information from a number of secret Soviet correspondents; but any reference to them is ruled out, since in each case the information was furnished us with the strict proviso that its source remain anonymous—for obvious reasons having to do with the informant's personal security. Several items have not required citations, since they were generally known in those circles we frequented in Leningrad and Moscow (when we lived first in one capital, then in the other), regardless of whether they were known in the West. There was even less need to cite sources for facts furnished by the Moscow correspondents of American and West European newspapers and weeklies or TV journalists; and the same goes for a speech by Andropov or the verse of an "official" poet taken from the Soviet press—whether "central," "republican," or local. The conversations between Khrushchev and Gomulka, Beria and Matyas Rakosi, Brezhnev and Andropov; the results of the voting in the Politburo on the question of Czechoslovakia; and several other events were reconstructed on the basis of rumors. Those rumors, however, were so persistent that they could be taken as fact—not merely because nothing more reliable was available to us but because they fit into the context of events contemporaneous with them and stand up to historical, political, and psychological analysis. We have also cited several other rumors, only (as Suetonious said) "in order not to leave out anything, and not because I regard them as true or likely." This does not mean that we consider them unlikely; but we had no way of checking their veracity.

These minimal notes provide information that we think is indispensable but with which we did not want to burden the basic text.

1   THE HUNGARIAN DÉBUT

The events of the Hungarian revolution and the role played by Yuri Andropov in its suppression have been reconstructed on the basis of the following: the contemporary Hungarian, Soviet, West European, and American periodical press; the reminiscences of participants—both published and furnished to the authors *viva voce*; papers read at a conference of scholars held at New York University on October 23, 1981, on the twenty-fifth anniversary of the revolution; material from the quarterly *Problems of Eastern Europe* (Frantishek and Larisa Silnitsky, eds.) and the *New Hungarian Quarterly* (Ivan Boldizsar, ed.); and several retrospective articles that appeared in Western periodicals following Andropov's coup d'état. The "Hungarian" chapter's concluding remarks—from Sandor Kopacsi, Georg Heltai, Bela Kiraly, and Miklos Vasarhelyi—are quoted from articles in *Time* (November 29, 1982), the *New York Times* (December 28, 1982), and the *Wall Street Journal* (November 15, 1982).

We would also like to thank Bela Kiraly—now professor of history at Brooklyn College, who at the time of the Hungarian revolution was chairman of the Revolutionary Council of National Defense—for consultation on various controversial questions. This was essential because during the quarter century since it happened, the Hungarian revolution has been shrouded in legend—especially with respect to the then Soviet ambassador's role. For example, several authors have stated that Pal Maleter, minister of defense in the Nagy government, was arrested during a banquet given in his honor by the Soviet ambassador, Andropov. That is not true. Pal Maleter was arrested at a Soviet military base in the village of Tokol, on Csepel Island, during talks with a Soviet military delegation. There is no need, it seems to us, to add dark colors to a portrait that is none too bright-hued in any case. All we allowed ourselves to borrow from the reminiscences of people who had met Andropov in Budapest were a few of his personal traits: his fondness for gypsy music, "heartrending" love songs, Hungarian ballads, and so on. (We are not altogether convinced that they correspond to reality, but they seem quite likely.)

Khrushchev's recollections of the events in Hungary are quoted from a typescript of his tape-recorded memoirs on file at the Russian Institute of Columbia University. (We had access to them while serving as visiting scholars at that institute.) Tito's account of his meeting with the Soviet leaders in the summer of 1956 is based on a speech of his published on November 16 of that same year in the Yugoslav Party newspaper, *Borba*.

2 A LUCKY TICKET: THE KGB

In addition to the sources cited in the text, we have used: an interview with Vladimir Sakharov published in the *New York Times* (June 13, 1982); an article by Aishe Seitmuratova in the quarterly *Problems of Eastern Europe* (Nos. 3 and 4, 1978); and an article by the former Soviet general Petr Grigorenko, "That Democrat, Andropov," published in the *Novoye russkoye slovo* (July 29 and 30, 1982), in which Grigorenko retells the story of Mikola Sharygin-Bodulyak's meeting with Andropov—an account of which Sharygin-Bodulyak published in the Parisian émigré newspaper, *Russkaya mysl*. The events of 1968 in Czechoslovakia were reconstructed on the basis of the contemporary periodical press; the transcription, under the title of "An Unfinished Conversation," of a tape recording made by one of the leaders of the "Prague Spring," Iosef Smrkovsky; the reminiscences of another of its leaders, Zdenek Mlynar, "*Mráz přichází z Kremlu*" ("A Cold Wind Blows from the Kremlin," *Index*, 1978); articles by, and interviews with, Irzhi Pelikan, Ota Shik, Lyudek Pakhman.

3 RUSSIAN NATIONALISM: THE KGB'S IDEOLOGICAL STAKE

While still living in Moscow, we devoted several years to investigating Russian nationalistic tendencies in the present-day political and ideological climate of the USSR; and some of the material we gathered was used in articles we published in American newspapers and in the following magazines: *Novy Mir* (No. 2, 1972), *Literaturnoye Obozreniye* (No. 7, 1976), *Vremya i My* (Nos. 24, 32, and 44), *Midstream* (October 1980), the *Partisan Review* (No. 2, 1981, and No. 1, 1982), and *Dissent* (Winter 1981).

4 ANDROPOV'S CAUCASIAN "REHEARSALS"

The "Azerbaijani" part of this chapter was written on the basis of material published in the newspaper *Bakinskiy rabochiy* during the past twelve years, and on eyewitness accounts of Geidar Aliyev's "police government." The "Georgian" part is based not only on similar material in the Tbilisi newspaper *Zarya Vostoka* but on the authors' personal observations and on interviews with many people close to Eduard Shevardnadze, ranging from his classmates to his speech writers, members of the Georgian Central Committee, and his ministers. (We smuggled our "Georgian Notes"—about seventy-five pages—out of the USSR.)

5 THE CRUSHING OF DISSENT AND THE CAMPAIGN AGAINST DÉTENTE

We got our list of the murders in the Ukraine from the aforementioned article by Petr Grigorenko, "That Democrat, Andropov"; and Vladimir Voinovich's speech at the graveside of the murdered Konstantin Bogatyrev was taken from Lydia Chukovskaya's book *Protsess isklyucheniya*, published in Russian by the YMCA Press in 1979. We have given a more detailed account of Soviet dissent in articles published in the *New York Times* (October 4, 1977) and the *Michigan Quarterly Review* (Winter 1980).

6 ANDROPOV IN THE POLITBURO: AT HOME AMONG STRANGERS, A STRANGER AT HOME

We do not have (nor can we ever have) any hopes of obtaining tape recordings of Politburo sessions. Because if anyone has tapes of its members' private conversations, it is our hero, who is hardly likely to share such information with his biographers. Nonetheless, there are certain leaks, which come—strange as that may seem—more from the

KGB, which keeps watch over the Central Committee, than from the CC itself. As for the CC, we have information only from its ex-members, who have had nothing more to do than gossip and reminisce. One example is Khrushchev, who dictated his memoirs. And the same thing has recently been happening with a number of Party officials who lost their jobs along with their chiefs—rivals of Andropov whom he overcame. In particular, the account of Andropov's youth is based on information from one of those pensioners.

The sparse and fragmentary information about Andropov's family life has transpired in two ways: first, indirectly, thanks to the university classmates of his daughter, Irina; second, thanks to the loose tongues of Moscow actors, to whose milieu Andropov's son-in-law belonged. We decided to take a psychological approach in this chapter (a rather restrained one), in view of our hero's fondness for psychological devices, which in his hands served as a powerful weapon in Kremlin intrigues.

The line from "Epigraph on a Tyrant," from *Collected Poems of W. H. Auden*, copyright © 1940, renewed 1968 by W. H. Auden, is reprinted by permission of Random House.

7   THE ALLIANCE WITH THE MILITARY AND THE INVASION OF AFGHANISTAN ON CHRISTMAS EVE 1979

Roy Medvedev's hypothesis as to the "Ustinov-Andropov alliance" has been set forth by Medvedev himself in an article written for the *Los Angeles Times* (reprinted in *Newsday*, January 9, 1983), and in many interviews with Western correspondents in Moscow. (Cf., for example, Andrey Nagorski's article, "The Making of Andropov," in *Harper's*, February 1983.) His viewpoint is also expressed in the book *Andropov*, published under the name of "Zhores Medvedev."

8   THE DNEPROPETROVSK MAFIA AND THE DEFEAT IN POLAND

Naturally, neither of the present writers has ever been in Andropov's former office on Dzerzhinsky Square. And the same goes for John Barron and the defector Vladimir Sakharov, in whose words the author of *KGB* describes that office as follows: ". . . a big, ornate room with rich oriental carpets, embroidered sofas, mahogany-paneled walls, a high ceiling, and tall windows overlooking the square on Marx Prospekt." This office, resembling an Eastern seraglio or a set used in a James Bond movie, is something quite impossible in reality. First, because of Andropov's austere tastes. Second, and more important, because in any Soviet institution the interiors—ranging from Brezhnev's study to the office space occupied by ministries, city committees, and oblast committees (even if they are located in what were once the private residences of nobles)—are always impersonal, bureaucratically dull and colorless. So that even if Andropov had had a weakness for Oriental rugs and embroidered sofas, as a secretive "underground man" he never would have allowed himself to display that weakness on the job. Moreover, he was so absorbed in his favorite kind of work, and his head was so full of plans and operations, that he had little time or inclination left for expressing himself as a human being or giving things a personal touch. There was good reason why many people who met him had noticed that he had something about him of a graven image—an "absence of presence." And what he preferred above all, in the layout of his own office, was functionalism and not decorative traits.

As for the iron shutters and the concealed button for raising and lowering them, one of the present writers (Vladimir Solovyov) saw such things in the "Big House" at 4 Liteiny Prospekt in Leningrad, the local KGB headquarters, when it was visited by a large group of writers, artists, and actors. One of the guides assigned to the group, proud of this technical innovation, boasted: "Now we have such things everywhere—even in the office of the chairman of the Committee of State Security." We are taking him at his word.

11   A FAREWELL GLANCE FROM LENIN'S TOMB;
      OR, AN OBITUARY OF BREZHNEV

Joseph Brodsky's epitaph on the death of Brezhnev, which was used as one of the epigraphs for this chapter, is reprinted with permission from the *New York Review of Books*, copyright © 1982 Myrev, Inc.

In conclusion we note that, just as rapidly as this book was written in Russian, it was translated into English, chapter by chapter, by our friend Guy Daniels in close collaboration with the authors—a process involving some heated arguments and much joint searching for English phraseology accurately reflecting the Russian original.

Index